The Newspapers of Nevada

OTHER BOOKS BY RICHARD E. LINGENFELTER

*Lying on the Eastern Slope: James Townsend's
Comic Journalism on the Mining Frontier*
(Coauthor, Richard A. Dwyer)

Steamboats on the Colorado River, 1852–1916

*The Hardrock Miners: A History of the Mining Labor
Movement in the American West, 1863–1893*

Songs of the American West
(Coauthor, Richard A. Dwyer)

Presses of the Pacific Islands, 1817–1867

The Songs of the Gold Rush
(Coauthor, Richard A. Dwyer)

The Newspapers of Nevada

A HISTORY AND BIBLIOGRAPHY, 1854-1979

Richard E. Lingenfelter
and
Karen Rix Gash

University of Nevada Press
Reno
1984

GRATEFUL ACKNOWLEDGMENT IS HEREBY MADE TO
THE GANNETT FOUNDATION FOR HELPING TO
MAKE PUBLICATION OF THIS BOOK POSSIBLE.

UNIVERSITY OF NEVADA PRESS, RENO, NEVADA 89557 USA
© 1984 RICHARD E. LINGENFELTER AND KAREN RIX GASH
ALL RIGHTS RESERVED
BOOK AND JACKET DESIGN BY DAVE COMSTOCK
PRINTED IN THE UNITED STATES OF AMERICA

LIBRARY OF CONGRESS CATALOGING IN PUBLICATION DATA
LINGENFELTER, RICHARD E.
   THE NEWSPAPERS OF NEVADA

   INCLUDES INDEX.
   1. AMERICAN NEWSPAPERS—NEVADA—BIBLIOGRAPHY.
   2. AMERICAN NEWSPAPERS—NEVADA—HISTORY. I. GASH,
KAREN RIX, 1947–   II. TITLE.
Z6952.N49L56 1983   011'.35'09793   83–16790
[PN4897.N45]
ISBN 0–87417–075–3

Contents

Preface   xvii
Introduction   xix
Location Symbols   xxiii
Reference Abbreviations   xxv

THE NEWSPAPERS OF NEVADA

ACME (MINERAL COUNTY)
    Nevada Copper News 1907   1
ATWOOD (NYE COUNTY)
    Fairplay Prospector 1907   1
AURORA (MINERAL COUNTY)
    Esmeralda Star 1862–4   1
    Aurora Weekly Times 1863–5   4
    Esmeralda Union 1864–8   4
    Esmeralda Herald 1877–83   6
    Aurora Star 1886   6
    Aurora Borealis 1905–6   7
AUSTIN (LANDER COUNTY)
    Reese River Reveille 1863+   7
    Austin Republican 1868   9
    Spark of Genius 1879   9
    Democrat 1882–3   9
    Austin Holiday Review 1882   10
    People's Advocate 1890–3   10
    Nevada Progressive 1924–6   11
    Austin Sun 1933–4   11
BATTLE MOUNTAIN (LANDER COUNTY)
    Measure for Measure 1873–5   11
    Battle Mountain Messenger 1877–84   12
    Lander Free Press 1881–2   12
    Central Nevadan 1885–1907   13
    The Little Joker 1887   14
    Battle Mountain Herald 1907   14
    Battle Mountain Herald and Central Nevadan 1907–11   14
    Battle Mountain Scout 1913–62   14
    Nevada Progressive 1924–6   15
    Battle Mountain Bugle 1976+   15
BEATTY (NYE COUNTY)
    Beatty Bullfrog Miner 1905–9   16
    Beatty Bulletin 1947–56   16
    Beatty Newsbits 1977+   16

BELLEHELEN (NYE COUNTY)
    Bellehelen Record 1907   17
BELLEVILLE (MINERAL COUNTY)
    Belleville Times 1877–8   17
BELMONT (NYE COUNTY)
    Silver Bend Reporter 1867–8   17
    Mountain Champion 1868–9   19
    Belmont Courier 1874–1901   20
BETTY O'NEAL (LANDER COUNTY)
    Betty O'Neal Concentrator 1924–5   20
BLAIR (ESMERALDA COUNTY)
    Blair Press 1906–10   21
    Blair Booster 1907   21
BOULDER CITY (CLARK COUNTY)
    Boulder City Journal 1931–41   21
    Boulder City Age 1932–3   22
    Boulder Dam Challenge 1936   22
    Boulder City Reminder 1938–40   22
    Boulder City News 1940+   22
    Oasis Advertiser 1960   23
    Dam Informer 1962   23
    Desert Rat Review 1968   23
BOVARD (MINERAL COUNTY)
    Bovard Booster 1908   23
BRISTOL (LINCOLN COUNTY)
    Bristol Times 1881–2   24
BULLFROG (NYE COUNTY)
    Bullfrog Miner 1905–6   24
CALIENTE (LINCOLN COUNTY)
    Caliente Progress 1904   25
    Caliente Express 1905–6   25
    Caliente Lode-Express 1906–8   26
    Prospector 1909–13   26
    Caliente News 1920–5   27
    Caliente Record 1925   27
    Caliente Herald 1928–68   27
CAMP SIBERT (CLARK COUNTY)

The Desert Scorpion (The Sibert Scorpion) 1941–3	28
CANDELARIA (MINERAL COUNTY)	
True Fissure 1880–6	28
Chloride Belt 1890–2	29
CARLIN (ELKO COUNTY)	
Commonwealth 1908–12	29
Western Home Builder 1914–6	30
Nevada Democrat 1917	30
Carlin Courier 1976	30
CARRARA (NYE COUNTY)	
Carrara Obelisk 1913–6	31
Carrara Miner 1929	31
CARSON CITY (ORMSBY COUNTY)	
Territorial Enterprise 1859–60	31
Silver Age 1860–2	32
Carson Daily Independent 1863–4	33
The Daily Morning Post 1864–5	34
State Democrat 1864	35
Nevada Appeal 1865–70;1872+	35
Nevada State Journal 1866	36
The Daily State Register 1870–2	37
The Daily Nevada Tribune 1872–96	37
Nevada Pulpit 1874	38
Daily Evening Herald 1875	39
Nevada Patriot 1876	39
Parish Guide 1876–8	40
The Portfolio 1878	40
Carson Times 1880–1	40
Daily Index 1880–7	41
The Daily Bee 1882	42
Carson Free Lance 1885–7	42
The Carson Boys 1885–6	43
Carson Post 1885	43
Nevada Union 1886–7	43
Nevada Index-Union 1887–8	43
The Sun 1889–91	44
Carson City News 1891–1930	44
The Weekly 1891–9	45
Carson Press 1892–6	45
Celebration Gazetteer 1892	46
The White Ribbon 1894	46
Parish Rubric 1897–1904	46
Ormsby County Ledger 1900	47
Carson Weekly 1900–18	47
Yogi 1910–1	47
Karson Sity Gazoot 1911	48
Greater Nevada 1912	48
Carson Evening Gazette 1914	48
Carson City Enlightener 1914	48
Nevadian Times 1931–5	49
Carson Chronicle 1935+	49
The Rainbow 1936–7	50
Nevada State Veteran 1949	50
Nevada Capitol News 1949–50	50
Las Vegas Playgirl 1960–1	51
Carson City News 1961	51
Nevada Statesman 1966	51
Carson Review and Advertiser 1970–7	51
Desert News 1973	51
Silver State Forum 1975	52
The Donoghue Letter 1977–8	52
Carson Times 1977+	52
Prospector 1978+	52
CHAFEY (HUMBOLDT COUNTY)	
Chafey News 1908–9	52
CHERRY CREEK (WHITE PINE COUNTY)	
The Independent 1878–9	53
White Pine News 1881–5	53
Cherry Creek Miner 1903	54
CLAROIS	
Clarois Review	54
CLOVERDALE (NYE COUNTY)	
Cloverdale Budget 1893	54
COLUMBIA (ESMERALDA COUNTY)	
Goldfield Review 1904–7	55
Columbia Topics 1908–9	55
COLUMBUS (ESMERALDA COUNTY)	
Borax Miner 1873–8	55
COMO (LYON COUNTY)	
Como Sentinel 1864	56
CONTACT (ELKO COUNTY)	
Contact Miner 1913–6	57
Nevada-Contact Mining Review 1924–5	57
COPPERFIELD (MINERAL COUNTY) (See ACME)	
CRESCENT (CLARK COUNTY)	
Crescent Times 1905	58
CRYSTAL BAY (WASHOE COUNTY)	
Villager 1961–3	58
North Tahoe World 1969–70	58
DAYTON (LYON COUNTY)	
Lyon County Sentinel 1864–6	58
Lyon County Times 1880–1901	59
News Reporter 1886–7	59
Dayton Advocate 1904–5	60
DEETH (ELKO COUNTY)	
Deeth Tidings 1896	60
Commonwealth 1912–4	60
DELAMAR (LINCOLN COUNTY)	
The Ferguson Lode 1892–3	61

The De Lamar Lode 1894–1906	61
Local Messenger 1899–1901	62
De La Mar Roaster 1900	62
DIVIDE CITY (ESMERALDA COUNTY)	
Divide City Times 1919	62
DUCK VALLEY (ELKO COUNTY)	
Duck Valley News 1886	62
DULUTH (NYE COUNTY)	
Duluth Tribune 1907	63
DUTCH CREEK (MINERAL COUNTY)	
Dutch Creek News 1907	63
DYER (ESMERALDA COUNTY)	
Esmeralda Star 1956–7	63
EAST ELY (WHITE PINE COUNTY)	
White Pine News 1908–23	64
ELKO (ELKO COUNTY)	
Elko Independent 1869+	64
Elko Chronicle 1870	65
Elko Leader 1873	66
Elko Post 1875–81	66
The Free Press 1883+	67
Nevada Silver Tidings 1896–9	68
Daily Argonaut 1897–9	68
The Telegram 1909	69
Elko Enterprise 1916–7	69
Nevada Farmer and Stockman 1921–2	69
ELLENDALE (NYE COUNTY)	
Ellendale Star 1909	69
Ellendale Lode 1909	70
ELY (WHITE PINE COUNTY)	
White Pine News 1888–1908	70
White Pine Miner 1902–3	71
Amateur Outlook 1904	71
The Ely Record (The Mining Record) 1905+	71
Ely Mining Expositor 1906–15	72
Ely Post 1907	73
White Pine Suffragist 1914	73
Ely Daily Times 1920+	73
EMPIRE CITY (ORMSBY COUNTY)	
Empire City Globe 1867	74
EUREKA (EUREKA COUNTY)	
Eureka Sentinel 1870+	74
The Cupel 1874	76
Eureka Daily Republican 1877–8	76
Silver Plume 1877; 1882	77
Eureka Daily Leader 1878–85	77
Republican Press 1884–5	78
The Eureka Tri-Weekly Standard 1885–6	79
Eureka Miner 1971–3	79
FAIRPLAY (NYE COUNTY)	
(See ATWOOD)	
FAIRVIEW (CHURCHILL COUNTY)	
Fairview News 1906–8	80
Fairview Miner 1906–7	80
FALLON (CHURCHILL COUNTY)	
Fallon Standard (Churchill County Standard) 1903–58	81
Fallon Herald 1905–6	81
Fallon Eagle 1906–58	82
Ballot Box 1911–3	82
Co-operative Colonist 1916–8	83
Nevada Colony News 1917	83
Lahontan Valley Shopper 1957–8	83
Fallon Eagle-Standard 1958+	84
Churchill County Courier 1961–2	84
Fallon Citizen 1963–7	84
Lahontan Valley News 1970+	84
Desert Roundup 1977–79	85
The Shopper 1979+	85
FERNLEY (LYON COUNTY)	
Enterprise 1919–20	85
Nevadian Times 1931	85
The Fernley Newspaper 1957	86
Tri-Town Times 1957–8	86
FORT HALLECK (ELKO COUNTY)	
Halleck Gossip 1885	86
GABBS (NYE COUNTY)	
Gabbs Valley Enterprise 1974–6	86
GARDNERVILLE (DOUGLAS COUNTY)	
Gardnerville Press 1896	87
Douglas County Silverite 1896	87
Gardnerville Record 1898–1904	87
Courier 1899–1904	87
Record-Courier 1904+	88
Nevada Lutheran 1918–42	88
Air Age News 1966–7	89
GENOA (DOUGLAS COUNTY)	
The Scorpion 1857	89
Territorial Enterprise 1858–9	89
Carson Valley Farmer (Nevada Republican) 1865	91
Douglas County Banner 1865	91
Carson Valley News 1875–80	91
Genoa Journal 1880	92
Genoa Weekly Courier 1880–99	92
The Bugle 1888	93
Nevada Prohibitionist 1888–9	93
GERLACH (WASHOE COUNTY)	
Gerlach Express 1914	93
Valley Press 1961–2	94
GILBERT (ESMERALDA COUNTY)	

Gilbert Record 1925–6	94	*Goodsprings Gazette* 1916–21	110
GOLCONDA (HUMBOLDT COUNTY)		GRANITE (MINERAL COUNTY)	
Golconda Illustrated Gazette 1881	94	*Granite Times* 1908	110
The News 1899–1900	95	GRANTSVILLE (NYE COUNTY)	
Nevada Miner 1902	95	*Grantsville Sun* 1878–9	110
Rustler 1910–1	96	*Grantsville Bonanza* 1880–4	111
GOLD CENTER (NYE COUNTY)		GREENFIELD (LYON COUNTY)	
Gold Center News 1906–7	96	(See YERINGTON)	
GOLD CREEK (ELKO COUNTY)		HAMILTON (WHITE PINE COUNTY)	
Gold Creek News 1896–7	96	*Inland Empire* 1869–70	111
GOLD HILL (STOREY COUNTY)		*White Pine News* 1870–80	112
Gold Hill Daily News 1863–82	97	HARRIMAN (WASHOE COUNTY)	
Daily Morning Message 1864	98	(See SPARKS)	
The People's Tribune 1870	99	HAWTHORNE (MINERAL COUNTY)	
The People's Paper 1870	100	*The Oasis* 1881	113
The Golden Echo 1874	100	*Walker Lake Bulletin* 1883–1926	114
Fraternal Visitor 1881	100	*Esmeralda Herald* 1883–4	115
Gold Hill News 1974–8	100	*Esmeralda News* 1887–9	115
GOLDFIELD (ESMERALDA COUNTY)		*Hawthorne-Lucky Boy News* 1909	148
Goldfield News 1904–56	101	*Hawthorne Herald* 1909	115
Weekly Market Letter 1904	102	*Hawthorne-Lucky Boy Post* 1909	116
Market Letter 1904–7	102	*Hawthorne News* 1928–35	116
Weekly Market Review 1904–7	102	*Mineral County Independent* 1933+	116
Goldfield Vigilant 1905	103	*The Rocket* 1945–7	117
The Goldfield Sun 1905–6	103	*Mineral County Forum (Mineral*	
The New Nevada 1905	103	*County Democrat)* 1960–1	117
Semi-Monthly Bulletin 1905–6	103	*The Times of Mineral County*	
Nevada Mining and Market Review		1978+	117
1906	103	HAZEN (CHURCHILL COUNTY)	
Traders' Daily Gossip 1906	104	*Hazen Harvest* 1905–6	118
Nevada Mining Securities Review		HELENE (LINCOLN COUNTY)	
1906	104	(See DELAMAR)	
Nevada Mining News 1906	104	HENDERSON (CLARK COUNTY)	
Sporting Bulletin 1906	104	*Basic Bombardier (Big Job–Basic*	
Goldfield Tribune 1906–30	105	*Magnesium Newsletter)* 1942–4	118
Goldfield Gossip 1906–8	105	*Hendersonian* 1942–3	118
Mines and Market 1906	106	*Henderson Herald* 1946	118
Goldfield Chronicle 1906–9	106	*Henderson Home News* 1947+	119
Nevada Mining Bulletin 1906–7	107	*Henderson Star* 1958–9	119
The Little Mining Bradstreet 1907	107	*Nevada Jewish Chronicle* 1961–4	119
Goldfield Review 1907–9	107	HERCULES (CHURCHILL COUNTY)	
Nevada Workman 1907–8	108	*Hercules Miner* 1906–7	119
Goldfield Hotel Life 1909	108	HORNSILVER (ESMERALDA COUNTY)	
Goldfield News Letter 1910–5	108	*Hornsilver Herald* 1908	119
Sprague's Newsletter 1912–6	108	INCLINE VILLAGE (WASHOE COUNTY)	
Goldfield Post 1912–4	109	*North Lake Tahoe Bonanza* 1976+	120
Field of Gold 1915	109	*High Sierra Times* 1976–8	120
Goldfield Enterprise & Esmeralda		IONE (NYE COUNTY)	
County News 1958	109	*Nye County News* 1864–7	120
GOLDYKE (NYE COUNTY)		*The Advertiser* 1864	121
Goldyke Sun 1907	109	JARBIDGE (ELKO COUNTY)	
GOODSPRINGS (CLARK COUNTY)		*Jarbidge Miner* 1912	122

JESSUP (CHURCHILL COUNTY)
   Jessup News 1908 — 122
JOHNTOWN (LYON COUNTY)
   Gold Cañon Switch 1854 — 122
JUMBO (WASHOE COUNTY)
   Jumbo Miner 1908 — 123
JUNCTIONVILLE (LINCOLN COUNTY)
   Bugle 1880 — 123
KEARNS (EUREKA COUNTY)
   Nevada Slogan 1909 — 123
KENNEDY (PERSHING COUNTY)
   Nevada New Era 1894 — 123
KIMBERLY (LANDER COUNTY)
   Kimberly News 1910 — 124
KINGSTON (LANDER COUNTY)
   Ghost Town Gazette 1934 — 124
LAKE PEAK (MINERAL COUNTY)
   Lake Peak News 1906 — 125
LANDER (LANDER COUNTY)
   (*See* TENABO)
LAS VEGAS (CLARK COUNTY)
   Las Vegas Times 1905–6 — 125
   Advance 1905–6 — 125
   Las Vegas Age 1905–47 — 126
   Las Vegas Review (Clark County Review) 1909–29 — 126
   The Bulletin 1914 — 127
   Keys to Hidden Treasure 1926 — 127
   The Argus 1926–7 — 127
   Las Vegas Journal 1929 — 128
   Las Vegas Review-Journal 1929+ — 128
   Desert Sun 1931 — 129
   Las Vegas Times 1932 — 129
   Nevada Mining Bulletin 1932–6 — 129
   The Cloudburst 1933–4 — 129
   Las Vegas News 1941 — 129
   Las Vegas Tribune 1943–6 — 130
   Nevada Life 1945–6 — 130
   Las Vegas Hangover 1946 — 130
   Nevada Veteran 1946 — 130
   The Shopper 1947 — 131
   Free Press 1950 — 131
   Fabulous Las Vegas Magazine 1949–73 — 131
   Las Vegas Sun 1950+ — 131
   Nevada Citizen 1951–6 — 132
   Magazine Las Vegas 1951–6 — 132
   Independent 1955 — 132
   West, The Voice of Western America 1956+ — 132
   Nevada Democrat 1958–76 — 133
   The Nellis Century 1958–73 — 133
   Southern Nevada Labor Beacon 1958–69 — 133
   Las Vegas Magazine 1960–6 — 133
   Southern Nevada Labor News 1961–9 — 133
   This Is Las Vegas 1961+ — 134
   Las Vegas Playground 1962–4 — 134
   Las Vegas Voice 1963+ — 134
   Vegas Visitor 1964+ — 134
   Las Vegas Israelite 1965+ — 134
   Veteran's Journal 1965–71 — 135
   Las Vegas Life Magazine 1966–7 — 135
   Las Vegas Changing Times 1968 — 135
   Las Vegas Panorama 1968+ — 135
   Nevada Report 1969 — 135
   Quarterly Las Vegas Review 1969 — 136
   The Star (Las Vegas Star) 1969+ — 136
   La Verdad 1969–77 — 136
   Las Vegas Free Press 1970–1 — 136
   Beat of the Boulevard 1970–2 — 136
   Cabaret Magazine 1971 — 137
   Earth 1971 — 137
   Democratic News 1971–2 — 137
   Western Business News (Nevada Business News) 1973–5 — 137
   Vegas Wild 1973 — 137
   The GOPaper 1974–7 — 137
   The Democrat 1975–8 — 138
   Official Las Vegas Entertainment and Events Guide 1975–8 — 138
   We Are Free 1975–9 — 138
   Spring Mountain Gazette 1975–6 — 138
   What's Happening 1975–6 — 138
   The Bee Hive 1975+ — 139
   The Overlay 1975+ — 139
   Las Vegas Today 1975+ — 139
   Casino Post 1976+ — 139
   Nevada's Senior Journal 1976 — 139
   Las Vegan 1976+ — 140
   The Green Felt 1977+ — 140
   Las Vegas Mirror 1978+ — 140
   Las Vegas Fun Times 1978 — 140
   Vegas Gay Times 1978+ — 140
   Backstage 1978 — 140
   Vida Nueva 1979+ — 141
   Frontline 1979+ — 141
   The News 1979 — 141
   Off the Strip 1979+ — 141
   Las Vegas West 1979 — 141
LATHROP WELLS (NYE COUNTY)
   Desert News 1979+ — 142
LEWIS (LANDER COUNTY)

Lewis Herald 1881–3	142	Mineral County News 1928	155
LIDA (ESMERALDA COUNTY)		MINDEN (DOUGLAS COUNTY)	
Lida Enterprise 1905–6	142	Minden Times 1936–42	155
LOGANDALE (CLARK COUNTY)		The Nevada Magazine 1945–9	155
Lower Taxes 1917–20	143	MONARCH (NYE COUNTY)	
The Oak 1920–1	143	Monarch Tribune 1906	155
Sain's Weekly Letter 1926–7	143	MOTTSVILLE (DOUGLAS COUNTY)	
Lake Mead Monitor 1979+	143	Mottsville Star 1879	156
LORENA (MINERAL COUNTY)		MOUNTAIN CITY (ELKO COUNTY)	
Lorena Miner 1908	144	Weekly 6 Shooter 1869	156
LOVELOCK (PERSHING COUNTY)		Mountain City Times 1898	156
Nevada New Era 1892–4	144	Mountain City Mail 1938–9	157
Lovelock Tribune 1898–1912	144	NATIONAL (HUMBOLDT COUNTY)	
Lovelock Standard 1900	145	National Miner 1910–3	157
The Argus 1900–5	145	NELSON (CLARK COUNTY)	
Lovelock Review 1908–10	145	Eldorado Canyon Miner 1917	157
Lovelock Review-Miner 1911+	146	NIXON (WASHOE COUNTY)	
Northern Nevada Weekly Mine Review 1915	146	Firewheel (Pyramid Lake News) 1972–3	158
Nevada Legionnaire 1932–50	147	NORTH LAS VEGAS (CLARK COUNTY)	
LUCKY BOY (MINERAL COUNTY)		North Las Vegas News 1949–59	158
Luckyboy Mining Record (Walker Lake Mining Record) 1908–9	147	North Las Vegas Sun 1950–1	158
Hawthorne-Lucky Boy News 1909	148	Las Vegas Family Shopper 1958–9	159
Hawthorne-Lucky Boy Post 1909	116	Nevada Times (Nevada Mobile Home Times) 1958+	159
MANHATTAN (NYE COUNTY)		North Las Vegas Valley Times 1959+	159
Manhattan Mail 1906–11	148	Bullseye 1974+	159
Manhattan News 1906–7	149	OLINGHOUSE (CHURCHILL COUNTY)	
Manhattan Times 1907	149	Olinghouse Miner 1905	160
Manhattan Post 1910–4	149	ORO CITY (MINERAL COUNTY)	
The Knocker 1911	150	Oro City Times 1907	160
Manhattan Magnet 1917–22	150	OROVADA (HUMBOLDT COUNTY)	
MASON (LYON COUNTY)		Orovada Weekly Journal 1924–5	160
Mason Valley News 1909–14	150	OSCEOLA (WHITE PINE COUNTY)	
MAZUMA (PERSHING COUNTY)		Osceola Nugget 1903	160
Mazuma Herald 1907	151	OVERTON (CLARK COUNTY)	
Mazuma World 1907–8	151	Moapa Valley Herald 1975+	161
Seven Troughs District News 1908–9	151	Lake Mead Monitor 1979+	161
Seven Troughs Miner 1909–10	151	PACKARD (PERSHING COUNTY)	
MCGILL (WHITE PINE COUNTY)		Rochester-Packard Miner 1917–9	220
Copper Ore 1909–14	152	PAHRUMP (NYE COUNTY)	
METROPOLIS (ELKO COUNTY)		Pahrump Valley Times 1971+	161
Metropolis Chronicle 1911–3	152	Pahrump Valley Star 1972+	161
MIDAS (ELKO COUNTY)		Desert Living 1979+	162
Gold Circle Miner 1908	153	Pahrump Tribune 1979+	162
Gold Circle News 1908	153	PALMETTO (ESMERALDA COUNTY)	
Gold Circle Porcupine 1914	153	Palmetto Herald 1906	162
MILLERS (ESMERALDA COUNTY)		PARADISE (HUMBOLDT COUNTY)	
Millers Booster 1907–8	154	Paradise Reporter 1879–80	162
MINA (MINERAL COUNTY)		Paradise Sunshine 1905–6	163
Western Nevada Miner 1907–30	154	PINE GROVE (LYON COUNTY)	

CONTENTS / xi

Pine Grove News 1868	163	*Reno Democrat* 1883–4	180
PIOCHE (LINCOLN COUNTY)		*Daily Morning Star* 1884–5	180
Lincoln County Record (Pioche Record)		*Sagebrush Stockman* 1886–7	181
1870+	164	*The Free Lance* 1889–91	181
Pioche Review 1872	165	*The Snowbound* 1890	181
Pioche World 1874	166	*Cyclone Occasional* 1891	182
Pioche Journal 1874–6	166	*The Plaindealer* 1895–9	182
Local News 1876	166	*The Daily Nevada Tribune* 1896	182
Pioche Boomlet 1888	166	*Nevada Citizen* 1897	183
The Memorandum 1891	167	*Reno Ledger* 1899–1904	183
The Lode 1893–4	167	*Pandora* 1900	183
Local Messenger 1898–9	167	*Mining and Industrial Review*	
Pioche Times 1902	167	*(Nevada Miner)* 1902–3	184
Chronicle 1910–1	168	*Evening Telegram* 1903	184
Lincoln County Independent 1938–41	168	*Nevada Observer* 1904–7	184
Pioche People's Press 1944	168	*The Star* 1904	185
Slipstream 1946	168	*Amateur Outlook* 1904	185
PIONEER (NYE COUNTY)		*Progressive West* 1905–7	185
Pioneer Topics 1909	169	*Reno Federation* 1906	185
Pioneer Press 1909	169	*Reno Call* 1906	186
Pioneer Market Letter 1909	169	*Nevada Mining Investor* 1906–7	186
Pioneer Times 1909	170	*Nevada Mining Market Outlook*	
PITTMAN (CLARK COUNTY)		1906–7	186
Pittman Key 1942–3	170	*Carnival News* 1906	186
POTOSI (LINCOLN COUNTY)		*Nevada Mining News* 1907–9	187
East of the Nevada; or the Miner's		*The Reveille* 1907–10	187
Voice from the Colorado 1861	170	*Fortnightly Market Review* 1907–8	187
Potosi Nix Cum Rouscht 1861	171	*Corriere di Nevada* 1907–8	188
QUARTZ MOUNTAIN (NYE COUNTY)		*Lantern* 1907–28	188
Quartz Mountain Miner 1926–7	171	*Hot Stuph* 1908	188
RAMSEY (STOREY COUNTY)		*Daily American* 1908	188
Ramsey Recorder 1906–8	172	*Reno Record* 1908	189
RAWHIDE (MINERAL COUNTY)		*Italian-French Colony* 1908–9	189
Rawhide Rustler 1907–9	172	*Mining Digest* 1908	189
Rawhide Times 1908	173	*Nevada Churchman* 1908–12	189
Rawhide News 1908–9	173	*Nevada-California Miner* 1909	190
Rawhide Daily Press 1908	173	*Mining Financial News* 1909	190
Rawhide Press-Times 1908–11	174	*Nevada Mines and Farms* 1909–13	190
Telegraph Gossip 1908	174	*Reno Whooperup* 1909–10	190
Rawhide Miner 1908	174	*Reno Industrial Journal* 1910	191
RENO (WASHOE COUNTY)		*Reno Nevada Weekly* 1910–1	191
Reno Crescent 1868–75	175	*Voice of the People* 1910–1	191
Nevada State Journal 1870+	175	*Nevada Mining News* 1911–6	192
Daily Nevada Democrat 1875	177	*Truth* 1911	192
Reno Evening Gazette 1876+	177	*Nevada Bugle* 1912	192
Nevada State Fair Herald 1877;		*New West* 1912	192
1881; 1885	178	*Nevada News Letter and Advertiser*	
Daily Evening Record 1878	179	1914–27	193
Reno Annual Advertiser 1878	179	*Nevada Rockroller* 1914	193
The Plaindealer 1881–4	179	*Nevada Socialist* 1914	193
Reno Times 1882	180	*Nevada Democrat* 1914–5	194
Reno Bazaar 1882–3	180	*Reno Amusements* 1915	194

xii / THE NEWSPAPERS OF NEVADA

Western Miner 1915–6, 1919, 1927	194
Bollettino del Nevada 1915–44	195
Nevada Federationist 1916–19	195
Western Financier 1916	195
Nevada Socialist 1916	195
The Nevadan 1916	196
Nevada Home Builder 1917–21	196
Nevada Federationist 1917	196
Nevada Observer 1917–8	197
The Fighting Mechanic 1918	197
Nevadan 1918	197
Nevada Mining Press 1918–31	198
Nevada Stockgrower 1919–33	198
Nevada Topics and Advertiser 1920	198
Elks Show Message 1921	198
Theatre Herald 1921–2	198
Nevada Searchlight 1921–2	199
Sagebrush Legionnaire 1922	199
Intermountain Liberal (Nevada Liberal) 1924–31	199
Nevada Voice 1926–7	200
Tri-State Miner 1926	200
Western Mines and Markets 1927	200
Nevada Review Monthly 1928	200
Reno News 1930	201
Nevada State Builder 1931–2	201
Nevada Labor Record 1932–3	201
Reno State Economist 1932	201
Nevada Register 1932+	202
News Advertiser 1934–6	202
Nevada Veteran and Labor News 1935	202
Desert, A Nevada Magazine 1936	202
Reno Life 1936	202
Town Talk 1938	203
Nevada Independent 1938	203
Mining Press 1938–49	203
Shopping News 1939–48	203
Here and Now 1940	203
Nevada State Labor News 1941–51	204
The Pry 1942–3	204
Flyer 1943	204
Destinies 1943–4	205
Reno Reminder 1945	205
Mountain Magic 1947–8	205
Reno Reporter 1947–50	205
CAPReno 1948–9	206
Nevada Hunting and Fishing 1948–9	206
Shopping News Reminder 1949	206
Reno Fundial 1949–52	206
Nevada Independent and Reno Reporter 1950	207
Donner Trail Reporter 1950	207
Nevada State News 1951–7	207
Reno This Week 1952	207
Nevada Beverage Index 1952+	207
Reno Pace 1952–3	208
Boots and Chutes 1954–5	208
Friday 1954	208
The Independent 1955–8	208
Vigilant Reporter 1957	208
Sierra Magazine 1959–61	209
Flight Times 1959–63	209
The Sentinel 1959–75	209
Reno News 1959	209
Action 1960–71;1977+	210
Washoe County Citizen 1960–1	210
KOLO Times 1961	210
Cupid's Destiny 1961–77	210
Nevada Veterans' Journal 1962–6	210
Native Nevadan (Newsletter) 1964+	211
Northern Nevada Labor News 1964–79	211
Camels Coming 1965–8	211
The Citizen 1965–6	211
Many Smokes 1966–77	212
The Camels Hump 1966	212
View Magazine 1966–7	212
Air Age News 1967–8	212
Home and the Range 1968	212
Love 1968	213
West Coast Poetry Review 1971–7	213
Showtime 1971+	213
Nevada Mobile Home News 1973	213
Impact 1973–9	213
Our Town 1974	214
Fun and Gaming 1974–5	214
Northern Nevada Shopping News 1974	214
Silver Circle Mobile Home News 1975	214
The Nevada Outdoor Adventure 1975+	214
Nevada Sage 1975+	214
Nevada Profiles 1976	215
Reno Magazine 1976	215
Northern Nevada Home 1976	215
The Sierra Scene 1976	215
Cathouse News 1977	216
Western Wildlife 1977–8	216
Nevada Horse Life 1977+	216
Discover Magazine 1977–8	216

The Green Sheet (Green Felt News)		*Lyon County Times* 1874–80	228
1978–9	216	*Mining Reporter* 1876	229
Key Magazine 1978+	217	*Reporter* 1876	229
Nevadian 1979+	217	SILVER PEAK (ESMERALDA COUNTY)	
Arcadian 1979	217	*Silver Peak Post* 1906–7	229
Reno Magazine 1979+	217	SKOOKUM (LANDER COUNTY)	
The Local Picture 1979+	217	*Skookum Times* 1908	230
RHYOLITE (NYE COUNTY)		SPARKS (WASHOE COUNTY)	
Rhyolite Herald 1905–12	218	*Harriman Herald* 1904	230
Bullfrog Miner 1906–9	218	*Sparks Headlight* 1904–5	230
Rhyolite Daily Bulletin 1907–9	219	*Sparks Dispatch* 1905	230
Death Valley Magazine (Death Valley Prospector) 1907–8	219	*The Forum (Nevada Forum)* 1906–10	231
ROCHESTER (PERSHING COUNTY)		*Corriere di Nevada* 1907	231
Rochester Miner 1913–4	219	*Nevada Methodist* 1907	231
Rochester Journal 1913	220	*Headlight* 1908	232
Rochester Mining News 1913	220	*The Magnet* 1909–10	232
Rochester Paycrack 1916–7	220	*Sparks Tribune* 1910+	232
Rochester-Packard Miner 1917–9	220	*Saturday Reporter* 1915	233
ROSEBUD (PERSHING COUNTY)		*Nevada Legionnaire* 1950–8	233
Rosebud Mining News 1907	221	*Nevada Sportsman* 1956–7	233
ROUND MOUNTAIN (NYE COUNTY)		*Sparks Advertiser* 1958	233
Nugget 1906–10	221	*Nevada Federal Journal* 1964	234
RUBY HILL (EUREKA COUNTY)		*Nevada State Public Observer* 1964	234
Ruby Hill Mining Report 1878–9	221	*Hearth and Home* 1966	234
Ruby Hill Mining News 1880–4	222	*Air Age News* 1968	234
RUBY VALLEY (ELKO COUNTY)		*Big Nickel* 1968+	234
Ruby Valley News 1975+	222	*Key* 1971	235
SAFFORD (EUREKA COUNTY)		*Nevada Rancher* 1971+	235
Safford Express 1883	223	*Valley Green Sheet* 1972	235
SCHELLBOURNE (WHITE PINE COUNTY)		*Sierra Shopper* 1976–7	235
Schell Creek Prospect 1872–3	223	STATE LINE (CLARK COUNTY)	
SCHURZ (MINERAL COUNTY)		*Mining News* 1902	235
The Indian Call 1939	224	*State Line Oracle* 1903	236
Agai Dicutta Yuduan (Paiute) 1975–7	224	STATELINE (DOUGLAS COUNTY)	
News Notes 1977–9	224	*Tahoe Chronicle* 1967–8	236
Neh-Muh News (Numa News) 1979	224	STEWART (ORMSBY COUNTY)	
SEARCHLIGHT (CLARK COUNTY)		*Indian Advance* 1899–1903	236
Searchlight Bulletin (The Searchlight) 1902–13	224	*New Indian* 1902–7	236
Searchlight News 1907–8	225	*Nevada American* 1913–5	237
Searchlight Enterprise 1917–8	225	SUN VALLEY (WASHOE COUNTY)	
Searchlight Journal 1946–7	225	*Valley Outlook* 1972–3	237
Searchlight News-Bulletin 1951	226	SUTRO (LYON COUNTY)	
SHERMANTOWN (WHITE PINE COUNTY)		*Sutro Independent* 1875–80	237
White Pine Evening Telegram 1869	226	TAYLOR (WHITE PINE COUNTY)	
Shermantown Reporter 1869–70	226	*White Pine Reflex* 1884–5	238
SILVER BOW (NYE COUNTY)		*White Pine News* 1885–8	238
Silver Bow Standard 1905–6	227	TENABO (LANDER COUNTY)	
SILVER CITY (LYON COUNTY)		*Bullion District Miner* 1907	239
Washoe Times 1861	227	TOBAR (ELKO COUNTY)	
		Eye-Opener 1912	239
		Tobar Times 1916	239

TONOPAH (NYE COUNTY)
    Tonopah Bonanza 1901–29   240
    Tonopah Miner 1902–21   240
    Tonopah Sun 1904–10   241
    Tonopah Nevadan 1912–3   242
    Tonopah Daily Times 1915–29   242
    The Net 1918   243
    Tonopah Mining Reporter 1921–9   243
    Nevada Mining Record 1926–9   243
    Tonopah Times-Bonanza 1929+   243
    Nevada Mining Record & Reporter 1929–32   244
    Bombing and Gunnery Range 1942–3   244
    Nevada Democratic Record (Nevada Record) 1962+   245
    Nevada Veterans' Journal 1966+   245
TRANSVAAL (NYE COUNTY)
    Transvaal Miner 1906   245
    Transvaal Tribune 1906   245
TREASURE CITY (WHITE PINE COUNTY)
    White Pine Gazette 1868   246
    White Pine News 1868–70   246
TUSCARORA (ELKO COUNTY)
    Tuscarora Times 1877   247
    Mining Review 1877   247
    Tuscarora Times-Review 1878–1903   247
    Mining News 1883   248
    Tuscarora Mining News 1907–8   248
    Business Talks 1908   249
TYBO (NYE COUNTY)
    Tybo Sun 1877–80   249
UNIONVILLE (PERSHING COUNTY)
    Humboldt Register 1863–9   249
    Humboldt Register and Workingman's Advocate 1869   250
    Silver State 1870–4   251
    Mining Topics 1921–6   251
VERNON (PERSHING COUNTY)
    Vernon Miner 1907   252
    Vernon Review 1907   252
    Seven Troughs Miner 1907–9   252
VIRGINIA CITY (STOREY COUNTY)
    Territorial Enterprise 1860–1916   253
    Virginia Daily Union 1862–7   255
    Virginia Evening Bulletin 1863–4   256
    Democratic Standard 1863   256
    The Occidental 1864   257
    Nevada Pionier 1864   257
    The Daily Old Piute 1864–5   257
    Washoe Stock Circular 1864   258
    Daily Evening Washoe Herald 1864   258
    The Daily Constitution 1864–5   259
    Nevada Staats Zeitung 1864   259
    Local Advertiser 1865   259
    Two O'clock News 1865   259
    Deutsche Union 1866   260
    The Daily Trespass 1867–8   260
    The Daily Safeguard 1868–9   260
    City Review 1868–9   261
    Virginia Evening Chronicle 1872–1927   261
    The Footlight 1872–87   262
    Pacific Coast Advertiser 1873   263
    Nevada Mining Review 1873   263
    The Daily Independent 1874–5   263
    Nevada Post 1874   264
    Nevada Staats Zeitung 1875   264
    Comstock Record 1876   264
    Stock Report 1877–8   265
    Nevada Statesman 1877   265
    The Lariat 1877   265
    Stock Ledger 1877–9   266
    The Stage 1878–80   266
    Rushlight 1878   266
    Nevada Monthly 1880   267
    The Occasional 1886   267
    Comstock Union 1886   267
    The Evening Report 1887–1904   268
    The Orphans' Appeal 1887–90   268
    Republican Principles 1888   268
    Comstock Miner 1889   269
    Campaign Notes 1900   269
    Monday Budget 1917–8   269
    Monday Budget 1927–9   269
    Virginia City News 1930–51   270
    Territorial Enterprise 1946   270
    Territorial Enterprise and Virginia City News 1952–196 9   271
    Virginia City Times 1958–61   271
    Virginia City Chronicle 1962   271
    Sun Mountain Sentinel 1964–5   271
    Virginia City Times Bonanza 1969   272
    Virginia City Legend 1970–3   272
    Virginia City Crier 1974–5   272
    We, The People 1975   272
WABUSKA (LYON COUNTY)
    Wabuska Mangler   273
WADSWORTH (WASHOE COUNTY)
    Wadsworth Dispatch 1892–1904   273
    The Dispatch 1920   274
    Nevadian Times 1927–31   274
WARD (WHITE PINE COUNTY)
    Ward Miner 1876–7   274

Ward Reflex 1877–84	275	*Winnemucca Republican* 1902–4	283
WASHOE CITY (WASHOE COUNTY)		*Humboldt Standard* 1903	283
Washoe Times 1862–3	275	*Humboldt Star* 1906–1962	283
Old Pah Utah 1863–4	276	*Silver State News* 1907–8	283
Washoe Weekly Star 1864–5	276	*Humboldt Bulletin* 1961–72	284
Washoe Weekly Times 1865	277	*Humboldt Star & Battle Mountain*	
Eastern Slope 1865–8	277	*Scout* 1962–7	285
WELLS (ELKO COUNTY)		*Nevada Mining Record* 1966	285
Wells Index 1896	277	*Territorial Enterprise* 1969–70	285
Nevada State Herald 1897–1933	278	*Humboldt Sun* 1972+	286
Wells Progress 1936+	278	*Winni Minimart* 1977+	286
WHITE PLAINS (CHURCHILL COUNTY)		WONDER (CHURCHILL COUNTY)	
Churchill News 1888	279	*Wonder Mining News* 1906–12	286
WHITNEY (CLARK COUNTY)		*Wonder Miner* 1907	287
Whitney News 1942–3	279	*American Enterprise* 1908	287
WINNEMUCCA (HUMBOLDT COUNTY)		YERINGTON (LYON COUNTY)	
Winnemucca Argent 1868	279	*Mason Valley Tidings* 1893–4	287
Humboldt National 1869	280	*Yerington Rustler* 1895–1900	287
Humboldt Register 1869–76	280	*Lyon County Monitor* 1900–1902	288
The Silver State 1874–1925	281	*Yerington Times (Lyon County Times)*	
Humboldt Mail 1886	282	1901–32	288
People's Advocate 1898–9	282	*Lyon County Wasp* 1912–3	289
The Nevada Magazine 1899–1900	282	*Mason Valley News* 1914+	289
Nevada News 1900–1	283	*Numu Ya Dua' (Numa Ya'-Dua)*	
		1973–6; 1979+	289

THE BORDER NEWSPAPERS

ARIZONA			
Mohave County	292	*Placer County*	305
CALIFORNIA		*San Bernardino County*	305
Alpine County	293	*Sierra County*	307
Eldorado County	294	IDAHO	
Inyo County	295	*Owyhee County*	308
Kern County	298	OREGON	
Lassen County	299	*Lake County*	308
Modoc County	300	UTAH	
Mono County	302	*Tooele County*	309
Nevada County	304	*Washington County*	309

Bibliography   311

Index   313

Preface

This new study of the newspapers and selected periodicals of Nevada supplants a previous work, *The Newspapers of Nevada, 1858–1958.* We survey here about 800 publications which appeared from 1854 through 1979, adding some 320 papers not previously listed (roughly half of which were started since 1958) and providing new material on about 400 others. We have included nearly every type of newspaper and periodical published in Nevada during this period—not only traditional newspapers, but also weekly advertisers and penny shoppers, amateur and organizational publications, literary and news magazines, comic and campaign sheets, stock market reviews and promoters' tip sheets, entertainment and matrimonial guides, and even two fictitious papers, the *Clarois Review* and *Wabuska Mangler,* which had a life only in the columns of other papers. Each of these diverse periodicals had its place in recording life in Nevada. We have, however, excluded government serials, school papers, and house organs which were published primarily for use by employees.

We hope that this work will serve not only as a history of the Nevada periodical press, but also as a guide to primary sources for research into Nevada's history. For the latter purpose we have listed microfilm holdings.

Each newspaper and periodical is listed under the town in which it was published, in chronological order of its establishment. This necessarily means that the histories of some peripatetic papers, such as the *White Pine News,* which moved from town to town five times in its career, will appear under the various towns where they were published. The towns appear alphabetically, and their current county locations are indicated in the table of contents. Each publication is listed by the actual name on its masthead. Where the masthead names underwent minor changes over the years, we have used the name as it last appeared. When there was a major change in the name of a paper, we have taken that to mark the commencement of a new paper, except in those cases when the management remained the same and the serial numbering of the original paper continued. For each publication we give a brief historical sketch and a list of known holdings. The citation "film" indicates duplicate microfilm holdings at each of the four major libraries in the state: the University of Nevada, Reno; the University of Nevada, Las Vegas; the Nevada Historical Society, Reno; and the Nevada State Library, Carson City.

This new study of the Nevada press resulted indirectly from the filming of the state's newspapers. The filming was begun in 1963 by the Nevada Newspaper Microfilming Project (NNMP), which was organized for the specific purpose of microfilming all of the newspapers known to have been published in Nevada. The NNMP was a cooperative effort among the state's four major libraries, the University of Nevada, Reno, being responsible for all papers prior to 1950, and the Nevada State Library for those after that date. In the course of preparing the papers for filming, issues were read and changes of title, place, frequency, editor, and publisher were noted. This review provided much of the new material included in the present study as well as the stimulus for undertaking it.

For their aid in making this study possible, we would like to express our gratitude to Robert Armstrong, Linda Reichlin, Judy Verstuyft, and Kenneth Carpenter. Appreciation is also extended to Mary Ellen Glass, former UNR oral historian, Richard Datin of the Nevada State Museum, Guy Rocha of the Nevada State Archives, and Ruth Donovan and Robert E. Blesse of the UNR Library. Lee Mortensen was extremely helpful in locating physical issues of newspapers at the Nevada Historical Society. Anna Dean Kepper at the University of Nevada, Las Vegas, gave invaluable aid for southern Nevada publications, and Vivian Fisher of the Bancroft Library pleasantly provided valuable information on that institution's holdings. We are also grateful to David F. Myrick and Gil Schmidtmann for their generous assistance.

Errors will inevitably be found in any study of this nature, and new papers are bound to turn up. Any additional information or corrections will be gratefully received by the authors. Please address comments to them in care of the University of Nevada Press.

KAREN RIX GASH
RICHARD E. LINGENFELTER

Introduction

The bulk of the newspapers and periodicals founded in Nevada have folded, and the history of the Nevada press can leave one with a sense of tragedy and futility. Indeed, most Nevada editors would seem either to have lacked good judgment or to have suffered more than their share of insanity. Of the roughly 800 publications started in Nevada in the last 125 years, half failed in a year or less, and only 70 were still being published in 1979. Roughly half of Nevada's papers were published in mining camps, and many others were pulbished in farming or ranching communities or in railroad shipping points dependent on the mining camps for a market.

Although the failure of some newspapers may be traced to the overoptimism of editors, failures were more often linked to the decline and failure of mining camps. It was not the judgment, energy, or sacrifice of the editor that molded the fate of a paper; its success or failure was already cast in the extent of the ore bodies which lay hidden beneath the earth. Only the miner's pick and blasting cap could speak the fate of the camp and the press.

All guesses at the size of an ore body were based on the merest of superficial evidence, but everyone, the capitalist, the editor, and the day-wage miner alike, took the gamble. Some lodes like the Comstock endured for years, while others lasted barely beyond the first telling. Behind the excitement of every new discovery was the realization that, no matter how large the lode might be, it was still finite. Someday, in a month or in twenty years, the veins would pinch out and the camp would die. Until this day came, and while ore was still to be mined, the camp lived and the press prospered.

Not all camps reached the size and degree of prosperity necessary to support the press. Probably only one out of every ten mining camps ever boasted a newspaper; but thousands of camps were founded, and of these, hundreds reached large proportions before they collapsed. There, newspapers flourished, fulfilling their duties to the community as long as they were needed. Only a very few camps survived the boom period to enter a more stable era as supply centers or county seats.

Despite the ephemeral nature of any particular camp, the mining region as a whole remained strikingly constant. Throughout the history of the region, the total population and number of camps remained fairly stable. The death of one camp was accompanied by the birth of another, and the population and institutions simply shifted. The newspapers, too, moved from camp to camp. Some papers such as the *White Pine News,* which changed locations five times, retained the same name throughout their careers, changing only the dateline. Usually, however, management provided a new name for a paper when it moved to a new location, even though the press and material often remained the same.

Several factors enabled so large a number of newspapers to be established in the remote mining camps of Nevada. These were: the low cost of equipment, the small staff required to run a paper, and the ease with which a plant could be transported. Many a mining-camp weekly was issued by a one-man staff from a small hand press and a few fonts of type. The material and press required to issue a small four-page weekly cost only $1,000, and the plant for a daily ran about $3,000. When a camp declined, the entire newspaper plant could usually be loaded into one wagon and hauled to the next boom.

Although a small weekly newspaper required little capital investment, it was also rather unremunerative. Indeed, many an editor explained the failure of his paper with the statement that he would have liked to continue the paper, but he had not brought enough money with him. As a result, many editors had other sources of income to support, if not wholly to sustain, their editorial careers. Some were lawyers, like C. C. Powning and C. N. Harris; assayers, like Conrad Weigand and T. E. Picotte; architects, like S. F. Hoole; saloon keepers, like W. J. Forbes; and even part-time clowns, like Orlando (Dan) Jones. Such men drifted in and out of the editorial profession, working for a time at some other occupation until they accumulated enough money to establish a newspaper and then, when it failed, returning to their previous careers.

Many times it took even more than a large bankroll and incurable optimism to keep a newspaper alive. On many a dull day the editor was called upon to create news where none existed. On these occasions some of Nevada's earliest literary endeavors were born, as tall tales and anecdotes flowed from the pens and fell into type at the hands of Dan De Quille, Mark Twain, Fred Hart, James W. E. Townsend, Sam P. Davis, and many others. They created in their legends the proudest legacy of the Nevada press.

When wit and imagination failed, many an editor resorted to filling his columns with items clipped from other papers. For some this practice became so common that it seemed their principal tools were not a press and type, but a pair of scissors and a pastepot. This was accepted practice so long as proper credit was given the source. If this sacred trust was violated, however, the offender was forced to bear the full forensic wrath of his wronged contemporary. The Reno *Gazette* and the Virginia City *Chronicle* had several duels over such a failure, during one of which the *Gazette* editor complained, "The Virginia *Chronicle* evidently favors the 'no credit' system. At least, it copies copiously from the *Gazette* without credit." The *Gazette* editor was rightfully aggravated, since the *Chronicle* had credited his rival, the *Nevada State Journal,* as the source for a Wadsworth suicide story, which had cost the *Gazette* $3.05 to get by telegraph. In 1895, the news-gathering facilities of many Nevada papers were united, with the formation of the Nevada Press Association. As a means of enforcing solidarity, those papers that did not join were supposed to be deprived of complimentary exchange subscriptions from members. Eventually most of the papers in the state joined the association. When silver became a major political issue three years later, another organization, the Bi-Metallic Newspaper League of Nevada, was formed by those editors favoring the sixteen-to-one ratio of silver coinage.

In all, the mining-camp press served many valuable and creative purposes. Most obviously, the press furnished national and local news to the miners and promoted the mines and the district abroad. Locally, it served as a civilizing and socializing vehicle, aiding the establishment of political and judicial institutions. Nationally, it acted in the interest of organized politics and mining. Finally, but not least important, the press was an art form, providing a certain cultural elegance in the fragile metaphors which it created in the wasteland.

In recent decades, gambling and tourism have come to dominate Nevada's economy, and the rash of Las Vegas papers reflect that change. But despite increasing prosperity, the larger newspapers in both cities and small towns have been absorbed by a very few newspaper chains. Such a course was the natural consequence of rising labor and printing costs, and radio and television competition, but it has taken a great toll on the diversity and individuality that once characterized the Nevada press. There are indications, however, that the great reductions in printing costs recently made possible by photo offset processes are bringing about a resurgence of small community papers and a renewed diversity in the Nevada press.

Location Symbols

In listing periodical holdings, a short dash denotes a continuous run, brackets denote a broken file, and a comma or semicolon denotes a break. The following symbols indicate the location of the holdings.

Az	Arizona State Department of Library and Archives, Phoenix, Ariz.
AzTP	Arizona Historical Society, Tucson, Ariz.
AzU	University of Arizona, Tucson, Ariz.
C	California State Library, Sacramento, Calif.
CAltu	Modoc County Free Library, Alturas, Calif.
CBaK	Kern County Library, Bakersfield, Calif.
CBiI	*Inyo Register* Office, Bishop, Calif.
CBrC	Mono County Recorder, Bridgeport, Calif.
CHi	California Historical Society, San Francisco, Calif.
CIE	Eastern California Museum, Independence, Calif.
CInI	Inyo County Free Library, Independence Calif.
CL	Los Angeles Public Library, Los Angeles, Calif.
CLCM	Los Angeles County Museum of Natural History, Los Angeles, Calif.
CLSM	Southwest Museum, Los Angeles, Calif.
CLU	University of California, Los Angeles, Calif.
CMrC	Alpine County Recorder, Markleeville, Calif.
CoU	University of Colorado, Boulder, Colo.
CP	Pasadena Public Library, Pasadena, Calif.
CPom	Pomona Public Library, Pomona, Calif.
CQCL	Plumas County Free Library, Quincy, Calif.
C-S	California State Library, Sutro Branch, San Francisco, Calif.
CSaT	San Francisco Theological Seminary, San Anselmo, Calif.
CSd	San Diego Public Library, San Diego, Calif.
CSfCP	Society of California Pioneers, San Francisco, Calif.
CSfWF-H	Wells Fargo Bank, History Room, Library, San Francisco, Calif.
CSmH	Henry E. Huntington Library, San Marino, Calif.
CSto	Stockton and San Joaquin County Public Library, Stockton, Calif.
CSuLas	Lassen County Free Library, Susanville, Calif.
CTeN	*Tehachapi News* Office, Tehachapi, Calif.
CtY	Yale University, New Haven, Conn.
CU	Main Library, University of California, Berkeley, Calif.
CU-BANC	University of California, Bancroft Library, Berkeley, Calif.
CYoM	Yosemite Museum, Nature Library, Yosemite, Calif.
DI-GS	United States Geological Survey, Reston, Va.
DLC	Library of Congress, Washington, D.C.
DNA	United States National Archives and Records Service, National Archives Library, Washington, D.C.

film	Microfilm available at Nv, NvHi, NvU, and NvULV.
ICHi	Chicago Historical Society, Chicago, Ill.
KHi	Kansas Historical Society, Topeka, Kans.
MH	Harvard University, Cambridge, Mass.
MnHi	Minnesota Historical Society, St. Paul, Minn.
MWA	American Antiquarian Society, Worcester, Mass.
N	New York State Library, Albany, N.Y.
NbHi	Nebraska Historical Society, Lincoln, Neb.
NcD	Duke University, Durham, N.C.
NHi	New York Historical Society, New York, N.Y.
NN	New York Public Library, New York, N.Y.
NNG	General Theological Seminary, New York, N.Y.
Nv	Nevada State Library, Carson City, Nev.
NvBC	Lander County Recorder, Battle Mountain, Nev.
NvCC	Ormsby County Recorder, Carson City, Nev.
NvEC	Elko County Recorder, Elko, Nev.
NvEHi	Northeastern Nevada Historical Society, Elko, Nev.
NvElC	White Pine County Recorder, Ely, Nev.
NvEuC	Eureka County Recorder, Eureka, Nev.
NvFC	Churchill County Museum, Fallon, Nev.
NvFE	*Fallon Eagle-Standard,* Fallon, Nev.
NvGC	Esmeralda County Recorder, Goldfield, Nev.
NvGM	Mormon Station State Park, Genoa, Nev.
NvHC	Mineral County Recorder, Hawthorne, Nev.
NvHi	Nevada Historical Society, Reno, Nev.
NvLR	*Lovelock Review-Miner,* Lovelock, Nev.
NvMC	Douglas County Recorder, Minden, Nev.
NvMiD	Douglas County Library, Minden, Nev.
NvMus	Nevada State Museum, Carson City, Nev.
NvPC	Lincoln County Recorder, Pioche, Nev.
NvRW	Washoe County Library, Reno, Nev.
NvRWR	Washoe County Recorder, Reno, Nev.
NvTC	Nye County Recorder, Tonopah, Nev.
NvU	University of Nevada, Reno, Nev.
NvULV	University of Nevada, Las Vegas, Nev.
NvWC	Humboldt County Recorder, Winnemucca, Nev.
OClWHi	Western Reserve Historical Society, Cleveland, Ohio
Or	Oregon State Library, Salem, Ore.
OrHi	Oregon Historical Society, Portland, Ore.
OrU	University of Oregon, Eugene, Ore.
P	Pennsylvania State Library, Harrisburg, Penn.
pub	Publisher's file
pvt	Private collections
UHi	Utah State Historical Society, Salt Lake City, Utah
USlGS	Church of Jesus Christ of Latter Day Saints, Genealogical Society, Library, Salt Lake City, Utah
UStgD	Dixie College, St. George, Utah
WaPs	State College of Washington, Pullman, Wash.
WHi	State Historical Society of Wisconsin, Madison, Wis.

Reference Abbreviations

Angel	Myron Angel, ed., *History of Nevada*
ANR	*American Newspaper Reporter*
AO	Ely *Amateur Outlook*
AS	*Austin Sun*
Averett	Walter R. Averett correspondence
Ayer	*Ayer Directory of Publications*
BB	*Bulletin of Bibliography*
BBM	*Beatty Bullfrog Miner*
BC	*Belmont Courier*
Beebe	Lucius Beebe, *Comstock Commotion*
BFP	*Bodie* (California) *Free Press*
Bishop	*Bishop's Directory of Virginia City* ...
BMHCN	*Battle Mountain Herald and Central Nevadan*
BM	*Bullfrog Miner*
BMM	*Battle Mountain Messenger*
CA	Carson *Appeal*
Cargile	Lee M. Cargile correspondence
CCS	*Churchill County Standard*
CI	Carson *Index*
CIU	Carson *Index-Union*
CL	*Cheyenne* (Wyoming) *Leader*
CLE	*Caliente Lode-Express*
CO	*Carrara Obelisk*
CSMI	Colorado Springs (Colorado) *Mining Investor*
CTF	Candelaria *True Fissure*
CVN	*Carson Valley News*
CW	Carson *Weekly*
De Quille	Dan De Quille, *History of the Big Bonanza*
DL	*De Lamar Lode*
DMR	Denver *Mining Record*
DNN	*Directory of Nevada Newspapers*
DNT	*Daily Nevada Tribune*
Doten	*The Journals of Alfred Doten*
Drury	Wells Drury, *An Editor on the Comstock Lode*
ECM	*Eldorado Canyon Miner*
EFP	Elko *Free Press*
EI	*Elko Independent*
EN	*Esmeralda News*
ES	*Eureka Sentinel*
FE	*Fallon Eagle*
files	Information derived directly from newspapers on file in repositories

FN	*Fairview News*
Folkes	John G. Folkes, *Nevada's Newspapers: A Bibliography*
GaN	*Golconda News*
Gash	Karen Rix Gash files
GC	*Goldfield Chronicle*
GeC	*Genoa Courier*
GHN	*Gold Hill News*
GN	*Goldfield News*
GR	*Goldfield Review*
Greenspun	Herman M. Greenspun, *Where I Stand*
GT	*Goldfield Tribune*
Hazlett	Fanny G. Hazlett and Gertrude Hazlett Randall, "Historical Sketches . . . of Dayton"
Hensher	Alan Hensher, "Earle Clemens and the Rhyolite Herald"
HR	*Humboldt Register*
II	*Inyo Independent*
IR	*Inyo Register*
Jackson	W. Turrentine Jackson, *Treasure Hill*
Jensen	Rex Jensen correspondence
L	*Lantern*
LA	*Lovelock Argus*
LAS	*Los Angeles Star*
LCT	*Lyon County Times*
LFP	*Lander Free Press*
LO	Logandale *Oak*
LRM	*Lovelock Review-Miner*
LT	*Lovelock Tribune*
LVA	*Las Vegas Age*
MCI	*Mineral County Independent*
McMurtrie	Douglas C. McMurtrie, *A Bibliography of Nevada Newspapers*
MER	San Francisco *Mining and Engineering Review*
Mildren	Edgar E. Mildren correspondence
MM	Denver, *Miners' Magazine*
MT	*Mining Topics*
Murbarger	Nell Murbarger correspondence
MVN	*Mason Valley News*
Myrick	David F. Myrick correspondence
NE	*Needles* (California) *Eye*
NeT	*Nevada Tribune*
NF	*Nevada Forum*
NMI	*Nevada Mining Investor*
NMN	*Nevada Mining News*
NSJ	*Nevada State Journal*
NT	*Nevadian Times*
Polk	R. L. Polk, *Nevada State Gazetteer*
PR	*Pioche Record*
PSND	*Pacific States Newspaper Directory*
PT	*Pioneer Topics*
PTR	*People's Tribune*
pub	Information received from publisher
RC	*Reno Crescent*

RDP	*Rawhide Daily Press*
RG	Reno *Gazette*
RH	*Rhyolite Herald*
Rice	George G. Rice, *My Adventures With Your Money*
Ritter	Betsy Ritter, *Life in the Ghost City of Rhyolite, Nevada*
Rogers	Franklin R. Rogers, "Washoe's First Literary Journal"
RPT	*Rawhide Press-Times*
RR	Reno *Reveille*
RRR	*Reese River Reveille*
SA	*Silver Age*
SB	*Searchlight Bulletin*
SFAC	San Francisco *Alta California*
SFE	San Francisco *Examiner*
Shepperson	Wilbur S. Shepperson, *Retreat to Nevada*
SPP	*Silver Peak Post*
SS	*Silver State*
TB	*Tonopah Bonanza*
TE	*Territorial Enterprise*
TM	*Tonopah Miner*
TMR	*Tonopah Mining Reporter*
Trego	Peggy Trego correspondence
TS	*Tonopah Sun*
TTR	*Tuscarora Times-Review*
Twain	Mark Twain, *Roughing It*
VC	Virginia City *Chronicle*
WD	*Wadsworth Dispatch*
WLB	*Walker Lake Bulletin*
WM	*Western Miner*
WNM	*Western Nevada Miner*
WPN	*White Pine News*
Young	Janie Young correspondence

The Newspapers of Nevada

ACME

Nevada Copper News

The weekly *Nevada Copper News* was begun on March 15, 1907, at the height of a copper boom at Acme, also known as Copperfield, a station on the Southern Pacific Railroad. J. Holman Buck of the *Western Nevada Miner*, at Mina, nine miles farther down the tracks, was editor and proprietor, and continued it for only a few months.

Nevada Copper News: (Mar 15 1907–c. May 1907)
  No issues located.
Ref: TS Mr 13 1907; GT Ap 11 1907; RG My 1, 3 1907

ATWOOD

Fairplay Prospector

Following his suspension of the *Nevada Copper News* at Acme, J. Holman Buck established the *Fairplay Prospector* at the new camp of Atwood, some thirty miles to the northeast of Mina. The *Prospector* was issued weekly at $4 a year, and competed with Lindley Branson's neighboring *Goldyke Sun* for the scant patronage of the district. This venture also proved short-lived and the paper was undoubtedly suspended before the end of 1907.

Fairplay Prospector: (c. 1907)
  No issues located.
Ref: Polk 1907–8

AURORA

Esmeralda Star

The *Esmeralda Star*, the pioneer paper of Esmeralda County, was started at Aurora on May 17, 1862. It was Republican in politics and sold at a subscription price of $12 per year. Edwin A. Sherman and Co. appeared as publishers, with U. B. Freaner, a secessionist, being the other half of the partnership. This created tension until March 7, 1863, when Sherman bought Freaner's interest and became sole proprietor.

  The *Star* was published weekly until June 24, 1863, when it was expanded to a semiweekly. On September 23, it also changed the name of its location. Previously, many had supposed that Aurora was in Mono County, California, but with the completion of the boundary line survey it was determined to be in Esmeralda County, Nevada, and the *Star* changed accordingly.

On November 18, 1863, John Hatch joined Sherman in the publication of the *Star*. After nearly being assassinated by a rebel desperado, Sherman decided that he had had enough, and he sold his interest to Hatch. Through political difficulties the *Star* had come to have a bad name, and Hatch wanted to make a fresh start. Thus in March of 1864, he suspended the *Star*, and later that same month, used the press and material to found the *Esmeralda Daily Union*.

The colorful history of the Washington press, upon which the paper was printed, was told by Sherman in the *Star* of May 2, 1863:

> The press and a very small part of the present material formerly belonged to the late and lamented J. Judson Ames, and from which was issued the San Diego *Herald*. This press was brought across the Isthmus of Panama in 1850 by Judge Ames, and in coming up the Chagres River was thrown overboard by the upsetting of the canoe in which it was being conveyed to Gorgona. The natives being unable to lift the heavier part of it from the bottom of the stream which had a very rapid current, the Judge, who was a very powerful man, jumped overboard and lifted it out himself and placed it in the canoe, much to the astonishment of his dark-skinned companions. This being a No. 3 Washington press, its weight can be more accurately estimated by the members of the craft than by others; at any rate it will suffice for our readers to know that it weighs more than four hundred pounds. He succeeded in getting it to Panama after much difficulty; and soon after issued at that place the Panama *Star* for a very short period, and then brought it to San Francisco.
>
> By the advice of his friends he was induced to move it to San Diego, as that point was then advocated as the western terminus of the Pacific Railroad; and it was desired by speculators in town lots to have a newspaper published there, to induce immigration and give an importance to the place. At that time there were but few papers published in California, and as the members of Congress were of Southern proclivities and intent on having a Pacific Railroad for the exclusive benefit of the Southern route, their aid and encouragement of every enterprise in that portion of the State was given to that end; hence the encouragement of the San Diego *Herald* to that end. For ten long years Ames continued its publication, excepting at times when the immortal "John Phoenix", alias "Squibob", during the Judge's absence, would carry it on in his own inimitable style, playing all sorts of pranks, and scattering gems of wit. The cuts out of which he formed the *Pictorial Herald*, we still retain. The garrison being removed from San Diego, and the county exporting nothing but hides, its commercial importance died entirely away. The Mormons having left San Bernardino to go to Salt Lake, at the call of Brigham Young, the Americans in that valley sent to Ames in San Diego, offering to pay the entire expense of moving it to their village, and as Ames said "they were skinning everything in San Diego County, he thought that perhaps they might commence on him, and in order to save his own hide he would accept the offer of the San Bernardinos, before he was flayed alive." He accordingly, in the summer of 1859, moved his press to San Bernardino and published the *Herald* there.

Unfortunately for him the population was too small to support a paper, and his printers not being willing to take *truck* in payment for their services, he was compelled to let out his press to other parties, who in turn failed to make anything for themselves, or pay him for the use of the press. Disheartened in every respect, the flower of his life having been thrown away in endeavoring to sustain the fruitless project of making San Diego the western terminus of the Pacific Railroad, the blasting of all his hopes of prosperity to be realized in its completion, and the failure of men who broke their promises with him, all added their weight to his sorrow, and J. Judson Ames, the true friend and social companion, died of a broken heart.

Previous, however to his death, the press and material passed into our hands, and with it we received this admonition from him. "If ever you let this press be used in publishing a rebel sheet, or dispose of it to a traitor, my ghost shall haunt you as long as you live, and when you die 'Squibob' shall act as foreman in sculling you across the 'Styx'." Alas, both are now lying 'neath the green turf.

In April, 1861, we commenced the publication of the San Bernardino *Patriot*. The Holcombe Valley mines having induced a considerable emigration to that part of the country, the prospects for publishing a paper were at that time somewhat flattering. But difficulties soon intervened. The Mormons nearly all returned, the mines were not so rich as they promised to be, large numbers of horse thieves and other outlaws made it their resort, and more than all, armed bodies of secessionists were formed all through that section, and it was extremely hazardous to publish a Union paper among such a people. In October of that year, the press was leased for a certain time, but the lessee was totally unable to succeed, and throwing up the contract it was deemed best in February, 1862, to remove it to Esmeralda; and accordingly it was packed up and brought to Aurora by the Owen's River route. While on the way it narrowly escaped destruction from the hostile Indians; but owing to the kindness of Colonel Evans and Lieutenant Noble of the Second Cavalry California Volunteers, an escort was furnished and it finally reached here on or about the first of May last. At that time we were in Sacramento and learning that it had arrived, we started from that place on the ninth of May and reached here on the seventeenth. On our arrival we were astonished to find the first number of the *Star* already issued without giving the publishers' names; and surprised to find it expressing sentiments entirely antagonistic to the principles we cherish. We also found that a heavy sacrifice had to be made on our part before we could get possession of the press and material in order to publish a loyal paper; and that was, to give a bill of sale of one-half of it in order to get control of the whole, both editorially and financially. We made that sacrifice, and for nine months and a half had to struggle against secession enemies in front and at the same time be yoked with one by compulsion in business.

Following this, the press was used on the *Esmeralda Union* until that paper folded in 1868. The press was then sold to Chalfant and Parker, who took it back to Owens Valley, where it was used for many years to publish the *Inyo Independent* at Independence, Inyo County, California. The old Washington now rests in the Henry Ford museum in Dearborn, Michigan.

Esmeralda Star: (May 17 1862–Mar 1864)
  CU-BANC — S 20 1862; N 18 1863
  NvHi — Jl 5 1862; D 30 (supp) 1863

OClWHi — My 17 1862
film — My 17, Jl 5, S 20 1862; N 18, D 30 (supp) 1863
Ref: files; Angel 295-7; McMurtrie 294

Aurora Weekly Times

Early in April of 1863, Robert E. Draper and Robert Glen issued the first number of the *Aurora Weekly Times* on the press and material of the former *El Dorado Times* of Georgetown, California. The paper was printed every Saturday, at the *Times* office on the east side of Silver Street, as a twenty-four-column weekly that sold for $6 a year. The new journal was well received and within a month it was enlarged to become the *Aurora Daily Times*. It continued as such for nearly a year, until a general business decline forced its reduction to a weekly around the first of April, 1864. About this same time, Glen sold his interest to Draper, who then became sole editor and proprietor. Draper continued the paper until the summer of 1864, when he sold the establishment to George O. Kies and Robert Ferral. In early July of 1864, the new owners enlarged the paper again to a daily, issuing it as a Democratic campaign organ. On November 7, 1864, the day before the election, the *Times* was suspended and Ferral removed the press to the new camp of Montgomery in Mono County, California. There he used it to commence the short-lived *Montgomery Pioneer* on November 26. This venture quickly proved a failure and Ferral soon returned to Aurora, where he revived the *Times* as a weekly. The *Esmeralda Union* was already well entrenched, however, and the *Times* was forced to suspend for the last time, apparently in the summer of 1865.

The history of the *Times* was made eventful by a duel between the editor, R. E. Draper, and Dr. W. H. Eichelroth. It was fought on October 5, 1863, at the Bodie Ranch, six miles west of Aurora. The weapons were shotguns loaded with ball and fired at a distance of forty yards. At the second shot Draper was severely wounded in the foot, whereupon the parties shook hands and honor was satisfied. The duel had resulted from some trivial matter, but Draper was crippled for life.

The press and material were subsequently taken to Winnemucca to issue the *Argent,* and then on to Silver City, Idaho, to produce the *Tidal Wave.*
Aurora Weekly Times: (Apr 1863-Nov 7 1864; c. Jan-c. Jul 1865)
  pvt — N 27, 28, D 12 1863
  CSmH — D 9, 11 1863
  CU-BANC — Je 11, O 7 1864
  NvU — N 30, D 1 1863
  film — N 27, 28, 30, D 1, 9, 11, 12 1863; Je 11, O 7 1864
Ref: files; HR N 19 1864; Angel 297, McMurtrie 294, 311

Esmeralda Union

After the suspension of the *Star,* John Hatch and Co. immediately used the press and material to found the *Esmeralda Daily Union.* The first number was issued on March 21, 1864, with the Reverend J. B. Saxton, pastor of the First Baptist Church at Aurora, as chief editor, and J. G. McClinton as city editor. In August of the same year, Saxton retired from the paper and McClinton succeeded him as editor. He held that position until the summer of 1866, when John W. Avard became sole proprietor and editor.

In the spring of 1864, Aurora was at the height of its boom, and was able to support two dailies—the *Union* and the *Times.* By the fall of 1864, the boom had collapsed, and the *Times* temporarily suspended after the election. Shortly thereafter, on November 14, the *Union* was reduced to a triweekly; then, on December 30, to a semiweekly; and finally, to a weekly the following year. By early 1867, J. W. Avard was not only sole proprietor and editor, but also sole compositor, pressman, and devil. He was even forced to carry and distribute the paper to his patrons. Exhausted, Avard suspended the paper in June, 1867. Aurora still wanted a paper, however, and a group of citizens raised enough money to help Avard revive the paper on November 23, 1867. The *Union* was continued as a weekly for a little more than a year, but its fate was cast, and it finally suspended on October 3, 1868. In the spring of 1870, the old press and material were sold to Pleasant A. Chalfant and James E. Parker. They removed the plant to Independence, Inyo County, California, where they used it to found the *Inyo Independent.*

This press was the one upon which were printed many of the most remarkable pranks of Lieutenant Derby, alias John Phoenix. One of the most notable of these tricks was that of converting the Democratic *San Diego Herald* into a roaring advocate of the Whig cause. Derby did this while left in charge of the paper by its editor, Judge Ames. John Bigler, at that time the Democratic candidate for governor of California, pretended not to see any humor in the joke, but he probably enjoyed it as much as anyone—once he was certain that he had been elected. It is a curious coincidence that in 1868, the old press repeated this trick. Avard went away from Aurora for a vacation, and left his Republican *Esmeralda Union* temporarily in charge of the Honorable Joe Wasson and another man. They thought that the sleepy old town needed waking up, so without notice to anyone they brought the paper out as a rabid Democratic sheet, with the name of Governor Haight flying at the masthead for President. The hoax was transparent, but the *State Capitol Reporter* of Sacramento, then edited by ex-Governor Bigler, swallowed the whole thing and royally welcomed the new convert—probably without reading the leading editorial, as its ironical character was clearly apparent.

Esmeralda Union: (Mar 21 1864–Jul 1867; Nov 23 1867–Oct 3 1868)
   CSmH — [Mr 23 1864–Mr 15 1865]
   CU-BANC — N 23 1867–F 23, Mr 8–Ap 4, 18–25, My 9–Ag 8, 22–O 3 1868
   NvHi — Mr 31 1864; F 8 1868
   film — [Mr 23 1864–O 3 1868]
Ref: files; Angel 297

Esmeralda Herald

Aurora experienced a rebirth of activity in the late 1870's and early 1880's, as a result of the development of the Bodie mines, a few miles to the west, across the California line. On October 13, 1877, Frank Kenyon started a twenty-four-column Republican weekly, the *Esmeralda Herald*, at Aurora. At the same time, he commenced the neighboring *Bodie Standard*, which he sold in September, 1878, to T. S. Harris and Fred Elliott. That winter, leaving his editor, John M. Dormer, in charge of the *Herald*, Kenyon sailed for Guatemala to establish an English newspaper in Guatemala City. However, he developed jaundice and died on board ship, the day before landing.

Dormer managed the *Herald* for Kenyon's estate until December 6, 1879, when Malcom M. Glenn assumed the editorship. On March 6, 1880, Glenn purchased the paper, becoming sole editor and proprietor. Glenn's brother Hugh purchased a half interest on April 9, 1881, but sold it back on August 6. The decline of Aurora finally forced the *Herald*'s suspension on August 4, 1883, though Glenn promised it was "Not Dead But Sleeping." The plant was moved to the railroad town of Hawthorne, but after less than a year in its new location the *Herald* was dead. Glenn fared little better; four years later he was declared insane, and committed to the asylum at Stockton, California. (See Hawthorne, *Esmeralda Herald*.)

Esmeralda Herald: (Oct 13 1877–Aug 4 1883)
   CIE — S 17 1881
   CU-BANC — N 3 1877–Jl 29 1882
   NvGC — Complete
   film — [O 20 1877–Ag 3 1883]
Ref: files; BMM Ag 11 1883; EN My 4 1887

Aurora Star

After abandoning the short-lived *Oasis* at Hawthorne, Orlando Ezra Jones moved his equipment to Bodie in Mono County, California. Here he ran an unsuccessful weekly, *The Opinion,* and then established the *Bodie Evening Miner* in April of 1882, in partnership with John J. Curry. This paper flourished and Jones soon bought out Curry, becoming sole editor and proprietor.

In 1886, at the height of the *Bodie Miner's* prosperity, Jones decided to expand his domain to the nearby town of Aurora. In March of that year he began the *Aurora Star*. Jones issued the paper every Saturday as a 22 by 30-inch, independent weekly, for which he claimed a circulation of 250. The local zeal of Aurora was insufficient to support even a weekly, however, and the *Star* expired sometime within the same year.

Aurora Star: (Mar 1886–c. 1886)
   No issues located.
Ref: IR Mr 11 1886; II Mr 16 1886; PSND

Aurora Borealis

The first number of the *Aurora Borealis* was issued on November 18, 1905, by J. Holman Buck and E. R. Brooks, who were at that time publishing the *Bodie Miner,* only a few miles across the state line, in California. Buck held the editorial post, while Brooks served as business manager. They published the *Borealis* every Saturday, as a four-page, six-column weekly that sold for $3 a year. The paper did well and probably survived until June of 1906, when Buck removed a portion of the *Bodie Miner* plant to Mina to establish the *Western Nevada Miner.*

Aurora Borealis: (Nov 18 1905–c. Jun 1906)
   NvHi — D 23 1905
   film — D 23 1905
Ref: files; GN F 9 1906

Reese River Reveille

W. C. Phillips arrived in the new town of Austin in the spring of 1863, with a press and material for a newspaper. He gave his new venture the alliterative title of *Reese River Reveille* and issued the first number on May 16, 1863. Phillips was an able writer, as well as a practical printer, and served as both publisher and editor. Among the pioneers of Austin was a skillful printer, Oscar L. C. Fairchild, who became an assistant of Phillips. These two men put up the press, arranged the office, and pulled the first newspaper in the wilderness of central Nevada.

The *Reveille* was issued as a four-page, six-column weekly at prices commensurate with the expenses and the opportunity — 50¢ a number or $24 a year in gold coin for a subscription, and for advertising, all that the advertiser would stand. Surprisingly enough, the paper survived; the town was booming and no one minded the extortionary prices. A newspaper was a novelty in such a wild, isolated region, and the *Reese River Reveille* was widely circulated, spreading the fame of the new mines. After the third issue, in keeping with the progress of the town, the paper was advanced to a semiweekly, on June 3. On November 27, it became a triweekly.

Declining health soon compelled Phillips to seek a milder climate, and on October 3, 1863, he leased the office to the brothers, O. L. C. and J. D. Fairchild, who engaged Adair Wilson as editor. In December, Myron Angel joined the *Reveille* as assistant editor. Wilson served as editor until February of 1864, when he was succeeded by Angel, who retained the position until January of 1868. Phillips returned to Austin in May, 1864, still in feeble health and evidently ill with consumption. Unable to resume the burden of managing a growing newspaper, he sold the paper to his lessees, the Fairchilds, and retired to his former home in Illinois, where he died the following autumn.

The new owners purchased complete material for a large daily paper, and on May 24, 1864, J. D. Fairchild issued the first number of the *Daily Reese River Reveille.* It was a morning paper of nine columns to the page, as large as the *Sacramento Daily Union.* On April 30, 1868, J. D. Fairchild sold his interest in the paper to O. L. C. Fairchild. From May 29 to September 11, 1869, the paper was temporarily reduced to a weekly. O. L. C. Fairchild sold out to Andrew Casamayou and John H. Dennis on August 14, 1871. Since both men were Democrats, they changed the once Republican *Reveille* to an independent. Dennis sold his interest to John Booth on September 9, 1873, and Casamayou assumed the editorial post. Two years later Casamayou died, on December 8, 1875. On December 21, John Booth and Co. appeared as proprietors, with Fred H. Hart as editor and Andrew Maute as business manager. Hart was a brilliant writer and made the *Reveille* famous with his tales of the Sazerac Lying Club. On March 26, 1877, Hart became a part owner of the *Reveille,* but he sold out to Booth on November 23, 1878, and returned to Virginia City. Booth managed the paper as sole editor and proprietor until January 30, 1882, when Alf Doten took over the editorship, to be followed by John W. Maddrill on January 3, 1883.

After Booth's death on March 13, 1884, his widow continued the *Reveille* under Maddrill's editorship until November 17, 1886, when George A. Carpenter took over the post. On January 28, 1889, George A. Carpenter and Co. purchased the paper. Carpenter continued as editor until June 30, 1890, when the Lander Publishing Company appeared as proprietor, with George W. Rutherford as editor and manager. Two weeks later, on July 18, C. W. Hinchcliffe and John H. Dennis became publishers, and Rutherford remained as editor. On November 21, 1890, the *Reveille* was reduced to a weekly and Alfred H. Phillips succeeded to the post of editor and manager. C. W. Hinchcliffe became sole publisher the following December, continuing the paper as a weekly. A. H. Phillips bought the paper on January 20, 1893, and sold it five days later to W. D. Jones, who formed the Reveille Publishing Company and immediately enlarged the paper to a semiweekly.

Fifteen years later, on July 4, 1908, Lester W. Haworth of the *Manhattan Mail* became editor and manager, continuing until his death on May 11, 1917, when his wife Alice took over the helm. W. W. Ellis followed her on November 1, 1919, and was in turn succeeded by Doug H. Tandy on December 17, 1921. T. H. Dalton bought the *Reveille* on July 29, 1922, but Tandy stayed on as editor until January 10, 1925, after he had started the rival *Nevada Progressive.* Dalton hired Ray J. Chatelle to replace Tandy, but finally engaged Tandy to resume the editorship on May 23, 1926, even though the latter was still running the rival *Progressive.* On December 25, 1926, Tandy bought out Dalton, suspended his own paper, and became sole editor and publisher of the *Reveille.* He in turn sold out to William M. Thatcher, of the rival *Austin Sun,* on June 30, 1934.

After sixteen years, Thatcher finally retired to Oakland in 1950. He sold the paper to Jock Taylor, who had become editor in June of 1949. Ira N. Jacobson of Tonopah bought the *Reveille* in 1962, making it part of his newspaper combine. Thereafter it was printed in Tonopah, but Taylor remained as editor in Austin until 1964. He was followed by Gerald Roberts, who edits all of the Jacobson papers from Tonopah.

Reese River Reveille: (May 16 1863+)
   pub — 1863+
   pvt — D 22 1869
   C — N 22 1864–Jl 13 1865; My 22 1866–My 21, D 21 1868; N 1888; Je 1889; My 16 1952
   CHi — N 7 1896
   CSmH — O 29 1872
   CU-BANC — My 16 1863–S 20, O 17, 30 1873; F 5 1878–Ja 8 1881; [D 31 1885–D 31 1886]; Ja 3 1887–D 25 1891; Ja 25 1893–D 28 1899; D 19 1900
   KHi — N 11 1922
   MWA — Jl 18 1863
   NHi — Ap 3 1873
   NvBC — 1863+
   NvHi — Jl 18 1863; S 13 1865; Jl 16 1880; Ja 2 1884–N 16 1886; F 10 1908+
   NvMus — [O 17 1887–D 31 1904]
   NvU — 1867–78; 83–1923+
   OClWHi — S 13 1869
   film — [My 16 1863+]
Ref: files; Angel 304–5

Austin Republican

The *Austin Republican* was a short-lived newspaper published in 1868, probably during the election campaign. It left little record beyond a mention in Rowell's *American Newspaper Directory* for 1869.

Austin Republican: (c. 1868)
  No issues located.
Ref: McMurtrie 295

Spark of Genius

The *Spark of Genius* was an eight-column juvenile monthly founded in April of 1879, by Vienna Dollarhide, an Austin primary teacher. It scintillated with the "literary genius of the youthful climbers of the ladder of learning," but soon faded from the firmament.

Spark of Genius: (Apr 1879–c. 1879)
  No issues located.
Ref: GHN Ap 17, 27 1879

Democrat

While John Booth held the reins of the *Reveille* with a strong Republican hand, his son, William, founded an opposition paper during the election of 1882, under the firm name of W. W. Booth and Co. The daily *Democrat* was started in Austin on August 8, 1882, with Joseph P. Joachimsen as editor. After the election George E. Miller replaced Joachimsen, and William tried to continue the paper as a regular daily. He was soon deep in debt, however, and on February 27, 1883, Miller and others attached the paper for back wages and sundry debts. Two local businessmen, restaurant owner Louis Loustalot and shoemaker Robert Hogan, paid the debts, and immediately leased the paper to S. F. Clark, who took over on February 28, 1883, under the name of the Democrat Publishing Company. Joachimsen again assumed the editorship, but Austin was simply unable to support two papers. The *Democrat* finally suspended on July 10, 1883, "from lack of adequate sustenance."

Democrat: (Aug 8 1882–Jul 10 1883)
   C — Ag 13–26, 30–31, O 6 1882–Ja 19, 31–F 3, 8–28, Mr 6–7, 22–Ap 7, 11–29, My 2–Jl 3, 8 1883
   CU-BANC — Ag 9 1882–Jl 8 1883
   film — Ag 9 1882–Jl 8 1883
Ref: files; Doten 1439, 1464

Austin Holiday Review

The *Austin Holiday Review* was published in December, 1882, by J. A. Wright as an "advertising medium."

Austin Holiday Review: (Dec 1882)
  No issues located.
Ref: LFP D 8 1882

People's Advocate

As the People's Party gained popularity in the West, party organs were established throughout the mining region. On December 3, 1890, the *People's Advocate* was founded in Austin by the politically sponsored People's Advocate Company. W. D. Jones, a local attorney, was employed as editor and manager. The paper was a four-page, six-column, 12 by 18-inch weekly, selling for $5 a year. In less than a month, on January 28, 1891, the paper's financial success prompted its owners to enlarge it to a semiweekly.

The *Advocate* continued to prosper, making such inroads into the rival *Reese River Reveille's* support that its owners finally agreed to sell out. On December 31, 1892, Jones resigned the editorship of the *Advocate* to become editor and proprietor of the *Reveille*. F. H. Triplett became editor of the *Advocate* on January 4, 1893, only to close it down on the twenty-first of the same month. There was talk of reviving the *Advocate* at Battle Mountain, but nothing came of it.

People's Advocate: (Dec 3 1890–Jan 21 1893)
  CU-BANC — D 10 1890–Ja 21 1893
  NvU — D 3 1890–D 31 1892
  film — D 3 1890–Ja 21 1893
Ref: files

Nevada Progressive

On December 31, 1924, the *Nevada Progressive* was founded simultaneously at Battle Mountain and Austin by Doug H. Tandy of the Progressive Publishing Company at Austin. The paper was issued each Wednesday from the printing plant at Austin and sold for $2.50 a year. Its combined circulation provided a substantial income, and it continued until about December 23, 1926, when Tandy purchased the *Reese River Reveille* at Austin and suspended the *Progressive* to combine the material with the *Reveille*.

Nevada Progressive: (Dec 31 1924–c. Dec 23 1926)
   CSmH — D 31 1924–D 30 1925; Mr 17 1926
   NvHi — [D 31 1924–O 2 1926]
   film — [D 31 1924–O 2 1926]
Ref: files

Austin Sun

The *Sun,* a weekly which illuminated Austin only briefly, rose on September 2, 1933. William M. Thatcher edited it for nearly a year before it was eclipsed on June 23, 1934. On June 30, 1934, Thatcher acquired the *Reese River Reveille* and merged the two papers to form the *Reese River Reveille and the Austin Sun.*

Austin Sun: (Sep 2 1933–Jun 23 1934)
   NvU — S 2 1933–Je 23 1934
   film — S 2 1933–Je 23 1934
Ref: files

~(BATTLE MOUNTAIN)~

Measure For Measure

The first number of the Battle Mountain *Measure for Measure* was issued by William J. Forbes on November 22, 1873. Forbes was sole editor and proprietor, and published the paper on a dilapidated press that had formerly been used to publish the *Reese River Reveille,* the *Silver Bend Reporter,* the *White Pine News* and the *Schell Creek Prospect.*

   Measure for Measure was a rather quaint title for a newspaper, but Forbes was a rather quaint person. He was distinguished among the journalists of the Pacific Coast for his genial humor, ability as an editor, and skill as a printer. He sought originality in all things, desiring particularly to avoid standard names for his papers. Among the papers he founded were the *Trespass* of Virginia City and the *New Endowment* of Salt Lake. The name of the first was suggested by his act of trespassing upon a field already occupied, since there were several strong newspapers in Virginia City when he established his. *New Endowment* was adopted as a challenge to the Mormons of Salt Lake City. His Battle Mountain paper was named after a passage in Shakespeare, "As ye measure unto us, so will we measure unto you." The paper was issued weekly and poured out vitriolic comments until Forbes's untimely death on October 31, 1875.

Measure for Measure: (Nov 22 1873–Oct 30 1875)
   CU-BANC — Ag 28 1875
   NvU — [Mr 6–O 9 1875]
   film — [Mr 6–O 9 1875]
Ref: files; GHN N 24 1873; SFAC O 31 1875; Angel 306–7; McMurtrie 295

Battle Mountain Messenger

Mark W. Musgrove founded the *Battle Mountain Messenger* on May 19, 1877, but transferred the paper to E. A. Scott the following August. On July 6, 1878, the office of the paper was destroyed by fire. New material was ordered immediately and publication was resumed on August 31. On November 16 of the same year, Scott leased the *Messenger* to W. W. Robins and John Sterling, for a period of six months. This firm dissolved after two months, on February 8, 1879, and Robins assumed the lease, hiring S. H. Fulton as editor. They, too, failed, and Scott once more resumed control as editor and publisher. On December 13, 1879, Scott again leased the office, this time to Charles H. Sproule and Walter H. Davis. With Sproule as editor, this partnership ran the paper for a year and a half, enlarging it to a semiweekly on September 11, 1880.

Scott again took control on June 25, 1881. The following week he acquired a partner named Mahoney, who lasted only a month, withdrawing from the partnership on August 3. Following this setback Scott reduced the paper to a weekly again on September 17. After continuing alone for another eighteen months, Scott finally gave up, and the paper passed on to the Messenger Publishing Company on March 3, 1883. E. T. George, formerly of the *Lewis Herald,* served as editor for one year. He was followed on February 23, 1884, by John H. Dennis, who had just sold out his interest in the *Tuscarora Times-Review.* Dennis made a valiant attempt to expand the *Messenger,* increasing it to a semiweekly on April 26. Soon after the election, however, on November 15, he reduced it to weekly again. Six weeks later, the day after Christmas, 1884, the paper suspended, a victim of the deepening depression in silver mining.

Battle Mountain Messenger: (May 19 1877–Dec 26 1884)
   CU-BANC — D 15 1877; [Ja 5–O 26 1878; Ja 4–N 15 1879]; N 20, D 4–18 1880;
     Jl 23–N 12, 26 1881; [F 25 1882–D 26 1884]
   NvU — Je 4 1881–D 26 1884
   film — [D 15 1877–D 26 1884]
Ref: files

Lander Free Press

After ending his lease of the *Battle Mountain Messenger* on June 1, 1881, Charles H. Sproule undertook to start his own paper at Battle Mountain.

He purchased an office on Front Street, a short distance from the *Messenger* office, and on the first of July, 1881, started the *Lander Free Press*. The paper was issued weekly on Fridays, a day earlier than the *Messenger,* and was a four-page, Republican sheet, twice the size of his opponent's. E. A. Scott of the *Messenger* did not appreciate the competition. With his new partner, Mahoney, he began issuing his paper semiweekly, in an attempt to drive out the *Free Press.* However, the semiweekly could not be sustained, and the two weeklies were rivals until the *Free Press* suspended on December 28, 1882. Sproule removed the material to Elko, where he used it to found the Elko *Free Press* on January 5, 1883.

Lander Free Press: (Jul 1 1881–Dec 28 1882)
   NvU — Jl 8 1881–D 28 1882
   film — Jl 8 1881–D 28 1882
Ref: files

Central Nevadan

For three weeks following the suspension of the *Battle Mountain Messenger* on December 26, 1884, the town and surrounding mines were without a newspaper. Finally public demand and the promise of new support induced John H. Dennis to reenter the publishing business at Battle Mountain.

On January 16, 1885, the newly organized firm of Dennis and Ellsworth began publication of the weekly *Central Nevadan.* The paper was a four-page, six-column sheet, selling at a subscription price of $5 per year. The promised support was provided and the paper prospered.

With the commencement of the second volume on January 7, 1886, Dennis became sole editor and proprietor. He continued to run the paper until October 3, 1889, when he leased the establishment to J. D. Park. The lease lasted for less than three months, and on January 2, 1890, J. A. Blossom purchased the *Central Nevadan,* hiring George W. Rutherford as editor. Six months later Rutherford quit to become editor of the Austin *Reese River Reveille.* Frank Francis became editor on July 30, 1890, serving for nearly two years. Ownership passed to R. C. Blossom on September 11, 1890.

When Francis left for Lovelock to start a paper of his own, Fred E. Woolcock took over the editorial chair on July 21, 1892, and remained there until the final suspension of the paper, except for a two-month substitution by L. M. Biersmith in August and September, 1905. Blossom managed the paper until May 9, 1901, when he sold the firm to H. R. Lemaire. On January 7, 1904, it passed to A. D. Lemaire, in whose hands it suspended on December 5, 1907, to be merged with the *Battle Mountain Herald.* (See *Battle Mountain Herald and Central Nevadan.*)

Central Nevadan: (Jan 16 1885–Dec 5 1907)
   CU-BANC — Mr 17 1887; Jl 4, 25, D 12 1889; Ja 9–23, F 6 1890; O 15 1891
   NvHi — S 22, O 20, N 10–17 1892

NvMus — [D 12 1895; 1896–1904]
NvU — [Ja 16 1885–8; 1891–1907]
film — [Ja 16 1885–D 5 1907]
Ref: files

The Little Joker

The Little Joker was a "bright and newsy" little amateur paper published by Alfred Brown at Battle Mountain from March of 1887 through July or later.
The Little Joker: (Mar 1887–c. Jul 1887)
   No issues located.
Ref: RRR Mr 28, Ap 13, 19, My 2, Ag 1 1887; ES My 26 1887

Battle Mountain Herald

On October 10, 1907, Tom C. Parker launched the weekly *Battle Mountain Herald* in hot competition with the *Central Nevadan*. It was a quick fight, and in less than three months, on December 12, 1907, Parker bought out the *Central Nevadan* to form the *Battle Mountain Herald and Central Nevadan.*
Battle Mountain Herald: (Oct 10 1907–Dec 12 1907)
   No issues located.
Ref: BMHCN D 19 1907

Battle Mountain Herald and Central Nevadan

On December 19, 1907, Tom C. Parker, having bought out the *Central Nevadan,* combined it with his *Battle Mountain Herald* to commence the weekly *Herald and Central Nevadan.* The paper prospered for several years under his editorship but finally suspended on May 18, 1911.
Battle Mountain Herald and Central Nevadan: (Dec 19 1907–May 18 1911)
   NvHi — [Ja 30–Jl 30 1908; S 9 1909]
   NvU — [1908–11]
   film — [D 19 1907–My 18 1911]
Ref: files

Battle Mountain Scout

Following the suspension of the *Herald and Central Nevadian* in mid–1911, Battle Mountain was without a newspaper until A. B. Gibson arrived from Goldfield to commence the *Battle Mountain Scout* on July 2, 1913. The paper prospered, but became a jinx for its owners. Its founder died in less than a year, on April 7, 1914, and the paper passed to Charles H. Gibson, who died on November 19 of the following year. Thereafter it had a multitude of owners, changing hands an average of once every two to three years. F. H. Mitchell served as editor for the Gibson estate till Raymond F. Burt bought the *Scout* on September 9, 1916. Lester W. Haworth took over from him on April 7, 1917, but he turned in his chips the following January, and his widow, Alice, took the helm.

On February 7, 1921, R. E. L. Windle and A. L. Brackett of the Winnemucca *Humboldt Star* bought the paper, hiring F. H. Triplett as editor, a position he held for five years. R. C. Stitser bought Windle's half interest on July 22, 1922, and Brackett's two years later, becoming sole proprietor on July 21, 1924. He, in turn, sold the paper to Noble H. Getchell on May 22, 1926. During Getchell's tenure, W. C. Hancock was editor. Stitser bought back the *Scout* on January 20, 1933, retaining Hancock as business manager, and taking on Ethel Estes as editor. With Stitser's death on January 29, 1939, the *Scout* passed to his widow, Mrs. Avery D. Stitser, who, with Estes as editor, carried it on until October 13, 1960. On that date Elizabeth Michael Rieck became its last editor, and Edwin B. Brown became general manager. He was followed in that post in quick succession by Charles Bridge, Gene Dilkes, and Mike Payette. In their hands the *Scout* was merged, in late October or early November of 1962, with the Winnemucca *Humboldt Star* to form the *Humboldt Star and Battle Mountain Scout.* (See *Humboldt Star and Battle Mountain Scout.*)

Battle Mountain Scout: (Jul 2 1913–c. Oct-Nov 1962)
   CHi — F 6, Mr 6, Ag 14, N 13 1915; F 12 1916
   NvHi — [Ja 7 1914–24]
   NvU — Jl 2 1913–7; Mr 9–23 1918; 1919–N 16 1934; D 26 1957–61; F 1–My 24 1962
   NvWHL — Jl 1925–31; 1935–60
   film — [Jl 2 1913–My 24 1962]
Ref: files

Nevada Progressive

The weekly *Nevada Progressive* was founded simultaneously at Austin and Battle Mountain on December 31, 1924, by Doug H. Tandy of the Progressive Publishing Company. The paper was published every Wednesday at Austin and sold for $2.50 per year. In December of 1926, Tandy purchased the *Reese River Reveille,* and suspended the *Progressive* about December 23.

Nevada Progressive: (Dec 31 1924–c. Dec 23 1926)
   CSmH — D 31 1924–D 30 1925; Mr 17 1926
   NvHi — [D 31 1924–O 2 1926]
   film — [D 31 1924–O 2 1926]
Ref: files

Battle Mountain Bugle

The Battle Mountain Bugle is a fortnightly paper begun on May 27, 1976, by Terri Keyser-Cooper and David Shire.

Battle Mountain Bugle: (May 27 1976+)
   NvHi — My 27 1976+
   film — My 27 1976+
Ref: files

BEATTY

Beatty Bullfrog Miner

Early in March of 1905, soon after commencement of the rush to the Bullfrog Mining District, C. W. Nicklin issued a sample paper for the new district, dubbing it the *Bullfrog Miner*. Within a few weeks Nicklin arrived at the booming town of Beatty with a press and material, and on April 8, 1905, he published the first regular issue of the *Bullfrog Miner*. During the previous week, Frank P. Mannix had started a paper of the same name at the rival camp of Bullfrog, and for several weeks the two fought over title to the name. Finally, on May 13, 1905, Nicklin renamed his paper the *Beatty Bullfrog Miner*, but the animosity continued. T. G. Nicklin of the *Las Vegas Age*, who replaced C. W. as editor on June 17, continued the squabble until January 12, 1907, when he sold the paper to Clyde R. Terrell and Dan G. McKenna. Ownership was shuttled back and forth again when T. G. Nicklin resumed proprietorship on June 8, only to turn it back to Terrell on February 22, 1908. Nicklin then took over again, but sold out in May of 1909, to Earle R. Clemens of the *Rhyolite Herald*. Clemens finally suspended the *Miner* in July.

Beatty Bullfrog Miner: (Apr 8 1905–Jul 1909)
   NvHi — Ap 8 1905–O 24 1908
   NvU — Je 7-S 27, O 11 1907–S 12 1908
   film — [Ap 8 1905–O 24 1908]
  Ref: files; TS My 4, 24 1905; RH My 19 1909; PT Jl 24 1909

Beatty Bulletin

After a hiatus of nearly half a century, Robert A. Crandall of the *Goldfield News* started a new paper, the *Bulletin,* at Beatty on April 25, 1947. It was issued as the flip side of the *Goldfield News,* which was simply folded inside-out for Beatty distribution under the *Bulletin* masthead. Beatty news was provided by Dorothy Dorothy. Crandall continued the *Bulletin* for nearly a decade, until December 28, 1956, when he merged the *Tonopah Times-Bonanza* with his *Goldfield News*.

Beatty Bulletin: (Apr 25 1947–Dec 28 1956)
  See *Goldfield News* for holdings.
Ref: files

Beatty Newsbits

Jo and Jerry Mundt began the little typewritten fortnightly *Beatty Newsbits* about March, 1977, as "a courtesy publication for the people of Beatty."

Beatty Newsbits: (c. Mar 1977+)
   NvULV — O 15 1978+
Ref: files

⊱❨ BELLEHELEN ❩⊰

Bellehelen Record

The *Record* was a short-lived weekly, founded in April of 1907, to promote the new camp of Bellehelen in the Kawich Range, some fifty miles east of Tonopah. It apparently collapsed with the boom before the end of the year.
Bellehelen Record: (Apr 1907–c. 1907)
    No issues located.
Ref: NE Ap 13 1907

⊱❨ BELLEVILLE ❩⊰

Belleville Times

Mark W. Musgrove brought a press and material to Belleville in the fall of 1877, and in late October he began publication of the *Belleville Times.* Musgrove was sole editor and proprietor, and issued the paper semiweekly at $7 per annum. He continued the paper until the following April, when he sold the plant to D. M. Brannan. The *Times* died in Brannan's hands about six weeks later, in June of 1878. The material was purchased by John M. Dormer, who brought it to Aurora and later used it to start the *Bodie Daily Free Press* in California.
Belleville Times: (Oct 1877–Jun 1878)
    No issues located.
Ref: Angel 298; Doten 2241

⊱❨ BELMONT ❩⊰

Silver Bend Reporter

With the first rush to Belmont, in the Silver Bend District, Mahlon Dickinson Fairchild, a younger brother of the *Reese River Reveille* owner, moved a quantity of surplus material and a press from Austin, in February of 1867. The weather was cold, not conducive to fast freighting, and houses in the primitive new town were not easily secured, nor when secured were they the best protection against the rigors of winter at an altitude of 7,000 feet above the sea. These handicaps somewhat delayed the appearance of the new paper, but on March 30, 1867, the *Weekly Silver Bend Reporter* came into existence, published by Oscar L. C. Fairchild and Co. Mahlon Fairchild was editor, manager, and mechanical operator, assisted only by a small boy.

Fairchild began his venture in the austere waste with the following eloquent salutatory:

> Citizens of Belmont, of Silver Bend and of Eastern Nevada, we to-day introduce ourselves by presenting to your consideration the first number of

the *Weekly Silver Bend Reporter,* and with it our compliments and best wishes, and in turn ask your friendship and your patronage. American pioneers, intelligent and enterprising, carry with them the press and type, and wherever they pitch their tent, be it in the wilderness of the interior, among the snow covered peaks of the Sierra or on the sunny sea beach of the Pacific, there too must the newspaper appear, with its political discussions; its disquisitions upon men, morals, law and religion; its advocacy of the resources of its section; its details of local and foreign news; its tales, stories and jokes, and last though not least in importance and interest, its advertisements. It is the newspaper that links the pioneer with his home—the subtle, invisible wire over which courses the constant stream of intelligence, civilizing influences and sweet memories, drawing the wanderer back into the world, and assimilating ideas. Here, in this bright offshoot of civilization, surrounded by a vast ocean of wilderness, shall be a newspaper. In young, vigorous and beautiful Belmont, we have set up our altars, and amidst the crags and mountain peaks veined with untold treasures, and assisted by the brave pioneers, our companions, we tell the story of Silver Bend. Rich beyond all comparison, beyond the El Dorados of ancient or modern times we know our section to be, and to make this known to the world, point out the approaches, to present every resource, and to tell how we live, shall be the aim and object —the specialty of the *Reporter.* We have no jealousies of localities, no favored place to advocate to the injury of another, but while particularly representing Belmont, shall, in the broadest sense, advocate the every interest of all, of Silver Bend, of Nye County, of Eastern Nevada and of the State at large. We are in the midst of a mining region, the wealth of which the world can not yet comprehend. In extent it is greater than many States of the East, or than many of the kingdoms of Europe. A future of unequaled prosperity a prodigal Nature assures us, and in this bright hope and confidence we are inspired to reach beyond the narrow circle of our vision and include in our grasp all the "Great East" and hold it up to the light of the world. All interests— mining, milling, agricultural, manufacturing and mercantile—shall receive notice, and whatever instruction in any of these various pursuits we may be able to impart from our knowledge, or that we may learn from others, will be given, and the best interests of all advocated and protected. Believing in the power and efficacy of the press, its influence at home and abroad, and that the paper is taken as the representative of the people where published, we shall endeavor that the *Reporter* shall have the power and be a representative well approved by the people.

The new candidate for public favor was well received, and thrived with the booming times at Silver Bend. On April 4, 1868, M. D. Fairchild bought out his brothers, becoming sole proprietor. He enlarged it to a semiweekly on June 6, to give it a competitive advantage over its newly established opponent, the weekly *Mountain Champion.* But the wonderful tales of the new White Pine District soon lured Fairchild away. On July 29, 1868, he suspended the *Reporter* and struck out for the new district, where he went into the more profitable lumber business.

Silver Bend Reporter: (Mar 30 1867–Jul 29 1868)
  CHi — Ap 6 1867
  CU-BANC — [Mr 30–Jl 6], D 14 1867–Jl 29 1868
  DLC — Mr 30 1867–Jl 29 1868

NvHi — Je 8 1867
NvTC — Mr 30 1867–Jl 29 1868
NvU — Mr 30 1867–Jl 29 1868
film — Mr 30 1867–Jl 29 1868
Ref: files

Mountain Champion

In accordance with the rule governing political appointments, Nye County, or rather the "Great East," as that entire portion of the state was termed by the press, was entitled to name the next candidate for Congress. Thomas Fitch, foreseeing this, had moved to Belmont early to spread out his political net. As the time for conventions approached, the necessity of securing an "organ" became apparent. The editor of the *Reporter* was an unpurchasable Democrat, and so long as he controlled the sheet, Fitch had no hope in that quarter. Consequently, in the spring of 1868, overtures were made by the Fitch interests to induce Joseph E. Eckley to publish a Republican paper in Nye County. Promises of money were made and Eckley began negotiating to purchase the *Reporter.* However, when these promises were not kept, the purchase fell through.

Fitch was persistent in his effort to have an "organ" to advance his political interests. Since the *Reporter* had more material than it could use, still lying in boxes as it had left the type foundry, and since it also had an extra press, which had formerly been used in printing the *Nye County News* at Ione, Mahlon Fairchild consented to sell Fitch and Co. a printing outfit. Thus on June 3, 1868, the Fitch paper, the *Mountain Champion,* began publication at Belmont as a weekly. W. F. Myers was listed as editor, and H. M. Barnes as business agent. They waged a brief battle with the *Reporter,* which ended in triumph with suspension of the *Reporter* and the nomination of Fitch.

The *Mountain Champion* continued to advocate Fitch until after his election in November. Upon election, Fitch rewarded Myers with a federal appointment and Barnes with the ownership of the *Mountain Champion* on November 7, 1868. Barnes hired Edward F. McElwain as editor, and induced him to buy the paper on January 9 of the following year. Within a few months McElwain, like Fairchild, became infected with White Pine fever, and on April 24, 1869, he suspended the *Mountain Champion.* He shipped the entire plant, including that of the *Reporter,* to Shermantown, where he started the *White Pine Telegram.* Eventually he sold the old press to Pat Holland, who used it to issue the *Shermantown Reporter.*

Mountain Champion: (Jun 3 1868–Apr 24 1869)
CU-BANC — Je 3–N 28, D 12 1868–Ap 10 1869
NvTC — Je 3 1868–Ap 24 1869
NvU — Je 3 1868–Ap 24 1869
film — Je 3 1868–Ap 24 1869
Ref: files

Belmont Courier

Following the initial excitement, the prosperity of Belmont waned, and for five years after the suspension of the *Mountain Champion* the camp was without a newspaper. Renewed mining activity prompted Andrew Casamayou and John Booth of the *Reese River Reveille* to reestablish a newspaper in 1874. On February 14 of that year they commenced publication of the *Belmont Courier,* an independent weekly with Republican tendencies. On November 30, 1875, Casamayou died and his widow took over the partnership, which continued under the firm name of John Booth and Co. It remained as such until December 23, 1876, when Andrew Maute, former business manager of the *Reveille,* became sole proprietor of the *Courier.* Samuel Donald purchased a half interest in the establishment from Maute on December 4, 1880. This partnership lasted for over eight years, until March 30, 1889, when Maute again became sole proprietor. In 1898, Maute was elected state printer, and he leased the *Courier* to F. G. Humphrey on December 24. The paper folded in Humphrey's hands on March 2, 1901, but Maute won reelection in 1902.

Belmont Courier: (Feb 14 1874–Mar 2 1901)
  CU-BANC — O 7–18, D 9, 23 1876; My 5, 19, Je 2–16, 30 1877; Je 8, 22–Ag 17 1878; My 8 1880; F 25 1882; Jl 6–20, S 21, O 29 1889; Ja 4–25 1890
  ICHi — Je 9 1876
  MnHi — Jl 14 1876
  NvHi — [1882–91]
  NvTC — [F 14 1874–Mr 2 1901]
  NvU — 1890–2; 1897
  film — [F 14 1874–Mr 2 1901]
Ref: files

~(BETTY O'NEAL)~

Betty O'Neal Concentrator

On February 9, 1924, N. W. Cockrell commenced publication of the *Concentrator* at the Betty O'Neal Mine, approximately fourteen miles south of Battle Mountain. The paper was published each Saturday, at a price of $2 a year, by the Concentrator Publishing Company, with Cockrell serving as editor. The *Concentrator* had a rocky career, however, and by June, Noble H. Getchell was editor and Alta Ashcraft was local editor. Apparently Cockrell's subscribers, advertisers, and creditors had taken over the publishing company, as the paper proclaimed it was "the only newspaper edited and published by the citizens of any mining camp in the state."

Betty O'Neal Concentrator: (Feb 9 1924–c. 1925)
  pvt — Je 14 1924
  NvHi — Je 21 1924
  film — Je 21 1924
Ref: files

⊱❊ BLAIR ❊⊰

Blair Press

Following the suspension of the *Lida Enterprise* and its companion, the *Palmetto Herald,* in October of 1906, Newman H. Mix moved his material on to Blair to try his luck. There he founded the *Blair Press,* about November 3, 1906. The *Press* did well for a time, but, by July 23, 1909, Mix had become discouraged with its prospects and suspended the paper. H. F. Kane leased the plant and revived the paper on September 3, 1909, but the venture was doomed. Within a year, on June 17, 1910, he was forced to suspend.

Blair Press: (c. Nov 3 1906–Jun 17 1910)
   NvHi — Ja 18 1908–Je 17 1910
   NvU — Ja 4–D 26 1908; Ja 9 1909–Je 17 1910
   film — Ja 4 1908–Je 17 1910
Ref: files

Blair Booster

In January of 1907, W. W. Booth moved his *Silver Peak Post* plant to Blair, continuing the paper under that name until March 13, when he rechristened it the *Blair Booster.* Under the masthead he boasted, "This paper is different from other newspapers and I thank the Gods of Verse and Prose that it's different." C. E. Day was manager of the paper until May 29, when William P. Clearly assumed the post. But Newman Mix had already monopolized the field with his *Press,* and the *Booster* failed on June 12, after the support promised it by mining and real estate speculators was not forthcoming. Booth, an inveterate booster, moved the plant to Millers to try again.

Blair Booster: (Mar 13 1907–Jun 12 1907)
   pvt — Mr 13–Je 12 1907
Ref: files; SPP Ja 16 1907; LT Je 28 1907

⊱❊ BOULDER CITY ❊⊰

Boulder City Journal

Soon after construction began on Hoover Dam, Frank F. Garside and A. E. Cahlan of the *Las Vegas Review-Journal* commenced a Boulder City edition of their paper, under the name of the *Boulder City Journal.* It started on September 24, 1931, as the second section of the *Review-Journal* and finally became a separate edition in 1935. Elton M. Garrett was local news editor for Boulder City for a time. The *Journal* ceased being issued as a separate edition on December 12, 1941, and was reincorporated into the *Review-Journal.*

Boulder City Journal: (Sep 24 1931–Dec 12 1941)
    film — [S 24 1931–D 12 1941] with *Las Vegas Review-Journal*
Ref: files

Boulder City Age

Not to be outdone by the *Review-Journal,* Charles P. Squires of the *Las Vegas Age* began the *Boulder City Age* about May 14, 1932. W. H. Buntin served as editor, issuing the *Age* as a Tuesday weekly; but the venture was a losing proposition, and Squires suspended it about 1933.

Boulder City Age: (c. May 14 1932–c. 1933)
    NvHi — My 14, 24, 1932; Ag 1 1933
    film — My 14, 24 1932; Ag 1 1933
Ref: files

Boulder Dam Challenge

The *Boulder Dam Challenge,* the "Mite-y Midget News-gazine of Model City on the Marge of Lake Mead," was a typewritten sheet issued by Elton M. Garrett. It commenced about February 28, 1936, and probably ceased late that spring.

Boulder Dam Challenge: (c. Feb 28 1936–c. Jun 1936)
    NvULV — My 22 1936
    film — My 22 1936
Ref: files

Boulder City Reminder

Boulder City's next hometown newspaper was the modest little mimeographed daily, the *Reminder,* begun on June 21, 1938, by Allen J. "Bud" O'Hara and Thomas C. Kaufman. They issued the paper for barely two months before selling its good will to Eliza Carter and Jane Cooke, in whose hands it prospered. On April 19, 1940, they renamed it the *Boulder City News.* (See *Boulder City News.*)

Boulder City Reminder: (Jun 21 1938–Apr 18 1940)
    pub — [Je 21 1938–Ap 18 1940]
    film — [Je 21 1938–Ap 18 1940]
Ref: files

Boulder City News

On April 19, 1940, Eliza Carter and Jane Cooke renamed their *Reminder* the *Boulder City News,* as they slowly expanded it to a full-fledged daily. In December of 1941, they sold it to Robert E. Carter and R. W. Brann. Carter became the publisher and Brann the editor. Elton M. Garrett later replaced Brann and served as editor until the end of November, 1946, when Marvin E. Carter assumed the editorship. Then, on July 1, 1948, it was purchased by Morry M. Zenoff, who became both editor and proprietor. He reduced it to a weekly in 1950, when he began a second paper, the *Home News,* at nearby Henderson. William Gillis served briefly as editor from 1956 to 1957, but the *News* was still published by Morry Zenoff in 1979.

Boulder City News: (Apr 19 1940+)
   pub — Ap 19 1940+
   NvU — 1942+
   film — Ap 19 1940+
Ref: files; Ayer 1944+

Oasis Advertiser

The *Oasis Advertiser* was a weekly sheet published at Boulder City and distributed there and at Henderson in 1960.

Oasis Advertiser: (1960)
  No issues located.
Ref: Folkes 24

Dam Informer

Ken Bouton started the weekly *Dam Informer* at Boulder City in 1962. He changed its name to the *Boulder Dam Informer* with the second number, but it never got beyond its third issue.

Dam Informer: (c. 1962)
  No issues located.
Ref: Folkes 24

Desert Rat Review

The *Desert Rat Review* was begun at Boulder City in August, 1968, by Robert Freeman, and may not have lived past its first issue. It was a campaign publicity paper, sporting the slogan "Plagiarism is the Key to Success."

Desert Rat Review: (Aug 1968)
   NvULV — Ag 1968
   film — Ag 1968
Ref: files

BOVARD

Bovard Booster

In the spring of 1908, William W. Booth of the *Tonopah Bonanza* shipped the old Blair and Millers *Booster* plant to the new camp of Bovard, some ninety miles northwest of Tonopah. There, on April 28, 1908, William Stuart Webster and Charles H. White, acting in behalf of Booth, revived the *Booster* once again. Booth was proprietor of the paper and Webster and White served as managing and assistant editors, respectively. They published the *Booster* every Tuesday at Bovard as a four-page, six-column weekly, which sold at the rather steep price of $5 a year. Despite, or possibly as a result of, the *Booster*, Bovard's boom proved brief and the paper was quickly suspended, probably during the following month.

Bovard Booster: (Apr 28 1908–c. May 1908)
 NvHi — Ap 28 1908
 film — Ap 28 1908
Ref: files

Bristol Times

In 1879, the camp of Bristol sprang into existence, approximately thirty-three miles north of Pioche, and for nearly five years it supported a population of several hundred miners. In late November of 1881, during the last flush period of the camp, Eugene J. Trippel and D. M. Brannan commenced the weekly *Bristol Times.* It was printed on the material of the former *Tybo Sun,* and prospered for slightly more than a year before the decline of the camp forced its suspension in mid-December of 1882. With the following obituary the *Times* chronicled its own demise:

> Bury us deep under the fragrant sagebrush. Let the festive hog and rollicking chipmunk sing sweet lullably to our departed memory. The many-hued lizard will drop a sorrowing weep upon the lonely mound. Don't stay the pensive donkey from braying a tender obituary notice over our "dead" corpse. Let the sympathizing coyotes gather about our grave. Let them yelp a mournful dirge over what was but is not. Ta-ta. Vale! Vale! Vale!!!
>
> >Down we go cheerfully,
> >   Nary a sigh.
> >Sober not beautifully —
> >   Thus do we die.
> >Yet we're not kicking,
> >   Though called rather soon.
> >Plant our toes sticking
> >   Straight up at the moon.
> >We ran with the "devil,"
> >   And paid pretty dear;
> >Rewarding our evil,
> >   They planted us here.

Trippel later drifted to Arizona, where he founded the *Yuma Times* in 1890.

Bristol Times: (Nov 1881–Dec 1882)
 No issues located.
Ref: SS N 12 1881; Myrick

Bullfrog Miner

The rush to the Bullfrog Mining District led to a heated controversy between two editors there, each of whom started a newspaper called the

Bullfrog Miner — one published in Bullfrog and the other in Beatty. Early in March of 1905, C. W. Nicklin of the *Las Vegas Age* printed a sample paper called the *Bullfrog Miner,* which he mailed to potential subscribers in the district. While Nicklin was lining up a printing plant to ship to Beatty, the Bullfrog Townsite Company approached Frank P. Mannix to start a paper in their camp. On March 31, 1905, Mannix commenced his paper, printed at Tonopah, appropriating the name *Bullfrog Miner.* The following week, Nicklin, who had arrived with his press at Beatty, printed the first regular issue of his *Bullfrog Miner* there. Mannix soon after brought in a press from Los Angeles.

Nicklin charged plagiarism, and the battle for the name began, growing more heated each week. Their exchanges began referring to them as *Bullfrog Miner No. 1* and *No. 2*, but they argued incessantly over who was *No. 2*. Both refused to give up the name. As one observer noted, "There is a superstition in nine-tenths of the mining camps of the west that a paper must be called the *Miner* to take well enough with the real working men to make a go of it," and the name Bullfrog was "so very catchy that they both had to have it," too. The dispute was at last settled, however, "without bloodshed or loss of perspiration," when Nicklin added Beatty to the masthead, making his the *Beatty Bullfrog Miner.*

Ironically, the town of Bullfrog proved to be a bust, and on March 23, 1906, at the end of his first year, Mannix issued his last *Miner* in Bullfrog. He moved the plant to neighboring Rhyolite, where he continued the paper, needless to say, under that hard won name *Bullfrog Miner.*

Bullfrog Miner: (Mar 31 1905–Mar 23 1906)
  NvHi — Je 9 1905; Ja 12, F 23, Mr 9–23 1906
  film — [1905–6]
Ref: files; BBM My 6, 13 1905; TS My 4, 24 1905

CALIENTE

Caliente Progress

In early October of 1904, the weekly *Caliente Progress* was commenced by the Lincoln County Democratic Party, to "boost" J. A. Denton's bid for reelection to the state assembly. H. William Dunn, a San Francisco newspaper man hired as editor, made it a "newsy little sheet," but it lasted less than three months, suspending in mid-December after Denton's defeat. The plant was purchased by A. C. Hose, to found the *Caliente Express* three weeks later.

Caliente Progress: (c. Oct 1904–Dec 1904)
  No issues located.
Ref: PR O 7, 21, 28, N 4 1904, Ja 6 1905; SB Ja 13 1905

Caliente Express

The first number of the *Caliente Express* was issued as a Democratic weekly on January 5, 1905, by A. C. Hose, from the plant of the defunct *Progress.*

Hose had no better luck than his predecessor, however, and on August 3 he suspended the paper. James Brown of the *Las Vegas Times* then bought the plant, and with G. R. McCoy revived the *Express* on August 31, emphasizing "the new management as separate, distinct and in no way connected with the past ownership of the paper." McCoy quickly became disenchanted with Caliente, and quit after two weeks. But Brown held out until June 20, 1906, when he sold the plant to the Lincoln County Publishing Company. This company immediately suspended the *Express* and, combining the material with that of the former *De Lamar Lode,* they commenced the *Caliente Lode-Express* on the following June 30. (See *Caliente Lode-Express.*)

Caliente Express: (Jan 5 1905–Jun 20 1906)
   CLCM — Mr 2 1905
   film — Mr 2, Ag 31 1905–My 31 1906
Ref: files; PR Ja 6 1905; CLE Je 30 1906; LCT Jl 14 1906

Caliente Lode-Express

On June 30, 1906, ten days after the suspension of the *Caliente Express* and eleven days after the suspension of the *De Lamar Lode,* the two plants were combined to issue the *Caliente Lode-Express.* This new sheet was issued every Saturday as a six-page weekly by the Lincoln County Publishing Company, editors and proprietors. On January 19, 1907, Charles W. Patterson became editor, and on November 9, he became publisher, with Harry W. Preston assuming the editorship. Under their guidance, however, the paper soon foundered, and on December 12, 1908, O. H. P. Hendrix took over the management, noting that his predecessor had "sunk into dark oblivion." But its new owner did no better, as the paper suspended two weeks later on December 26, 1908.

Caliente Lode-Express: (Jun 30 1906–Dec 26 1908)
   NvHi — Ja 5 1902–N 2 1907; Ag 1–S 5, D 12 1908
   NvPC — [Je 30 1906–D 26 1908]
   NvU — [Je 30 1906–D 26 1908]
   film — [Je 30 1906–D 26 1908]
Ref: files

Prospector

Following the suspension of the *Lode-Express,* the old plant lay idle only a short time before it was purchased by Robert Graham to commence the Caliente *Prospector* on March 20, 1909. Graham was sole editor and proprietor of the paper and issued it as an eight-page, 15 by 22-inch weekly, dedicated almost wholly to local mining interests. The *Prospector* prospered for only a few years. Graham sold out on March 9, 1912, to H. B. Thompson, and on July 27, a syndicate of Lincoln county citizens temporarily took over the paper. Thompson regained control of it on September 10, but soon sold it to W. F. Connell. He finally suspended publication on February 1, 1913.

Prospector: (Mar 20 1909–Feb 1 1913)
   NvHi — Mr 20, Jl 3 1909–F 1 1913
   NvU — Mr 20 1909–F 1 1913
   film — Mr 20 1909–F 1 1913
Ref: files

Caliente News

For seven years after suspension of the *Prospector*, Caliente was without a newspaper. On May 27, 1920, the Pioche Record Publishing Company filled this void with the establishment of the *Caliente News*. E. Charles D. Marriage was editor of the *News*, and he issued the paper every Thursday as an independent weekly, which sold for $3 a year. By 1923, Marriage had acquired enough money to purchase the establishment from the Record Company and he became sole editor and proprietor. Two years later he engaged in an editorial battle with the *Pioche Record* and its short-lived satellite, the *Caliente Record*. This duel ended finally with the purchase of the *News* by the Pioche Record Company, who suspended it on June 27, 1925.

Caliente News: (May 27 1920–Jun 27 1925)
   NvCh — 1922–5
   NvHi — F 5 1925
   film — [O 21 1920–Ap 2 1925]
Ref: files; PR Je 27 1925

Caliente Record

The weekly *Caliente Record* was published briefly in April of 1925, by the Pioche Record Publishing Company, to compete with the *Caliente News*. It engaged in a spirited editorial duel with the *News*, but proved only partially successful and was suspended within the month.

Caliente Record: (Apr 1925)
   NvU — Ap 1925
Ref: files

Caliente Herald

In less than two years after he was driven from the editorial field in Caliente by the *Pioche Record*, E. Charles D. Marriage had rallied his resources for a new attack, and on January 12, 1928, he reentered the field with the establishment of the *Caliente Herald*. The paper was published every Thursday as an independent weekly by the Caliente Publishing Company, with Marriage serving as editor. This venture proved a success and the *Herald* flourished. Marriage took Philip J. Dolan as partner and business manager on August 6, 1931, and turned the editorship over to him on June 13, 1935. Together they ran the *Herald* until January 3, 1946, when it was purchased by David S. and Edna D. Williams of Milford, Utah. It subsequently was sold to Mr. and Mrs. J. Westover about 1956. In 1960, they in turn sold the *Herald* to Francis L. Peters, editor of the *Pioche*

Record. He continued it as a separate paper for several years, although it was printed in Pioche. He finally suspended it on May 30, 1968, merging it with the *Pioche Record* to form the *Lincoln County Record.*
Caliente Herald: (Jan 12 1928–May 30 1968)
  NvHi — [Ag 14 1941–My 30 1968]
  NvU — [Mr 22 1928–My 30 1968]
  film — [Mr 22 1928–My 30 1968]
Ref: files; Ayer 1955–68

CAMP SIBERT

The Desert Scorpion (The Sibert Scorpion)

The *Sibert Scorpion* was a semimonthly, with the motto "The Sting is in the Tale." It was begun on November 1, 1941, by the soldiers at Camp Sibert near Boulder City. Pfc. Sherwin Garside was its first editor. After the Army renamed the base Camp Williston, they considered calling the paper the *Williston Womeo,* but finally changed it simply to the *Desert Scorpion* on January 30, 1943. It apparently suspended two months later.
The Desert Scorpion: (Nov 1 1941–c. Mar 27 1943)
  NvULV — N 1 1941–Ja 17, F 21–Ap 4, My 2–D 5 1942; Ja 2–Mr 27 1943
  film — [N 1 1941–Mr 27 1943]
Ref: files

CANDELARIA

True Fissure

After helping to start the *Free Press* at Bodie, John M. Dormer disposed of his interest in the paper to H. Z. Osborne. With a new press and material he came to the camp of Candelaria, where he commenced publication of the *True Fissure* on June 5, 1880. The paper was a twenty-four-column, Republican weekly, which sold for $5 a year. Dormer was sole editor and proprietor and, aided for a time by Wells Drury, who became assistant editor on October 9, 1880, Dormer made the paper a strong Republican advocate. He was rewarded in 1882 by the party's nomination as Nevada secretary of state. He won the election that fall, but continued the *True Fissure* until, with the decline of the camp, he decided to lease it to John C. Todman on November 7, 1885. In Todman's hands the *True Fissure* pinched out on December 4, 1886, but only after helping to reelect Dormer to a second term as secretary of state. The plant was moved to Hawthorne, where it was used to publish the unsuccessful *Esmeralda News,* after which it was returned to Candelaria to commence the *Chloride Belt.*
True Fissure: (Jun 5 1880–Dec 4 1886)
  CU-BANC — Je 12 1880–Ja 29, F 26–Je 11, 25–Jl 30, Ag 20–D 31 1881; Ja 7–Jl 29 1882; F 10 1883

NvMus — Ja 2 1886
NvU — [Ja 1 1881–1886]
 film — [Je 12 1880–D 4 1886]
Ref: files

Chloride Belt

In 1890, the Candelaria region experienced a rebirth of mining activity. W. W. Booth, sensing the opportunity to establish a newspaper, purchased the material of the old *Esmeralda News,* brought it back to Candelaria, and set it up in a building on the west end of Main Street. On June 21, 1890, he issued the first number of his new paper, the *Chloride Belt.* Booth was sole editor and proprietor, issuing the paper as a four-page, six-column, 15 by 22-inch weekly, at $5 a year. Under Booth's hand the *Chloride Belt* carried on a spirited battle with the neighboring *Walker Lake Bulletin* of Hawthorne. At the height of this forensic duel, Alfred McCarthy of the *Bulletin* fired: "The *Chloride Belly Band* made an unusually silly spectacle of itself last week—it is bad enough ordinarily, but its last issue was a marvelous mixture of bad English and untruths. We always believed the 'editor' of that sheet to be an ass, but we did not know before that he was a malicious liar."

Within a short time Booth lost faith in the prospects of Candelaria, and on the first of December of 1890, he sold the paper to D. L. Sayre. Under Sayre's management the paper lost its spirit and became a relatively drab affair, containing a patented front and back page and poorly printed locals on the inside. In 1892, a year-long miner's strike dealt a death blow to Candelaria's prosperity, and on December 24 of that year Sayre suspended the *Chloride Belt.* Tired of the uncertainty of mining booms, he removed the press and material to the farming community of Yerington, where he commenced the *Mason Valley Tidings.*

Chloride Belt: (Jun 21 1890–Dec 24 1892)
  NvHi — Ag 20–O 8, 29–N 19 1892
  NvU — [D 10 1890–D 24 1892]
  film — [D 10 1890–D 24 1892]
Ref: files; RG My 20, N 19 1890; WLB S 24 1890

CARLIN

Commonwealth

On September 8, 1909, the *Commonwealth* was founded at Carlin, located on the Southern Pacific Railroad, by the Nevada Publicity Company. A. B. Gray served as editor, issuing the *Commonwealth* each Wednesday as an eight-page, 15 by 22-inch, Democratic weekly, which was primarily a booster paper. It sold at the low rate of $1.50 a year. By 1912, however, Gray had run out of praises to sing of Carlin, and on February 21 he published his last issue there. He moved the plant fifty-five miles up the tracks to Deeth, where he revived the paper the following week. (See Deeth, *Commonwealth.*)

Commonwealth: (Sep 8 1909–Feb 21 1912)
  NvHi — [D 28 1910–F 21 1912]
  NvU — [S 14 1910–F 21 1912]
  film — [S 14 1910–F 21 1912]
Ref: files

Western Home Builder

The first issue of the *Western Home Builder* was published at Carlin on June 6, 1914, by W. T. McNeil. McNeil was sole editor and publisher, issuing the paper every Thursday as an independent weekly at $3 a year. Like its predecessor, the *Commonwealth,* the *Home Builder* was a promotional paper, which was born at Carlin but at an early age moved on to greener pasture. On November 23, 1916, McNeil suspended the *Home Builder* at Carlin and removed the plant to Reno, where he revived it as the *Nevada Home Builder* on January 19, 1917. (See Reno, *Nevada Home Builder.*)

Western Home Builder: (Jun 6 1914–Nov 23 1916)
  NvU — [Je 6 1914–N 23 1916]
  film — [Je 6 1914–N 23 1916]
Ref: files

Nevada Democrat

After W. T. McNeil moved the *Western Home Builder* to Reno in November 1916, Carlin was without a paper until the peripatetic Joe Camp commenced his *Nevada Democrat* on February 9, 1917. With the blessing of McNeil, who was listed as associate editor for the first few issues, Camp labeled his paper, "successor to *Nevada Home Builder,*" and continued the numbering of the latter, even though it was very much alive in Reno. Carlin, however, was simply no longer able to support a paper, and the *Democrat* succumbed within a few months.

Nevada Democrat: (Feb 9 1917–c. Apr 1917)
  NvU — F 23, Ap 13 1917
  film — F 23, Ap 13 1917
Ref: files

Carlin Courier

The weekly *Carlin Courier* was launched on May 7, 1976, by Chuck and Jan Bunning, with the latter as editor. It was the first attempt at running a newspaper in Carlin in nearly sixty years, but it was an abortive one. The paper died in less than three months.

Carlin Courier: (May 7 1976–Aug 4 1976)
  NvHi — My 7–Ag 4 1976
  film — My 7–Ag 4 1976
Ref: files

⚜ CARRARA ⚜

Carrara Obelisk

On May 8, 1913, with a brass band and an exhibition baseball game, the American Carrara Marble Company opened the townsite of Carrara on the Las Vegas and Tonopah Railroad just below its marble quarry south of Beatty. To promote both the town and the company, A. B. Perkins, brother of the company's general manager, also commenced a weekly paper, the *Obelisk,* the same day. Perkins, as editor and manager, filled each issue with local and mining news from his office at Carrara. But the paper was actually printed in Salt Lake City and the Ohio stockholders of the company made up most of its subscribers. It suspended in the fall of 1916, shortly before the quarry shut down.

Carrara Obelisk: (May 8 1913–c. Sep 1916)
  NvU — [F 7 1914–S 9 1916]
  film — [F 7 1914–S 9 1916]
Ref: files

Carrara Miner

The short-lived *Carrara Miner,* printed in Los Angeles, was launched about June 16, 1929, by Bernard M. Stone to help promote a mining excitement and sell stock in the evanescent Gold Ace Mining Company.

Carrara Miner: (c. Jun 16 1929–c. Jul 1929)
  NvU — Jl 11 1929
  film — Jl 11 1929
Ref: files; TMR Je 29 1929

⚜ CARSON CITY ⚜

Territorial Enterprise

The *Territorial Enterprise* holds several firsts in Nevada newspaper history. Aside from being the first paper to be published in Nevada Territory, it was successively the first paper to be issued in Genoa, Carson City, and Virginia City. The *Enterprise* was founded at Genoa on December 18, 1858, by Alfred James and W. L. Jernegan. In August of 1859, Jonathan Williams purchased James's interest and the paper was continued under the firm name of W. L. Jernegan and Co. Jernegan anticipated the growth of Carson City and, suspending publication at Genoa, he revived the *Enterprise* at Carson City on Nov. 26, 1859. While at Carson City the paper was continued as a twenty-column, 21 by 28-inch weekly, selling for 25¢, or $5 a year. The printing office of the *Enterprise* occupied half of the second story of Major Ormsby's adobe building on Carson Street, between Second and Third, overlooking the Plaza. Jernegan handled his financial affairs poorly and in July of 1860, his creditors seized his interest in the paper and sold it to Henry DeGroot. Williams eventually bought out DeGroot to become sole proprietor. With the rapid boom of Virginia City, the *Enterprise* moved once more. In October of 1860, Williams suspended the paper at Carson City and removed the plant to Virginia City, where he revived the *Enterprise* the following month. There the paper flourished.

Jernegan always felt that he had been cheated of his interest in the paper, and swore he would get even. Twenty years later, on his deathbed in White Pine County, he left a legacy of malediction for the *Enterprise* — it was all he had to leave anybody. "I call on God to curse the *Enterprise* and all, dead or alive, who robbed me," he wrote in his diary, "and I also call down the curses of the Great Jehovah on Nevada by quarter sections and subdivisions." Jonathan Williams had already committed suicide in Pioche four years earlier, and the *Enterprise* eventually ceased publication in 1916.

(See Virginia City, *Territorial Enterprise.*)

Territorial Enterprise: (Nov 12 1859–Oct 1860)
  pvt — D 17 1859
  CU-BANC — N 26, D 10, 24–31 1859; Ja 14, 28, F 18, Mr 3–10,
    31, Ap 14–My 5, 19, Je 2, Jl 14, Ag 4 1860
  film — [N 26 1859–Ag 4 1860]
Ref: files; Angel 312; SFE Ja 22 1893; Beebe

Silver Age

The departure of the *Territorial Enterprise* from Carson City was hastened, if not determined, by the indiscretion of a drunken foreman sent from Quincy, in Plumas County, California, by John C. Lewis of the *Argus,* to investigate the territory for a favorable locality to establish a newspaper. The foreman, on looking over the field, decided upon Virginia City and wrote his employer to that effect. Lewis immediately set out with a complete plant to start a paper there. Upon reaching Carson City, however, he found that the *Enterprise* had flanked his lieutenant and taken possession of the promised land. This left Lewis with only two alternatives, either go back to California or locate in Carson City. He decided upon the latter.

Therefore, within a month of the *Enterprise* exodus, its place was filled in Carson City with a new weekly. John C. Lewis commenced publication of the *Silver Age* about December 1, 1860. The paper was published in a carpenter's shop, facing the southeast corner of the plaza. It was Union in politics, and measured 24 by 36 inches. It was well received, and on August 26, 1861, it was enlarged to a daily of twenty columns, at a subscription price of $16 per year, thus becoming the first daily in Nevada. Within a few weeks Lewis added G. T. Sewall as a partner, and about six months later they sold the paper to the Age Association, consisting of John Church, S. A. Glessner and J. L. Laird. On November 2, 1862, this association suspended the *Silver Age* and moved the establishment to Virginia City. There they started the *Virginia Daily Union* on November 4, 1862.

The press of the *Silver Age* continued to have a transient history. In the fall of 1868, the *Union* was purchased by that strange genius, William J.

Forbes, who gave it the name, *Trespass*. Eventually the material and press were taken to White Pine County by J. J. Ayers and C. A. V. Putnam, to be used at Hamilton in publishing the *Inland Empire*. Then, Governor Lewis R. Bradley became proprietor and transferred the wandering establishment to Holmes C. Patrick, who removed it to Stockton, California. John Church, in one of his more lucid moments, suggested that, in that move, the material should have been accompanied by all of its former proprietors, whom he considered proper occupants of the insane asylum at that place.

The *Stockton Republican* was printed on the old *Silver Age* material for three years prior to its suspension in 1873. The *Narrow-Gauge,* edited and published by W. N. Glenn, succeeded the *Republican*. The office was then bought by L. F. Beckwith, who issued the *Daily Courier,* a seven-day newspaper, supporting the election of Newton Booth for Governor. In April, 1874, Mrs. Laura De Force Gordon purchased the wreck to print a paper called the *Daily Leader.* It was a Democratic sheet, edited with ability, and, according to Rowell's newspaper directory, was at that time the only daily in the world edited and conducted by a woman. In November of 1875, the establishment was removed to Sacramento, where the publication was continued until June, 1876. The press was then taken to Oakland and used in the publication of the short-lived *Daily Democrat.* Following this it fades into obscurity and no record of it is preserved.

Silver Age: (c. Dec 1 1860 – Nov 2 1862)
  pvt — Jl 4 1862 (extra)
  CU-BANC — O 2 1862
  DNA — Jl 13, 19, Ag 10, 26, S 15, O 20 1861
  film — Jl 13, 19, Ag 10, 26, S 15, O 20 1861; O 2 1862
Ref: files; Angel 312–3; McMurtrie 296

Carson Daily Independent

The first number of the *Carson Daily Independent* was issued on July 27, 1863, nine months after the *Silver Age* had been moved to Virginia City. W. W. Ross, proprietor of the paper, was unequivocally Union in sentiment. The *Independent* was a twenty-four column, 21 by 27-inch sheet, issued every morning except Monday, at a subscription price of $16 per annum or one bit per single copy. On August 31 of the same year, Israel Crawford became manager. The paper was soon enlarged in size, and on October 20, Crawford purchased the establishment.

Four months later, on February 28, 1864, Crawford sold the paper to the firm of G. W. Calwell and Co., an association of printers consisting of G. W. Calwell, George A. Edes, Andrew Maute, and Charles J. Miller. The new firm reduced the *Independent* to its original dimensions within two weeks after purchase. On March 29, only one month after selling, Crawford's name again appeared as editor and proprietor. In July, a weekly publication replaced the daily, but the daily resumed on August 13 without explanation. The paper appears to have suspended on October 11, 1864, with Israel Crawford still its proprietor.

Part of the office material and the press were used to start the *Genoa Valley Farmer* in September of 1865, and the remainder of the plant was taken to Elko. That portion taken to Genoa finally passed into the hands of A. T. Hawley, who used it to issue the *Douglas County Banner*.

Carson Daily Independent: (Jul 27 1863–Oct 11 1864)
  CSfWF-H — D 5 1863
  CU-BANC — Je 17 1864
  NvHi — Je 5 1864
  NvMus — S 1, D 20 1863
  film — S 1, O 8, D 5, 20 1863; Je 5, 17 1864
Ref: files; HR Mr 5 1864; Angel 313; McMurtrie 296

The Daily Morning Post

On August 27, 1864, the first number of the *Daily Morning Post* was issued at Carson City by H. W. Johnson and Co. It was the successor of the *Daily Morning Message,* run for a short time that year at Gold Hill. The *Post* contained twenty-eight columns and was printed on paper measuring 23 by 32 inches. Although it was declared to be Union in sentiment, it tried to refrain from supporting any party nominations. John C. Lewis, former editor and proprietor of the *Silver Age,* was employed as editor, but, because he became too independent, his chair was filled with one more subservient to the policy of the proprietors.

Johnson and Co. continued the paper until the last of October in 1864, after which Lewis purchased the establishment. The *Post* was published through the election campaign of 1864, but suspended early in January of 1865. Within two weeks, however, the paper was revived by E. F. McElwain and Co., who continued it until sometime in April or May of that year, when McElwain founded the *Carson Daily Appeal.*

On December 9, 1865, Lewis started a weekly paper at Washoe City, called the *Eastern Slope.* It was printed on the old *Post* material until it, too, suspended in 1868. In July of 1868, Lewis moved the press to Reno and used it to print the *Crescent* until 1875, when he sold the plant to J. C. Dow. That same year Dow started the *Nevada Democrat,* which lasted until mid-1878. After the suspension of the *Democrat,* the short-lived *Reno Daily Record* was issued from this material until September, 1878, when it was taken to Bodie, California, to start the Bodie *News.*

The Daily Morning Post: (Aug 27 1864–c. May 1865)
  pvt — Mr 16 1865
  CU-BANC — D 28 1864
  NvHi — Mr 16, Ap 15 (extra) 1865
  NvMus — Ap 15 (extra) 1865
  film — D 28 1864; Mr 16, Ap 15 (extra) 1865
Ref: files; Angel 313; McMurtrie 296

State Democrat

Colonel Adrian C. Ellis started a daily campaign paper, the *State Democrat,* at Carson City on October 25, 1864. It supported General George McClellan for President, and as had been planned at the start, was suspended with the close of the campaign.

State Democrat: (Oct 25 1864–Nov 1864)
   No issues located.
Ref: Angel 313; McMurtrie 297

Nevada Appeal

Carson City, the state capital, was again left without a newspaper, but only for a short time. On May 16, 1865, E. F. McElwain, J. Barrett, and Marshall Robinson commenced a Republican paper, the *Carson Daily Appeal.* The first number brought news of the capture of Jefferson Davis, and the people of Carson City celebrated by hanging the ex-Confederate President in effigy. Henry R. Mighels was engaged as editor, and on November 28, 1865, he and Robinson purchased Barrett's and McElwain's interests in the paper. Robinson and Mighels managed the *Appeal* until the end of December, 1870, when C. L. Perkins and H. C. Street purchased the paper and suspended it, changing its politics to Democratic and its name to the *Daily State Register.*

But the *Appeal* would rise again. Henry R. Mighels returned with financial backing from senatorial aspirant John P. Jones and started the *New Daily Appeal* on September 9, 1872. After the election, on December 12, Marshall Robinson again became a partner, and three days later they bought out the rival *State Register,* combining its plant with theirs. *New* was dropped from the masthead on March 11, 1873. Mighels again became sole proprietor of the paper on January 1, 1878. That September, he was nominated by the Republican Party as lieutenant governor, but failed to be elected. He died at his home in Carson City on May 27, 1879.

Upon Mighels's death, editorial management of the *Appeal* fell to his widow, Nellie V. Mighels, but on August 8 of the following year, S. H. Fulton of the *Elko Post* assumed those duties. Sam P. Davis relieved Fulton of the editorship on October 5, 1880, and later married Mrs. Mighels. Davis continued as editor until he was elected state controller in 1898. Henry R. Mighels, Jr., son of the former proprietor, then leased the paper until June 1, 1906, when Irwin G. Lewis took up the lease. On July 8, 1907, the Appeal Publishing Company took over, with Dean K. Smith as editor and James T. Green as manager.

The *Appeal* was leased briefly by Irwin Lewis and Edwin E. Roberts in 1909, before reverting back to Smith and Green. Then T. D. Van Devort became editor for the Nevada Printing Company on November 3, 1913, and he ran it for nearly a decade. The *Appeal* next passed to L. J. Blake as editor and publisher on January 4, 1922. He sold the paper back to Henry R. Mighels, Jr., on January 6, 1927, and Mighels bought the rival *News* on May 1, 1930, merging it with the *Appeal*. On April 4, 1933, ownership passed to Ida B. Mighels, who hired E. T. Clyde as editor. Amos O. Buckner bought the paper on October 17, 1938, retaining Clyde as editor until about 1943, when F. J. Neddenriep took over the post.

Wesley L. Davis, Jr., became publisher on May 2, 1944, running the paper until January 2, 1947, when Arthur N. Suverkrup bought it and rechristened it the *Nevada Appeal*. He sold it, on August 2 of the following year, to George H. Payne, who also bought the weekly *Chronicle* and combined their plants, although he continued both papers. Neal Van Sooy purchased both papers about 1952, but eventually sold them to Edwin B. Brown in 1961. The following year, Donald W. Reynolds of the *Las Vegas Review-Journal* added them to his empire, bringing in a succession of editors: James Leavy, E. Gorton Covington, Michael Kruglak, Zane Miles, John S. Miller and Steven R. Frady. (See Carson City, *Daily State Register*.)

Nevada Appeal: (May 16 1865 — Dec 28 1870; Sep 9 1872+)
　pvt — Ag 2 1865; D 30 1866; My 15, O 8 1867; N 21 1875; N 24 1886; N 26, 1896
　C — O 10 1868
　CSfWF-H — Ja 16 1866
　CSmH — O 9–N 15 1867; Ja–Mr, My–D 1868; Ja–D 1870; Mr 1–D 30 1876; 77–80
　CU-BANC — My 16 1865–D 28 1870; S 14 1872–Ap 30, Je 1–D 31 1880; Ja 9, 11 1881; Jl 12, D 29 1882; Je 7–26 1883; F 5, My 1 1884; Ja 26–N 8 1885; Ja 1 1886–D 31 1891; Ja 5, S 16 1892
　ICHi — Ag 15, 27 1865
　MWA — Ja 16 1867; O 29 1868
　NvCC — Ja 2 1907–O 30 1913; Ja 6 1914–D 31 1915; Ap 9 1918–Ap 29 1919; Ja 1930+
　NvHi — D 7 1865; Je 16 1866; Ja 5, N 16 1867–N 14, 21 1868–N 25, D 27 1873– N 1892; Je 1 1911+
　NvU — My 16 1865–D 28 1870; S 9 1872+
　OClWHi — O 2 1881
　film — [My 16 1865–D 28 1870; S 9 1872+]
Ref: files; Angel 313–5; Doten 2239; Ayer 1940+

Nevada State Journal

After helping to establish the *Carson Daily Appeal* at Carson City, E. F. McElwain retired from that firm, and on May 14, 1866, issued the first number of the *Nevada State Journal*. McElwain was publisher and issued the paper as a daily, with the "Old Piute," John K. Lovejoy, serving as editor. The *Journal* was a lively concern, but not a financial success. It survived a little more than a week, folding on May 23.

Nevada State Journal: (May 14 1866–May 23 1866)
　NvU — My 15–23 1866
　film — My 15–23 1866
Ref: files; RRR My 18, 31, 1866; McMurtrie 297

The Daily State Register

When Charles L. Perkins and H. C. Street took control of the *Carson City Daily Appeal,* they promptly changed its name to the *Daily State Register.* The first number of the *Register* was issued on December 29, 1870, announcing that "the subscribers of the late Carson *Appeal* today receive the paper under a new name and under different management." It contained the same number of columns as had the *Appeal,* but they were lengthened about two inches, possibly reflecting the somewhat elongated structure of the new editor, Mr. Street. The ensuing March 5 saw a return to the old size of the paper, and the announcement that the paper would only be issued twice a week in the future. However, two days later, the daily format was resumed, in accordance with the wishes of many of the citizens.

On February 13, 1872, John Booth, late owner of the Unionville *Silver State,* became proprietor of the *Register* and Street retired as editor. After the revival of the *Appeal* by Mighels in September, Booth faced stiff competition for subscribers and advertisers. Thus, when Mighels finally offered to buy him out, he accepted. The *Register* was suspended on December 15, with the announcement that Carson could not yet support two dailies, so it was better to have just one, "and sustain it handsomely than to accord to two merely a starvation living." (See Carson City, *Nevada Appeal.*)

The Daily State Register: (Dec 29 1870–Dec 15 1872)
  CU-BANC — D 29–30 1870; F 21 1871–D 15 1872
  DLC — D 29 1870–Mr 5, D 2 1871–Mr 6 1872
  NvHi — O 31 1871
  NvMus — O 24 1871; S 5 1872
  NvU — [1870–2]
  film — [D 29 1870–N 30 1872]
Ref: files; GHN D 16 1872; Angel 314; McMurtrie 298

The Daily Nevada Tribune

The *Nevada Tribune* was started at Carson City as a semiweekly on July 16, 1872, by R. R. "Deacon" Parkinson, his eldest son, Edward J. Parkinson, and Joseph McClure, under the firm name of McClure and Parkinson. Deacon edited the paper, which prided itself in being both "Spicy and Newsy." It was well received, and on January 26, 1874, it was enlarged to a daily, the front page masthead being changed to *Daily Nevada Tribune* on August 9, 1875. Although the *Tribune* was avowedly Republican, it remained independent in its support of candidates. On March 17, 1875, Ed Parkinson became sole proprietor, but Deacon continued to hold the editorial chair for many years. Ed served as both reporter and business manager, while his younger brother and three sisters did all the rest.

Deacon Parkinson was born in England and had spent his youth upon the seas, arriving in San Francisco in 1850. Two years later he was married, and Edward J. Parkinson, the oldest of his eight children, was born in San

Francisco in late 1852. He moved with his family to Carson City about 1865, and became very active politically.

For many years a fierce rivalry raged between the *Tribune* and the *Appeal*. The Deacon had a particular dislike for young David Sessions, a South Carolinian and Princeton alumnus, known even among the unlettered for his familiarity with the classics. Sessions held the local editorship of the *Appeal,* acting as the brevity and levity man.

On one occasion in 1874, Henry Mighels went to San Francisco on business and turned the editor's chair over to Sessions. Immediately Sessions dashed off a scathing editorial, referring to the old man of the *Tribune* as a "chance scribbler of foreign birth who shocks you by committing murder on his Sovereign's English at every breath." The Deacon fairly boiled and stormed out the door of his office, bumping into David Sessions. He hurled all of the usual epithets at Sessions and then threw in a few of his own invention. With this the young scholar, who was ordinarily a cultured and unaggressive individual, started swinging with both fists.

Upon hearing of this outrage, Ed Parkinson gave public notice that he would settle with Sessions personally. On April 9, they met on the street and both opened fire with revolvers. Sessions suffered a shattered hand and Parkinson fell, wounded in the left flank. Both recovered quickly to continue the feud along literary lines.

In later years Deacon Parkinson carried on the rivalry with Sam Davis, who succeeded Mighels on the *Appeal*. The feud at last faded when the Parkinsons leased the plant to H. A. Lemmon on November 19, 1894, and moved to Seattle. H. C. Dunn, foreman of the State Printing Office, joined with Lemmon on March 11, 1895, but they gave up the lease on November 1 and bought the rival *Carson City News*. Parkinson suspended the *Tribune* on April 5, 1896, and sold an interest in the plant to C. A. Norcross and Company, who moved it to Reno. There it struggled on under the same name from April 22 until its final suspension on July 15, 1896. (See Reno, *The Daily Nevada Tribune*.)

The Daily Nevada Tribune: (Jul 16 1872–Apr 5 1896)
   pvt — N 25 1881; Mr 3 1887; Je 1 1888
   CHi — S 22 1893; Jl 12 1894
   CSmH — My 1 1882–My 31 1883
   CU-BANC — [S 17 1873–My 15, Jl 27 1875; S 1879–80]; Je 11 1881; Mr 9, Ap 9 1883; Ap 2 1887; Jl 24 1891
   ICHi — O 5 1876
   NvHi — O 5 1875; [1876]; Je 4 1886; F 1 1887; Jl 15 1890; [1892]
   NvU — Mr 1875–Ap 5 1896
   film — [S 17 1873–Ap 5 1896]
Ref: files; Angel 315; McMurtrie 297; Doten 1916–7, 2239

Nevada Pulpit

The *Nevada Pulpit,* Nevada's second monthly, was founded in January of 1874, by the Reverend George B. Allen, Episcopal rector of St. Peter's

Parish in Carson City. Allen issued the magazine as an eighteen-page, thirty-six-column monthly, measuring 8½ by 5½ inches, at a subscription price of $1 per year. The *Pulpit* was ably edited, advocated no creed, and was liberal and independent in its views, inviting free expression of opinion from all sides. About September 1, Allen was thrown from a horse and disabled for some time, causing the September number to be delayed and issued as a double with the October issue. The magazine prospered, but Allen was forced to suspend it with the December issue, when he was called to northern California. However, the success of the *Nevada Pulpit* prompted Allen to return to Carson City two years later and attempt to publish a weekly, the *Nevada Patriot*.

Nevada Pulpit: (Jan 1874–Dec 1874)
   pvt — Ja–D 1874
   CLU — Ja–D 1874
   CSaT — Ja–D 1874
   CSmH — Ja–D 1874
   NvU — Ja–D 1874
Ref: files

Daily Evening Herald

The *Daily Evening Herald* was a short-lived enterprise that attempted to break into an already packed field. It was founded by Wells Drury and Co. in Carson City on August 9, 1875, during the height of the rivalry between the *Appeal* and *Tribune*. Drury had been out of college only two years and was excessively optimistic. He chose Charles A. V. Putnam as editor and managed the paper very well. In a short time, however, he realized the effort was vain and, on September 3, he sold the doomed establishment to Charles Lee, who changed the firm name to the Herald Publishing Company. The following month, the paper was suspended.

Daily Evening Herald: (Aug 9 1875–Oct 1875)
   NvU — [Ag 20–S 9 1875]
   film — [Ag 20–S 9 1875]
Ref: files; Angel 315; McMurtrie 298

Nevada Patriot

The Reverend George B. Allen returned to Carson City from northern California in the summer of 1876, and decided to reenter the editorial field. On July 11, 1876, he issued the first number of the weekly *Nevada Patriot*. Allen intended for the *Patriot* to be the vehicle of free expression for the entire state and issued 3000 copies of the first number, hoping to increase the circulation to 5000. The paper was an eight-page, forty-column sheet, selling at a subscription price of $1 for three months. In a glowing editorial, Allen devoted the paper to the "material, educational, social, political and moral interest of the Silver State." The venture received certain opposition from struggling local papers throughout the state, who were reluctant to share a portion of their subscribers with the *Patriot.* Dejectedly, Allen suspended the paper in early August of the same year.

Nevada Patriot: (Jul 11 1876–Aug 1876)
   CU-BANC — Jl 11 1876
   NvHi — Jl 11–Ag 3 1876
   film — Jl 11–Ag 3 1876
Ref: files

Parish Guide

The Reverend H. L. Foote was Episcopal rector of St. Peter's Parish in Carson City from October 11, 1876, until May 11, 1878. During his incumbency, he issued a small paper called the *Parish Guide,* for the exclusive use of the Episcopal churches of Nevada.

Parish Guide: (c. 1876–1878)
   No issues located.
Ref: Myrick

The Portfolio

The *Portfolio* was a small monthly begun at Carson City by young amateur printers in July of 1878. It sold for 50¢ a year and lasted through its fourth issue, but nothing else is known of it.

The Portfolio: (Jul 1878–c. Nov 1878)
   No issues located.
Ref: CA Ag 21, S 26, N 21 1878; TE N 23 1878

Carson Times

On March 18, 1880, the first number of the daily *Carson Times* was issued by Edward Niles. The *Times* was started as a modest 12 by 18-inch paper, but it was later enlarged to 21 by 28 inches. It was Republican in politics and sold for $10 a year. Niles was sole editor and proprietor and filled the *Times* with scintillating passages of wit and satire. However, the *Times* was forced to suspend on June 11, 1881, for reasons well explained in the following obituary by Niles, which was published in the Carson *Index* on June 15:

> I started the business with limited capital and incurred a debt of $2,500 for press, type and necessary outfit. During the past year I have paid on the material, including freight charges, fully $1,200, and nearly $4,000 for composition. My material was supplied by Messrs. Miller & Richards, through their San Francisco Agency.
>
> Other payments fell due recently. The Scotch firm above mentioned declined to extend further accommodation, notwithstanding the fact that they were fully protected and have been paid nearly one-half the value of the property. Aided by a zealous and unusually strict incumbent of our shrievalty, they pinched me so hard that I decided not to throw any more good money after bad, concluded that discretion was the better part of valor in this case, and quietly retired, for the present, from the arena of Carson's paper knights.
>
> Conscious of having ministered faithfully to a generous army of advertis-

ers, a valued corps of subscribers and a cheerful squad of deadheads, and also with the belief that the *Times* has been lively, enterprising and moderately entertaining, its editor and publisher extends his sincere thanks to all who so generously aided its vigorous career, and with malice toward none, and all that sort of thing, will soon enter a new field of labor, trusting, at some future time, to profit by experience and with ample capital again enter the editorial ranks.

Carson, June 14, 1881   E. Niles

Carson Times: (Mar 18 1880–Jun 11 1881)
 CSfWF-H — F 5 1881
 CU-BANC — [Ap 9 1880–Je 11 1881]
 NvU — Jl 10–D 31 1880
 film — [Ap 9 1880–Je 11 1881]
Ref: files; CI Je 15, 1881

Daily Index

On December 25, 1880, Marshall Robinson commenced publication of the *Daily Index* at Carson City. The paper was to be issued every morning except Monday, at a subscription price of $5 a year. The first number was printed on a 14 by 20-inch sheet and contained twenty columns, nine of which were blank. The blank columns were held in anticipation of future advertising. Judge Charles N. Harris was editor and managed the position with exceptional ability. In the first number he clearly defined the aims of the *Index:*

> Editorially we have no pronunciamento to make. Our columns will reflect matters of current interest. We have no friends to reward nor enemies to punish, our mode of expression will usually be definite and to the point, we shall have opinions to express now and then. Politically, our accent is Republican and our persuasion Stalwart. Religiously, we are tolerant. Socially, we are bland and accommodating. Our appreciation of the fine points of modern civilization is second only to that of a *railroad president.* Financially, we are not a bonanza; and commercially we acknowledge ourself a proper subject for the grand bounce. Our diurnal comfort is principally derived from our knowledge that a good many of the people of Nevada are fixed up about as we are. We know of no good reason to fear for the success of our venture. The times couldn't be worse or harder, nor the people much more impoverished. Everything is to be won, and there is nothing more to be lost. We can't lose much on advertisements, for we have started publication without any. We can't lose any money, for the reason that none has been paid to us. It must be apparent, therefore, that the *Index* is planted upon the bedrock foundation of public esteem, and its future consequently secure.

The paper was indeed well founded, and it flourished for many years under the pen of Judge Harris. Harris and George B. Hill leased the paper for six months starting on November 21, 1882, but Robinson resumed control at the end of the time. On July 1, 1886, Robinson sold the *Index* to Wells Drury, and Harris took up the editorship of the new rival *Nevada*

Union. Drury edited the *Index* until November 10, 1886, when James W. E. Townsend became editor and publisher. Townsend enlivened its columns for only a few months before he, too, sold out on January 27, 1887, to the Index Publishing Company. This firm continued the *Index* until July 1, 1887, when it was purchased again by Marshall Robinson. Four days later Robinson merged with C. N. Morris's Nevada Union Publishing Company, which combined the *Index* with the *Nevada Union* to form the *Nevada Index-Union.* (See Carson City, *Nevada Index-Union.*)

Daily Index: (Dec 25 1880–Jul 5 1887)
   NvCC — D 25 1880–Je 1886
   NvHi — F 22, O 27 1882; [Ja–Je 1887]
   NvU — D 25 1880–Jl 5 1887
   film — D 25 1880–Jl 5 1887
Ref: files; Angel 316

The Daily Bee

The Carson City *Daily Bee* was founded about April 10, 1882, as a campaign organ for the Democratic Party, by A. J. Mills and A. P. Jones, editors and proprietors. The paper was a small sheet, measuring 7 by 10 inches, and containing four pages of three columns each. It sold to the most optimistic for $1.50 for three months and to the more skeptical for 50¢ a month. After the close of the election campaign on November 18, the *Bee* buzzed off.

The Daily Bee: (c. Apr 10 1882–Nov 18 1882)
   pvt — Jl 14 1882
   NvHi — S 22, O 28, 31, N 2, 6, 18 1882
   NvMus — Jl 17 1882
   film — Jl 14, 17, S 22, O 28, 31, N 2, 6, 18, 1882
Ref: files

Carson Free Lance

In February of 1885, A. C. Pratt purchased a small office east of Rail's Hardware Store in Carson City, where, on March 2, he published the first number of the *Carson Free Lance.* Pratt was sole editor and proprietor and issued the paper as a four-page, five-column, 14 by 20-inch weekly, at $2.50 per year. The paper prospered for a time and on the following July 13, Pratt sold the establishment to C. S. Young at a substantial profit. Young continued the *Free Lance* until the summer of 1887, when he suspended the paper, selling out to the Reno *Gazette.*

Carson Free Lance: (Mar 2 1885–c. 1887)
   NvHi — Mr 23, Ap 6–My 18, Je 1–29, Jl 13, Ag 17, 31, S 14, O 5–12, 26–N 3, 30, D 31 1885; F 1, 22–Mr 1, 22–29, Je 14, Jl 19, Ag 2–9, S 20, O 11, N 8–15, 29 1886
   NvMus — O 5 1885
   NvU — [Mr 2 1885–N 8 1886]
   film — [Mr 2 1885–N 29 1886]
Ref: files; RG S 15 1887

The Carson Boys

In late 1885, a small Democratic sheet, *The Carson Boys,* was established at Carson City by the firm of Merigold and W. L. Corbett. The paper was issued semiweekly, on Wednesdays and Saturdays, and measured 10½ by 14 inches. Merigold and Corbett recruited 550 subscribers from the ranks of the Democratic Party and these carried the paper for several months, into 1886. However, the paper was not a financial success and *The Carson Boys* closed shop by mid-1886.

The Carson Boys: (1885–1886)
  NvMus — S 16 1885 (clipping); My 12 1886
  film — S 16 1885 (clipping); My 12 1886
Ref: files; Myrick

Carson Post

The *Carson Post* was a 7 by 9-inch amateur monthly published by two-twelve-year-old boys, Billy Cowan and Si Adams, for four months, probably in the mid-1880's.

Carson Post: (c. 1885)
  No issues located.
Ref: Doten 2239

Nevada Union

The *Nevada Union* was begun at Carson City on August 4, 1886, by the Nevada Union Publishing Company, with Charles N. Harris as editor, and W. A. Geft as manager. The paper was issued every evening except Sunday, as a four-page, six-column, 14 by 21-inch daily, selling at a subscription rate of $8 a year. Harris became both editor and manager of the *Union* after Geft resigned the following March 14. On July 5, 1887, the Nevada Union Publishing Company purchased the *Index* and merged it with the *Nevada Union* to form the daily *Nevada Index-Union.* (See Carson City, *Nevada Index-Union.*)

Nevada Union: (Aug 4 1886–Jul 5 1887)
  pvt — Ag 4 1886
  NvHi — Ag 25 1886
  NvU — [Ag 4 1886–Jl 5 1887]
  film — [Ag 4 1886–Jl 5 1887]
Ref: files

Nevada Index-Union

On July 5, 1887, the Nevada Union Publishing Company purchased the Carson City *Daily Index* and merged the two firms to commence publication of the *Nevada Index-Union* on July 6. Judge Charles N. Harris continued to be editor and manager, issuing the paper every morning except Monday, as a four-page, six-column, 14 by 21-inch daily, at a subscription rate of $8 a year. The financial status of the firm was poor, however, and on January 1, 1888, the daily *Nevada Index-Union* was reduced to a weekly at $3 a year. The subscribers demanded that the daily be revived and promised additional support. On February 1, 1888, the daily *Index-Union* was reestablished and the weekly was continued. The daily was issued on a smaller scale, measuring only 10 by 15 inches and containing four pages of four columns each, but still sold at $8 per year. The promised support failed to materialize, however, and the paper was finally forced to suspend on July 3, 1888.

Nevada Index-Union: (Jul 6 1887–Jul 3 1888)
   NvHi — [Jl 6–D 1887]
   NvU — [Jl 6 1887–Jl 3 1888]
   film — [Jl 6 1887–Jl 3 1888]
Ref: files

The Sun

In June, 1889, two brothers, I. and Selig Olcovich, twelve and ten years old, respectively, started a small semiweekly "story paper," *The Sun.* The paper was well patronized by friends and a sympathetic community, and on the following October 17, it was enlarged from notepaper size to 8 by 10 inches. However, interest gradually waned and the *Sun's* appearance became less frequent. On August 17, 1891, George T. Davis, Jr., aged twelve years, joined the partnership, and they commenced a new paper, *The Weekly.* (See Carson City, *The Weekly.*)

The Sun: (Jun 1889–Jul 1891)
   No issues located.
Ref: CW F 29, Ag 8 1892

Carson City News

On June 21, 1891, Edwin T. Dupuis, a young Carson lawyer, issued the first number of the *Carson City News.* The paper was published every morning except Monday, as a four-page, twenty-four-column, Republican daily, at a subscription price of $8 per year. Dupuis ran the *News* for less than a year, selling on May 17, 1892, to Annie H. Martin, who became both editor and proprietor. She issued the paper until November 2, 1895, when she sold it to H. C. Dunn and Hal A. Lemmon, former lessees of the *Nevada Tribune.* They changed the publication to evenings, and increased the subscription rate to $12. Lemmon became sole editor and proprietor on September 17, 1904, but the Nevada Press Company took over the paper the following February 1. They hired William McClure Gotwaldt as editor about June 1, but sold out to George L. Sanford on July 17, 1906. Sanford and Gotwaldt served as joint editors for a month until August 19, when the latter quit to take charge of the *Manhattan News.*

   Sanford sold the *News* on November 15, 1908, to James T. Shaw. George A. Montrose became associate editor, and leased the paper himself on the following August 31. Montrose continued the lease for six years before turning it over to George M. Anderson, on May 1, 1915. Peter V. Felesina and Harry Gifford leased the *News* on March 1, 1918. Felesina eventually raised enough money to buy the paper, and on January 1, 1922, the Carson City News Printing Company took over. Felesina was president and E. T. Clyde was editor. Control of the company soon passed to Samuel Platt, who sold it to H. R. Mighels, Jr., of the rival *Appeal,* on April 18, 1930. Two weeks later, on May 1, Mighels suspended the *News* to merge it with his *Appeal.*

Carson City News: (Jun 21 1891–May 1 1930)
   pvt — Mr 17 1897; My 12 1898; S 1 1908–Je 30 1913
   CHi — S 22 1893
   CSmH — Ap 1 1914
   CU-BANC — D 15 1897; Jl 20 1927–My 1 1930
   NvCC — N 1 1913–Ja 4 1914; Ja 2 1916–Ap 12 1917; Ja 2 1921–My 1 1930
   NvMus — N 11 1918
   NvU — [Je 21 1891–1928]
   film — [Je 21 1891–My 1 1930]
Ref: files; Doten 1904, 2239

The Weekly

In July of 1891, I. and Selig Olcovich, aged fourteen and twelve respectively, suspended their semimonthly paper, *The Sun,* and in partnership with George T. Davis, Jr., age twelve, began publication of a new paper, *The Weekly,* on August 17. The paper, measuring 5½ by 8 inches and containing four pages of three columns each, was published every Monday at a nominal subscription price of $1 per year. Within a year, *The Weekly* was enlarged three times, finally measuring 8 by 11 inches. On December 10, 1894, Davis retired from the partnership, and the firm name became Olcovich and Olcovich, editors and proprietors. *The Weekly* continued to prosper for a time, and on May 4, 1898, it was enlarged to eight pages. Money became tight, however, and on June 20, 1898, the paper was reduced to four pages and the subscription rate was increased to $1.50 per year. This step heralded its doom. *The Weekly* suspended publication January 2, 1899, and was absorbed by the Carson *Appeal.*

The Weekly: (Aug 17 1891–Jan 2 1899)
   pvt — N 30 1891
   CHi — N 7 1897
   NvMus — [Ag 17 1891–6]
   NvU — [Ag 17 1891–Ja 2 1899]
   film — [Ag 17 1891–Ja 2 1899]
Ref: files; Doten 2015

Carson Press

On January 1, 1892, William L. Lee commenced a small, spicy, Friday weekly, the *Carson Press.* Unlike Lee's former short-lived juvenile weekly, the Reno *Morning Star,* the *Press* was destined to gain wider and more enduring support. It was suspended temporarily on September 16, 1893, when Lee went east, but was revived again on December 2, by his brother, A. W. Lee. The latter continued to issue it somewhat spasmodically for two and one-half more years, until its final suspension in January of 1896. That year Will Lee resurrected the *Press* once more at Gardnerville. (See *Gardnerville Press*.)

Carson Press: (Jan 1 1892–Jan 1896)
    pvt — Ja 9 1892
    CSmH — Ja 1 1892–Je 30, D 2–30 1893
    NvMus — Jl 4 1892
    film — [Ja 1 1892–D 30 1893]
Ref: files

Celebration Gazetteer

The *Celebration Gazetteer* was a daily program of the Independence Day parade and festivities, issued by the Carson City *Appeal* from July 3 to 6, 1892.

Celebration Gazetteer: (Jul 3 1892–Jul 6 1892)
    CU-BANC — Jl 3–6 1892
    film — Jl 3–6 1892
Ref: files

The White Ribbon

The White Ribbon was founded in Carson City on July 6, 1894, during the great Pullman strike, with the announcement, "You have before you the initial number of the WHITE RIBBON. It is published that the residents may learn the latest telegraphic news from all over the world until communication with the East and West shall again be established. When the strike is ended and trains are again running the WHITE RIBBON will have fulfilled its mission and its publication will be discontinued." The paper was published every evening by the White Ribbon Publishing Company, consisting of W. M. David, H. A. Lemmon, and L. A. Jacobs. It was printed on the Olcovich brothers' *Carson Weekly* press. *The White Ribbon* was no larger than a letter sheet, and consisted of four pages of only three columns each. It contained no advertisements and sold for 25¢ a week or 10¢ a copy. Most all the items were of an editorial nature, and the paper published many of Arthur McEwen's acid comments about Ambrose Bierce and M. H. DeYoung. It suspended about July 21.

The White Ribbon: (Jul 6 1894–c. Jul 21 1894)
    pvt — Jl 7 1894
    NvHi — Jl 6–9, 12–14, 17, 19 1894
    NvMus — Jl 21 1894
    film — [Jl 6–21 1894]
Ref: files

Parish Rubric

The *Parish Rubric* was a free monthly commenced in 1897, by the vestry of St. Peter's Church. It flourished at least until 1904.

Parish Rubric: (1897–c. 1904)
   NvU — [1901–4]
   film — [F 1898–1904]
Ref: files

Ormsby County Ledger

After their suspension of the *Weekly,* the Olcovich brothers ventured into the publishing business at least once again, with the issuance of the *Ormsby County Ledger.* This paper was little more than an advertiser, with stories and advertisements for the Olcovich brothers' store, but no news. It sold for 5¢ a copy, and claimed to be a monthly, but was undated. It probably appeared about 1900, or a little after, but its actual date and duration are unknown.

Ormsby County Ledger: (c. 1900)
   CU-BANC — undated issue
   film — undated issue
Ref: files

Carson Weekly

Exactly one year after the suspension of the Olcovich boys' *Weekly* on January 2, 1899, a new paper was commenced by two fourteen-year-olds, Dean K. Smith and Horace Meder. On January 28, 1900, they issued the first number of their new *Carson Weekly,* as an eight-page, three-column, 10 by 14-inch, Monday morning weekly, which they sold for $1.50 a year. This little sheet gained as enthusiastic a following as its predecessor had, and it was ultimately to grow from a small juvenile sheet to a large and mature enterprise.

On May 7, 1900, a youngster named Vieira replaced Meder as Smith's partner, but he quit on April 8 of the following year, leaving Smith sole owner. Smith finally sold the *Weekly* on March 9, 1903, to W. T. King, who ran it for over a decade. On May 4, 1914, he leased it to Ed G. Hummel for six months. Finally, on January 6, 1916, King sold the *Weekly* to A. B. Gray of the Nevada Publicity Company, formerly the publisher of the Deeth *Commonwealth.* With Gray as editor, the *Weekly* continued for only two years more, ultimately suspending on November 7, 1918.

Carson Weekly: (Jan 28 1900–Nov 7 1918)
   CHi — Ja 24 1918
   NvCC — Ap 12 1917–Ap 4 1918
   NvHi — S 16 1907–Je 27 1918
   NvU — [Ja 28 1900–N 7 1918]
   film — [Ja 28 1900–N 7 1918]
Ref: files; Doten 2057

Yogi

While awaiting trial on mail fraud charges, the irrepressible Sidney Flower, alias Parmenter Kent, former editor of the *Goldfield Gossip,* commenced a new monthly magazine, *Yogi,* on July 19, 1910. It was published by Guy Guinan of Carson City. Flower's firsthand accounts of life in the local jail attracted a sufficient number of eastern readers that the paper prospered. But in April, 1911, he moved the *Yogi* to Sierra Madre in southern California, where it lasted only one month, suspending in May.

Yogi: (Jul 1910–Apr 1911)
  CtY — Ja 1911
  NN — Jl 19 1910–My 1911
  film — Jl 19 1910–My 1911
Ref: files; CA Ag 8 1910

Karson Sity Gazoot

Around March of 1911, the entertainment committee of the Leisure Hour Club issued a comic paper, the *Karson Sity Gazoot,* to help promote their show "The Big Noise." Its "chief editor and muckraker" was James Sweeney.

Karson Sity Gazoot: (c. Mar 1911)
  NvMus — c. Mr 1911
  film — c. Mr 1911
Ref: files

Greater Nevada

The illustrated monthly booster magazine *Greater Nevada* was started in Carson City in January, 1912. Its editor, publisher, and duration are unknown.

Greater Nevada: (Jan 1912–c. 1912)
  No issues located.
Ref: BB vol. 7 no. 2

Carson Evening Gazette

The daily *Carson Evening Gazette* was an ambitious, but short-lived little typewritten paper, begun on July 21, 1914, most likely by Dorothy and Margaret Bartlett, daughters of District Judge and former Congressman George A. Bartlett. It apparently died with its second number, though it was briefly resurrected in spirit in the *Carson City Enlightener,* the following month. (See *Carson City Enlightener.*)

Carson Evening Gazette: (Jul 21 1914–Jul 23 1914)
  NvU — Jl 21–23 1914
  film — Jl 21–23 1914
Ref: files

Carson City Enlightener

Following the untimely death of the *Gazette,* the Misses Dorothy and Margaret Bartlett joined forces with Miss Eleanor Siebert and Masters Ogden Monahan, Frederick Siebert, and Kenneth Raycraft to launch a new weekly venture, the *Carson City Enlightener,* on August 5, 1914. This time they issued five numbers before calling it quits on September 4.

Carson City Enlightener: (Aug 5 1914–Sep 4 1914)
   NvHi — S 4 1914
   NvU — [Ag 5–21 1914]
   film — [Ag 5–S 4 1914]
Ref: files

Nevadian Times

The *Nevadian Times* was founded on July 1, 1927, at the railroad town of Wadsworth, by A. E. Haines. After four years at Wadsworth, Haines decided to move on to more promising prospects at nearby Fernley, but in scarcely a year he was again on the move, bringing the paper to Carson City on October 9, 1931. There he continued the paper under the same name, issuing it each Friday for $2.50 a year. Haines served as editor while his wife, V. E. Haines, became owner and publisher. They ran the *Times* until July 5, 1935, when they sold the establishment to George B. Russell and Herbert C. Sproule, and moved to Minden to found a new *Times* the following year. The new owners continued the paper for only a few weeks under the old name before they changed it to the *Carson Chronicle* on August 9. (See Carson City, *Carson Chronicle*.)

Nevadian Times: (Oct 9 1931–Aug 2 1935)
   NvU — O 9, N 27 1931; My 18, Je 15 1934
   film — O 9, N 27 1931; My 18, Je 15 1934; Mr 22–Jl 26 1935
Ref: files

Carson Chronicle

On August 9, 1935, soon after their purchase of the *Nevadian Times,* George B. Russell and Herbert C. Sproule renamed the paper the *Carson City Chronicle.* In order to ease the transition, they included both names for the first three issues. Russell was editor, issuing the paper every Friday as a Republican journal. Then Denver S. Dickerson, son of the former governor, bought the paper on November 5, 1937. He became sole editor and proprietor and changed its politics to Democratic. On September 10, 1943, Dickerson leased the paper to Wesley L. Davis, Jr., and it passed rapidly through several hands. On April 21, 1944, E. Norman Johnson took over the lease, and on July 13, 1945, he became the owner. The following week he leased it to John M. Taylor, who was soon followed by Alvin D. Mann on December 7. Mann gave up the lease suddenly on April 26, 1946, and Johnson struggled with the paper until July 19, when he signed up James R. Armour. But Armour quit abruptly on September 27, and Johnson finally convinced Wesley L. Davis, Jr., to buy the paper on January 10, 1947.

The following year, on August 20, Davis sold the *Chronicle* to George H. Payne, who had just purchased the daily *Appeal.* Payne combined the management and printing plants of the two papers, and the *Chronicle* has since been the weekly edition of the *Appeal.* R. E. Carpenter, of Wichita Falls, Texas, bought both papers on March 23, 1951, and sold them the following year to Neal Van Sooy, who renamed the weekly edition the *Carson-Tahoe Chronicle.* This name was dropped about 1956, when William R. Smith was made separate editor of the *Chronicle.* Edwin B. Brown bought the papers in 1961, but sold them the following year to Donald W. Reynolds of the *Las Vegas Review-Journal.* Reynolds hired James Leavy as editor of both papers, and on April 26, 1962, renamed the weekly the *Tahoe-Carson Chronicle.* This name was continued when his Don Rey Operating and Trading Company took over about 1965, with William Dolan as editor. In 1966, the paper's name was shortened to the *Carson Chronicle,* and then just to the *Chronicle* a few years later. The *Tahoe Chronicle* was issued separately from October, 1967, to November 25, 1968. From 1972, Donald Reynolds, himself, was listed as editor.

Carson Chronicle: (Aug 9 1935+)
  NvHi — S 5 1941–6; [1947–51]
  NvU — [Ag 9 1935+]
  film — [Ag 9 1935+]
Ref: files; Ayer 1951+

The Rainbow

The *Rainbow* appeared in Carson City in 1936 and 1937. True to its name, it vanished without a trace.

The Rainbow: (c. 1936–1937)
  No issues located.
Ref: NvMus (receipt for advertising)

Nevada State Veteran

In March of 1949, Ray A. Williams commenced the monthly *Nevada State Veteran* at Carson City, as the official publication of the Nevada Veterans of Foreign Wars. Williams was both editor and publisher for the first few months, before Bill Hann took over the editor's chair. The *Veteran* skipped a few issues and apparently suspended publication with its sixth number, in December of the same year.

Nevada State Veteran: (Mar 1949–Dec 1949)
  NvU — Mr, My–Je, N–D 1949
  film — Mr, My–Je, N–D 1949
Ref: files

Nevada Capitol News

The *Nevada Capitol News* began about 1949, in Carson City. K. C. Jones was publisher and Jules Henry was Reno representative. It probably suspended about December of 1950.

Nevada Capitol News: (c. 1949–c. Dec 1950)
  NvMus — D? 1950 (partial copy)
  film — D? 1950 (partial copy)
Ref: files

Las Vegas Playgirl

In August of 1960, Charlie Julian commenced a 48-page slick magazine, the *Las Vegas Playgirl,* patterned after *Playboy.* Despite its title, it was published in Carson City by Las Vegas Playgirl, Inc., and despite the hopes of its founder, it failed to catch on. It was intended as a monthly, but Julian published only two issues in 1960, and one in March of 1961, before it suspended.

Las Vegas Playgirl: (Aug 1960–Mar 1961)
 pvt — Ag 1960, Mr 1961
Ref: files

Carson City News

On January 5, 1961, C. F. and Pauline Brandi commenced the free weekly, *Carson City News.* Their editor, Walter Little, vowed to give the almost century-old *Appeal* "a little competition," but apparently it was too little, for the *News* soon succumbed.

Carson City News: (Jan 5 1961–c. Apr 1961)
 film — Ja 5–Ap 27 1961
Ref: files; TE F 10 1961

Nevada Statesman

The weekly *Nevada Statesman* was launched in Carson City on January 26, 1966, by Clayton Darrah of the Humboldt Bulletin Company, with John Wintersteen as editor and manager. It apparently ceased publication in April.

Nevada Statesman: (Jan 26 1966–c. Apr 22 1966)
 Nv — Ja 26–Ap 22 1966
Ref: files

Carson Review and Advertiser

Zane Miles launched the weekly *Carson Review* on November 25, 1970, but sold it eighteen months later to Donald and Lynn Woodward, publishers of the *Sparks Tribune* and the Gardnerville *Record-Courier.* They renamed it the *Carson Review and Advertiser* on May 10, 1972, and ran it for five years, with Janis Higginbotham as editor, before they moved it to Gardnerville in 1977, to make it an advertising supplement to the *Record-Courier,* under the head *Carson-Tahoe Advertiser.*

Carson Review: (Nov 25 1970–1977)
 film — N 25 1970–N 9 1973
Ref: files; DNN 74/5, 77/8

Desert News

Desert News, "Nevada's Off Road Vehicle Newspaper," was started on

June 5, 1973, by Don Woodward, with Tom Wixon as editor. It was distributed free throughout northern Nevada and northeastern California, but apparently suspended after its fourth issue in October.
Desert News: (Jun 5 1973–c. Oct 1973)
   film — Je 5–O 1973
Ref: files

Silver State Forum

The monthly *Silver State Forum* was started in February of 1975, by Forum Publishers, Ltd., with J. R. Goldman as general manager, and Kenneth Ambrose as feature editor. It appears to have ended with its second issue in March.
Silver State Forum: (Feb 1975–c. Mar 1975)
   NvHi — Mr 1975
Ref: files

The Donoghue Letter

The Donoghue Letter, "a newsletter for the gaming industry," began in Carson City in April, 1977. It was edited and published monthly, except for February and March, by Arthur Kenneth Donoghue and sold for a stiff $50 a year. It cashed in its chips in November, 1978.
The Donoghue Letter: (Apr 1977–Nov 1978)
   NvULV — Ap–N 1978
Ref: files

Carson Times

Donald W. Reynolds, publisher of the *Nevada Appeal* and *Carson Chronicle,* began a third paper, the *Carson Times,* on August 10, 1977, for the purpose of "enlarging the publication pattern." John S. Miller was editor.
Carson Times: (Aug 10 1977+)
   film — Ag 10 1977+
Ref: files

Prospector

The *Prospector,* a weekly advertiser distributed free in Carson City and Reno, was begun at Carson City in June, 1978, by Prospector Publishing, Inc., Dick Borghi, president.
Prospector: (Jun 1978+)
   No issues located.
Ref: pub

~(CHAFEY)~

Chafey News

The first number of the *Chafey News* was published on September 26, 1908, by W. T. Voorhees, a tramp printer from Rhyolite. Voorhees was sole editor and proprietor and issued the *News* every Saturday as a four-page, six-column weekly, selling at $3 a year. With the third number, Voorhees hired Anthony McCauley as editor and personally assumed the position of manager. On December 5 of the same year, McCauley bought out Voorhees's interest, becoming both editor and manager. McCauley held control for only a month, however, and about January 16, 1909, the *News* was purchased by the Chafey Publishing Company with Jno. Q. Critchlow, president; Arthur Prill, managing editor; W. H. Tobin and J. Q. Critchlow, associate editors. Unfortunately, the venture was doomed by the quick decline of Chafey. Only two issues later, on January 23, 1909, the *News* was probably suspended.

Chafey News: (Sep 26 1908–Jan 23 1909)
  NvHi — [S 26 1908–Ja 23 1909]
  NvU — [O 10 1908–Ja 23 1909]
  film — [S 26 1908–Ja 23 1909]
Ref: files

CHERRY CREEK

The Independent

The town of Cherry Creek was founded in 1873, and it experienced such sustained prosperity that by 1877, even the most cautious deemed it a stable locale for a newspaper. In the winter of 1877, Benjamin M. Barney arrived at Cherry Creek with a small hand press and purchased a building on the corner of Main and D Streets. He had ordered other material, but when it failed to arrive, he decided to start a paper with what he had available. On about the first of January, 1878, he issued the first number of the triweekly *Independent*. The paper contained only ten columns and was printed on a half-sheet for nearly a month until the remainder of the material arrived. Barney was sole editor and proprietor and published the paper every Sunday, Tuesday and Friday, at 50¢ a week or $10 a year. In February, 1878, A. V. Hoyt, an attorney at Cherry Creek, purchased a half interest in the firm and the paper was reduced to a weekly. About a month later, Barney retired from the paper and moved to Reno, where he helped to found the *Reno Daily Record*. Hoyt continued the *Independent* as a weekly, but was unable to make a success of it and finally suspended the paper on April 19, 1879.

The Independent: (c. Jan 1 1878–Apr 19 1879)
  CU-BANC — Ja 18, F 24 1878
  film — Ja 18, F 24 1878
Ref: files; GHN My 1 1879

White Pine News

With the collapse of the mining boom at Hamilton in 1878, A. Skillman suspended the *White Pine News* and shifted his capital to the *Eureka Senti-*

nel. For two years the paper passed through a fitful period of revivals and suspensions. On December 23, 1880, W. L. Davis and W. R. Forrest suspended the *News* at Hamilton for the last time. The following week they moved the press and material to Cherry Creek, where they revived the paper under the old name of *White Pine News,* on January 1, 1881. The paper was issued every Saturday as a four-page, five-column, 12 by 17-inch weekly, at a subscription price of $5 a year. On July 9, 1881, Davis bought out Forrest's interest in the paper and became sole editor and proprietor. Davis continued the *White Pine News* at Cherry Creek until August 15, 1885, when he removed the paper to the new boom camp of Taylor. (See Taylor, *White Pine News.*)

White Pine News: (Jan 1 1881–Aug 15 1885)
   CU-BANC — Ja 8 1881–Jl 29 1882
   NvELC — 1885
   NvU — Ja 1 1881–Ag 15 1885
   film — Ja 1 1881–Ag 15 1885
Ref: files

Cherry Creek Miner

About February of 1903, J. M. Lynch suspended the *White Pine Miner* at Ely and removed the plant to Cherry Creek, some fifty-five miles to the north. He revived the paper as the *Cherry Creek Miner* on March 25, 1903, under the name of the Miner Publishing Company. The brief revival of mining activity at the old camp was not sufficient to sustain a paper for long, however, and the *Miner* was forced to suspend later the same year.

Cherry Creek Miner: (Mar 25 1903–c. 1903)
   film — Ap 15 1903
Ref: files

CLAROIS

Clarois Review

The *Clarois Review* was a fictitious newspaper published in a fictitious town. The story was devised by John L. Considine and James F. Haley of the Reno *Reveille*. In the *Reveille* of December 15, 1908, they cited the *Clarois Review* as their source for a tall tale about two skeletons found underground in a fully stocked grocery store of the 1860's.

Clarois Review
   Nonexistent.
Ref: RR D 15 1908

CLOVERDALE

Cloverdale Budget

The *Cloverdale Budget* was a little sheet apparently published at the camp of Cloverdale, southwest of the Toiyabe Range, in 1893. One surviving weatherstained issue, bearing the date of April 14, 1893, found in the crotch of a sagebrush by a prospector named Mort D. McManon, was described in the *Goldfield Review* of October 27, 1907, and subsequently lost to oblivion again.

Cloverdale Budget: (1893)
  No issues located.
Ref: GR O 26 1907

~(COLUMBIA)~

Goldfield Review

About October 27, 1904, T. D. Van Devort commenced the *Goldfield Review* at Columbia, Goldfield's northern suburb. Van Devort was sole editor and publisher, and he issued the *Review* every Thursday as an eight-page, independent weekly, selling at $5 a year. The *Review* was published at Columbia for over two years, until March of 1907, when Van Devort moved the plant into Goldfield. (See Goldfield, *Goldfield Review.*)

Goldfield Review: (c. Oct 27 1904–Mar 1907)
  NvU — [Je 29 1905–Mr 9 1907]
  film — [Je 29 1905–Mr 9 1907]
Ref: files

Columbia Topics

On October 14, 1908, T. Lowe issued the first number of the *Columbia Topics.* Lowe was editor and manager of the paper, which was published as a Wednesday weekly by the Columbia Publishing Company, an affiliate of the neighboring *Goldfield News.* The *Columbia Topics* prospered for nearly a year, during which time Lowe also established another *Topics* at Pioneer, some fifty miles to the south. The newspaper field around Goldfield was already saturated, however, and the *Columbia Topics* was forced to suspend about June 24, 1909, followed one month later by its Pioneer brother.

Columbia Topics: (Oct 14 1908–c. Jun 24 1909)
  NvHi — [O 14 1908–Je 24 1909]
  film — [O 14 1908–Je 24 1909]
Ref: files

~(COLUMBUS)~

Borax Miner

On August 9, 1873, William W. Barnes issued the first number of the *Borax Miner* at Columbus. Barnes was sole editor and proprietor, publishing the paper as a Democratic weekly from his small office on Davis Street. The *Miner* contained twenty columns, measured 12 by 19 inches and sold for

$5 per annum. In 1875, the Pacific Borax Company ceased operations at Columbus and moved their works ten miles south to Fish Lake Valley. This precipitated the decline of Columbus, but the *Miner* held out for over two years until its final suspension early in 1878. In the later part of 1878, or early 1879, Barnes moved the material to Benton, across the California line, where he started the *Messenger.* This endeavor lasted only a few months, when he again moved the plant, this time farther west to Mammoth City, and there issued the *Herald,* which flourished until early 1881.

Borax Miner: (Aug 9 1873–c. 1878)
   CIE — O 18 1873
   NvU — [F 20 1875–My 19 1877]
   film — O 18 1873; [F 20 1875–My 19 1877]
Ref: files; Angel 298; McMurtrie 298

Como Sentinel

In January of 1864, T. W. Abraham arrived in the booming camp of Como, eight miles southeast of Dayton. He was interested in establishing a newspaper in Lyon County and was impressed by the prospects of the new town. After a brief survey of the surrounding mines, he purchased office space and returned to California for his press. On March 22, he telegraphed that the press was on the road from Dayton, and the townsfolk prepared a jubilant welcome. The ensuing revelry is described by Alf Doten in his diary:

> At various times during the day, passers on the road, arriving, reported the progress of the teams with the press — preparations made to receive them in good style — PM the Como "brass band" turned out — got a light spring wagon for band wagon — Alex' mule, and Hunt's big mule — both dressed out with . . . plumes & c — J B Witherell drove — Hunt and Jacobson rode also and supported pole with Cross's big flag — 6 of us in all — played down through town and up — drove down to Palmyra — played down through — met teams just below town — stopped & treated teamsters to some cocktails we had along — gave them 3 cheers — escorted them up, playing lively airs — all stopped at Arnhold's — He treated & we treated — drove on up —gave Basye a tune — stopped at Rappahannock shaft — got all the boys out — treated them — gave them a tune — they gave us 3 cheers — all the miners on all sides left the diggin's for Como, to see the fun — as the plumes of our mules appeared over the divide the anvils commenced firing — 2 batteries of them — 1 at each end of town — fired just as fast as they possibly could — regular "anvil chorus" — tried to outdo each other — train preceded by the band, playing "Hail Columbia" and "Yankee Doodle," passed gaily down Main st, past Cross's & up 5th Avenue to printing office — Citizens gave us lots of cheers — jolly time — The Dayton folks tried hard to induce the press to stop there, but couldn't

Abraham's partner, H. L. Weston, formerly of the *Petaluma Journal,* arrived the following week, and on April 16, 1864, they ran off the first issue of the *Como Sentinel.* In the opening number the proprietors announced their intention to support the administration; to decapitate the leaders of all wicked cliques and ungodly political alliances; to publish a weekly, twenty-four-column sheet; to help hold up the hands of the mining Aarons of Como; and to charge $6 a year for their paper. Doten took private pride in having written four columns of the material in the first issue: the mining summary, obituary and part of the salutatory. But the Como bubble quickly collapsed. With the thirteenth number, on July 9, Weston and Abraham suspended the *Sentinel* at Como, and within a week they removed the printing plant to Dayton. There they continued the paper on the ensuing Saturday, as the *Lyon County Sentinel*. At Dayton the paper survived for nearly two years, until it was destroyed by fire in the summer of 1866. (See Dayton, *Lyon County Sentinel*.)

Como Sentinel: (Apr 16 1864–Jul 9 1864)
  CU-BANC — Ap 16–Jl 9 1864
  NvU — Ap 16–Jl 9 1864
  film — Ap 16–Jl 9 1864
Ref: files; Doten 770–1, 774, 791; Angel 308; McMurtrie 298

CONTACT

Contact Miner

J. V. Marshall founded the *Miner* about March 20, 1913, at the booming town of Contact, in Nevada's northeastern corner. Marshall was both editor and proprietor of the Miner Publishing Company, which issued the paper every Thursday as a four-page, six-column, 13¼ by 19¾-inch, Democratic weekly, selling for $2.50 a year. The career of the paper was halted briefly in mid-1915, when Marshall made a trip east, but on his return the paper was promptly revived. About the end of 1915, Marshall sold the *Miner* to E. H. Childs, who changed its politics to independent and almost immediately suspended it.

Contact Miner: (Mar 30 1913–c. 1916)
  CHi — Je 4 1914; F 4 1915
  film — Je 4 1914; F 4 1915
Ref: files

Nevada-Contact Mining Review

The *Nevada-Contact Mining Review* was established at Contact in 1924, by Ed A. Strong, sole editor and proprietor. The paper was issued every Saturday, dedicated to mining and local news, and sold for $2.50 a year. Its life was brief, however, and it was suspended probably sometime the following year.

Nevada-Contact Mining Review: (1924–c. 1925)
  No issues located.
Ref: Myrick

COPPERFIELD

(See ACME)

CRESCENT

Crescent Times

On June 26, 1905, James Brown and Frank L. Reber of the *Las Vegas Times* founded the weekly *Times* at the new camp of Crescent, nearly fifty miles to the south. The paper was undoubtedly printed in Las Vegas and delivered to Crescent by stage. The following month, however, Crescent's need for a paper seems to have vanished, and the *Times* was suspended.

Crescent Times: (Jun 26 1905–Jul 1905)
  No issues located.
Ref: PR Je 30 1905; LVA Jl 8 1905

CRYSTAL BAY

Villager

The weekly *Villager* was begun by James Graham on January 13, 1961, at Crystal Bay, on the north shore of Lake Tahoe. It subsequently was run by Gilbert Landel, James Hecht, and F. D. Jeans, and ceased publication on January 11, 1963.

Villager: (Jan 13 1961–Jan 11 1963)
  film — Ag 18 1961–D 28 1962; Ja 4, 10 1963
Ref: files

North Tahoe World

Stub and Bobbie Stollery of the Tahoe City, California, *World,* started the weekly *North Tahoe World* at Crystal Bay on May 1, 1969. They sold out three months later to Bob Rapida of the Western Nevada Publishing Company, and Ruth Balling replaced Stub as editor. The paper shut down the following year.

North Tahoe World: (May 1 1969–Apr 17 1970)
  film — My 1 1969–Ap 17 1970
Ref: files

DAYTON

Lyon County Sentinel

Following their suspension of the *Sentinel* at Como, H. L. Weston and T. W. Abraham moved the plant to Dayton, where they revived the paper on

July 16, 1864, as the *Lyon County Sentinel.* Just five weeks later, on August 13, Weston leased his interest to his partner, and returned to California, leaving Abraham as sole editor and proprietor. With the commencement of the second volume, on April 15, 1865, Abraham was joined by B. F. Cooper and C. S. Paine, under the firm name of T. W. Abraham and Co. They guided the *Sentinel* until its untimely death on July 1, 1866, when fire destroyed the entire establishment. Only three short, four-column numbers were issued after the fire, on salvaged material, to fulfill obligations on several legal notices. (See *Como Sentinel.*)

Lyon County Sentinel: (Jul 16 1864–Jul 21 1866)
   CU-BANC — Jl 16 1864–O 6, 20 1865–Ap 7, Je 30 1866
   NvU — Jl 16–Ag 6, 20–S 24 1864
   film — [Jl 16 1864–Je 30 1866]
Ref: files; Angel 308; McMurtrie 298–9; Hazlett 68

Lyon County Times

John M. Campbell suspended the *Lyon County Times* at Silver City on December 11, 1880, and removed the press and material to Dayton. Here, he revived the paper one week later, on December 18. Campbell was sole editor and proprietor, and issued the *Times* every Saturday as a four-page, Republican weekly at a subscription price of $5 a year. Two years later, on January 20, 1883, Campbell was joined by Fred W. Fairbanks. This partnership ran the paper until June 27, 1885, when Fairbanks became sole editor and proprietor. Fairbanks continued the *Times* at Dayton until July 27, 1901, when he removed the plant to Yerington. The *Lyon County Times* finally suspended publication at Yerington on January 22, 1932. (See Yerington, *Lyon County Times.*)

Lyon County Times: (Dec 18 1880–Jul 27 1901)
   CU-BANC — D 18–25 1880; Je 25 1881; Jl 1, 22 1882; S 22–29, O 13 1883; F 9, Mr 15–D 27 1884; Jl 7 1888–D 26 1891
   NvHi — Ag 20, S 3, 17–O 8, 29, N 12 1892
   NvU — D 18 1880–Jl 27 1901
   film — [D 18 1880–Jl 27 1901]
Ref: files

News Reporter

The weekly *News Reporter* was founded at Dayton on March 4, 1886, by J. E. Ridgway, in an effort to break the monopoly of the *Lyon County Times.* Ridgway soon lost his enthusiasm for the fight and sold the paper on April 1, to Gordon A. Rice. The latter struggled for a year before he finally folded on June 30, 1887.

News Reporter: (Mar 4 1886–Jun 30 1887)
   NvU — Mr 4 1886–Je 30 1887
   film — Mr 4 1886–Je 30 1887
Ref: files

Dayton Advocate

Three years after the suspension of the *Lyon County Times,* George M. Smith and James T. Green attempted to revive a paper at Dayton. In mid-August of 1904, they commenced the *Dayton Advocate.* Smith and Green were editors and publishers, issuing the paper every Friday, as a four-page, 13 by 20-inch, Silver-Democratic weekly, at a subscription price of $3 a year. Dayton could no longer support a paper, however, and the *Advocate* ceased publication, probably early in 1905.

Dayton Advocate: (Aug 1904–c. 1905)
   No issues located.
Ref: TM Ag 20 1904

Deeth Tidings

About late January of 1896, the Reverend Merchant S. Riddle issued the first number of the *Tidings* at the small railroad town of Deeth. Riddle was sole editor and proprietor and made the *Tidings* a strong advocate of Free Silver politics. The paper was published every Saturday as an eight-page, four-column weekly and sold for $2 a year. By the fall of the year Riddle realized that, despite generous public support, the town was too small to support even a weekly newspaper. He suspended the *Tidings* at Deeth and shipped the press and material down the tracks to the much more prosperous and populous town of Elko. There he promptly revived the paper as the *Nevada Silver Tidings,* which he continued successfully for several years. (See Elko, *Nevada Silver Tidings.*)

Deeth Tidings: (c. Jan 1896–c. Sep 1896)
   No issues located.
Ref: Ayer

Commonwealth

On February 28, 1912, one week after his suspension of the *Commonwealth* at Carlin, A. B. Gray revived the paper at Deeth, fifty-five miles up the tracks. The *Commonwealth* was continued as a Democratic weekly, issued every Wednesday at $1.50 a year. It was well received, and extolled the virtues of its new resting place for over two years until its suspension on October 28, 1914. Gray then moved to Carson City where he purchased the once juvenile *Carson Weekly.*

Commonwealth: (Feb 28 1912–Oct 28 1914)
   NvHi — [F 28 1912–O 28 1914]
   NvU — [F 28 1912–O 28 1914]
   film — [F 28 1912–O 28 1914]
Ref: files

~(DELAMAR (HELENE))~

The Ferguson Lode

On September 5, 1892, the Lode Publishing Company issued the first number of the *Ferguson Lode,* at the camp of Helene, later renamed Delamar, fifty-five miles southwest of Pioche, in the Ferguson Mining District. Herbert Francis was editor and N. P. Dooley was manager of the paper. It was published every Monday as a four-page, six-column, 15 by 22-inch weekly, selling for $5 a year. By early 1893, it became evident that the new camp was not yet able to support a newspaper, and on February 27 the *Ferguson Lode* suspended at Helene. Dooley removed the plant to Pioche, where he revived the paper as the *Lode,* issuing it there for more than a year before returning to Helene, then known as Delamar. (See Pioche, *Lode.*)

The Ferguson Lode: (Sep 5 1892–Feb 27 1893)
 NvHi — [S 19 1892–F 27 1893]
 film — [S 19 1892–F 27 1893]
Ref: files

The De Lamar Lode

On June 16, 1894, one week after the suspension of the paper at Pioche, N. P. Dooley revived the *Lode* at its place of birth, rechristened Delamar, but formerly Helene. Dooley was sole publisher and proprietor, and continued the paper as a four-page, six-column weekly, selling for $5 a year. On January 6, 1896, the paper passed to the Lode Publishing Company, and this firm managed it until February 3, when Eugene Goodrich became publisher and proprietor. With increased prosperity, on April 20, 1898, Goodrich commenced a separate daily edition of the *Lode* and hired Charles James Pettee as editor. The daily edition was called first the *Daily Lode* and then the *Evening Lode.* It could not be sustained, however, and it was discontinued on June 4.

 Goodrich soon became discouraged with the entire venture, and on August 9 of the same year he sold the *Lode* plant to Pettee, who then became sole editor and proprietor. On the following September 6, Pettee enlarged the paper to a semiweekly, but reduced it to a weekly again on December 6. Pettee continued the *Lode* until March 3, 1903, when it passed to the Lincoln County Publishing Company, with H. W. Miles editor. This company suspended the *Lode* on June 19, 1906, and removed the plant to Caliente to merge with the *Express.* (See *Caliente Lode-Express.*)

The De Lamar Lode: (Jun 16 1894–Jun 19 1906)
 NvHi — Je 16–Ag 27, D 3–24 1894; Ja 27 1895–D 26 1905
 NvU — Ja 7 1895–Mr 30 1896; Ja 3 1899–1906
 film — [Je 16 1894–Je 19 1906]
Daily Lode (Evening Lode): (Apr 20 1898–Jun 4 1898)
 NvHi — Ap 20–Je 4 1898
 film — Ap 20–Je 4 1898
Ref: files

Local Messenger

On May 23, 1899, N. P. Dooley suspended the *Local Messenger* at Pioche and leased the plant to A. Clifford, who revived the paper at Delamar on the following June 3. Clifford issued the paper as a four-page, seven-column weekly, at a subscription price of $2.50 a year. By January of 1901, Wilkes J. Campbell had purchased the *Messenger* and became sole editor and proprietor. Delamar was unable to support two papers, however, and the *Local Messenger* was forced to suspend, probably within the year.

Local Messenger: (Jun 3 1899–c. 1901)
   NvHi — F 12–19, D 3 1900; Ja 5 1901
   film — F 12–19, D 3 1900; Ja 5 1901
Ref: files

De La Mar Roaster

Ed Thompson fired up the neatly printed little *Roaster* on March 18, 1900, just to blast the *Messenger* editor for his criticism of British action in the Boer War.

De La Mar Roaster: (Mar 18 1900)
   NvHi — Mr 18 1900
   film — Mr 18 1900
Ref: files

DIVIDE CITY

Divide City Times

When Divide City, six miles south of Tonopah, commenced to boom, Frank F. Garside of the *Tonopah Times* decided to honor the camp with a newspaper. On March 29, 1919, he issued the first number of the *Divide City Times* as an independent, Saturday weekly, selling for $3.50 a year. *Divide City* proved unable to support a paper, however, and the *Times* undoubtedly suspended when the boom collapsed that summer.

Divide City Times: (Mar 29 1919–c. 1919)
   NvHi — Mr 29–Ap 12 1919
   NvU — Ap 19 1919
   film — Mr 29–Ap 19 1919
Ref: files

DUCK VALLEY

Duck Valley News

The *Duck Valley News* was apparently a small, short-lived, amateur weekly begun about March 24, 1886. John S. Mayhugh, Jr., was editor, his parents were reporters, and H. Nelson did the printing. It survived at least to its second issue on March 31.

Duck Valley News: (c. Mar 24 1886–c. 1886)
  No issues located.
Ref: TTR Ap 6 1886

⟨ DULUTH ⟩

Duluth Tribune

In 1907, during the brief boom of Duluth, some forty-five miles northeast of Mina, J. Holman Buck of the Mina *Western Nevada Miner* commenced the *Duluth Tribune,* to be distributed at the new camp. Buck was sole editor and proprietor, issuing the paper as a Saturday weekly, costing $4 per year, while the boom lasted.

Duluth Tribune: (1907)
  No issues located.
Ref: Polk 1907–8

⟨ DUTCH CREEK ⟩

Dutch Creek News

With the first rush to Dutch Creek, on the southwestern shores of Walker Lake, William Stuart Webster arrived with a press and material for a newspaper. On about January 1, 1907, he commenced the *Dutch Creek News.* Webster was sole editor and proprietor and claimed to issue the little paper every Monday, but in fact issued it only every month. The Dutch Creek boom did not last and the *News* suspended with its May 1 number. Webster moved on to join forces with W. W. Booth of the *Tonopah Bonanza,* commencing the *Rawhide Rustler* that fall and the *Bovard Booster* the following year.

Dutch Creek News: (Jan 1 1907–May 1 1907)
  NvHi — F 1, Ap 1 1907
  NvU — My 1 1907
  film — F 1, Ap 1–My 1 1907
Ref: files; TB Ja 19, F 2 1907; TS Ap 5 1907

⟨ DYER ⟩

Esmeralda Star

The *Esmeralda Star* was a mimeographed monthly issued at Dyer, in Fish Lake Valley, by Olaf G. Barnard, around 1956–57. The paper sold for $1.50 a year and lasted about eighteen months.

Esmeralda Star: (c. 1956–1957)
  No issues located.
Ref: Averett

EAST ELY

White Pine News

In November of 1908, the peripatetic *White Pine News* moved once again, this time only a short distance from Ely to neighboring East Ely, where it resumed on November 24. During its previous thirty-nine years of publication, the *News* had been published in five successive camps: Treasure City, Hamilton, Cherry Creek, Taylor, and Ely. Now at middle age it moved to its sixth and final resting place.

A. Valjean continued as editor for the White Pine News Publishing Company until July 3, 1910, when he, C. S. Crain, and S. C. Patrick leased the paper under the name of the Investment News Bureau, with Arthur Smith as editor. At the same time they reduced the daily to a weekly. The former weekly edition, the *Mining Review,* started in 1907, had been absorbed back into the daily on December 25, 1909. Crain and Valjean subsequently retired, but Patrick retained control of the *News* for over a decade. He finally sold it to A. A. Sherman, who took over as editor and manager on October 17, 1920. In his hands the old journal which had seemed almost indestructible finally died, on December 30, 1923.

White Pine News: (Nov 24 1908–Dec 30 1923)
   NvHi — [N 1908–D 30 1923]
   NvMus — D 24 1911
   NvU — [N 24 1908–D 30 1923]
   film — [N 24 1908–D 30 1923]
Ref: files

ELKO

Elko Independent

In May of 1869, E. D. Kelley bought the plant of the *Humboldt Register and Workingman's Advocate* at Unionville and moved it to the new railroad town of Elko, on the Central Pacific Railroad. There, on June 19, 1869, E. D. Kelley and Co., with Judge George G. Berry as a silent partner, started the semiweekly *Elko Independent.* Kelley quickly became discouraged with the slow progress of the town, and he sold his interest to Berry and Charles L. Perkins on July 21. H. C. Street joined the partnership on January 1, 1870, but in the fall of 1870, when Perkins was elected state printer, he and Street moved to the state capital and purchased the *Appeal.* They still retained an interest in the *Independent,* but the firm name became Berry and Co. on January 14, 1871. J. C. Davis and William B. Taylor were hired to run the paper, which had been reduced to a weekly on December 30. Taylor became proprietor on June 1, 1872, with Berry continuing as a silent partner, but Taylor left for Pioche that fall.

S. S. Sears and C. C. S. Wright took over the *Independent* on January 4, 1873, and added a daily edition on August 17, 1875. Sears became sole proprietor on October 10, 1876, and ran it for another decade before selling to C. W. Grover on December 31, 1886. On April 6, 1891, W. W. Booher leased the paper from Grover, and bought it on January 1, 1892. Booher ran it for over two decades before he retired on September 18, 1914.

Charles H. Keith and Howard N. Riddle then became the publishers and suspended the weekly edition in December 1914. Riddle sold his interest to George B. Russell on November 7 and Keith did likewise on the following February 1. Russell was forced to reduce the paper to a triweekly a year later, and on September 11, 1920, he finally sold it to Harold P. Hale, who ran it successfully for nearly two more decades.

On March 1, 1937, Warren L. Monroe and R. C. Stitser of Winnemucca's *Humboldt Star* bought the *Independent,* with Monroe buying Stitser's interest in the Elko firm six months later. Monroe remained as sole editor and proprietor until January 1, 1974, when he sold it to Max and Barbara Wignall. Monroe stayed on as editor until May, 1975. In 1979, he still wrote a column, entitled "Hot Copy," in the then weekly *Independent.*

Elko Independent: (Jun 19 1869–Dec 1914, Feb 1919+)
    pub — 1870+
    C — Ag 10 1872
    CU-BANC — [Je 19 1869–Jl 30 1882]; Mr 3–17, Je 30, O 13 1889
    MWA — Je 19–Jl, Ag 7–11, 28–S 29 1869
    NvEC — 1869+
    NvU — 1869–71; 1877+
    film — Je 19 1869+
Daily Independent: (Aug 17 1875–Jan 1919)
    CU-BANC — Ja 4 1877; [78–Ag 3 1882]; Mr 1, O 11, D 26–28 1889
    DLC — Jl 1885–F 19 1887
    NvHi — Ag 17 1875–D 30 1899; [1904–15]
    NvU — 1915
    film — Ag 17 1875–99; [1904–15]
Ref: files; Angel 294; McMurtrie 299

Elko Chronicle

The *Elko Chronicle* was born as a Republican organ during the political campaign of 1870. It was edited by T. J. Butler and owned by the Chronicle Publishing Company. The first number was issued on June 5, 1870. The *Chronicle* was a semiweekly of twenty-four columns and sold for $8 a year. On June 24, William B. Taylor became business manager. The paper carried on a spicy banter with the Democratic *Independent,* whose proprietor,

Charles L. Perkins, was running for state printer. After Perkins was elected, Butler sold the paper to Taylor, who took over on November 27, 1870, and reduced it to a weekly. But Perkins, who was fearful of losing subscribers to his rival once he took his post in Carson City, offered Taylor the job of running the *Independent* while he was away. Taylor accepted, and with his second issue, on December 4, 1870, he suspended the *Chronicle*.

The material of the office was removed to Pioche in August of 1872, when Taylor, in partnership with Frank Kenyon, established the *Pioche Review*. At the end of the political campaign that year, the *Review* suspended and the material was absorbed in the *Pioche Record*.

Elko Chronicle: (Jan 5 1870–Dec 4 1870)
   CU-BANC — Je 5–N 20 1870
   NvEHi — 1870
   film — Je 5–D 4 1870
Ref: files; Angel 294; McMurtrie 299

Elko Leader

The *Elko Leader* was begun at Elko near January 1, 1873, and it probably folded within the same month. The Austin *Reese River Reveille* referred to it as a "sprightly and well-edited sheet," but aside from that, it left little record.

Elko Leader: (c. Jan 1873)
   No issues located.
Ref: McMurtrie 299

Elko Post

On September 11, 1875, the weekly *Elko Post* was commenced by E. A. Littlefield and C. C. Powning. Littlefield was editor of the Republican paper, and purchased Powning's interest on October 7, 1876, to become sole proprietor. On March 10, 1877, while publishing the *Post,* Littlefield established the *Times* at Tuscarora, but sold that paper in the fall. He continued as sole proprietor of the *Post* until May 8, 1880, when he was joined by his brother, L. B. Littlefield. The size of the paper was reduced and the firm of E. A. Littlefield and Co. continued the *Post* until its suspension on April 30, 1881. E. A. Littlefield then moved to Ogden, Utah, where he started the Ogden *Pilot,* which lasted some three years.

Elko Post: (Sep 11 1875–Apr 30 1881)
   CU-BANC — Ja 15–22 [Ap 22 1876–D 29 1877; Je 15–D 28 1878]; Mr 15, Ap 5–Ag 23, O 11–18, N 1 1879; Je 26 1880
   NvEHi — [1875–81]
   NvU — [S 11 1875–S 2 1877]
   film — [S 11 1875–Ap 30 1881]
Ref: files; Angel 294; McMurtrie 299

The Free Press

In December of 1882, Charles H. Sproule suspended the *Lander Free Press* at Battle Mountain and removed the press and material to Elko. On January 5, 1883, he commenced publication of the Elko *Free Press*. The paper was issued on Fridays, as a four-page, Republican weekly, measuring 22 by 30 inches, at a subscription price of $5 per year, the same size and price as the former *Lander Free Press.*

During the political campaign of 1884, Sproule issued the paper daily from September 10 to November 12. He repeated the practice from October 14 to November 10, 1886, and October 15 to November 8, 1890. In the latter campaign, Sproule ran successfully on the Republican ticket for the state assembly. Sproule ran the paper at Elko for twenty-one years without missing a single issue, but on September 3, 1904, ill health finally compelled him to retire. A group of Elko businessmen purchased the plant as the Free Press Publishing Company. They installed George B. Russell as editor and manager the following week, and began a separate daily edition about September 17.

Russell won election to the assembly in 1906, but retained the editorship until November 30, 1908, when he retired to devote his full attention to the *Luckyboy Mining Record,* which he and his brother had started in July. The publishing company promptly appointed Dr. Edwin J. Clark as editor, but he resigned on November 14, 1910. E. M. Steninger replaced Clark, and purchased control of the Free Press Publishing Company. The weekly edition was suspended on February 15, 1917, and the daily edition was reduced to triweekly on March 3, 1919. Steninger apparently lost financial control of the paper on August 28, 1925, and Harold P. Hale, publisher of the rival *Independent,* took brief control on December 31, 1927. But Steninger again assumed the editorship on January 2, 1928, continuing as such until February 26, 1941, when he became publisher, and Chris H. Sheerin became editor.

On June 15, 1931, the paper was again enlarged to a daily, and continued as such to 1979, with only a momentary lapse to a triweekly from February 7 to 18, 1944. E. M. Steninger finally retired from the paper on January 2, 1945, selling it to his son Eber B. Steninger and Chris H. Sheerin, the latter continuing as editor. They, in turn, retired in 1969, and Mel Steninger and Earl A. Frantzen became the publishers, with the former taking the editor's chair.

The Free Press (weekly): (Jan 5 1883–Feb 15 1917)
   pub — Ja 5 1883–F 15 1917
   CU-BANC — [F 16–Ap 27], N 30 1883; Mr 14–28, My 9 1884; Ag 31, D 28 1889; [Ja 11–My 21, Ag 20–O 26 1892]; O 7 1893; F 3, [Mr–Je], Jl 14–21 1894
   NvEHi — 1883–1901; Mr 5 1909–Mr 14 1913
   NvHi — [S 1892]; F 18 1899; F 16 1906; O 1907–F 15 1917
   NvU — 1883–F 15 1917
   film — [Ja 5 1883-Mr 14 1913]

Free Press (daily): (c. Sep 17 1904+)
  pub — S 24 1904+
  NvU — S 24 1904–16
  film — S 24 1904+
Ref: files

Nevada Silver Tidings

Following the suspension of the *Tidings* at Deeth, Merchant S. Riddle moved the plant to Elko, where he revived the paper as the *Nevada Silver Tidings* in the fall of 1896. The revival was financed by F. O. Williams, who became publisher, while M. S. Riddle and Sons served as editors. The paper was issued every Saturday as an eight-page, four column, 11 by 18-inch weekly, selling for $2 a year. Near the end of 1896, M. S. Riddle and Sons purchased the establishment, becoming editors and proprietors. In August of 1898, the *Tidings* was enlarged to a semiweekly, issued every Wednesday and Saturday. M. S. Riddle took charge of the Winnemucca *People's Advocate* on March 15, 1899, and sold the *Nevada Silver Tidings* to Phil S. Triplett and Howard N. Riddle. This firm ran the paper until June 17, 1899, when Triplett retired. The following week Riddle reduced the *Tidings* to a weekly and continued it as such until its suspension on July 15, 1899. At that time he retired to "more lucrative employment" elsewhere.

Nevada Silver Tidings: (c. Sep 1896–Jul 15 1899)
  NvHi — Ag 3, O 26 1898
  NvU — [Ja 2 1897–Jl 15 1899]
  film — [Ja 2–D 25 1897]; Ag 3, O 26 1898; [Ja 4–Jl 15 1899]
Ref: files

Daily Argonaut

The Elko *Daily Argonaut* was established about September of 1897, by the Elko Publishing Company. E. C. Snyder was editor and business manager, issuing the paper every evening except Sunday, as a four-page, five-column, 13 by 16-inch daily that sold for $7 a year. During the patriotic furor of the Spanish American War the printers enlisted, and the paper was suspended from May 4 to 10, 1898, until a new crew could be found. Snyder then severed his connection with the paper, and it was without an editor or manager until October 11, 1898, when Samuel T. Porter took over the helm. The following day, a weekly edition was added to the daily. George B. Russell and Charles H. Keith purchased the *Argonaut* on January 3, 1899. They ran the paper until February 6, when they suspended publication at Elko and removed the plant to Golconda to commence the *News*.

Daily Argonaut: (c. Sep 1897–Feb 6 1899)
  NvU — [Ja 3 1898–F 6 1899]
  film — [Ja 3 1898–F 6 1899]
Ref: files

The Telegram

On May 31, 1909, Erskine and S. C. (Babe) Mayer commenced the short-lived *Telegram,* the "Only Paper in Eastern Nevada Publishing Daily Telegraphic News."

The Telegram: (May 31 1909–c. Jun 1909)
   pvt — Je 2 1909
   film — Je 2 1909
Ref: files

Elko Enterprise

On December 1, 1916, D. N. Wheeler, editor of the *Elko Independent,* styling himself the Elko Enterprise Publishing Company, commenced the *Enterprise* as a Friday weekly. Wheeler, lacking a press of his own, had the paper printed in the *Independent* office, giving a bond insuring publication for six months. But in little over two the *Enterprise* had "gone to the boneyard."

Elko Enterprise: (Dec 1 1916–Feb 9 1917)
   NvU — D 1 1916–F 9 1917
   film — D 1 1916–F 9 1917
Ref: files; EI F 21 1917

Nevada Farmer and Stockman

The *Nevada Farmer and Stockman* was a monthly agricultural and livestock journal, founded by the Free Press Publishing Company in 1921. Evidently it was not a financial success, however, for it was suspended the following year.

Nevada Farmer and Stockman: (1921–c. 1922)
   No issues located.
Ref: Myrick

ELLENDALE

Ellendale Star

With the boom of Ellendale, some thirty miles east of Tonopah, in the spring of 1909, Lindley C. Branson of the *Tonopah Sun* decided once more to try to expand his journalistic empire. On June 12, he commenced the weekly *Ellendale Star.* The camp received much criticism from some of the Bishop, Rhyolite, and Goldfield papers, whose editors claimed that the whole thing was a swindle. As a result, the *Star* folded within a few months, but the mines are said ultimately to have yielded about a million dollars worth of bullion.

Ellendale Star: (June 12 1909–c. Aug 1909)
   No issues located.
Ref: TM Je 19 1909

Ellendale Lode

On June 13, 1909, less than twenty-four hours after the founding of the *Ellendale Star,* Kenneth Booth and W. J. Fording commenced a rival booster paper, the *Ellendale Lode,* from the office of the *Tonopah Miner.* Its editor observed that "if papers can make a district, Ellendale surely has a good start," but scandal brought the boom down quickly.

Ellendale Lode: (Jun 13 1909–c. Aug 1909)
   No issues located.
Ref: TM Je 19 1909

~(ELY)~

White Pine News

On September 15, 1888, a year after Ely became the White Pine county seat, W. L. Davis removed the *White Pine News* from the fading camp of Taylor and established it at Ely. Davis continued the *News* as a four-page, four-column weekly, at a subscription price of $5 per year. After managing the *News* through its leanest years, Davis sold the paper to L. L. Elliott on February 3, 1894, and retired to Redwood City, California. Elliott ran the paper for four years until September 11, 1897, when E. H. Decker purchased the paper under the name of the White Pine News Publishing Company.

Decker was a recent graduate of the University of Michigan, and was making his first attempt at publishing. Ill health forced him to sell the *News* on December 27, 1900. For the next six years the *News* passed through a rapid succession of hands. The Reverend George F. Plummer became editor and manager on January 3, 1901, followed by J. M. Lynch on April 18 — some three months later. Lynch, in turn, retired to start the rival *White Pine Miner,* and was succeeded by W. J. Stewart on October 16, 1902. J. D. Crossette became editor on April 21, 1904, while Stewart remained as business manager.

Denver S. Dickerson and Charles A. Walker purchased the *News* on November 24, 1904, and on October 19, 1905, Dickerson became sole editor and proprietor. He continued as such until May 8, 1906, when Houlden Hudgins took control, and Dickerson ran for lieutenant governor. On July 20, 1907, Roy W. Schenk briefly took the helm. Finally on November 4 of that year, the *News* management began to stabilize when A. Valjean took over as editor. He remained with the paper for many years.

The *News* prospered with the copper boom at Ely, increased to a semi-weekly on February 13, 1906, and eventually to a daily on December 25, 1906. A separate weekly edition, the *White Pine News Weekly Mine Review,* later renamed the *Weekly Mining Review,* was begun on January 12, 1907. On November 24, 1908, Valjean moved the *News* to East Ely, where it remained until its final suspension on December 30, 1923. (See East Ely, *White Pine News.*)

White Pine News: (Sep 15 1888–Nov 22 1908)
  CHi — My 21 1892; F 3 1894
  CSfWF-H — Jl 19 1890
  CU-BANC — Jl 6 1889–Ja 4 1890
  NvHi — Ja 4–D 27 1890
  NvU — Ja 4 1890–N 22 1908
  film — [S 15 1888–N 22 1908]
Ref: files

White Pine Miner

In October of 1902, J. M. Lynch retired from the *White Pine News* to commence a new paper at Ely, the *White Pine Miner,* probably the following month. Lynch was sole editor and publisher, and issued the *Miner* as a Saturday weekly. He soon discovered that Ely was not yet able to support two papers, however, and was forced to suspend the *Miner* about February of 1903. Lynch removed the material to Cherry Creek, reviving the *Miner* on March 25. (See *Cherry Creek Miner.*)

White Pine Miner: (c. Nov 1902–c. Feb 1903)
  No issues located.
Ref: Myrick.

Amateur Outlook

In July of 1904, C. M. McDonald moved his little monthly, *Amateur Outlook,* from Reno to Ely. He printed two issues there before returning to the university that fall. (See Reno, *Amateur Outlook.*)

Amateur Outlook: (Jul 1904–Aug 1904)
  CU-BANC — Ag 1904
  NvU — Jl–Ag 1904
  film — Jl–Ag 1904
Ref: files

The Ely Record (The Mining Record)

On March 4, 1905, John D. Crossette, former editor of the *White Pine News,* commenced a rival paper at Ely, the *Mining Record.* Crossette served as editor, issuing the paper as a Democratic weekly. On June 3, Benjamin Dial bought a half interest in the paper, but sold it back barely two months later, on September 16. Crossette then induced M. G. Foster to become co-publisher. On July 7, 1906, the Ely Publishing Company took over the paper, changing the politics to Republican and hiring William B. Root as editor.

  W. A. Leonard became editor on February 23, 1907, and on January 1, 1909, he trimmed the name to the *Ely Record.* Leonard became president of the publishing company on September 28, and held that post and the editorship until February 6, 1925. N. H. Chapin then assumed the presidency and H. P. Bagley became editor, but on July 10 of the same year U. C. Herr became editor. He was followed by Charles H. Russell on August 30, 1929.

Russell used the paper to further his political career, winning six consecutive terms in the Nevada legislature, beginning in 1935. Republican Russell finally retired as editor on December 6, 1946, when Democratic Governor Vail M. Pittman of the rival *Times* bought out the *Record*. But Russell moved on to the U.S. Congress and then replaced Pittman as governor. Pittman hired Paul Leonard as manager of the *Record* and Maurya Wogan as editor. Walter Wilcox became editor on November 21, 1947, and was succeeded the following year by Lloyd Leonard.

In 1951, the managements of the daily *Times* and weekly *Record* were officially combined, when Donald W. Reynolds of the *Las Vegas Review-Journal* added the papers to his growing empire. Thereafter the editor of the *Record* was the same as that of the *Times*.

The Ely Record: (Mar 4 1905+)
  NvHi — Ap 14 1906; [My 4 1907–56]
  NvU — [Mr 4 1905+]
  film — [Mr 4 1905+]
Ref: files

Ely Mining Expositor

In the fall of 1906, Denver S. Dickerson sold his interest in the *White Pine News*, and formed the Expositor Printing and Publishing Company, to commence the *Ely Mining Expositor* on October 11, 1906. The *Expositor* was issued every Thursday as a Silver-Democratic weekly, with Dickerson as editor. The paper was well received and grew rapidly, a daily edition being added on May 15, 1907. Following Dickerson's election as lieutenant governor, J. W. Connella took the editorial helm, holding it until February of 1908, when he was suddenly bitten by the "Rawhide Fever," and moved to that camp.

Dickerson leased the papers for a year on August 31, to L. G. Schwalenberg and H. C. Reilly. He resumed control on September 1, 1909, under the name of the Expositor Printing and Publishing Company, installing George A. Flannigan as editor. James F. Haley bought an interest in the paper and became the editor on May 2, 1910, but after the expiration of his term of office, Dickerson resumed the editorship on February 15, 1911. On May 22, 1912, he turned the editorial chair over to L. G. Schwalenberg.

The *Expositor's* career was waning. On December 26, 1912, the weekly edition was suspended, and on November 22, 1914, the daily *Expositor* was reduced to a weekly. As such it continued only two months until its final suspension on January 31, 1915.

Ely Weekly Mining Expositor: (Oct 11 1906–Dec 26 1912)
  CHi — [1914]

NvHi — O 11–18, D 15 1906–D 26 1907; F 13 1908; Jl 8 1909–D 26 1912
NvU — Je 1907–12
film — [O 11 1906–D 26 1912]
Ely Daily Mining Expositor: (May 15 1907–Jan 31 1915)
  CHi — Ag 24, 31 1914
  NvHi — O 28 1907–Jan 31 1915
  NvU — F 12 1908–D 20 1914
  film — [O 28 1907–Ja 31 1915]
Ref: files

Ely Post

The *Ely Post* was a weekly begun about February 15, 1907. It lasted at least a month, but probably not much longer.
Ely Post: (c. Feb 15 1907–c. Mar 1907)
  pvt — Mr 15 1907
Ref: files

White Pine Suffragist

The *White Pine Suffragist,* edited by Mrs. W. E. Collins, was apparently a one-issue paper, published at Ely on October 31, 1914. It supported the woman's suffrage amendment, which was approved in the election the following week.
White Pine Suffragist: (Oct 31 1914)
  NvHi — O 31 1914
  film — O 31 1914
Ref: files

Ely Daily Times

Nearly five years after the suspension of the *Expositor,* Vail M. Pittman bought the old Expositor Printing and Publishing Company and began the daily *Times* on April 19, 1920. Pittman held the editorial chair for over a quarter of a century, but the Times Printing and Publishing Company became the owner on August 12, 1930. Pittman became sole editor and publisher again on January 6, 1938. With the *Times* as a base he ran successfully for the lieutenant governorship in 1942.

When Governor Carville resigned to take a U.S. Senate seat in 1945, Pittman succeeded to the governorship; he was reelected to the office the following year. On July 13, 1946, he hired Walter Wilcox as editor of the *Times,* then replaced him with Paul A. Leonard in December. On December 6, Pittman also bought out his only rival, the *Record,* which he continued as a weekly edition of the *Times.* In 1951, Pittman finally retired from publishing, selling the *Times* and the *Record* to Donald W. Reynolds of the *Las Vegas Review-Journal.* Reynolds consolidated the management of the *Times* and *Record,* but hired a new editor every few years, in succession: John Hamlyn, James A. Dement, Peter Mygatt, Jay E. Steed, Darwin Lambert, Roy Cauley, Wayne Spencer, Hugh Clark, E. Gorton Covington, John S. Miller, and Rich Parker.

Ely Daily Times: (Apr 19 1920+)
   pub — 1920+
   CU — S 19 1925
   NvEC — [1927+]
   NvHi — [Je 10 1920+]
   NvU — [Ap 19 1920+]
   film — [Ap 19 1920+]
Ref: files

◢(EMPIRE CITY)◣

Empire City Globe

Empire City's only newspaper — if it actually existed — was the *Empire City Globe,* mentioned in the Gold Hill *News* of January 7, 1867, as containing "Gov" Hal Clayton's proclamation extraordinary to convene the "Third House of the Legislature" in the Carson City Theater at eight o'clock that evening. The proclamation burlesqued the actual convening of the State Legislature the same day and was said to have filled all four pages of the *Globe* and a supplement. The publishers of the *Globe* were not mentioned, but the officers of the Third House were "Gov" Clayton, President; Sam Brown, President *pro temp;* Capt. Jim, Sgt.-at-arms; and Mark Twain, Ass, despite the fact that the latter had left Nevada in 1864.

Empire City Globe: (c. Jan 7 1867)
   No issues located.
Ref: GHN Ja 7 1867

◢(EUREKA)◣

Eureka Sentinel

When Archibald Skillman closed the *Shermantown Reporter* in early June of 1870, following the death of his partner, G. A. Brier, he moved the old press and material to the new camp of Eureka. There, he formed a partnership with Dr. L. C. McKenney, who had had some previous journalistic experience and was anxious to reenter the field. On July 16, 1870, they commenced publication of the *Eureka Sentinel,* under the firm name of A. Skillman and Co. The paper was a twenty-four-column weekly, edited by Dr. McKenney, who proved to be a facile writer and devoted himself to a description of the boundless mining resources of the district. The town grew rapidly and the paper prospered with it, becoming a daily on May 23, 1871.

On September 29, 1871, the establishment was purchased by Fred Elliott and George W. Cassidy; the former was a practical printer as well as a writer, and the latter was the late editor of the *Inland Empire* at Hamilton. The *Sentinel* was enlarged to a triweekly and made an active Democratic organ. Elliott retired from the firm on May 29, 1872, leaving Cassidy sole editor and proprietor. On December 3, 1874, a half interest was purchased by John H. Dennis, late of the Austin *Reese River Reveille.* Dennis became the principal editor, allowing Cassidy the time to fulfill his political aspirations and perform his duties as state senator and later congressional representative.

The paper continued to prosper and was enlarged to a daily. Late in 1876, Skillman returned to Eureka from Hamilton, where he was publishing the *White Pine News.* On December 28, 1876, he purchased Dennis's interest in the *Sentinel.* The firm of Cassidy and Skillman continued the paper for many years, until Cassidy's death on June 24, 1892. Skillman became sole editor and proprietor on May 20, 1893. On August 30, 1879, a weekly was added to the daily, and the two editions ran until 1887, when the daily suspended.

Early in its career the *Sentinel* survived a baptism of fire and water. On November 20, 1873, the greater portion of Eureka was destroyed by fire and with it the entire office and material of the *Sentinel.* Only a few sheets of damaged paper and one or two galleys of type were saved. From this was published the *Eureka Daily Sentinel Supplement,* which continued the legal notices and thus enabled the paper to perform its legally required duties. New material was ordered from San Francisco and arrived soon, but the total loss to the proprietors was estimated at $12,000, with no insurance.

In July of 1874, a tremendous storm deluged all of central Nevada and sent a flood sweeping down the narrow canyon where Eureka is situated, destroying everything in its path. The *Sentinel* office, too, was flooded, but the damage was not so great as before and much of the material was saved. In April, 1879, the office was again ravaged by fire, but a portion of the building was fireproof and the total loss was negligible.

Following Archibald Skillman's death on August 1, 1900, the paper passed to his son, Ed A. Skillman, on September 8. He carried on the paper as sole editor and proprietor for forty years before passing it on to his son, Willis L. Skillman, on December 28, 1940. On November 18, 1944, the *Sentinel* finally left the Skillman family after nearly seventy-five years, when E. J. Moyle purchased the paper. Moyle ran the paper until his death in June, 1960, when it became a part of Ira N. Jacobson's combine. Since that time it has been printed at Tonopah. In March, 1975, William G. Roberts purchased the *Sentinel* and became both editor and publisher.

Eureka Sentinel (daily): (Jul 16 1870–Oct 1 1887)
   C — Ap 20 1872; Mr 8, My 31 1881; Mr 2, 5, 7, 9, 11, Ap 26, O 6, N 3, 9, 23, 1882
   CSmH — O 31 1872
   CU-BANC — N 12, 26 1870; [Ap 29 1871–N 18 1873]; My 14 1874; Ja 7 1875–D 22 1880; F 1 1881; Ja 1–Jl 30 1882; F 12, Mr 19 1884
   ICHi — Ag 24 1876
   NcD — O 17 1877

NvEuC — 1873–Ag 30 1879
NvFC — [S 10–D 31 1880; O 31 1885]
NvHi — O 23, Ja 29 1873
NvMus — S 28 1881; N 1, D 25 1885; Ja 26, F 14 1886
NvU — [Ag 1875–O 1 1887]
film — [N 12, 1870–O 1 1887]
Eureka Sentinel (weekly): (Aug 30 1879+)
C — Mr 11, S 9 O 7–14, N 25 1882
CU-BANC — Ag 30–S 6, 27 1879; N 14, D 5–26 1885; Ja 2–30, F 20–Jl 17, 31–Ag 14, 28–D 25 1886; Ja 1–Mr 26, Ap 9–30, My 14–N 5, D 3–17, 31 1887; Ja 21–Ap 28, My 12–Je 30 1888; Ja 12–D 28 1889; Ja 4–Ag 2, 16, 30, S 13–D 27 1890; Ja–D 1891; Ja 2 1892
NvHi — S 3–O 15, N 12–19 1892; [1908+]
NvU — [J 7 1888+]
film — [Ag 30 1879+]
Ref: files; Angel 298–9; Doten 1823; McMurtrie 299–300

The Cupel

The *Cupel* was an ephemeral Republican daily, begun at Eureka on March 23, 1874, by William B. Taylor. The press on which the *Cupel* was printed was an ancient affair, which first did service in Nevada in 1863, printing the *Carson Independent,* and was later used by Taylor to issue the *Elko Chronicle* and the *Pioche Review.* The *Cupel* lasted for nearly four months, until two o'clock on the afternoon of July 24, 1874, when a raging wall of flood water swept down Eureka canyon. The *Cupel* office and many other buildings were torn from their foundations, smashed and carried far down the canyon. Taylor survived, but Roger Robinette, reporter on the *Cupel,* was drowned in the flood.

The name, *Cupel,* had special significance to the people of the mining community, as explained by Wells Drury:

> Eureka was a camp in which all the ores required smelting, and in order to make a test the assayer was compelled to make use of the *cupel,* a little receptacle of bone-ash in which the precious metals, mixed with the base metals, were placed and subjected to a high degree of heat. The *cupel* absorbed or eliminated the base metals, leaving on top a shining button of pure gold and silver, ready for weighing and showing accurately the value of the ore. It would be difficult to select a name more appropriate for a true newspaper — one that fills the requirements of the profession, which is honor bound to show forth the truth and to cast away the mixtures of prejudice and misrepresentation.

The Cupel: (Mar 23 1874–Jul 24 1874)
No issues located.
Ref: GHN Mr 23, 28 1874; Drury, 184

Eureka Daily Republican

In December of 1876, following the suspension of the *Humboldt Register* at Winnemucca, John C. Ragsdale removed a portion of the material from that office to Eureka. There, on January 4, 1877, he issued the first number of the *Daily Republican.* On July 2, 1877, the Republican Publishing Company was formed, with Ragsdale as manager and editor. When he retired from the firm on December 1 of that year, H. B. Loomis became the unofficial editor. Alfred Chartz was named as editor and manager on March 21, 1878, and soon after, on April 18, he leased the paper in partnership with W. W. Watts and McCrosky. Chartz gained recognition for his witticisms, some of them at the expense of Edward Rickard, a conductor on the Eureka and Palisade Railroad. The latter threatened retaliation, and on June 16, 1878, he and Chartz quarreled on the street in Eureka. When Chartz fatally shot Rickard, who died two days later, the people of Eureka became so outraged that the *Republican* was forced to suspend publication on June 24. Chartz was tried and sentenced to life imprisonment in the state penitentiary and McCrosky and Watts left Eureka to try their luck elsewhere. In 1886, Alfred Chartz was released from the penitentiary and returned to journalism, publishing the *Evening Report* at Virginia City. The material of the *Republican* was purchased by C. L. Canfield and F. E. Fisk, who used it to start the *Leader* on June 25.

Eureka Daily Republican: (Jan 4 1877–Jun 24 1878)
  CU-BANC — [Ja 4 1877–Je 24 1878]
  NbHi — My 17 1876
  NvEuC — [Mr–Je 1878]
  NvHi — [Ja 8 1877–8]
  film — [Ja 8 1877–Je 24 1878]
Ref: files; Angel 299–300

Silver Plume

The *Silver Plume* was an amateur monthly begun at Eureka in May of 1877, by Wesley Kellogg and Edward D. Vanderlieth. They were assisted in the editorial work by J. Story and A. Taylor. They increased it to a semi-monthly in July, but it probably suspended after the September 1 issue, when they all went back to school. It was revived only briefly in February 1882.

Silver Plume: (May 1877–Sep 1 1877; Feb 1882)
  NvMus — Jl 4, Ag 1–S 1 1877
  film — Jl 4, Ag 1–S 1 1877
Ref: files; NeT F 6 1882

Eureka Daily Leader

As a result of the notoriety connected with the shooting of Edward Rickard by Alfred Chartz, part owner of the *Republican,* the proprietors of that paper were forced to discontinue its publication, and sold the establishment to Charles L. Canfield and Fred E. Fisk. On June 25, 1878, the day following the suspension of the *Republican,* Canfield and Fisk began publication of the *Eureka Daily Leader*. The *Leader* was exactly the same as the former *Republican;* only the title lead was changed. This firm continued the paper until October 4, 1879, when William W. Hobart purchased Fisk's interest. Hobart managed the editorial department and Canfield took over the locals. On April 16, 1880, Canfield retired from the firm.

The office was destroyed by a fire that August, but the rival *Sentinel* allowed Hobart to print a small sheet of legal advertisements on its press for two weeks in order to keep the paper alive. Hobart resumed regular publication on September 8, and took in C. A. Morden as a partner on November 9. The following year, on October 1, James E. Anderson bought out Hobart and Morden, but he sold the plant to H. Muller on August 31, 1882. Anderson remained as editor, however, and that fall he became involved in a hot political argument with the Republican candidate for school superintendent, George Reek. When they met on the street on November 3, both men opened fire; Anderson was fatally wounded and died three days later. Thereafter the paper passed rapidly through a number of hands.

Walter L. Marsden leased it from November 20 to December 28 of 1882. He was followed by Edward D. Vanderlieth and others, who hired Lambert Molinelli as editor. On June 6, 1883, S. M. Stenhouse became publisher, but his name was dropped less than a month later, and the management was unnamed until October 18, when William J. Penrose became editor. On November 19, 1884, Penrose retired from the *Leader* to start his own paper, the *Republican Press.* O. H. Grey leased the *Leader* on December 11, 1884. But Eureka had passed its boom and both the *Leader* and the *Republican Press* suspended the following May, leaving only the *Sentinel* to continue as a weekly.

Eureka Daily Leader: (Jun 25 1878–May 16 1885)
  CU-BANC — Je 25 1878–D 31 1880; Ja 6, Ap 9 1881
  MnHi — Ap 22 1879
  NvEuC — 1878–85
  NvFC — D 6 1881, S 26 1883
  NvHi — S 13–15, 24 1880
  NvMus — Ap 30 1883
  NvU — [1880–5]
  film — [Je 25 1878–My 16 1885]
Ref: files; Angel 300

Republican Press

William J. Penrose, editing the faltering Eureka *Leader* in addition to running his own *Mining News* at nearby Ruby Hill, quit the *Leader* on November 19, 1884. He moved the *Mining News* material to Eureka, where he used it to found the *Republican Press* on November 30. Penrose was sole editor and proprietor, and took pains to assure his readers that "the *Press,* as its name denotes, will be Republican in its utterances, but never ultra."

He issued the paper every Sunday, as a four-page weekly, for a subscription price of $5 a year. Eureka was unable to support three papers, however. The *Republican Press* suspended on May 9, 1885, and the *Leader* soon after. Penrose then moved to Butte, Montana, where with miner's union support he commenced a new paper, the *Mining Journal,* subsequently won election to the state house of representatives on the Democratic ticket, and was mysteriously murdered on a street corner on June 9, 1891.

Republican Press: (Nov 30 1884–May 9 1885)
 NvHi — N 30 1884–My 9 1885
 film — N 30 1884–My 9 1885
Ref: files

The Eureka Tri-Weekly Standard

The Eureka *Standard* was a relatively short-lived triweekly begun at Eureka on August 6, 1885, by F. G. Roney and A. J. Simpson. Roney was editor and, starting November 17, he was sole proprietor. The paper was issued from the *Standard* office on North Main Street and sold for $8 a year. The *Standard* struggled along for little more than a year before its suspension about September 15, 1886.

The Eureka Tri-Weekly Standard: (Aug 6 1885–c. Sep 15 1886)
 NvHi — [Ag 6 1885–S 15 1886]
 NvMus — F 12 1886
 film — [Ag 6 1885–S 15 1886]
Ref: files

Eureka Miner

In an effort to give Eureka a locally owned paper, Don and Linda Critchell began the weekly *Eureka Miner* on June 11, 1971. The *Miner* offered the *Sentinel* its first competition in eighty-five years, and it soon gained a larger share of Eureka's patronage. At first the type was set in Winnemucca and then driven to Carson City to be published by the *Appeal,* but eventually the typesetting was done in Eureka and the printing was done at Ely by the *Times.* Since the *Sentinel* was also not printed in Eureka, the Critchells pulled a clever coup by printing a supplement with a potato at Eureka. This qualified the *Miner* as the only paper printed in the county, thereby winning for it the right to publish all the county legal notices. In March of 1973, Ira Jacobson of the *Sentinel* finally bought the *Miner*'s name and good will, along with a promise from the Critchells that they would not publish another paper in the state of Nevada for five years.

Eureka Miner: (Jun 11 1971–Mar 16 1973)
 pvt — Je 11 1971–Mr 16 1973
 film — Je 11 1971–Mr 16 1973
Ref: pub

FAIRPLAY
(See ATWOOD)

FAIRVIEW

Fairview News

Early in February of 1906, Clyde C. Emerson of the *Fallon Herald* arrived in the new camp of Fairview, lured by the offer of a free lot for starting the camp's first newspaper. His tent was in fact the first in the camp. There, on March 3, 1906, he issued the first number of the *Fairview News,* though it was printed at his *Herald* plant in Fallon. With Emerson as editor, the Emerson Publishing Company issued the *News* every Saturday, as a four-page, independent weekly selling for $5 a year, advising "Invest Elsewhere if you will, but first see Fairview."

Confident of the camp's future, Emerson bought a new $5,000 printing plant in San Francisco, but before it could be shipped it was destroyed with much of the city in the earthquake and fire. The *News* was finally printed in Fairview on June 30, 1906, with the press and material of the former *Fallon Herald* plant, and Emerson became sole editor and publisher. The paper served Fairview throughout its boom, but finally succumbed when Emerson joined the rush to Rawhide. He started the *Rawhide News* on January 25, 1908, and on February 15, he suspended the *Fairview News* to move the plant to the new camp.

Fairview News: (Mar 3 1906–Feb 15 1908)
  NvHi — [Mr 3 1906–F 15 1908]
  NvU — Ap 1907 (anniv issue)
  film — [Mr 3 1906–F 15 1908]
Ref: files

Fairview Miner

On May 5, 1906, E. B. Clark commenced the ill-fated weekly *Miner* at Fairview. Clark soon expanded his journalistic empire with the establishment of two other *Miners* at the rival camps of Wonder and Hercules in the Wonder Mining District, some twenty miles to the northeast. He was also a man of extravagant tastes, which he indulged at the expense of neglected bills, and in October the sheriff seized the *Miner* plants for his creditors. Clark departed with whatever liquid assets he could get his hands on, leaving a trail of bad checks. He was finally arrested in New Orleans shortly before Christmas.

In the meantime, trying to recoup their losses from the paper, the creditors installed Louis A. Spellier as editor of the *Fairview Miner,* and resumed publication on December 26, 1906. They soon gave up and suspended the *Miner* on February 27. Spellier then went to work briefly as a reporter for the editors of the nearby *Wonder Miner*.

Fairview Miner: (May 5 1906–Oct 6 1906; Dec 26 1906–Feb 27 1907)
  No issues located.
  Ref: FE O 11 1906, Ja 3 1907; FN O 13, D 26 1906, Mr 2 1907; LT Ja 4, 1907

∽⁀(FALLON)⁀∽

Fallon Standard (Churchill County Standard)

Fallon's first paper, the *Standard,* was founded on December 19, 1903, by Fred W. Fairbanks of the Yerington *Lyon County Times.* Fairbanks published the weekly under the name of the Standard Publishing Company with R. Leslie Smaill as editor, until April 1, 1905, when William C. Black bought the paper and became both editor and proprietor. On February 20, 1908, Black leased the *Standard* to A. P. Bettersworth, formerly of the rival *Fallon Eagle.* Bettersworth changed the name to the *Churchill County Standard* two weeks later, and on July 7, he increased it to a semiweekly. On September 24, he turned over the lease to J. Otto Lee and C. J. Kinnear, who promptly cut the paper back to a weekly.

Lee soon departed for his home in Indiana, and on February 11, 1909, Kinnear became sole lessee. He lasted less than two months, and Black again became editor and proprietor on April 8. Black ran the paper until April 21, 1915, when Ernest L. Bingham bought it. On April 28, 1920, the name was shortened to the *Fallon Standard.* Black briefly bought back a half interest from Bingham, becoming co-publisher from January 21, 1920, to July 27, 1921. In late October, soon after Bingham died, his wife, L. H. Bingham, became the publisher. Her brother-in-law, C. E. Bingham, managed the paper until his own death in May of 1922. Then, on January 31, 1923, Mrs. Bingham hired H. R. Mighels, Jr., as editor. He served for three years until Claude H. Smith bought a half interest on May 5, 1926, and took over the editorship. Smith ran the paper for over thirty years, until his death in 1957. Ken Ingram then served as editor until William J. Cary, Jr., of the rival *Eagle,* bought the *Standard* and merged them into the *Eagle-Standard* on November 4, 1958. (See *Fallon Eagle-Standard.*)

Fallon Standard: (Dec 19 1903–Oct 28 1958)
  pub — Ap 1914–24; 1926–58
  NvFC — D 19 1903
  NvHi — [Jl 15 1909–55]
  NvU — Ja 1904–19; 1921; 1926–32; 1951–8
  film — [D 19 1903; Ja 1904–O 28 1958]
Ref: files

Fallon Herald

In May of 1905, Clyde C. Emerson issued the first number of the *Fallon Herald.* Emerson was editor and secretary and J. B. Young was president of the Emerson Publishing Company, which issued the paper as a Tuesday weekly. Attracted by the boom at Fairview, some forty miles to the east,

Emerson started a second paper, the *Fairview News*, on March 3, 1906. He printed both it and the *Herald* at Fallon, however, until June, when he finally decided Fairview had the more promising future. He then closed down the *Herald* and moved the printing plant to the new camp to continue the *News*.

Fallon Herald: (May 1905–Jun 1906)
  No issues located.
Ref: FN Je 30 1906

Fallon Eagle

The *Fallon Eagle* was founded on October 6, 1906, by A. P. Bettersworth and L. J. Leonesio, as the weekly *Churchill County Eagle*. Bettersworth became sole editor and proprietor on February 7, 1907. He sold the paper on October 3, 1907, to Delbert E. Williams, and bought the rival *Standard*. Williams ran the *Eagle* for over thirty years. On September 24, 1927, the banner was changed to the *Fallon Eagle*. After Williams's death in 1938, his widow became publisher and hired Allan K. Dalby as editor. After his death in 1945, Robert H. Sanford took over the editorship. About 1955, Mrs. D. E. Williams finally sold the paper to Calvin Sunderland, who, in turn, sold it a year later to William J. Cary, Jr. In 1958, Cary bought the rival *Standard*, and on October 31, 1958, he suspended the *Eagle*, merging the two papers to form the *Eagle-Standard* on November 4. (See *Fallon Eagle-Standard*.)

Fallon Eagle: (Oct 6 1906–Oct 31 1958)
  pub — O 6 1906
  CHi — Mr 20, My 22, Je 26 1915
  NvHi — S 12 1907–58
  NvU — My 23 1907–58
  film — [O 6 1906–O 31 1958]
Ref: files

Ballot Box

On April 15, 1911, Fred C. Sander, president of the Ballot Box Publishing Company, issued the first number of the *Ballot Box* at Fallon. John E. Worden was editor, secretary, and business manager. The *Ballot Box* was a Socialist paper, brandishing the slogan "Workers of the World Unite at the Ballot Box." It was printed at Lola, Kansas, and sent to Fallon every Saturday, as a four-page weekly selling at $1 a year. Only a few columns of each issue were devoted to local news, as national affairs and political commentary occupied most of its space. The *Ballot Box* prospered for nearly two years, but ultimately suspended on June 28, 1913.

Ballot Box: (Apr 15 1911–Jun 28 1913)
  NvHi — Jl 27 1912
  NvU — [Ap 15 1911–Je 28 1913]
  film — [Ap 15 1911–Je 28 1913]
Ref: files

Co-operative Colonist

The *Co-operative Colonist* was an erratic monthly paper begun at Fallon on March 20, 1916, by C. V. Eggleston, to promote his utopian Socialist colony at Nevada City, four miles to the east. Eggleston was editor, and his Union Security Company was officially the publisher. Starting in the fall of 1916, he was assisted editorially by nationally known Socialist writer Eli N. Richardson, who helped make the *Colonist* widely known. At the same time, it was reduced to publishing once every two months. Most of its subscribers were prospective colonists in the Midwest, and as out-of-state subscribers grew in number, Eggleston started a second paper, the *Nevada Colony News,* to serve the local interests of the Nevada City colonists. They finally concluded that Eggleston was much more concerned with his personal profits from land and stock sales than in the goals of the colony, however, and they voted him out in the spring of 1917.

L. V. Flowers became editor and publisher in March, but after barely three months he turned the publication over to an association of colonists known as "The Furtherance of Collective Ownership and Co-operation." They hired R. E. Bray, a former newspaperman from Oklahoma, to edit the paper. Monthly publication had resumed in May of 1917, but the gradual disintegration of the colony brought about a return to issues every two months in June of 1918. The paper finally suspended publication altogether that September. (See Fallon, *Nevada Colony News.*)

Co-operative Colonist: (Mar 1916–Sep 1918)
  NvU — [Jl 1916–Ag/S 1918]
  film — [Jl 1916–Ag/S 1918]
Ref: files; Shepperson 69–78, 119, 129

Nevada Colony News

The monthly *Nevada Colony News* was a short-lived local companion to the the *Co-operative Colonist,* begun in March of 1917, by C. V. Eggleston, to serve the local needs of the Socialist colony at Nevada City. It suspended with its second number in April, when Eggleston was ejected from the colony for his unutopian money grubbing.

Nevada Colony News: (Mar 1917–Apr 1917)
  NvU — Ap 1917
  film — Ap 1917
Ref: files; Shepperson 71–3

Lahontan Valley Shopper

In 1957, William J. Cary, Jr., commenced the *Lahontan Valley Shopper* as a weekly advertiser for his *Fallon Eagle.* It was issued every Wednesday, with a free distribution of 5000. It was discontinued in 1958, when the *Eagle* and *Standard* merged.

Lahontan Valley Shopper: (1957–1958)
   No issues located.
Ref: Ayer 1958

Fallon Eagle-Standard

In the fall of 1958, William J. Cary, Jr., of the *Fallon Eagle* bought the rival *Standard.* He merged the two on November 4, as the semiweekly *Eagle-Standard.* About 1960, the Fallon Publishing Company became proprietor, with Vern A. Miller as editor. Julius Vestergaard replaced Miller about a year later. On January 1, 1964, Norman Butler became the new owner, followed by Samuel E. Burgess in June of 1974. Burgess remained publisher until S. Dee Baughman became the owner in June, 1979, with Ken Snyder, owner-publisher of the Lindsay, California *Gazette,* as a minority partner.

Fallon Eagle-Standard: (Nov 4 1958+)
   pub — 1958+
   Nv — [1958+]
   NvU — [1958+]
   film — [1958+]
Ref: files

Churchill County Courier

On March 15, 1961, Monnie D. and Vern A. Miller, formerly editors of the *Eagle-Standard,* commenced a rival weekly, the *Churchill County Courier,* at Fallon. They failed to gain sufficient support, and after a year they finally closed down on May 30, 1962, though they promised, "It's not goodbye, it's just goodnight."

Churchill County Courier: (Mar 15 1961–May 30 1962)
   Nv — [Mr 15 1961–My 30 1962]
   film — [Mr 15 1961–My 30 1962]
Ref: files; TE Ap 7 1961

Fallon Citizen

On January 3, 1963, John Evasovich commenced the weekly *Fallon Citizen* in competition with the *Eagle-Standard.* The town proved unable to support two papers, however, and the *Citizen* succumbed on November 2, 1967.

Fallon Citizen: (Jan 3 1963–Nov 2 1967)
   film — [Ja 3 1963–N 2 1967]
Ref: files

Lahontan Valley News

Fallon's next newspaper, the weekly *Lahontan Valley News,* was begun on August 4, 1970, by Lahontan Valley Printing, Inc. Pat Stevenson was the first editor, followed by George Caudle, who took over on December 15, 1975. Caudle was followed in turn by Ed Harris, on June 2, 1976.

Lahontan Valley News: (Aug 4 1970+)
   pub — Ag 4 1970+
   film — Jl 3 1974+
Ref: files

Desert Roundup

The *Lahontan Valley News* published the weekly *Desert Roundup* from about July 1977 to the fall of 1979, for the public affairs office of the Fallon Naval Air Station. It was issued every other week until February 1978 when it became a weekly.

Desert Roundup: (c. Jul 1977–c. Oct 1979)
   Nv — Jl 15 1977–O 17 1979
Ref: files

The Shopper

The Shopper, which also carries considerable local news, was started at Fallon on March 28, 1979, by Curtis Tuck and Harry Copeland.

The Shopper: (Mar 28 1979+)
   pub — Mr 28 1979+
Ref: files

❦ FERNLEY ❦

Enterprise

The *Enterprise* was founded at Fernley on February 1, 1919, by Joe T. Camp, one of the last of Nevada's true tramp printers. Camp was sole editor and publisher, and issued the paper as a Saturday weekly for $2.50 a year. Like many of his previous ventures, the *Enterprise* was not destined to last long and was probably suspended about the middle of the following year, when he moved to Wadsworth to commence the *Dispatch*.

Enterprise: (Feb 1 1919–c. 1920)
   No issues located.
Ref: LRM Ja 3, F 7, 1919

Nevadian Times

A. E. Haines began the *Nevadian Times* at Wadsworth on July 1, 1927, but in early 1931, he removed the plant to Fernley. There, as sole editor and proprietor, he issued the *Times* every Friday as a Republican weekly. After publishing at Fernley for less than a year, he again packed up his material in September, and moved the plant on to Carson City. (See Carson City, *Nevadian Times*.)

Nevadian Times: (c. 1931–Sep 1931)
   No issues located.
Ref: NT Je 28 1935

The Fernley Newspaper

On March 14, 1957, unable to decide on an appropriate name for his new weekly, William J. Cary, Jr., launched it as simply the *Fernley Newspaper,* calling upon his readers to suggest names. It took three weeks, but he finally got a suggestion he liked. On April 4, he renamed it the *Tri-Town Times.* (See Fernley, *Tri-Town Times.*)

The Fernley Newspaper: (Mar 14 1957–Mar 28 1957)
  No issues located.
Ref: Ayer; TTT Ap 4 1957

Tri-Town Times

On April 4, 1957, William J. Cary, Jr., chose a new name, the *Tri-Town Times,* for his fledgling weekly, the *Fernley Newspaper.* At the same time he broadened its coverage to include Wadsworth and Silver Springs. Cary was editor and publisher, and printed the paper at Sparks. He was unable to rally sufficient support for the venture, and sold it on July 31, *1958,* to Walter Cox and Robert Sanford of the *Mason Valley News* at Yerington. It ceased as a separate paper in November, but it was continued as a section in the *Mason Valley News* until April 28, 1967.

Tri-Town Times: (Apr 4 1957–Nov 12 1958)
  film — Ap 4 1957–N 12 1958
Ref: files

FORT HALLECK

Halleck Gossip

The *Halleck Gossip,* a spicy little monthly, was started at Fort Halleck by Mrs. G. R. Kemp in February of 1885. It probably lasted less than a year as the fort was abandoned the following year.

Halleck Gossip: (Feb 1885–c. 1885)
  No issues located.
Ref: EFP F 6 1885

GABBS

Gabbs Valley Enterprise

The *Gabbs Valley Enterprise,* "the Biggest Little Newspaper in the West," was published irregularly at Gabbs from September, 1974, through April, 1976, but its editor and publisher were anonymous.

Gabbs Valley Enterprise: (Sep 1974–c. Apr 6 1976)
  NvHi — S 26 1974–F 29 1976
  film — My 22 1975–Ap 6 1976
Ref: files

⋙⋘(GARDNERVILLE)⋙⋘

Gardnerville Press

Following the suspension of the *Carson Press*, William L. Lee brought the plant to Gardnerville, where in September of 1896, he issued that town's first paper, the weekly *Gardnerville Press*. With the approach of the election, he changed its name to the *Douglas County Silverite*. (See Gardnerville, *Douglas County Silverite*.)

Gardnerville Press: (Sep 1896–c. Oct 1896)
  No issues located.
Ref: CW S 28 1896

Douglas County Silverite

Shortly after starting the *Gardnerville Press* in September of 1896, William L. Lee took Samuel J. Allen as a partner and converted the paper to a campaign sheet, the *Douglas County Silverite*. Allen became editor of the weekly, which apparently suspended at the close of the campaign in November.

Douglas County Silverite: (c. Oct 1896–c. Nov 1896)
  No issues located.
Ref: Myrick

Gardnerville Record

By the late 1890's, Gardnerville had become the most prosperous town in Douglas County and her citizens decided they needed a newspaper. In the summer of 1898, they raised enough money by subscription to purchase a small printing office. On July 12, 1898, George I. Lamy issued the first number of the weekly *Gardnerville Record*. On March 14, 1902, Dr. Stoddard Southworth purchased the *Record* from Lamy, and on October 10 of that year, his son, C. E. Southworth, became editor. When the plant was destroyed by fire in March of 1904, C. E. Southworth bought the rival *Courier* from George M. Smith, changing its name to the Gardnerville *Record-Courier*. (See Gardnerville, *Record-Courier*.)

Gardnerville Record: (Jul 12 1898–Mar 4 1904)
  NvHi — Ag 2 1898
  NvU — [Jl 12 1898–Mr 4 1904]
  film—[Jl 12 1898–Mr 4 1904]
Ref: files

Courier

George M. Smith and Delbert E. Williams suspended the *Courier* at Genoa on June 2, 1899, and removed the press and material to Gardnerville, where they revived the paper under the same name on June 9. Williams became discouraged with the prospects of the paper, and on May 25, 1903, he sold out to Smith. Then, in March of 1904, after his rival Charles E.

Southworth's *Record* was burned to the ground, Smith sold the *Courier* to Southworth. The name of the paper was changed to the *Record-Courier,* and as such it was still being published in 1979. (See Gardnerville, *Record-Courier.*)

Courier: (Jun 9 1899–Apr 1 1904)
  NvMC — My 25 1899–Ap 1 1904
  NvU — Je 9 1899–Ap 1 1904
  film — Je 9 1899–Ap 1 1904
Ref: files

Record-Courier

On April 8, 1904, after Dr. Stoddard Southworth's *Gardnerville Record* was destroyed by fire, Southworth purchased the rival Gardnerville *Courier* and changed its name to the *Record-Courier.* His son, Charles E. Southworth, was editor and manager, but Southworth sold it seven months later to W. C. Ezell and Bert N. Selkirk. Ezell became sole proprietor on April 6, 1906, but ill health forced him to sell the paper to George Springmeyer on December 21 of the same year.

Bert Selkirk bought the paper again on January 3, 1908, and with his wife Sue, settled down to stay. After nearly forty years, failing health finally forced the Selkirks to retire, and on November 3, 1944, Arthur N. Suverkrup purchased the paper. His son, John W. Suverkrup, assumed the editorship. In June, 1958, John A. McDermott bought the *Record-Courier.* He hired Abraham Protes as editor for a few years before taking over the position himself. Tony Payton and Tom Dickerson became the publishers in November, 1965, and ran it until February, 1970, when it was purchased by Frank Griffen, Jr. He published it less than two years. In October, 1971, Don Woodward bought the paper and still published it in 1979.

Record-Courier: (Apr 8 1904+)
  pub — 1904+
  NvHi — [Ap 8 1908+]
  NvMC — [Ap 8 1904+]
  NvU — [N 1914+]
  film — [Ap 8 1904+]
Ref: files; LCT Jl 21 1906

Nevada Lutheran

The *Nevada Lutheran* was a monthly religious magazine founded at Gardnerville about February of 1918, by the Reverend Frederick H. Menzel, F. E. Martens, and Waldemar E. Menzel. It was published by the Nevada Lutheran Publishing Company, with the Reverend Paul H. Felton as editor, and it prospered for twenty-five years, until its suspension in 1942.

Nevada Lutheran: (Feb 1918–1942)
  NvU — Je 10 1918
  film — Je 10 1918
Ref: files; Ayer

Air Age News

The *Air Age News* was begun at Gardnerville in January of 1966, as a monthly, with Bill Thorpe as editor. The paper prospered, became a semi-monthly on August 8, and eventually outgrew Gardnerville. It moved to Reno's Stead Airport on March 14, 1967. (See Reno, *Air Age News*.)

Air Age News: (Jan 1966–Feb 27 1967)
  Nv — Ja 1966–F 27 1967
  film — Ja 1966–F 27 1967
Ref: files

⌒⌒(GENOA)⌒⌒

The Scorpion

A few years after the demise of Joseph Webb's *Gold Cañon Switch,* Stephen A. Kinsey, who had settled in Carson Valley in 1851, commenced a second handwritten paper, the *Scorpion,* at Genoa. He issued the first number about February 1, 1857, bearing the motto, "Fear no man, and do justice to all." The *Scorpion* was published monthly and contained twelve columns of interesting news items, written in a large bold hand and generously illustrated with amusing caricatures. Although it made good reading, the paper probably died before its twelfth number. The following year the first press was packed over the Sierra to found Nevada's first printed paper, the *Territorial Enterprise.*

The Scorpion: (Feb 1 1857–c. Dec 1857)
  No issues located.
Ref: TE Ap 12 1871 (quotes from *Scorpion* Jl 1 1857)

Territorial Enterprise

The first newspaper to be printed in Nevada was begun at Genoa, when that village was the county seat of Carson County, Utah Territory. On December 18, 1858, William L. Jernegan and Alfred James issued the first number of the *Territorial Enterprise* from their makeshift print shop, a room in the Nevada Hotel, on Mill Street. Jernegan, who had just left behind a host of creditors in Yolo County, California, was looking for a remote spot to start anew, and Genoa was well suited to his purpose.

That fall he purchased a spare press and an assortment of material from Dan Gelwicks of the Placerville *Mountain Democrat.* The type was battered old bourgeois brought around the Horn from Norwich, Connecticut, by William Faulkner, to print the *Pacific News* in San Francisco in 1849. The press and type were brought over the Sierra by wagon, and arrived in Genoa on October 17. It was two months before the first paper was issued, because the type was thoroughly "pied." John A. "Snowshoe" Thompson helped bring in paper and California exchanges.

James assumed the editorial tripod, while Jernegan took care of business matters. The *Enterprise* was published weekly on Saturday mornings, and sold for 25¢ a copy or, more reasonably, for $5 a year. It was printed on paper measuring 21 by 28 inches, and contained four pages of five columns each. Advertising was $3 for a single insertion of ten lines and nearly half of the ads were from firms across the Sierra in Placerville and Sacramento.

The trials of pioneer printing are well described by Jernegan on the first anniversary of the *Enterprise:*

> One year ago to-day, the first number of the *Territorial Enterprise* was issued at Genoa. Our publishing room was in Singleton's Hall, Nevada Hotel, a room indiscriminately used by preachers, debating clubs, secret societies, and once at least, for a prison. Upon the latter occasion we had a man accused of crime chained to our printing press, with a leg chain, for two days and a half. What secrets that old Hall might tell, could it, by chance, be endowed with the gift of speech! Our establishment was removed to Carson City, on Thursday, Nov. 10, 1859. We now occupy half of the upper part of Major Ormsby's adobe building, southwest corner of the Plaza. Our volume is not yet completed by several numbers, owing to the fact that we have twice been compelled to suspend our issue for want of paper. During last winter, most of our paper was brought over on snow shoes, by attachés of this office. Many a time in the past year have we suffered for lack of fuel, and been pinched for want of actual necessities of life. But so far we have struggled on successfully, and to-day we find ourselves in more comfortable circumstances in many respects. To be sure we still have to descend from the editorial tripod to superintend the cooking of a beefsteak, the seasoning of a bean soup, or the concoction of a pot of coffee, (and in this line, let us indulge our vanity by saying that we yield to none other as a caterer to the *physical* man, whatever our shortcoming in regard to intellectual pabulum.) But as we have said, we feel that we have made a stop in advance. It has been and still is our aim, to lay the foundation of a reliable newspaper, such as the rapidly increasing population, and the developing interests of our pet New Territory demand. So far as literary ability is concerned, we make no claims for the past. The public can readily judge how far we *could* devote ourselves to the nice details of "fine writing," under the circumstances of physical difficulties and discomforts. What we do claim is, to have labored sincerely and earnestly for the interests of this people and this Territory, according to our understanding, ability and opportunities.

The *Enterprise* soon became a strong advocate of separate territorial organization for western Utah Territory, and Jernegan was an active member of the first constitutional convention, held for this purpose at Genoa in July of 1859. In August of 1859, Alfred James retired from the paper and the editorial chair was filled by Jonathan Williams who purchased James's interest, with financial backing from Major William M. Ormsby. Thereafter "Nevada Territory" was carried on the dateline, though its official creation was still nearly two years away. The rush to the newly discovered Washoe mines was passing Genoa by and on November 12, 1859, the last number of the *Enterprise* was issued at Genoa. The press and material were removed to Carson City, where the paper was revived on November 26. (See Carson City, *Territorial Enterprise.*)

Territorial Enterprise: (Dec 18 1858–Nov 12 1859)
   Facsimile of Jl 30 1859 in Myron Angel, *History of Nevada.*
   CU-BANC — Ja 8, 29, F 5–12, Mr 19–26, Ap 9–28, My 21–Jl 16, O 8 1859
   NvGM — Ja 1 1859
   film — [Ja 1–O 8 1859]
Ref: files; Angel 312, 317; TE D 17 1859; SFE Ja 22 1893; Beebe

Carson Valley Farmer (Nevada Republican)

In the late summer of 1865, J. H. Hill raised about $300 by subscription from the people of Douglas County for the purpose of starting a Union newspaper. With this money he purchased a portion of the material of the deceased *Carson Independent* and brought it to Genoa. Here, on September 16, 1865, he issued the first number of the *Carson Valley Farmer.* The paper had an extremely short and radical career. On the second number, Hill changed the paper's name to the *Nevada Republican,* and with the third number the concern died. The plant was purchased from Hill by a citizen of Genoa and leased to Richard Wheeler, who used it to publish the *Douglas County Banner.*

Carson Valley Farmer: (Sep 16 1865–Sep 30 1865)
   No issues located.
Ref: Angel 293; McMurtrie 300

Douglas County Banner

Following the three-issue existence of the *Carson Valley Farmer,* the material passed into the hands of one of Genoa's residents, who leased the establishment to Richard Wheeler. On October 7, 1865, Wheeler commenced publication of the *Douglas County Banner,* assisted by A. T. Hawley as editor. The paper was a Republican weekly of twenty-four columns and sold for $5 a year. Financial support was lacking, however, and with the twelfth number, on December 23, 1865, Hawley warned that "if the citizens of Douglas County desire the publication of the *Banner* to continue we must receive some assistance next week; otherwise we shall be compelled to discontinue." That was its last issue.

Douglas County Banner: (Oct 7 1865–Dec 23 1865)
   CU-BANC — N 18 1865
   NvU — O 7–D 23 1865
   film — O 7–D 23 1865
Ref: files; Angel 293; McMurtrie 300

Carson Valley News

No newspaper was published in Douglas County for nearly ten years until A. C. Pratt founded the *Carson Valley News* at Genoa on February 20, 1875. Pratt was sole editor and proprietor and issued the *News* every Friday morning as a Republican weekly of twenty-four columns, at a subscription rate of $5 per year. For a time the paper prospered. With the beginning of the third volume, on February 16, 1877, it was enlarged to a semiweekly. However, this prosperity was fleeting. On August 24 of the same year, the weekly was resumed, and on June 28, 1878, the paper suspended. Pratt stated that the suspension was due to insufficient patronage and that the paper would be resumed should circumstances improve. Three months later, on September 20, the *News* was revived on a smaller scale, as a twelve-column weekly. Pratt continued the paper until July 16, 1880, when the plant was purchased by Boynton Carlisle. He closed the *News* and used the material to commence the *Genoa Weekly Courier*.

Carson Valley News: (Feb 20 1875–Jul 16 1880)
    pvt — Je 28 1878
    CIE — S 19 1879
    CU-BANC — [O 2 1875–S 22 1877]–Je 8, D 6, 27 1878; Ja 10, Je 13, Ag 8–D 5 1879; Ja 2, 23–30, Mr 12, My 28, Jl 9 1880
    NvHi — Je 27 1877
    NvMiD — [F 20 1875–Ag 14 1877]
    NvU — 1875–F 1876
    film — [F 20 1875–Jl 16 1880]
Ref: files; TE Jl 2 1878; Angel 293; McMurtrie 300

Genoa Journal

On April 1, 1880, John H. Cradlebaugh commenced publication of a rival Democratic weekly, the *Genoa Journal*. Cradlebaugh was sole editor and proprietor, and struggled to make the venture solvent, but the town was unable to support two papers and he was forced to suspend in July. He received some new support from Democratic backers, who desired a paper to represent them in the coming political campaign, and in September of the same year he revived the *Journal* with George M. Smith as editor. At the close of the campaign, on November 1, 1880, Smith purchased the establishment and changed its politics to Republican. Smith continued the *Journal* until December 22, 1880, when he suspended it to combine the plant with that of the Genoa *Courier*, which he purchased on January 1, 1881.

Genoa Journal: (Apr 1–Jul 1880; Sep–Dec 22 1880)
    CU-BANC — O 13–D 22 1880
    film — O 13–D 22 1880
Ref: files; Angel 293; CVN Jl 2 1880

Genoa Weekly Courier

On July 16, 1880, Boynton Carlisle purchased the plant of the *Carson Valley News* at Genoa. On July 23, he changed the name to the *Genoa Weekly Courier*. The paper was a twenty-column, 16 by 22-inch, Republican weekly, selling for $3 a year. On January 1, 1881, Carlisle sold the firm to George M. Smith, who added to it the material of the former *Genoa Journal*. Smith ran the paper until August 31, 1883, when Jesse H. Dungan became editor and proprietor. On August 29, 1884, Dungan was succeeded by G. W. Oman, who managed the paper for two weeks and sold it to Delbert E. Williams on September 19.

George M. Smith again purchased the *Courier* on December 3, 1886. He turned it back over to Williams on June 6, 1890, and then took control once again on October 20, 1893. Finally, on June 2, 1899, Smith and Williams became joint publishers. They promptly suspended the *Courier* at Genoa and moved the plant to Gardnerville. (See Gardnerville, *Courier.*)

Genoa Weekly Courier: (Jul 23 1880–Jun 2 1899)
   pvt — Ja 28 1887; Jl 31 1891; Mr 11 1892
   CSPWF-H — N 18 1887
   CU-BANC — O 3–17 1890
   NvFE — Ag 1884–O 4 1895
   NvHi — Jl 8 1887; Ag 19–O 21, N 4–18 1892; Ap 19, O 4 1895
   NvMC — Jl 23 1880–My 18 1899
   NvU — [Jl 23 1880–9]
   film — [Jl 23 1880–Je 2 1899]
Ref: files

The Bugle

In June of 1888, Rev. C. H. Gardner launched a little monthly, the *Bugle*, at Genoa on a crusade of "social, moral and political reform." The following month, it became the official organ of the Women's Christian Temperance Union of Genoa and they renamed it the *Nevada Prohibitionist*. As such it flourished for about a year. (See Genoa, *Nevada Prohibitionist.*)

The Bugle: (Jun 1888)
  No issues located.
Ref: CIU Jl 3 1888

Nevada Prohibitionist

In July of 1888, the Women's Christian Temperance Union made the fledgling *Bugle* their official organ and renamed it the *Nevada Prohibitionist*. Its editors, the Rev. C. H. Gardner and Mrs. M. E. Latta, dedicated the paper "to the work of creating public sentiment against the evils of intemperence and in favor of pure homes society and politics." It was apparently issued monthly and sold for $1 a year, but it gave up its good work a year later and Gardner moved the press to Reno to start a new paper, the *Free Lance*.

Nevada Prohibitionist: (Jul 1888–c. Apr 1889)
  NvHi — Apr 1 1889
  film — Apr 1 1889
Ref: files; CIU Jl 3 1888; GEC Je 1 1888, Jl 26 1889

GERLACH

Gerlach Express

On June 12, 1914, Joe T. Camp commenced the first number of the *Express* at Gerlach, on the southern end of the Black Rock Desert. Camp was sole editor and publisher, issuing the paper every Friday as a four-page, six-column weekly, at $3 a year. It survived to its second number, but probably not too many more, undoubtedly suspending by July.

Gerlach Express: (Jun 12 1914–c. Jul 1914)
   CHi — Je 19 1914
   film — Je 19 1914
Ref: files

Valley Press

On December 15, 1961, George R. Lill of the *Sparks Tribune* commenced the *Valley Press* at Gerlach, numbering the first issue "volume 99, number 49," to make it the fanciful "successor to *Nevada Territory Comet* printed July 7, 1862 and *Prairie Junket* published 1871." Lill got little more support than Camp had nearly half a century before, and he suspended the *Press* around February 23, 1962.

Valley Press: (Dec 16 1961–c. Feb 23 1962)
   NvHi — [D 15 1961–F 23 1962]
   film — [D 15 1961–Ja 5, 19–F 23 1962]
Ref: files

❧(GILBERT)❧

Gilbert Record

With the boom of Gilbert, some thirty miles west of Tonopah, F. F. Garside of the *Tonopah Daily Times* decided to provide a newspaper for the camp. On February 21, 1925, he issued the first number of the *Gilbert Record* from the plant of the *Times* at Tonopah. Garside was sole editor and publisher, and issued the *Record* as a Saturday weekly, whose office was Post Office Drawer "H H" at Tonopah. By the end of the year Gilbert's boom had waned, and on May 8, 1926, Garside suspended the *Gilbert Record,* changing its name to the *Nevada Mining Record* at Tonopah. (See Tonopah, *Nevada Mining Record.*)

Gilbert Record: (Feb 21 1925–May 8 1926)
   NvHi — F 28–D 26 1925
   NvU — F 21 1925–My 8 1926
   film — F 21 1925–My 8 1926
Ref: files

(GOLCONDA)

Golconda Illustrated Gazette

The *Golconda Illustrated Gazette* was an ephemeral journal which flourished briefly in the spring of 1881, under the hand of some unknown editor. The

paper was issued as an illustrated weekly and, although it was very attractive, it seems to have been somewhat lacking in local news, prompting the editor of the nearby Winnemucca *Silver State* to observe that its "editor is more of an artist than a news gatherer." The lifetime of the *Gazette* was very short and its demise undoubtedly came in the spring of 1881.
Golconda Illustrated Gazette: (c. Mar. 1881–c. Apr 1881)
   No issues located.
Ref: SS Mr 31 1881

The News

Following the suspension of the Elko *Argonaut,* on February 6, 1899, George B. Russell and Charles H. Keith removed the plant to Golconda. There, in company with Clarence D. Van Duzer, they started the Golconda *News* the following week, on February 18. The *News* was issued as a semiweekly for about a month, whereupon it was reduced to a weekly. The weekly contained eight pages, half of which were preprinted patented material, and sold for $3 a year. Only a few weeks after the founding of the paper, Keith sold out to his partners. Some four months later, Van Duzer, who had been the editor, also retired from the firm, to start the *Nevada Magazine* in Winnemucca. As sole editor and proprietor, Russell continued the paper until July 14, 1900, when he, too, decided to move on "to cast our lot in Winnemucca." (See Winnemucca, *Nevada News.*)
The News: (Feb 18 1899–Jul 14 1900)
   CSmH — My 4 1899
   NvU — Jl 27 1899–Jl 14 1900
   film — F 18, My 4, Jl 27 1899–Jl 14 1900
Ref: files; EFP F 11, My 4 1899, Jl 14 1900; SS F 7, 20 1899; RG F 23 1899

Nevada Miner

On February 15, 1902, Clarence D. Van Duzer, having returned to Golconda, founded a semimonthly magazine, the *Nevada Miner.* It was a generously illustrated journal promoting statewide mining interests and, not incidentally, Van Duzer's successful campaign for Congress. As editor and publisher, assisted by Fred J. Cole as business manager, Van Duzer issued the *Miner* regularly until April 1, then "owing to unforeseen accidents," he skipped until July 1, when he suspended publication at Golconda and removed the plant to Reno. There he revived the paper in September. (See Reno, *Mining and Industrial Review*).
Nevada Miner: (Feb 15 1902–Jul 1 1902)
   CU-BANC — Jl 1 1902
   DLC — F 15–Jl 1 1902
   NvHi — Jl 1 1902
   NvU — F 15–Mr 15, Ap 1 1902
   film — F 15–Ap 1, Jl 1 1902
Ref: files; PR F 28 1902

Rustler

The *Rustler* was another of Joe T. Camp's short-lived ventures, begun at Golconda in 1910. Camp was sole editor and proprietor and issued the *Rustler* every Saturday as a four-page, Democratic weekly, at $2 a year. Golconda was no longer able to support a newspaper, however, and the *Rustler* was forced to suspend publication, probably sometime the following year.

Rustler: (1910–c. 1911)
  No issues located.
Ref: Ayer

GOLD CENTER

Gold Center News

At the height of the Bullfrog rush, the town of Gold Center was laid out a few miles south of the mines. There, on September 29, 1906, G. Harold Ellis founded the *Gold Center News*. Ellis was sole editor and proprietor and published the paper every Saturday, as a four-page, six-column weekly, at $2.50 a year. The *News* prospered for a few months during the boom of Gold Center, but stopped publishing early in 1907.

Gold Center News: (Sep 29 1906–c. 1907)
  NvHi — S 29 1906, Ja 12 1907
  film — S 29 1906, Ja 12 1907
Ref: files; GN Ja 12 1907; GT F 17 1907

GOLD CREEK

Gold Creek News

The *Gold Creek News* was begun at Gold Creek, seventy miles north of Elko, on December 24, 1896, by the Gold Creek News Publishing Company. The paper contained four pages with a patented inside, measured 15 by 22 inches, and sold for $2.50 a year. Charles MacKnight Sain, author of two novels, *Class of '95* and *An Expectant Heir to Millions,* was editor of the *News,* and used the front page to publish a serialized version of his third novel, *Tom Davis in Heaven*. About December 10, 1897, after nearly a year at Gold Creek, the *News* failed, and the plant was moved to Mountain City, where it was used to publish the *Times*.

Gold Creek News: (Dec 24 1896–Dec 10 1897)
  NvU — D 24 1896–D 10 1897
  film — D 24 1896–D 10 1897
Ref: files; RG D 23 1897

⇜❰GOLD HILL❱⇝

Gold Hill Daily News

The first number of the *Gold Hill Daily News* was issued on October 12, 1863, by Philip Lynch and his stepson, John H. Mundall, former publishers of the *Placer Courier* at Forest Hill, California. Its office was a solid brick building that had formerly housed Wells Fargo Express. Hiram R. Hawkins was editor. The *News* was a daily of 21 by 28 inches. It contained twenty-four columns, over eleven of which were advertisements, and sold for $16 a year. It did exceptionally well, and was enlarged by four columns after two months, remaining that size until its demise.

In the spring of 1865, Hawkins was appointed United States Consul to Peru, and resigned his editorial post on the *News* to owner Lynch on May 20. Lynch bought out Mundall to become sole editor and publisher on April 9, 1866. Mundall committed suicide by an overdose of morphine two years later.

Alf Doten became associate editor and reporter on November 14, 1867, and retained that position until the death of Philip Lynch on February 13, 1872. The following day Doten hoisted his name to the masthead as editor, in an attempt to preempt the position and forestall other would-be purchasers. Doten then wrote to aspiring senatorial candidate John P. Jones, to ask if he would either buy the paper or back Doten in doing so. When Jones declined, Doten convinced his political rival, William Sharon, to take a mortgage on the paper for $7,000. After raising $3,000 more through various loans, Doten bought the paper from Lynch's widow on March 9 for $10,000 — proudly counting it all out in $20 gold pieces. Thus he officially became sole editor and proprietor.

During the bonanza years of Gold Hill and Virginia City, the *News* was one of the leading political and mining journals of the state, but with the decline of the Comstock, the *News* also faded. By February of 1879, Doten was deep in debt, and when the paper was attached for $953.89, he was unable to borrow any more to pay it. Doten signed over full title to the *News* to politically ambitious Charles C. Stevenson in return for settling his debts. On February 21, proprietorship of the paper passed to Stevenson, under the firm name of the News Publishing Company, with Alf Doten remaining as managing editor, and W. P. Pratt as business manager.

The fortunes of the paper continued to decline, and on December 10, 1881, Doten left. Wells Drury, who worked with Doten on the *News*, tells the following tale of Doten's severance:

> Alf Doten was just placing the neck of the ginger-ale bottle across his thumb, as was his custom when called on to do his own pouring, when all at once his attention was attracted by a sign behind Charlie Price's bar. The sign read: "At Midnight All Drinks in this Saloon Reduced to Ten Cents."
> It was a terrible blow to the pride of Gold Hill, for up to that time the camp was able to boast the possession of one two-bit saloon.

"Thus passeth the glory of the world," exclaimed Alf.

"It doesn't seem to me that I can endure this humiliation," the veteran editor said, addressing a faithful companion who was always willing to stand by in such trying times.

The clock showed the hour to be 11:55. In a few minutes the brag of Gold Hill that it was able to support at least one first-class drinking place would be wiped out.

"I want to have the honor of buying the last two-bit drink in the old town," said Alf. He was asking a favor, but in this instance his companion was obdurate. "Let's shake dice to see who shall have the privilege," was the best he would grant.

So they rattled the bones and Alf won, but I never saw any winner more sorrowful.

The clock made a premonitory w-h-r-r-ing sound to indicate that the fateful hour was about to be struck.

"Here's to the departure of Gold Hill's glory and pride," was the toast they proposed, and they drank in silence.

"Not much use trying to run a nonpareil paper in a longprimer town any longer," said Doten. "I was willing to stick it out as long as there was a living chance, but now that there is nothing but ten-cent shebangs, the old *News* might as well suspend."

Thus, Alf Doten terminated his fourteen-year connection with the *News*. The following month, he left with his family for Austin to edit the *Reveille*. W. P. Pratt took over as editor with Pleasant Moore as local reporter. But four months later, on April 8, 1882, after what Doten termed "a lingering illness," the *News* died. Its costly plant was removed to Wood River, Idaho, where it was used to publish the short-lived Bellevue *Times*. Subsequently it was taken farther east, and ended up in a warehouse in charge of a Montana sheriff.

Gold Hill Daily News: (Oct 12 1863–Apr 8 1882)
 pvt — Ap 15 1865
 C — Ap 17 1865; N 6 1866; D 29 1868; F 2–3 1877
 CHi — Jl 4 1876
 CSmH — Jl 16, Ag 9 1864
 CU-BANC — O 12 1863–Ap 8 1882
 DLC — Ap 20–22, My 6–10, 24–29, 31, Je 2–10, 13–29, Jl 6–10, 13–14, 18, 20, 24, 31, Ag 22, S 1, 9, 12, 21, 23, 25, D 14 1865; Ap 21–D 1874
 ICHi — O 5 1876
 MWA — Ja 26 1866
 NNHi — My 2 1873
 NvHi — Ag 30, D 14 1866; N 3 1873; Ag 13 1874; Mr 4 1875; S 20 1881
 NvU — [Ap 11 1864–82]
 film — O 12 1863–Ap 8 1882
Ref: files; Doten 961, 1005, 1156–7, 1342–3, 1395, 1412–3; Angel 323–5; McMurtrie 300–1; Drury 237–8

Daily Morning Message

The daily Gold Hill *Message* was begun on May 23, 1864, by an association of printers, G. W. Bloor, D. M. Sandidge, J. S. M'Cann, and H. W. Johnson, under the firm name of George W. Bloor and Co. The *Message* was unable to break the monopoly already held by the Gold Hill *News,* and the paper was suspended after barely a month, on June 29, 1864. Shortly thereafter the material was taken to Carson City, where it was used for a time on the *Post.*

Daily Morning Message: (May 23 1864–Jun 29 1864)
   CU-BANC — Je 16 1864
   film — Je 16 1864
Ref: files; GHN My 23, Je 29 1864; Angel 325; McMurtrie 301

The People's Tribune

The first monthly to be published in Nevada was the *People's Tribune; Devoted to the Betterment of All Things, to the Defense of Right and to the People,* founded by Conrad Wiegand at Gold Hill. The prospectus, or sample copy, was issued on November 3, 1869, but regular issues did not commence until January of 1870. It was an eight-page affair, selling for 25¢ a copy. Wiegand was an assayer by profession and was intensely interested in the question of metals as a medium of exchange, writing copiously on this subject. Mark Twain had known Wiegand in Virginia City and several years later, in his book, *Roughing It,* Twain described him:

> If ever there was a harmless man, it is Conrad Wiegand of Gold Hill, Nevada. If ever there was a gentle spirit that thought itself unfired gunpowder and latent ruin, it is Conrad Wiegand. If ever there was an oyster that fancied itself a whale; or a jack-o'-lantern, confined to a swamp, that fancied itself a planet with a billion-mile orbit; or a summer zephyr that deemed itself a hurricane, it is Conrad Wiegand.

To Wiegand, the *Tribune* had a moral mission, it was a crusading magazine, which endeavored to become the "conscience of Washoe." Wiegand was both editor and proprietor and sent copies of the *Tribune* to prominent men throughout the nation, attempting to gain a wide circulation. However, his effort was unrewarded. To most, he was only fighting in a paper bag. The *Enterprise* job shop printed the first issue, but its business manager refused to have anything to do with subsequent issues, which he considered libelous. Wiegand responded with an extra edition accusing the *Enterprise* of trying to crush him. With the sixth number, in June of 1870, the *People's Tribune* spoke its last.

The People's Tribune: (Jan 1870–Jun 1870)
   CtY — Ja–Je 1870
   CU-BANC — F 1870
   MH — Ja–Je 1870
   MWA — Ap 1870
   NvHi — F 1870
   NvU — F 1870
   film — Ja–Je 1870
Ref: files; GHN N 3 1869, Ja 13 1870; TE F 1 1870; Twain 515

The People's Paper

In February of 1870, Conrad Wiegand, the quixotic editor and proprietor of the Gold Hill monthly magazine, the *People's Tribune,* announced:

> We have been urged to start an Evening Daily Paper. Upon reflection, and after ascertaining that it will be possible to secure the aid of experienced men in the business, we have decided to do so, provided we can secure nine hundred names as willing to take the papers ... and provided, also, we can obtain advertisements enough to pay. Thus far the names handed in do not much exceed *eight* hundred. The name of the paper is to be *The People's Paper.*

Whether he ever obtained sufficient subscribers or advertisers to start the paper is uncertain. If he did, it must have been very short-lived, for it seems to have left no other trace.

The People's Paper: (c. Feb 1870)
  No issues located.
Ref: PTR F 1870

The Golden Echo

The *Golden Echo* was a four-page literary paper published in October of 1874, during the fair at the Miner's Union Hall in Gold Hill, for the benefit of St. Patrick's Church. Mary Atchison, its editor, filled over half its columns with poetry.

The Golden Echo: (Oct 1874)
  No issues located.
Ref: GHN O 7 1874

Fraternal Visitor

The *Fraternal Visitor* was a small monthly started in April of 1881, at Gold Hill, by P. H. Mulcahy, Grand Secretary of the Independent Order of Good Templars, as the organization's statewide organ. It was printed at the *Enterprise* job shop in Virginia City, but distributed from Gold Hill.

Fraternal Visitor: (Apr 1881–c.1881)
  No issues located.
Ref: TE Ap 5 1881; GHN Ap 6 1881

Gold Hill News

On June 3, 1974, the *Gold Hill News* was revived by David W. Toll as a local color sheet. Aimed at the tourist trade, it tried to fill the place of the defunct *Territorial Enterprise.* The *News* was issued every fortnight until September 30, 1975, then suspended for eight months to be revived as a weekly on June 3, 1976. It continued as such until August 23 of the following year, then lay moribund for another year before issuing a final gasp on October 31, 1978.

Gold Hill News: (Jun 3 1974–Oct 21 1978)
   NvU — Je 3 1974–O 31 1978
   film — Je 3 1974–O 31 1978
Ref: files

~(GOLDFIELD)~

Goldfield News

In the spring of 1904, James F. O'Brien and R. E. L. Windle arrived at the booming tent camp of Goldfield with a press and material for the camp's first newspaper. Although most of their type was still buried in a freight jam on the road from Sodaville, they borrowed type and paper from the Tonopah *Miner* and recruited Rev. F. H. Robinson to help with the "type sticking." On April 29, they proudly issued the first number of the *Goldfield News,* to provide "All That's New and True in the Greatest Gold Camp Ever Known." O'Brien and Windle were joint editors and proprietors, issuing the *News* as an eight-page, six-column weekly. The *News* prospered, but poor health forced O'Brien's retirement, and on January 19, 1906, the paper was purchased by Charles S. Sprague, in the name of the Goldfield Publishing Company.

Sprague greatly enlarged the paper, making it the principal promotional paper for the southern Nevada mines and tripling its subscription list with *News* subscribers from every state and territory in the Union. On February 23, 1909, an evening edition, the *Daily News,* was added to the weekly. Both continued through the boom until March 18, 1911, when the rival Goldfield Tribune Printing Company purchased the *News* and John C. Martin became editor and manager. He suspended the daily edition and renamed the weekly the *Goldfield News and Weekly Tribune,* which he continued as an adjunct of the daily *Tribune.* V. L. Ricketts replaced Martin as editor and manager about January of 1914, and ran the paper until August of 1923. Two years later, the Esmeralda County Printing Company leased the paper and W. C. Lewis became editor.

On April 12, 1930, after the suspension of the daily *Tribune,* the Tribune Printing Company again took control, with W. H. Fording as editor and another name change for the weekly, to the *News and Tribune.* Al R. Hopkins became editor and manager on April 24, 1933. He was succeeded briefly by Amos H. Dow, on November 24, 1939, but returned to run the paper until about February of 1945. C. R. Terrell then bought the *News,* and sold it within a few months to a group known as the Prospector's Friend Inc., which installed Harold V. Lankford as editor.

On August 23, 1946, Robert A. Crandall took over as editor and proprietor. Hoping to gain new subscribers in Beatty, he began printing the inside of the paper as the *Beatty Bulletin* on April 25, 1947. After he purchased the *Tonopah Times-Bonanza,* in 1952, all of the printing was done there, and on December 28, 1956, he finally suspended the *News,* absorbing it into the Tonopah paper.

Goldfield News (weekly): (Apr 29 1904–Dec 28 1956)
  pvt — N 25, D 23 1904; Ja 27 1905
  CHi — Ja 26 1918
  CLCM — [F 1947–Jl 7 1950]

CSmH — Jl 1, 29 1904 [1911-29]
MWA — F 26 1926
NvHi — [1909-56]
NvMus — Ap 29, Je 17 1904
NvU — [1905-49]
film — [Ap 29 1904-56]
Goldfield News (daily): (Feb 23 1909-Mar 18 1911)
NvHi — [Ap 12 1909-Mr 18 1911]
NvU — [1909-11]
film — [Mr 9 1909-Mr 18 1911]
Ref: files

Weekly Market Letter

The first of the flood of brokers' promotional sheets to be issued from Goldfield was the *Weekly Market Letter,* sent out in the summer of 1904, by the firm of Elliott, Williams and Colburn, to entice potential investors and speculators. It was a small, 8 by 10-inch sheet, printed on one side only, and its longevity is unknown, but it probably lasted until the brokerage firm broke up in November.

Weekly Market Letter: (c. Aug 1904-c. Nov 1904)
NvMus — Ag 19 1904
Ref: files; BBM Ja 19 1907

Market Letter

In the fall of 1904, another Goldfield broker, G. S. Johnson, started a more enduring rival weekly *Market Letter.* It was an illustrated, four-page affair which promoted not only his Goldfield, but also Greenwater and Bullfrog, mining ventures. After he had sold all the stock he could, he finally suspended the *Letter* on April 20, 1907, announcing that the demand of the mining ventures on his time forced him to withdraw from the brokerage business.

Market Letter: (c. Fall 1904-Apr 20 1907)
pvt — [My 1906-Ap 20 1907]
Ref: files; DMR Ja 3, O 27 1905

Weekly Market Review

In November of 1904, C. H. Elliott joined with two other brokers, L. L. Patrick and Sol Camp, to form a new firm known as Patrick, Elliott and Camp, and they commenced a new promotional paper, the *Weekly Market Review.* Elliott died in February of 1906 but the firm and the paper lasted for at least another year.

Weekly Market Review: (c. Nov. 1904-c. 1907)
NvU — F, S 1906
Ref: files; DMR Ja 3 1905, Ap 2 1906, Ja 5 1907; BBM Ja 19 1907

Goldfield Vigilant

Goldfield's next paper was the exceedingly short-lived *Goldfield Vigilant,* which issued its first and possibly only number on January 30, 1905, under the banner "News of all that's new and true." No editor or publisher was listed, and although it contained considerable news, it may have been issued as an advertising sheet for the Kimball Development Company.

Goldfield Vigilant: (Jan 30 1905–c. 1905)
   CSmH — Ja 30 1905
   film — Ja 30 1905
Ref: files

The Goldfield Sun

Goldfield's first daily, the *Sun,* was founded on February 1, 1905, by Lindley C. Branson of the newly established daily *Tonopah Sun.* Branson was sole editor and proprietor and issued the paper every morning except Monday, as a four-page, 15 by 22-inch weekly at $12 a year. The *Sun* illuminated the scene for over eighteen months, but an I.W.W. boycott of the paper for its anti-union stance forced its suspension on September 22, 1906. The plant was purchased by J. M. Burnell, former business manager of the Denver *Rocky Mountain News,* to commence the daily *Tribune.*

The Goldfield Sun: (Feb 1 1905–Sep 22 1906)
   CSmH — [1905–6]
   film — [F 2 1905–S 22 1906]
Ref: files

The New Nevada

The New Nevada was a short-lived stock promotion weekly, started about May of 1905 by broker Volney B. Leonard. It boasted "The most complete list of stock quotations issued by any Goldfield operator."

The New Nevada: (c. May 1905–c. Jun 1905)
   No issues located.
Ref: DMR My 23, Je 5 1905

Semi-Monthly Bulletin

In the summer of 1905 the Goldfield Securities Company commenced its own promotional sheet, the *Semi-Monthly Bulletin.* It apparently folded early the following year.

Semi-Monthly Bulletin: (c. Aug 1905–c. 1906)
   No issues located.
Ref: DMR Ag 19, D 23 1905

Nevada Mining and Market Review

The *Nevada Mining and Market Review* was a weekly promotional sheet sent free to would-be investors and speculators in Nevada mining stocks, by the firm of D. MacKenzie and Co. of Goldfield, "mine operators and commission brokers," from the spring through fall of 1906.

Nevada Mines and Market Review: (c. Apr 1906–c. Oct 1906)
   pvt — O 22 1906
Ref: files; GN Ap 13 1906

Traders' Daily Gossip

The *Traders' Daily Gossip* was a speculator's tip sheet, issued by the brokerage firm of D. MacKenzie and Co., in the spring of 1906, as an adjunct of their weekly *Nevada Mining and Market Review.*

Traders' Daily Gossip: (c. Apr 1906)
   No issues located.
Ref: GN Ap 13 1906; DMR Ap 6 1906

Nevada Mining Securities Review

About the spring of 1906, the L. M. Sullivan Trust Company of Goldfield, a front for the infamous promoter Jacob S. Herzig, alias George Graham Rice, commenced a sixteen-page, free distribution monthly, the *Nevada Mining Securities Review.* It ran for nearly a year, luring investors to Rice's promotions, until he and Sullivan moved to Reno.

Nevada Mining Securities Review: (c. Apr 1906–c. 1907)
   No issues located.
Ref: GN My 11, S 29 1906; MT Je 15 1906

Nevada Mining News

The *Nevada Mining News,* containing the "Latest News from Bullfrog, Fairview, Goldfield, Manhattan, Searchlight, Round Mountain and all other Nevada Gold Camps," was started at Goldfield in the spring of 1906. No editor or publisher was listed but it was probably also the vehicle of George Graham Rice's Goldfield-Tonopah Advertising Agency. He ran the agency separately from his brokerage operation, the Sullivan Trust, which issued its own monthly promotional paper. Rice moved to Reno early in 1907 to start a new paper of the same name. (See Reno *Nevada Mining News*.)

Nevada Mining News: (c. Jun 1906–1906)
   NvMus — Je 14 1906
   film — Je 14 1906
Ref: files; MT Je 15, Jl 15 1906; BM Je 29 1907

Sporting Bulletin

The daily *Sporting Bulletin* was started at Goldfield about August 14, 1906, as part of the advance promotion for the Gans-Nelson fight. It was printed at the *Goldfield Review* office and published by Becker and Daly, who promised to expand to eight pages and an edition of 10,000 copies on the morning of the fight, September 3. The paper doubtless suspended that same day.

Sporting Bulletin: (c. Aug 14 1906–c. Sep 3 1906)
   NvMus — Ag 29 1906
   film — Ag 29 1906
Ref: files

Goldfield Tribune

The Goldfield *Tribune* was begun as a daily on September 24, 1906, on the former *Sun* plant, by J. M. Burnell and John C. Martin, with the former as manager and the latter as editor. Later in 1906, a Monday weekly was added to the daily edition, but in 1909, the John S. Cook bank attached the property. On August 25 the publishers became known as the Tribune Printing Company, with Martin continuing as editor. This firm purchased the *Goldfield News* in March of 1911, and, suspending the daily *News,* continued the weekly *News* as the weekly edition of the *Tribune.*

On April 19, 1916, V. L. Ricketts, who had been editing the *News,* also replaced Martin on the *Tribune,* and served as editor of both the *News* and *Tribune* until August 31, 1923. For the next two years no editor or manager was listed. During that time the paper was briefly suspended on October 18, 1924, when the plant was destroyed by fire, but revived on December 22, after citizens pledged $8,000 to form a new company. On August 28, 1925, W. C. Lewis leased the paper as the Esmeralda County Printing Company, and became editor. He ran the *Tribune* until "the shrinking popularity of Goldfield" forced its suspension on March 29, 1930. The weekly edition was still published as the *News.* (See *Goldfield News.*)

Goldfield Tribune (daily): (Sep 24 1906–Mar 29 1930)
   CHi — [F 6–O 18 1915] Ja 15 1916; Ja 25 1918
   NvGC — [1908–1930]
   NvHi — F 9, Ag 15, S 17 1907–Mr 29 1930
   NvU — [S 24 1906–Mr 29 1930]
   film — [S 24 1906–Mr 29 1930]
Ref: files; LCT F 27 1909; MVN N 8 1924

Goldfield Gossip

The first number of the *Goldfield Gossip,* "a monthly magazine devoted to extending knowledge of the mines and stocks of southern Nevada," appeared on October 1, 1906. Its editor was a charming rogue, Parmenter Kent, who doubled as a mining stock broker and used the paper to push his promotions, although he pretended that his advice "simply reflects the public opinion of Goldfield, as expressed on the street and in the clubrooms by the foremost men of the community." Goldfield was listed as the dateline, but it was actually printed in Carson City, and its subscribers were almost entirely from the East.

The *Gossip* was an interesting sheet, and it quickly grew from a monthly to a weekly, on January 18, 1907. Then, on March 9, apparently under pressure of exposure by his competitors, Kent surprised his readers by confessing that his real name was Sidney Flower and that he had previously been charged with mail fraud in a variety of schemes, including promotion of a nicotineless "health cigar," a chain of milk sanitariums, a magnetic ore separator, and a Colorado gold mine, through a magazine called *New Thought,* which he had published in the East. The implication, of course, was that he had now reformed, and many of his readers seem to have given him the benefit of the doubt. Although he had to cut the *Gossip* back to a monthly again in June, it did survive until the end of the speculative boom in January of 1908. The hushing of the *Gossip* may also have been hastened by U.S. postal authorities, who again brought mail fraud charges against Flower, alias Kent, but he simply started a new magazine, the *Yogi,* in Carson City. (See Carson City, *Yogi.*)

Goldfield Gossip: (Oct 1 1906–Jan 1908)
  DLC — O 1 1906–Ja 1908
  NvHi — Mr 16 1907
  NvU — Ap 3, My 4, 18 1907
  film — O 1906–S 1907
Ref: files; CA Ag 8 1910

Mines and Market

Mines and Market was a free weekly issued by Goldfield broker F. M. Dorsey in the fall of 1906, to advertise the stock in his pet promotions.

Mines and Market: (c. Oct 1906)
  No issues located.
Ref: CSMI O 22 1906

Goldfield Chronicle

The first number of the *Goldfield Chronicle* was published on November 22, 1906, by Horace A. Dunn of the Goldfield Chronicle Company. Dunn served as editor, issuing the paper every evening except Sunday, as an eight-page, 15 by 22-inch, Democratic daily. The *Chronicle* soon gained a circulation of 2,000, and on February 22, 1908, Dunn purchased the *Goldfield Review,* which he continued as the weekly edition of his daily under the firm name of the Goldfield Chronicle-Review Publishing Company, with George W. Long as manager. The new firm, however, was plagued by a $6,000 debt owed by the *Review* to the American Type Foundry. On February 22, 1909, the sheriff seized the paper for the John S. Cook bank, which took preemptive action, fearing an attachment by the foundry. Dunn and Long managed to get out a few more issues before the printing plant was sold, forcing suspension of the *Chronicle* on February 27. (See *Goldfield Review.*)

Goldfield Chronicle: (Nov 22 1906–Feb 27 1909)
  NvHi — [S 11 1907–F 27 1909]

NvMus — My 25 1907
NvU — [Je 5 1907–F 27 1909]
film — [My 25 1907–F 27 1909]
Ref: files

Nevada Mining Bulletin

In December of 1906, the short-lived *Nevada Mining Bulletin* made its debut in Goldfield. It was a free distribution, illustrated "Monthly Review of Mining in the Nevada Camps," published at 12-14 Ramsey Street by the Nevada Mining Bulletin Company. It was probably owned by the firm of M. B. Aston and Willis Sears, whose promotions it advertised, and whose office was at the same address.

Nevada Mining Bulletin: (Dec 1906–c. 1907)
NvU — D 1906
film — D 1906
Ref: files

The Little Mining Bradstreet

In March of 1907, Charles C. Coulter issued the first number of *The Little Mining Bradstreet* at Goldfield. It gave a critique of "200 of the best mining properties" in the Goldfield, Tonopah, Bullfrog, Manhattan, Wonder and Fairview areas. Coulter intended to issue it twice a year, in March and September, and sell it to the brokerage firms for distribution to their clients; but the second number apparently was never issued.

The Little Mining Bradstreet: (Mar 1907)
pvt — Mr 1907
Ref: files; CSMI Je 3 1907

Goldfield Review

T. D. Van Devort founded the *Goldfield Review* about October 27, 1904, at Columbia, Goldfield's northern suburb. He published the paper there for about three years, until March of 1907, when he moved the plant into Goldfield and revived the paper the following month. Forming the Review Publishing Company, he continued the *Review* as an eight-page, independent, Thursday weekly, selling at $5 a year.

Early the following year, on February 22, 1908, Van Devort sold the paper to Horace A. Dunn of the *Goldfield Chronicle,* who combined the two plants into the Chronicle-Review Publishing Company and continued the *Review* as a weekly edition of his daily *Chronicle.* Goldfield had become overcrowded with newspapers, however, having three weeklies and two dailies. On February 13, 1909, the *Review* was suspended, followed two weeks later by the *Chronicle,* which was sold under attachment by the sheriff. (See Columbia, *Goldfield Review.*)

Goldfield Review: (Apr 1907–Feb 13 1909)
NvHi — [S 28 1907; Ja 25 1908–F 13 1909]

NvU — [1907-8]
NvULV — Mr 7 1908
film — [Ap 20 1907-F 13 1909]
Ref: files; GC F 23, 26, 27 1909

Nevada Workman

The *Nevada Workman* was a short-lived venture commenced by the Goldfield local of the Industrial Workers of the World on August 17, 1907. It received limited support from the miners and was denounced by the *Goldfield Review* as the "mouthpiece of the radical and anarchistic element of the union." Phil S. Haley and Gladwin Bland shared the editor's chair and wrote its swan song, preserved in *Nevada, A Guide to the Silver State:*

> The editorial pork chop is becoming more and more elusive. The unprincipled but necessary advertiser is becoming more unprincipled and less willing. The enthusiatic subscriber grows more enthusiastic and beautifully less . . . All these circumstances render it improbable that the *Workman* will continue to be the weekly delight of its numerous intelligent and busted constituency. Vene, Vidi, Vici; which being interpreted in this case, means, "We came, we saw, we got it in the neck."

Nevada Workman: (Aug 17 1907-c. Feb 1908)
  NvU — S 7 1907
  film — S 7 1907
Ref: files; MM S 5 1907; GR F 15 1908

Goldfield Hotel Life

T. Lowe of the *Columbia Topics* issued the weekly *Goldfield Hotel Life* early in 1909. It was "devoted to the guests of Nevada's leading hotel . . . as exclusive medium for advertisers desirous of reaching a select clientage," but it apparently failed the same year.

Goldfield Hotel Life: (1909)
  No issues located.
Ref: PT F 24 1909

Goldfield News Letter

The *Goldfield News Letter* was another of the mining stock brokers' tip sheets that flowed from the camp. This one was published by J. C. Garinger and Co., from about October, 1910, to 1915.

Goldfield News Letter: (c. Oct 1910-c. 1915)
  NvHi — Ap 26 1915
Ref: files

Sprague's Newsletter

In 1912, following his sale of the *Goldfield News,* Charles S. Sprague commenced an irregular mining promotional sheet, *Sprague's Newsletter,* which lasted until 1916.

Sprague's Newsletter: (1912–1916)
   NvHi — 1912–6
Ref: files

Goldfield Post

On March 9, 1912, the *Goldfield Post* commenced with "a Hearty Invitation to the World to Come and Dig Wealth from the Nevada Hills." The *Post* was a Democratic weekly, published by the Goldfield Printing and Publishing Company, which consisted of P. J. Carney, Louis K. Koontz, John Knuz, and Dr. J. J. McCarthy. The paper prospered for a short while, but probably suspended sometime about 1914.

Goldfield Post: (Mar 9 1912–c. 1914)
   NvHi — My 25 1912
   film — My 25 1912
Ref: files; Folkes 53

Field of Gold

The *Field of Gold* was a booster paper begun at Goldfield, in September of 1915, by a promoter named Kingsland. Its editors promised to "confine themselves to the truth," which may have accounted for its brief career—apparently just a few months.

Field of Gold: (Sep 1915–c. Nov 1915)
   No issues located.
Ref: CO O 9, N 13 1915

Goldfield Enterprise & Esmeralda County News

Following the suspension of the *Goldfield News,* one brief attempt was made to revive a local paper. This was a diminutive, sixteen-page monthly, with the unwieldy title of the *Goldfield Enterprise & Esmeralda County News,* founded on February 1, 1958, by Oscar Morrisett, president and editor of Goldfield Enterprises Inc. It claimed to be the "biggest little newspaper in Nevada," and, selling for 20¢ a copy or $3 a year, it boasted a circulation of 10,000. Evidently the circulation was not entirely paid subscribers, however, as the *Enterprise* met its death the following November.

Goldfield Enterprise & Esmeralda County News: (Feb 1 1958–Nov 1958)
   pvt — F 1–N 1958
   film — F 1–N 1958
Ref: files

GOLDYKE

Goldyke Sun

Following the suspension of his *Goldfield Sun* in August of 1906, Lindley C. Branson of the *Tonopah Sun* attempted to extend his journalistic empire northward to the new camp of Goldyke, some sixty miles above Tonopah. There he established the short-lived daily *Goldyke Sun* in 1907, with postmaster Henry Trembly serving as editor. Lack of financial support and competition with J. Holman Buck's neighboring Atwood *Fairplay Prospector* caused its early suspension, however.

Goldyke Sun: (1907)
  No issues located.
Ref: Polk 1907–8; Folkes 114

⌒⁀(GOODSPRINGS)⁀⌒

Goodsprings Gazette

On May 20, 1916, during the World War I revival of mining activity at the old camp of Goodsprings, Frank A. Doherty issued the first number of the *Goodsprings Gazette.* Doherty was sole editor and proprietor, publishing the paper every Saturday as a four-page, six-column, Republican weekly, which sold for $2.50 a year. Doherty died within a year, and in February of 1917, his widow, Florence S. Doherty, took over as editor and publisher. The *Gazette* prospered for several years under her management, but finally suspended publication on May 21, 1921.

Goodsprings Gazette: (May 20 1916–May 21 1921)
  CHi — My 26 1917
  NvHi — [O 11 1919–My 14 1921]
  NvU — [Jl 29 1916–My 21 1921]
  NvULV — My 12 1917
  film — [Jl 29 1916–My 21 1921]
Ref: files

⌒⁀(GRANITE)⁀⌒

Granite Times

The *Granite Times* was a weekly begun at Granite on March 20, 1908, by Frank Eugene Bugbee. It was entirely handwritten, with pen and ink on brown paper, and illustrated with colored crayon drawings. Only seven copies of the first number were issued, but it attracted great interest in the camp and won advertising from several merchants. It apparently suspended with its seventh number, on May 1, 1908.

Granite Times: (Mar 20 1908–May 1 1908)
  NvHi — Ap 17, My 1 1908
  film — Ap 17, My 1 1908
Ref: files; WNM N 27 1909

⌒⁀(GRANTSVILLE)⁀⌒

Grantsville Sun

Grantsville was founded in 1863, but it was outshown by the radiance of Ione and Belmont until 1877, when the Alexander Company became interested in the mines in the vicinity. The company relocated the town and built a twenty-stamp mill. With the revival of Grantsville, D. L. Sayre moved a press and materials to the town, and on October 19, 1878, commenced publication of the *Grantsville Sun.* Sayre was sole editor and proprietor, and issued the *Sun* weekly for the "intellectual illumination of Nye County." Financial misfortune overtook him, however, and on April 16, 1879, "owing to the stringency of the times," and Sayre's "inability to make collections," the *Sun* set.

Grantsville Sun: (Oct 19 1878–Apr 16 1879)
  CU-BANC — O 19, N 30 1878–Ja 11, 22–F 19, Mr 6–Ap 16 1879
  film — [O 19 1878–Ap 16 1879]
Ref: files

Grantsville Bonanza

In late November of 1880, Samuel Donald purchased a half interest in the Belmont *Courier* from Andrew Maute, and two weeks later they extended their journalistic domain to Grantsville, thirty-six miles to the north. On December 11, 1880, they issued the first number of the *Grantsville Bonanza.* The paper was an independent weekly of twenty-four columns, 18 by 24 inches in size, dedicated to local interest. The *Bonanza* prospered under the wing of the *Courier,* and probably continued until the end of 1884.

Grantsville Bonanza: (Dec 11 1880–c. Dec 1884)
  pvt — My 7 1881
  NvHi — Jl 30 1881
  film — My 7, Jl 30 1881
Ref: files; BC N 27 1880

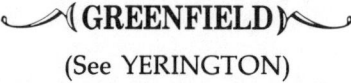
(See YERINGTON)

Inland Empire

In the winter of 1868, the promising bonanzas of the White Pine District were very attractive to two enterprising journalists, James J. Ayers and Charles A. V. Putnam. They purchased the entire plant of the Virginia City *Safeguard* and moved it to Hamilton, at great expense, in February of 1869. Here they established one of the most complete printing offices ever set up outside of a large commercial city. On March 27, 1869, they issued the first number of the daily *Inland Empire.* The paper was large and well conducted, prospering with the development of White Pine.

The following winter, Hamilton was named the county seat of White

Pine County, and in January of 1870, when the *White Pine News* moved down the hill from Treasure City, a fierce rivalry began. On January 18, Ayers wisely sold out his half interest to G. A. Brier. Within three months, on April 10, 1870, the *Inland Empire* suspended publication. Brier revived the *Shermantown Reporter* the following month, but died ten days later.

The *News* was a powerful Republican advocate, and during the gubernatorial campaign of 1870, the Democrats purchased the material of the *Empire* to support their cause. On October 4 of that year, George W. Cassidy revived the *Inland Empire,* continuing it until the end of the campaign. The paper finally suspended on November 9, 1870, and the material was sold to H. C. Patrick, who removed it to Stockton, California.

Inland Empire: (Mar 27 1869–Apr 10 1870; Oct 4 1870–Nov 9 1870)
   C — Ap 1 1869
   CU-BANC — Mr 27–D 31 1869; F 1–Ap 10, O 4–N 9 1870
   MWA — Mr 27 1869
   NvHi — Mr 27 1869
   NvU — Ap 15 1869–Ap 10 1870
   WHi — Je 16, S 21 1869
   film — [Mr 27 1869–Ap 10, O 4–N 9 1870]
Ref: files; Angel 330–1

White Pine News

The *White Pine News* was begun at Treasure City on December 26, 1868, by W. H. Pitchford and R. W. Simpson. Soon afterwards William J. Forbes assumed control, and, in January of 1870, he moved the daily *News* to the county seat at Hamilton, where it commenced on January 15. Under Forbes, the *News* was a strong Republican power and fought bitterly against the *Inland Empire,* forcing suspension of the latter in April. On April 22, W. H. Pitchford bought a half interest in the *News,* but sold it again, apparently the following year, leaving Forbes as sole editor and proprietor.

Forbes reduced the *News* to a weekly on November 23, 1872, and finally sold the paper on February 8, 1873, to Archibald Skillman and Fred Elliott. They changed its politics to Democratic. As the mines continued to decline, Elliott retired in 1875, and in November of 1878, Skillman at last suspended publication and transferred his capital and energy to the *Eureka Sentinel.* Several efforts were made to revive the *News* at Hamilton, but none were successful. The last attempt suspended on December 23, 1880, whereupon the plant was moved to Cherry Creek. (See Cherry Creek, *White Pine News.*)

White Pine News: (Jan 15 1870–Dec 23 1880)
   CU-BANC — Ja 15–Ag 1870; Mr 20–My 23 1872; O 16 1875–Ap 14 1877; Je 15 1878; My–D 16 1880
   ICHi — Jl 22 1876
   NvMus — Ja 20 1877
   NvU — [1870–6]

film — My 27–Ag 30 1870; [N 7 1872–S 13 1873; F 27 1875–D 2 1876]; Ja 20 1877
Ref: files; Angel 299, 330; McMurtrie 302

HARRIMAN
(See SPARKS)

HAWTHORNE

The Oasis

In the spring of 1881, the Carson and Colorado Railroad had its terminus at the south end of Walker Lake, where the railroad company laid out the townsite of Hawthorne. To promote the sale of town lots, the company held a special train excursion in April of that year, bringing 700 people down from the north to view the future metropolis. A number of members of the press took the excursion, and no fewer than five promised to found newspapers in the embryo community. As time passed, however, these threats proved to be merely hot air, and even the booming metropolis failed to mature as rapidly as was expected. By summer it contained only a few clapboard shanties, with little or no hope for the future.

Nonetheless, Orlando E. Jones decided to found a newspaper to share in the boom that he felt was sure to occur. In midsummer he moved the press and material of his former *Bentonian* from nearby Benton, California, to the dusty, new site of Hawthorne. There he set up his meager equipment, and on September 1, 1881, he commenced publication of a small weekly, the *Oasis*. It was yet to be a long time before the desert around Hawthorne would become an oasis, and it was nearly as distant a time before the town would need a newspaper. Still, Jones, a former circus clown, who would perform for even the smallest audience, was also willing to try to issue a paper for only a handful of subscribers. For six thankless weeks he produced a truly scintillating journal for the cluster of shanties that would someday be Hawthorne.

But the venture was hopeless and at last he admitted defeat. On October 6, he suspended the *Oasis*, lamenting:

> This is a world of sadness. It becomes the sad duty of the undersigned to announce that with this issue his connection with the *Oasis,* either as editor or manager, ceases. What may be the disposition of the paper hereafter will be the subject of a future announcement. The enterprise started as an experiment, and the experiment so far as this affiant is concerned, is a failure. It may be possible to publish a newspaper on one square meal a week; but to undertake to do so on one square a month, and hash only once in thirty-one days for the long months is a little more than human nature can stand. It might be done in Missouri but it will prove a dead failure every time in

Nevada. Hawthorne has a future before it, and we look for the building up of an inland town here of considerable importance. But printers, as a rule, are not wealthy enough to run newspapers for glory. If the *Oasis* should not be continued by other parties, and is really dead, it cannot be said that its life, though brief, was jolly. To those friends who have endeavored to aid the enterprise by patronage and encouragement we return our sincere thanks. Liberty and Nevada. Ta ta.

Orlando E. Jones

The *Oasis* was never revived, and sometime later Jones removed the material to Bodie, California, where he began an even shorter venture, the *Opinion*. This lasted for only three numbers in February of 1882, and the following month he used the material to commence the *Bodie Evening Miner*. This paper, at last, proved a success, providing Jones with a source of income for nearly a decade.

The Oasis: (Sep 1 1881–Oct 6 1881)
  NvHi — S 8 1881
  film — S 8 1881
Ref: files; BFP Ap 19, S 30, O 7 1881

Walker Lake Bulletin

On March 21, 1883, John M. Campbell began publication of the *Walker Lake Bulletin* at Hawthorne, although its masthead was dated one week earlier. Campbell was sole editor and proprietor, and published the paper every Wednesday, as a four-page, six-column weekly, selling it at a subscription price of $5 a year. During the election campaign of 1884, the paper was increased to a semiweekly from April 19 to November 5. On April 11, 1888, Campbell turned the editorship over to James T. Green, who held the post until July 4, after which he was replaced by Alfred J. McCarthy, brother of Denis E. McCarthy of the *Virginia Chronicle*.

McCarthy served as editor until December 24, 1890, when he purchased the plant from Campbell. As sole editor and proprietor, he ran the *Bulletin* until December 30, 1913, when his son, John A. McCarthy, became the publisher. John McCarthy enlisted in the army toward the end of World War I, and A. J. McCarthy again became sole editor and publisher on May 4, 1918. As such he continued the *Bulletin* until July 2, 1926, when the plant and the town were leveled by fire.

Walker Lake Bulletin: (Mar 14 1883–Jun 26 1926)
  pvt — Ap 17 1903
  CU-BANC — [Jl 4–D 26 1888]; O 9, D 25 1895
  NvHi — [1888–9]; S–O 1892; O 11 1919–D 15 1923
  NvU — [1883–5; 1889–1904]; Mr 21 1911–Ja 25 1919
  film — [Mr 14 1883–D 29 1905; Jl 3 1910; Mr 21 1911–O 25 1924]
Ref: files

Esmeralda Herald

On August 4, 1883, Malcolm M. Glenn suspended the *Esmeralda Herald* at Aurora, and sold the material, which was removed to the new town of Hawthorne. There the *Herald* was revived on August 18, by the Esmeralda Herald Publishing Company, with E. W. Taylor as business manager. They issued it as a four-page, 20 by 28-inch weekly, at a subscription rate of $5 per year. Hawthorne could not support two papers, however, and on November 24, 1883, the *Herald* passed into the hands of Oliver Needham, where it died on April 19, 1884.

Esmeralda Herald: (Aug 18 1883–Apr 19 1884)
  NvGC — 1877–82; 1884
  NvU — Ag 18 1883–Ap 19 1884
  film — [Oct 20 1877–Jl 29 1882]; Ag 18 1883–Ap 19 1884
Ref: files; EN My 4 1887

Esmeralda News

The *Esmeralda News* was begun at Hawthorne with the material of the former Candelaria *True Fissure,* on January 1, 1887, by the Esmeralda News Publishing Company. P. M. Bowler, Jr., served as editor, and S. H. Rosenthal as business manager. The paper was issued every Saturday, as a four-page, 23 by 32-inch weekly, at a subscription price of $5 a year. On September 22, 1888, Bowler retired from the editorship and Rosenthal became editor and manager. In the spring of 1889, Rosenthal was appointed clerk of Esmeralda County, and on May 18 of that year, he suspended the *Esmeralda News* to assume his new duties. The following year, W. W. Booth packed the material back to Candelaria, where he started the *Chloride Belt.*

Esmeralda News: (Jan 1 1887–May 18 1889)
  NvHi — Ja–D 1887
  NvU — [1887–9]
  film — [Ja 1887–My 18 1889]
Ref: files; CTF D 4 1886; PR Ja 15 1887; WLB My 21 1890

Hawthorne–Lucky Boy News

(See Lucky Boy, *Hawthorne–Lucky Boy News*)

Hawthorne Herald

In the spring of 1909, W. W. Booth suspended the *Rawhide Rustler* and moved the plant to Hawthorne, where he began the weekly *Hawthorne Herald* on April 23. Early the following month he bought the *Hawthorne–Lucky Boy News* and merged it with the *Herald,* renaming it the *Hawthorne–Lucky Boy Post.* (See *Hawthorne–Lucky Boy Post.*)

Hawthorne Herald: (Apr 23 1909–c. May 7 1909)
  No issues located.
Ref: RPT Ap 23 1909

Hawthorne–Lucky Boy Post

At the height of the boom at Lucky Boy, a short distance southwest of Hawthorne, W. W. Booth bought the plant of the *Hawthorne–Lucky Boy News* and combined it with his *Hawthorne Herald,* to form the *Hawthorne–Lucky Boy Post* on May 12, 1909. Booth was sole editor and publisher, printing the *Post* at Hawthorne as a Wednesday weekly and distributing it at Lucky Boy by stage. By October 2, 1909, the boom had collapsed and the paper suspended.

Hawthorne–Lucky Boy Post: (May 12 1909–Oct 2 1909)
   NvHi — My 12–O 2 1909
   NvMus — My 26 1909
   NvU — My 12–O 2 1909
   film — My 12–O 2 1909
Ref: files

Hawthorne News

After nearly twenty years' absence from the journalistic arena at Hawthorne, W. W. Booth reentered the contest with the establishment of the *Hawthorne News* on August 29, 1928. The early numbers of the *News* were printed at the *Bonanza* plant in Tonopah and shipped 106 miles to Hawthorne for distribution. Following his sale of the *Bonanza* to Frank Garside, in mid-November of 1929, Booth moved a portion of the *Bonanza* plant, together with the material of the defunct *Tonopah Miner,* to Hawthorne. There he continued the *News* as a Republican, Wednesday weekly, until October 3, 1934, when Joe Keno bought it. Keno ran the *News* for less than a year, suspending it on June 15, 1935, when he sold the plant to J. W. Connors and J. R. McCloskey of the *Independent.* They combined the two plants to form the *Mineral County Independent-News.* (See Hawthorne, *Mineral County Independent.*)

Hawthorne News: (Aug 29 1928–Jun 15 1935)
   pub — 1928–35
   NvHC — 1931–2
   NvHi — Ja 14 1931; My 24–Ag 23 1933; Ja 25–My 31 1935
   NvU — F 15–Je 14 1935
   film — Ja 14 1931; My 24–Ag 23 1933; Jl 18 1934–Je 14 1935
Ref: files

Mineral County Independent

In early 1933, J. W. Connors and Jack R. McCloskey quit the *Hawthorne News* and purchased the plant of the defunct Mina *Western Nevada Miner.* They moved it to Hawthorne to commence the rival *Mineral County Independent* on March 1, 1933. The first office of the *Independent* was an old frame building that had been hauled to Hawthorne from Lucky Boy several years earlier, to serve as a soft drink parlor during prohibition.

McCloskey served as editor, issuing the paper as a four-page, six-column, Republican weekly.

In June of 1935, Connors and McCloskey purchased the *Hawthorne News* and combined it with the *Independent,* changing its name to the *Mineral County Independent and Hawthorne News* on July 24. The paper prospered with the growth of Hawthorne. It was edited by Alvin D. Mann from November 24, 1943, until September 5, 1945, while McCloskey was in the service during World War II. Jack McCloskey became sole owner in 1954, and in 1979, the *Independent* was still owned and published by him, from a spacious brick office at 501 D Street.

Mineral County Independent: (Mar 1 1933+)
   pub — Mr 1 1933+
   NvHC — Mr 1 1933+
   NvHi — [Mr 8 1933+]
   film — [Mr 1 1933+]
Ref: files

The Rocket

The *Rocket* was launched in May, 1945, as a biweekly for the personnel of the U.S. Naval Ammunition Depot at Hawthorne. It was printed by the *Mineral County Independent,* with Paul Adams serving as editor.

The Rocket: (May 1945–c. 1947)
Ref: Gash

Mineral County Forum (Mineral County Democrat)

In January, 1960, R. M. Aalbu commenced the fortnightly *Mineral County Democrat* at Hawthorne, in competition with the *Independent.* He gained only marginal support, and in apparent hopes of attracting a wider audience, Aalbu changed its name on February 9, 1961, to the *Mineral County Forum,* explaining that "many people attach political connotation to the name Democrat." The name change had little effect, however, and he was forced to suspend the paper on September 6, 1961.

Mineral County Forum (Mineral County Democrat): (Jan 1960-Jan 26 1961)
   film — Ja 12–26, F 9, 23, Mr 8, My 17, Je–S 6 1961
Ref: TE F 10 1961; Folkes 102

The Times of Mineral County

Hawthorne's youngest paper, the *Times of Mineral County,* was begun on September 14, 1978, as a weekly, by the Aurora Investment Company, a group of seven local citizens led by Jo Gomez. A generously illustrated photo offset paper, edited by veteran newsman Fred S. Cook, it attracted a sustaining share of advertising.

The Times of Mineral County: (Sep 14 1978+)
   Nv — S 14 1978+

film — S 14 1978+
Ref: files

~(HAZEN)~

Hazen Harvest

The *Harvest* was founded at Hazen, a small ranching and farming community, on August 6, 1905, by J. R. Hunter and Reynolds of the Hazen Printing Company. They issued the *Hazen Harvest* as a nonpartisan weekly, selling for $1.50 a year. The paper's harvest was evidently not so large as they had hoped, however, and it was suspended, probably the following year.

Hazen Harvest: (Aug 6 1905–c. 1906)
  No issues located.
Ref: Ayer; TM Ag 5 1905; NSJ Ag 6 1905; WPN Ag 10 1905

~(HELENE)~

(See DELAMAR)

~(HENDERSON)~

Basic Bombardier (Big Job–Basic Magnesium Newsletter)

The weekly *Big Job–Basic Magnesium Newsletter* was begun on June 26, 1942, for the employees of the new Basic Magnesium plant at what is now Henderson. On May 7, 1943, it was renamed the *Basic Bombardier,* and was issued semimonthly, with W. Harold Kingsley as editor. On September 22, 1944, Guernsey Frazer took over the editorship, and in his hands it died on November 17, 1944.

Basic Bombardier: (Jun 26 1942–Nov 17 1944)
  Nv–Je 26 1942–N 17 1944
  film–Je 26 1942–N 17 1944
Ref: files

Hendersonian

Richard King also began a weekly, the *Hendersonian,* in 1942. But he soon surrendered the field to the rival *Big Job,* and moved to neighboring Las Vegas to start the *Tribune.*

Hendersonian: (c. 1942–c. Mar 1943)
  No issues located.
Ref: Folkes 25

Henderson Herald

(See Las Vegas, *Las Vegas Tribune*)

Henderson Home News

Morry M. Zenoff of the nearby *Boulder City News* commenced the *Henderson Home News* about October 24, 1947, as a weekly feature in the *Boulder City News.* He finally made it a separate paper in the 1950's.

Henderson Home News: (c. Oct 24 1947+)
  NvU — [S 3 1948–Ja 27 1950] in *Boulder City News;* [1959–68]
  film — [S 3 1948–Ja 27 1950]; 1958+
Ref: files

Henderson Star

The *Henderson Star* was an ephemeral weekly, begun in 1958, which lasted only about six months and disappeared in 1959.

Henderson Star: (c. 1958–c. 1959)
  No issues located.
Ref: Folkes 25

Nevada Jewish Chronicle

On August 18, 1961, Morry Zenoff of the *Henderson Home News* and *Boulder City News* launched a third paper, the *Nevada Jewish Chronicle,* the state's only "Anglo-Jewish Weekly." It apparently ceased publication in 1964.

Nevada Jewish Chronicle: (Aug 18 1961–c. 1964)
  pub — 1961–4
Ref: files

~(HERCULES)~

Hercules Miner

The *Miner* was a weekly that flourished briefly at the little camp of Hercules, which hoped for a time to rival Wonder as the principal camp of the Wonder Mining District. It was started about September of 1906, apparently by John L. Emerson and E. B. Clark, who ran the other *Miners* at Wonder and Fairview. Like the others, it undoubtedly folded after Clark decamped and was arrested on a bad check charge.

Hercules Miner: (c. Sep 1906–1907)
  No issues located.
Ref: FN N 11 1906; Polk 1907–8

~(HORNSILVER)~

Hornsilver Herald

On May 9, 1908, Earle R. Clemens of the *Rhyolite Herald* issued the first number of the *Herald* at Hornsilver, a camp that was then only two weeks old. Clemens was publisher and A. B. Gibson was mining editor. They issued the paper every Saturday, as a four-page, 15 by 22-inch, nonpartisan weekly. Within five weeks of its founding, Hornsilver boasted a population of 700 and an assortment of 220 frame buildings, tents, shacks, and sheds. The *Herald* shared in this brief but phenomenal growth then suspended sometime in the Fall.

Hornsilver Herald: (May 9 1908–c. Sep 1908)
   NvHi — [My 9–S 12 1908]
   film — [My 9–S 12 1908]
Ref: files

INCLINE VILLAGE

North Lake Tahoe Bonanza

The *North Lake Tahoe Bonanza* was started as a weekly on May 5, 1976, by Chapman Wentworth. In 1979 it was being published twice weekly, by David Trussell.

North Lake Tahoe Bonanza: (May 5 1976+)
   pub–My 5 1976+
Ref: pub

High Sierra Times

Larry Glickfeld of Avalanche Publishing, Inc., began the fortnightly *High Sierra Times* on November 26, 1976. John Wright was editor, promising to make it "A forum for politics, the environment, sports, social issues, literature and you." Wright was not editor for long, however, being followed in turn by Randy Dixon in March, 1977, Mike Sterling in May, 1977, and Michael Dougan in October, 1977. The *Times* apparently died about May, 1978.

High Sierra Times: (Nov 26 1976–c. May 1978)
   NvHi — N 26 1976–My 10 1978
   NvU — N 26 1976; Ja 19, S 1–14 1977
Ref: files

IONE

Nye County News

Three months after the organization of Nye County, Joseph E. Eckley and Henry De Groot moved a printing plant to the newly created county seat at Ione. There, on June 25, 1864, they issued the first number of the *Nye County News*. It was a Republican weekly of twenty columns, measuring 18 by 24 inches, and selling for $8 a year. In their first number, the publishers expressed doubt about the propriety of starting a paper at Ione at that time. These fears soon proved to be well founded and the paper was forced to suspend in less than two months.

Following the suspension of the *News,* John Booth issued a small paper, the *Advertiser,* for two months during the political campaign of 1864, but ceased publication after the election in November. Nye County was then without a paper until July 1, 1865, when Eckley revived the *Nye County News,* this time in a format nearer the size of the *Advertiser.* Eckley issued the paper each Saturday from his office on Main Street, as a single-sheet, ten-column weekly, at $8 a year. On August 26, he was joined by William Locker. Together they continued the paper until November of 1866, when Eckley was elected state printer. Locker apparently carried on the *News* alone until its final suspension in May of 1867. (See Ione, *The Advertiser.*)
Nye County News: (Jun 25 1864–Aug 1864; Jul 1 1865–May 1867)
   CSmH — Jl 2 1864
   CU-BANC — Je 25–Jl 9 1864; S 15 1866
   NvHi — Ag 11 1866
   NvTC — Jl 1–O 28 1865
   film — Je 25–Jl 9 1864; Jl 1–O 28 1865; Ag 11, S 15 1866
Ref: files; Angel 309; McMurtrie 302

The Advertiser

John Booth, a printer of practical experience in California, had come to Ione in the winter of 1863, but had very little luck in the mines. Following the suspension of the *Nye County News,* he decided to try to revive a paper in the county.

On September 17, 1864, he issued the first number of his new paper, *The Advertiser,* announcing: "The object for publishing the little 'ADVERTISER' is simply this, that as a matter of convenience for citizens of Nye county through which they may be enabled to advertise, mining notices, particularly, and speak of local matters, generally."

It was issued weekly on Saturdays as a Democratic journal. Booth tried to avoid the downfall of his predecessors by financing his paper solely on advertising and not being dependent on a rare, if not nonexistent, population of subscribers. He began the *Advertiser* on a small and cautious scale, planning to enlarge it as it became established. The first three numbers were printed on one side of a 9 by 12-inch sheet, but it was interestingly written and contained considerable news for its size.

On October 8, the Democratic County Convention was held at Ione, and John Booth was nominated for state assemblyman. With this incentive, he enlarged the paper to both sides of the sheet and began writing editorials slandering his Republican opponent, A. C. Bearss. Friends of Bearss soon retaliated by stealing the lever to Booth's hand press, thereby threatening suspension of the paper. However, Booth succeeded in replacing the lever with a piece of mountain mahogany, and the *Advertiser* was saved. Booth continued to defame his opponent up to the eve of the election. Then, wholly confident of success, he suspended the *Advertiser* on October 29 with the seventh number, and prepared to leave for Carson City. But Bearss was elected instead, and a dejected Booth returned for a time to California. Booth later returned to Nevada, and, after purchasing interests in several papers finally bought the Austin *Reese River Reveille,* which he ran until his death in 1886.

The Advertiser: (Sep 17 1864–Oct 29 1864)
   pvt — S 17–O 15, 29 1864
   NvTC — [S 17–O 29 1864]
   film — [S 17–O 29 1864]
Ref: files; RRR O 12 1864

⁓(JARBIDGE)⁓

Jarbidge Miner

Early in January of 1912, the *Miner* made a brief appearance at the new camp of Jarbidge, but its editor, publisher, frequency, and longevity are unknown.

Jarbidge Miner: (c. Jan 1912)
  No issues located.
Ref: RRR Ja 13 1912

⁓(JESSUP)⁓

Jessup News

The *Jessup News* was started in April of 1908, at the short-lived camp of Jessup, a dozen miles north of Huxley station on the Southern Pacific Railroad. Nothing is known of its owners or duration.

Jessup News: (Apr 1908–c. 1908)
  No issues located.
Ref: RH Ap 29 1908

⁓(JOHNTOWN)⁓

Gold-Cañon Switch

The first journalistic enterprise to be launched within the present bounds of the state of Nevada was a small, handwritten sheet, the *Gold-Cañon Switch.* It was started at Johntown, then in Utah Territory, about 1854, by Joseph Webb, a partner of "Old Virginy" Fenimore, for whom Virginia City was later named. Very little is known of this first paper except that it was probably issued monthly on letter paper and in a very small edition.

Gold-Cañon Switch: (c. 1854)
  No issues located.
Ref: De Quille 11

⸺(JUMBO)⸺

Jumbo Miner

George L. Sanford and W. P. Harrington founded the weekly *Miner* at the boom camp of Jumbo, in Washoe County, on April 4, 1908. During the few flush days, the editors proclaimed Jumbo to be, "one of the greatest coming young mining camps in the state of Nevada or the world," but they evidently suspended the paper with the first sign of decline, on July 25, 1908.

Jumbo Miner: (Apr 4 1908–Jul 25 1908)
  NvHi — [Ap 4–Jl 25 1908]
  NvU — [My 16–Jl 15 1908]
  film — [Ap 4–Jl 25 1908]
Ref: files

⸺(JUNCTIONVILLE)⸺

Bugle

The weekly *Bugle* was a manuscript paper started about February of 1880, at Junctionville, more commonly known as Bonelli's Ferry, on the Colorado River at the mouth of the Virgin River. It was written on letter sheets by the ferryman's son, Leonard Bonelli, who listed himself as editor and the Bugle Publishing Company as publisher.

Bugle: (c. Feb 1880–c. 1880)
  No issues located.
Ref: PR F 28 1880

⸺(KEARNS)⸺

Nevada Slogan

In September of 1909, the *Nevada Slogan* made its debut at the new camp of Kearns, in the Cortez Mining District. Its editor and publisher are unknown, and its duration was probably but a few months.

Nevada Slogan: (Sep 1909–c. 1909)
  No issues located.
Ref: NSJ S 27 1909

⸺(KENNEDY)⸺

Nevada New Era

The mines at Kennedy were discovered in 1891, and by 1894, several mining companies had begun operations and the boom was on. During the height of the excitement, Frank Francis closed down his weekly *Nevada New Era* at Lovelock and moved the plant to the new camp, where he revived it as the semiweekly *Nevada New Era* on June 23, 1894. Francis used the paper to promote not only the new camp but also his own campaign for the state assembly. Though the boom camp collapsed that winter, Francis, winning the assembly seat, closed up the paper about December 30, and headed for the capital.

Nevada New Era: (Jun 23 1894–Dec 30 1894)
   NvHi — Jl 14, Ag 4 1894
   film — Jl 14, Ag 4 1894
Ref: files; LA Je 29 1901; LRM Ja 7 1927

KIMBERLY (KIMBALL)

Kimberly News

The weekly *News* was commenced on February 17, 1910, to serve the new camp of Kimberly in Lander County. It was published by the Kimberly Publishing Company, and printed in Battle Mountain, twenty-four miles away. Because there was already a town of the same name in White Pine County, the Lander camp was renamed Kimball that fall. The paper, however, kept its original name until its suspension on December 17. Its editors claimed they were just taking a Christmas vacation, but they never resumed.

Kimberly News: (Feb 17 1910–Dec 17 1910)
   NvHi — [F 17–D 17 1910]
   NvU — [F 17–D 17 1910]
   film — [F 17–D 17 1910]
Ref: files

KINGSTON

Ghost Town Gazette

The *Ghost Town Gazette* was a small, mimeographed weekly that briefly brought life to a transient relief camp in Kingston Canyon in southern Lander County. It was begun in early May of 1934, by Don Laurie, who served as editor, assisted successively by Jay Divison and William Morgan, who enlivened its pages with cartoons. By summer, however, the ghosts had returned to Kingston Canyon.

Ghost Town Gazette: (May 1934–c. Jun 1934)
   No issues located.
Ref: NSJ My 13 1934; AS Je 9 1934

⁓❨ LAKE PEAK ❩⁓

Lake Peak News

When the Walker Lake Reservation was thrown open to mining on October 29, 1906, over two thousand prospectors and adventurers rushed in, in a wild dash reminiscent of the Oklahoma land rush. Most staked out mining claims, a few laid out townsites, such as Lake Peak, and one sat down with pencil and pad and dashed off the district's first newspaper, the *Lake Peak News*. Its enterprising publisher is unknown but he may have been F. Eugene Bugbee, who seventeen months later issued a little handwritten paper at Granite, just to the north.

Lake Peak News: (Oct 29 1906–c. 1906)
   No issues located.
Ref: CCS N 10 1906

⁓❨ LANDER ❩⁓

(See TENABO)

⁓❨ LAS VEGAS ❩⁓

Las Vegas Times

On March 25, 1905, James Brown and Frank L. Reber, from Montana, commenced the Las Vegas *Times,* the first newspaper at the huddle of tents that was to become Las Vegas. Brown and Reber both served as editors and issued the *Times* every Saturday, as a four-page, 16 by 22-inch, Republican weekly, at $3 a year. The *Times,* the *Advance,* and the *Age,* which appeared within the next two weeks, quickly engaged in a rivalry for subscribers and advertisers. But both the *Times* and the *Advance* ultimately yielded to the *Age,* and on November 3 of the following year, Brown and Reber suspended the Las Vegas *Times* after commencing the *Greenwater Times* on October 23, 1906.

Las Vegas Times: (Mar 25 1905–Nov 3 1906)
   NvU — [Ap 1 1905–N 3 1906]
   film — [Ap 1 1905–N 3 1906]
Ref: files; PR Mr 31 1905

Advance

The *Advance,* Las Vegas's second paper, was founded one week after the *Times,* on March 31, 1905, by W. W. Wallace, a well-known editor from Ogden, Utah. Wallace was sole editor and proprietor, issuing the paper every Friday as an eight-page, 13 by 20-inch, independent weekly, at $3 a year. The *Advance* soon lost out in the competition between the *Age* and the *Times*, and it was suspended probably the following year.

Advance: (Mar 31 1905–c. 1906)
  No issues located.
Ref: PR Ap 7 1905

Las Vegas Age

On April 7, 1905, only two weeks after the establishment of the *Times*, C. W. Nicklin founded the third newspaper, the *Age*, at the chaotic tent camp of Las Vegas, whose swelling population eagerly awaited the completion of the railroad from Salt Lake to make it the supply center for the new camps at Bullfrog and Greenwater. Nicklin further expanded his holdings the following day by founding the *Bullfrog Miner* at distant Beatty. The *Age* was edited and published by Nicklin each Saturday, as a six-page, independent weekly, at $2 a year. When the railroad reached Las Vegas two months later, the town boomed, carrying with it the *Age*, the *Times* and the *Advance*. A spirited journalistic duel among the three papers ensued, ending the following year in complete victory for the *Age*.

It was only a brief triumph, however, for the *Age* was soon involved in lengthy competition with new rivals. In the meantime, however, Nicklin left the paper in the hands of Charles C. Corkhill, manager and later editor, turning his attention to the *Beatty Bullfrog Miner*. Two years later, on June 20, 1908, he sold the *Age* to Charles P. Squires, who became sole editor and proprietor and stayed with the paper for nearly forty years.

On February 27, 1928, the *Age* was enlarged to a semiweekly, followed by a triweekly edition on April 24. Ultimately, on May 6, 1931, it became a daily, but on January 6, 1934, it was again reduced to a weekly. About 1943, ownership of the paper passed to Service Printers, Inc., and some two years later it was purchased by Frank F. Garside, publisher of the rival daily *Review-Journal*. Despite these changes, however, Squires was retained as editor, remaining until the suspension of the *Age*, on November 30, 1947.

Las Vegas Age: (Apr 7 1905–Nov 30 1947)
  CHi — F 6, Je 27 1915
  NvHi — Ap 7 1905–Jl 25 1907; Ag 15 1908–N 30 1947
  NvU — S 21 1907–N 30 1947
  NvULV — [Je 28 1913; Jl 1915–S 1917; F 1919–28; 1930–3; 1939–40, 1944]
  film — [Ap 7 1905–N 30 1947]
Ref: files; PR Ap 14 1905; SB Je 26 1908

Las Vegas Review (Clark County Review)

On September 18, 1909, Charles C. Corkhill, left without a job when C. P. Squires bought the *Age*, reentered the journalistic arena with a paper of his own, the *Clark County Review*. Corkhill published the paper as a Democratic weekly until March 3, 1922, when he leased it to his editor, T. S. Trebell, who dropped Clark County from the name and added Las

Vegas. On October 6 of the same year John H. Lightfoot and W. F. Rector leased the paper with Lightfoot serving as editor until March 2, 1923. Rector edited the paper by himself for only six weeks before Corkhill resumed control on April 20. Then his wife May Corkhill became publisher on October 3, 1924. She finally sold the *Review* on May 7, 1926, to Frank F. Garside, who hired A. E. Cahlan as editor. Garside increased the issue to a semiweekly on September 7, 1926, to a triweekly on March 26, 1928, and finally to a daily on January 28, 1929. Soon after he forced the capitulation of the new rival *Journal,* and on July 20, 1929, he combined the two papers to commence the *Review-Journal.* (See *Las Vegas Review-Journal.*)

Las Vegas Review: (Sep 18 1909–Jul 18 1929)
  pub — 1909–29
  CHi — F 6 1915; F 16 1918
  NvHi — [Ja 8 1910–Jl 18 1929]
  NvU — [S 18 1909–Ja 25 1919; 1920–Jl 18 1929]
  film — [S 18 1909–Jl 18 1929]
Ref: files

The Bulletin

The *Bulletin* was a short-lived paper begun at Las Vegas about April of 1914, by A. W. Jurdan. It was devoted to "exposing such rottenness as we have had" in public works contracts and was issued erratically.

The Bulletin: (c. Apr 1914)
  NvULV — Ap 20 1914
  film — Ap 20 1914
Ref: files

Keys to Hidden Treasure

Following the collapse of his billion-dollar railroad scheme through the bottom of the Grand Canyon, which he had promoted in his Logandale *Oak,* Charles MacKnight Sain moved to Las Vegas to launch a new promotion, the Argus Research Corporation. To further this endeavor, in September of 1926, he started an occasional magazine, *Keys to Hidden Treasure,* which he explained was the "House Organ of the Argus Research Corporation for the Information of Argus Stockholders and Propective Stockholders." Later that year or early the following year he renamed it simply *The Argus,* but its role remained the same. (See Las Vegas, *The Argus.*)

Keys to Hidden Treasure: (Sep 1926–c.1926)
  NvHi — S 1926
  film — S 1926
Ref: files

The Argus

In the latter part of 1926 or early 1927, Charles MacKnight Sain changed the name of his promotional organ for his Argus Research Corporation from *Keys to Hidden Treasure* to *The Argus*. As such, it apparently finally folded sometime later that year. (See Las Vegas, *Keys to Hidden Treasure*.)

The Argus: (c. 1926–c. 1927)
   NvHi — F 1927
   film — F 1927
Ref: files

Las Vegas Journal

The *Journal* was founded at Las Vegas on March 29, 1929, by former governor James G. Scrugham. George Ellis was editor and the paper was issued as an independent weekly. Since the paper was printed in Los Angeles and shipped to Las Vegas for distribution, it offered poor competition to Frank Garside's *Review*. Nonetheless, Garside soon bought out the paper, suspending it on July 13, 1929, and merging it with his own paper to found the daily *Review-Journal* on July 19. (See *Las Vegas Review-Journal*.)

Las Vegas Journal: (Mar 29 1929–Jul 13 1929)
   NvU — Mr 29–Ap 5 1929
   NvULV — Mr 29 1929
   film — Mr 29–Ap 5 1929
Ref: files

Las Vegas Review-Journal

Following his purchase of the weekly *Las Vegas Journal,* Frank F. Garside merged it with his *Review,* and on July 19, 1929, commenced the daily *Review-Journal,* with A. E. Cahlan continuing as editor. On April 1, 1949, Donald W. Reynolds purchased the paper, keeping Cahlan as editor, and later promoting him to managing director. The *Review-Journal* grew with the boom of Las Vegas, and by 1956, it had surpassed all other papers in the state in daily circulation. In the meantime Reynolds was expanding his publishing empire with the acquisition of the Ely *Times* and *Record* about 1951, and the Carson City *Nevada Appeal* and *Chronicle* in 1962.

When Cahlan retired in April of 1961, the managing directorship passed to Fred W. Smith. Robert Brown was editor in 1962, followed by Joe Digles in 1964. James Leavy, former editor of Reynolds's Carson *Appeal,* became editor about 1966, and was followed by Don Digilio about 1969.

Las Vegas Review-Journal: (Jul 19 1929+)
   pub — Jl 19 1929+
   C — Jl 1 1955+
   CLCM — S 17 1930
   NvHi — Jl 19 1929+
   NvU — Jl 19 1929+
   NvULV — [1930–74]
   film — Jl 1929+
Ref: files

Desert Sun

In August of 1931, the Desert Sun Publishing Company, with A. L. Fink, president and publisher, commenced the daily *Desert Sun* at Las Vegas. Trying to win support, it struggled for over two months before it failed.

Desert Sun: (Aug 1931–c. Oct 1931)
   NvULV — O 12, 21 1931
   film — O 12, 21 1931
Ref: files

Las Vegas Times

The name of Las Vegas's pioneer paper, the *Times*, was revived in July, 1932, by William E. Stinson, in an unsuccessful bid for a share of the town's newspaper patronage. The paper was published weekly by Stinson, with Charles S. Doherty as editor, but the new *Times* fared even more poorly than its namesake, folding on July 25, when it shut down for what was supposed to be only a two-week vacation.

Las Vegas Times: (c. Jul 1932–Jul 25 1932)
   NvULV — Jl 18, 25 1932
   film — Jl 18, 25 1932
Ref: files

Nevada Mining Bulletin

The *Nevada Mining Bulletin* was launched at Las Vegas, about December of 1932, by A. G. Hillen as sole editor and publisher. Hillen issued it twice monthly for about two years, cut it back to a monthly for a year, then to every two months, and finally stopped it entirely about May, 1936.

Nevada Mining Bulletin: (c. Dec 1932–c. May 1936)
   DI-GS — S 1, O 15 1934; Mr 15, Je 1935; Mr–My 1936
Ref: files

The Cloudburst

The *Cloudburst*, "Published Every Now and Then in the Interest of Highway 91," was begun at Las Vegas in 1933. Jim Woolley was editor and publisher and Bill Wallace was advertising manager. It dried up in 1934.

The Cloudburst: (1933–1934)
   NvULV — Ja 1934
   film — Ja 1934
Ref: files

Las Vegas News

The *Las Vegas News* was an ephemeral weekly begun on January 23, 1941, by the Nevada Publishing Company, with Bill Busick as editor. It was printed in Los Angeles and apparently folded within two months.

Las Vegas News: (Jan 23 1941–c. Mar 20 1941)
   NvULV — Ja 23–30, F 13–Mr 6, 20 1941
   film — Ja 23–30, F 13–Mr 6, 20 1941
Ref: files

Las Vegas Tribune

The *Las Vegas Tribune* was started as an independent weekly on April 2, 1943, by Richard King as editor and publisher. King published it for barely three months before he sold it, on July 11, to Joseph B. Bates, who hired L. V. "Lou" Africa as editor. Bates in turn sold the paper to the Tribune Publishing Company on August 8. They hired Marc Wilkinson as editor, and expanded it to a daily on November 21, as the *Morning Tribune.* Will Freeman bought the paper in 1944, and replaced Wilkinson as editor. The *Tribune* was never able to gain even as large a circulation as that of the waning *Age,* and about January, 1946, it was reduced to a weekly again, as the *Las Vegas Tribune and Henderson Herald,* with Richard King again editor. It folded soon after.

Las Vegas Tribune: (Apr 2 1943–1946)
   NvHi — [Ap 2 1943–My 27 1944]
   Nv — Jl 5, 12 1946
   film— [Ap 2 1943–Jl 12 1946]
Ref: files

Nevada Life

The monthly *Nevada Life* was started at Las Vegas in September, 1945, by Len Weissman, who was both its editor and its publisher. It suspended the following May but revived briefly in November with Louis Rangno added as editor.

Nevada Life: (Sep 1945–May 1946; Nov 1946)
   NvHi — S 1945–My 1946; N 1946
Ref: files

Las Vegas Hangover

On January 10, 1946, Harriet Merry started the *Las Vegas Hangover,* a lively weekly magazine that promised to give the "Low Down on Las Vegas." It was "circulated in every major Hotel, Auto Club, C. of C., Auto, Bus and Air Terminals in the eleven western states." Merry also hoped it would serve "as a guide post for Hollywood actors' agents," but it probably succumbed within a month.

Las Vegas Hangover: (Jan 10 1946–c. Feb 1946)
   NvULV — Ja 31 1946
Ref: files

Nevada Veteran

The *Nevada Veteran,* "Operated and Controlled by Nevada Veterans for Nevada Veterans," was a short-lived twice-monthly begun at Las Vegas in January, 1946. It was published by Desert Enterprises, Inc., with Kenneth O'Connell as advertising manager. No editor was listed.

Nevada Veteran: (Jan 1946–c. 1946)
   NvHi — Ap 17, 30 1946
   NvU — Ap 17, 30 1946
   film — Ap 17, 30 1946
Ref: files

The Shopper

The weekly *Shopper,* with Marge Kent as editor and publisher, first appeared on February 13, 1947. It disappeared a few months later.

The Shopper: (Feb 13 1947–1947)
   NvULV — F 13–27, Mr 13 1947
Ref: files

Free Press

In April of 1950, the printers of the International Typographical Union went on strike against the *Review-Journal,* and on May 3, they commenced an opposition daily, the *Free Press.* It was published for less than two months. Then on June 30, it was sold for $1,000 to Herman M. "Hank" Greenspun, who changed the name to the *Las Vegas Sun* the following day. (See *Las Vegas Sun.*)

Free Press: (May 3 1950–Jun 30 1950)
   NvULV — My 3, 5, 8, Je 28, 30 1950
Ref: files

Fabulous Las Vegas Magazine

Jack Cortez began the weekly *Fabulous Las Vegas Magazine* about April 16, 1949, as an entertainment guide. The publication passed to E. B. Cortez in April of 1967, and it ceased in 1973.

Fabulous Las Vegas Magazine: (c. Apr 1949–1973)
   NvULV — [Mr 4 1950–73]
Ref: files

Las Vegas Sun

Following his purchase of the *Free Press* plant, Herman M. "Hank" Greenspun commenced the daily *Las Vegas Sun* on July 1, 1950. Greenspun immediately engaged Al Cahlan of the *Review-Journal* in what was the liveliest and most vitriolic editorial duel witnessed in Nevada in some eighty years. Greenspun has been refreshingly outspoken on many issues, and probably the highest point in his career was his trial in 1955, for sending through the mail "matter of an indecent character tending to incite murder or assassination." Needless to say, this "matter" was a copy of his *Las Vegas Sun,* the January 8, 1954, issue of which contained a Greenspun editorial beginning, "I've never been one to make predictions but when a thing is inevitable, even I can foresee the future. Sen. Joe McCarthy has to come to a violent end. Huey Long's death will be serene and peaceful compared with the demise of the sadistic bum from Wisconsin." The trial was reported seriocomically in his paper, and his final acquittal was anticlimactic. Ever the crusader, Greenspun next took on Nevada Senator Patrick McCarran, then the underworld, and survived them all.

Las Vegas Sun: (Jul 1 1950+)
   pub — Jl 1950+
   C — Mr 20 1955
   NvULV — S 3 1961; Ag 30 1975
   film — Ja 5 1951+
Ref: files; Greenspun

Nevada Citizen

The *Nevada Citizen* was a labor weekly begun at Las Vegas in 1951. It was published by the Nevada State Federation of Labor and edited by B. J. Lydon. The paper suspended about 1956, but was soon revived, at least in spirit, by the *Southern Nevada Labor Beacon.*

Nevada Citizen: (1951–c. 1956)
   CU-BANC — 1955–6
   NvHi — Ap 10 1954–Je 18 1955
   NvULV — Ag 30 1952
   film — [Ap 17 1954–F 18 1956]
Ref: files

Magazine Las Vegas

Magazine Las Vegas was launched as a semimonthly on July 15, 1951, by Les Perry and Tom Magowan, but it was soon reduced to a monthly. In August, 1952, Magowan became sole editor and publisher, continuing as such until it ceased about May of 1956.

Magazine Las Vegas: (Jul 15 1951–c. May 1956)
   NvULV — [Jl 15 1951–My 1956]
Ref: files

Independent

On September 12, 1955, Guy D. Loucks commenced the *Independent* at Las Vegas, to do battle with Hank Greenspun's *Sun.* Loucks served as editor, issuing the paper as a Monday weekly, but the engagement was brief and the *Independent* suspended after about half a dozen issues.

Independent: (Sep 12 1955–c. Oct 1955)
  No issues located.
Ref: Averett

West, The Voice of Western America

West, a quarterly magazine, was begun in the fall of 1956, by Everett L. Storey, editor and president of West Magazine, Inc. It is a 64-page news and feature magazine.

West, The Voice of Western America: (Fall 1956+)
   pub — 1956+
   pvt — 1956+
Ref: files

Nevada Democrat

Dean W. "Diamond Tooth" Miller commenced the bimonthly *Nevada Democrat* at Las Vegas about May, 1958, and ran it until its demise in September, 1976.

Nevada Democrat: (c. May 1958–Sep 1976)
   Nv — [My 1969–S 1976]
   NvHi — Ag 4 1962; O 1974
   NvULV — [1962–9]; 70–5
Ref: files

The Nellis Century

The Nellis Century was launched in 1958, by Dick Arnst, publisher, and James E. Kosmo, editor, for free, weekly circulation among the personnel of Nellis Air Force Base. In 1963, it was published by Service Publications, Inc., and later in the 1960's by the *North Las Vegas Valley Times,* who continued it until December, 1973.

The Nellis Century: (1958–Dec 1973)
   NvU — N 15 1963
   film — N 15 1963
Ref: files

Southern Nevada Labor Beacon

George W. Wilkinson commenced the *Southern Nevada Labor Beacon* at Las Vegas in 1958. It was a Monday weekly, with Wilkinson as editor and publisher, and as the title indicates, was devoted to the interests of labor in the region. It apparently suspended about 1969.

Southern Nevada Labor Beacon: (1958–c. 1969)
   No issues located.
Ref: Ayer 1963–8

Las Vegas Magazine

Las Vegas Magazine was apparently started in the early 1960's, as a revival of *Magazine Las Vegas.* It was published monthly by Jack Murray until about 1966.

Las Vegas Magazine: (c. 1960–1966)
   NvULV — Jl 1964; Ja 1966
Ref: files

Southern Nevada Labor News

In 1961, the Building and Construction Trades Council of Las Vegas commenced their own paper, the *Southern Nevada Labor News,* with Glenn C.

Vaux as publisher, to rival Wilkinson's *Beacon*. The *News* was published monthly by an editorial committee of the council until 1979.

Southern Nevada Labor News: (1961–1979)
  Nv — 1970–9
  NvU — [1963]
  NvULV — [1965–8] 69–79
Ref: files

This Is Las Vegas

This Is Las Vegas was a slick entertainment magazine begun about 1961, by the Nevada Club of Las Vegas. It was published monthly in issues of 30,000 and distributed on Bonanza, Western, and Pacific Airlines.

This Is Las Vegas: (c. 1961–?)
  No issues located.
Ref: Myrick

Las Vegas Playground

Las Vegas Playground was a bimonthly magazine began in February, 1962, by United Publications, Inc., with Charles R. Bell, president, and Louis L. Kimzey, editor. Kimzey became editor and publisher for the Kimtex Corporation of Hollywood in October, 1963, but the magazine apparently folded soon after.

Las Vegas Playground: (Feb 1962–1964)
  NvULV — [F 1962–Ja 1964]
Ref: files

Las Vegas Voice

Dr. Charles I. West started the city's first black newspaper, the weekly *Las Vegas Voice,* about October of 1963. It gained solid support and prospered.

Las Vegas Voice: (c. Oct 1963+)
  film — Ja 1964–7
Ref: files

Vegas Visitor

The *Vegas Visitor* was begun as a monthly entertainment guide in December, 1964, by Herb Hanson and Robert Campbell, editors and publishers. It became a weekly in November, 1967. In 1979, Campbell was sole publisher and Bob Chavez was editor.

Vegas Visitor: (Dec 1964+)
  pub — D 1964+
  film — My 2 1969+
Ref: files

Las Vegas Israelite

The *Las Vegas Israelite,* "serving the welfare and growth of the Jewish

Community," was begun on January 29, 1965, by Jack Tell, editor and publisher. It has flourished under the slogan "for those who deserve the best."

Las Vegas Israelite: (Jan 29 1965+)
  film — Ja 29 1965+
Ref: files

Veteran's Journal

The monthly *Veteran's Journal,* "the only Nevada Veteran's Newspaper Published by Veterans," was apparently begun about April of 1965, by the Veteran's Journal, Inc., with Roland C. Bartlett as editor. It seems to have suspended about November of 1971, to become the *Democratic News.* (See Las Vegas, *Democratic News.*)

Veteran's Journal: (c. Apr 1965–c. Nov 1971)
  film — My–Je, Ag 1971
Ref: files

Las Vegas Life Magazine

Maury and Muriel Stevens launched the monthly *Las Vegas Life Magazine* in May, 1966, and Joy Hamann was listed as editor. The magazine died in November, 1967.

Las Vegas Life Magazine: (May 1966–Nov 1967)
  NvULV — My 1966–N 1967
Ref: files

Las Vegas Changing Times

The *Changing Times,* an "underground paper ... with ideals and goals and crusades of youth" began on April 1, 1968. It was issued weekly by George D. French and lasted until July 4.

Las Vegas Changing Times: (Apr 1 1968–Jul 4 1968)
  NvU — Ap 1–Jl 4 1968
Ref: files

Las Vegas Panorama

In 1968, the weekly entertainment guide, *Panorama,* moved from Miami Beach, Florida, to Las Vegas, as the *Las Vegas Panorama.* Ralph Petillo was editor and publisher until about 1979, when Gary D. DiCarlo took over.

Las Vegas Panorama: (1968+)
  NvULV — [1968+]
Ref: files

Nevada Report

Gabriel R. Vogliotti issued the first number of the monthly *Nevada Report* on July 15, 1969. There may never have been a second.

Nevada Report: (Jul 15 1969–1969)
   NvHi — Jl 15 1969
Ref: files

Quarterly Las Vegas Review

The first, and apparently only, number of the *Quarterly Las Vegas Review* was issued late in 1969, by E. Ricardo Villasenor — his avowed goal "to build that better mouth-trap in the form of honest, no-nonsense show-business journalism." But the world didn't beat a path to his door, so he made a new start with the *Star* in December. (See Las Vegas, *The Star*.)

Quarterly Las Vegas Review: (1969)
   NvULV — 1969
Ref: files

The Star (Las Vegas Star)

On December 5, 1969, after the failure of the *Quarterly Las Vegas Review*, E. Ricardo Villasenor commenced a biweekly, the *Las Vegas Star,* to spread the "News from the Entertainment Capital of the World." This time he succeeded. In May of 1977, he changed its frequency to monthly, its name to the *Star,* and expanded the coverage to include Reno and Tahoe.

The Star: (Dec 5 1969+)
   NvULV — [D 5 1969+]
Ref: files

La Verdad

La Verdad, the first Spanish weekly in Las Vegas, was begun about December 26, 1969, by Larraz and Jones Publications, with Rolando Larraz and Marsha Jones as editors. It apparently ceased about December, 1977.

La Verdad: (c. Dec 26 1969–c. Dec 1977)
   NvULV — [Ja 2 1970–D 1977]
Ref: files

Las Vegas Free Press

"Nevada's Fearless Newspaper," the weekly *Las Vegas Free Press,* "dedicated to total freedom of thought and expression," was begun on January 1, 1970, by Alice and Jay Tell. It ceased publication the day before Thanksgiving in 1971.

Las Vegas Free Press: (Jan 1 1970–Nov 24 1971)
   NvHi — [D 23 1970–Je 28 1971]
   NvULV — Ja 1 1970–N 24 1971
   film — Ja 1 1970–N 24 1971
Ref: files

Beat of the Boulevard

Dave Bradley published the monthly entertainment guide, *Beat of the Boulevard,* from January, 1970, until about February, 1972.

Beat of the Boulevard: (Jan 1970–c. Feb 1972)
   NvULV — Ja–Je 1971
Ref: files

Cabaret Magazine

Cabaret Magazine, an entertainment weekly, was started by Edwin L. Hart about April, 1971, and stopped in May.

Cabaret Magazine: (c. Apr 1971–May 1971)
   NvULV — My 1, 8 1971
Ref: files

Earth

Earth was an occasional mimeographed paper, put out by the Earth Free News Collective in the fall of 1971.

Earth: (1971)
   NvULV — 1971
Ref: files

Democratic News

In the fall of 1971, Roland C. Bartlett suspended the *Veteran's Journal* to commence the bimonthly Las Vegas *Democratic News* in December. It appears to have folded in the spring.

Democratic News: (Dec 1971–c. Apr 1972)
   film — D 1971–Ap 1972
Ref: files

Western Business News (Nevada Business News)

John Cronan launched the monthly *Nevada Business News* at Las Vegas in June, 1973. In September of 1974, he changed the name to *Western Business News,* in the hope of attracting a wider readership. It failed to do so, however, and one year later Cronan suspended the *News* to commence an entertainment guide under the title *What's Happening.*

Western Business News: (Jun 1973–Aug 1975)
   film — Je 1973–Ag 1975
Ref: files

Vegas Wild

Vegas Wild, a cartoon quarterly, "For Laughs Only," was started in July, 1973, by Mark S. Mennell. It apparently folded within the year.

Vegas Wild: (July 1973–1973)
   NvULV — Jl 1973
Ref: files

The GOPaper

The GOPaper was started in July of 1974 to put Republicans and Republican ideals before the Las Vegas community. William M. Laub, Jr., was publisher with Louis Sanchez as editor.

The GOPaper: (Jul 1974–c. Oct 1977)
   NvHi — Jl 1974–O 1977
   NvULV — [Jl 1974–Mr 1976]
Ref: files

The Democrat

In May of 1975, the Democratic party of Clark County commenced the monthly *Democrat* as their "Official Voice." Marguerite C. Segretti was editor.

The Democrat: (May 1975–c. Nov 1978)
   NvHi — Ag 1975–N 1978
Ref: files

Official Las Vegas Entertainment and Events Guide

In May 1975, Marvin Sellinger launched a small monthly called the *Official Las Vegas Entertainment and Events Guide.* It officially died in 1978.

Official Las Vegas Entertainment and Events Guide: (May 1975–1978)
   NvULV — My 1975–8
Ref: files

We Are Free

We Are Free, a monthly newsletter of the Libertarian party of Nevada, began in Las Vegas in July, 1975. No editor was listed but after a lapse in publication from March of 1976 until March of 1977, it resumed with John R. Sherwin as editor. It died in March of 1979.

We Are Free: (Jul 1975–Mar 1976; Mar 1977–Mar 1979)
   NvHi — Jl 1975–Mr 1979
Ref: files

Spring Mountain Gazette

The *Spring Mountain Gazette* was begun as a biweekly in August, 1975, by Marshall Taylor, publisher, and Fran Demers, editor. They reduced it to a monthly in November, and stopped it in January.

Spring Mountain Gazette: (Aug 1975–Jan 1976)
   NvULV — [Ag 1975–Ja 1976]
Ref: files

What's Happening

Failing to make a success of his *Western Business News,* John Cronan suspended that paper and started a monthly entertainment guide, *What's Happening,* in September, 1975. He had even less success with it, however, for it failed in only six months.

What's Happening: (Sep 1975–c. Apr 1976)
   film — S 1975–Ap 1976
Ref: files

The Bee Hive

The *Bee Hive,* "The 'Good News' Newspaper," is a monthly published at Las Vegas by Richard B. Taylor and Robert D. Best of the Bee Hive Press. It was started in October of 1975, and serves the special interest of some 35,000 members of the seven Southern Nevada Stakes of The Church of Jesus Christ of Latter-day Saints.

The Bee Hive: (Oct 1975+)
   pub — O (1975+)
   pvt — S 1979
   NvU — O 1975+
Ref: files

The Overlay

The *Overlay,* the bimonthly of the Gambler's Book Club, began sometime in 1975.

The Overlay: (1975+)
   NvHi—Summer 1977
   NvULV — 1975+
Ref: files

Las Vegas Today

Las Vegas Today, a weekly entertainment guide, was first issued on April 6, 1975, by Robert L. Brown of the Las Vegas Valley Publishing Company, publisher of the *North Las Vegas Valley Times.* It has been edited by A. D. Hopkins, Elliot S. Krane, and David Dearing.

Las Vegas Today: (Apr 6 1975+)
   NvULV — Ap 6 1975+
Ref: files

Casino Post

Cathy Post Field began the semimonthly *Casino Post,* "with news and views for hotel-casino employees," on February 14, 1976. Milt Bozanic later purchased it, changing it to a monthly.

Casino Post: (Feb 14 1976+)
   NvULV — [F 14 1976+]
Ref: files

Nevada's Senior Journal

In April, 1976, Ad-Vantage Advertising commenced publication of *Nevada's Senior Journal,* a monthly newspaper for senior citizens. It succumbed in November.

Nevada's Senior Journal: (Apr 1976–Nov 1976)
   NvULV — Ap–N 1976
Ref: files

Las Vegan

Las Vegan, the slick, monthly "City Magazine," was started in November, 1976, by Mike Millard. In 1979, it was published by Nancy Millard, with Jack E. Sheehan as editor.

Las Vegan: (Nov 1976+)
    NvULV — N 1976+
    LvPL — [1976] 77+
Ref: files

The Green Felt

In January, 1977, Richard B. Taylor and Robert D. Best commenced the monthly *Green Felt.* Taylor served as editor until Best bought him out and invited Mike O'Connor to fill the post.

The Green Felt: (Jan 1977+)
    NvULV — [Ja 1977+]
Ref: files

Las Vegas Mirror

The weekly *Las Vegas Mirror* was launched on January 27, 1978, by the Continental News Service, with Ralph Petillo as general manager, and William Millman as managing editor. In June, Galaxy Composition, Inc., took over the publication, but Millman remained as editor.

Las Vegas Mirror: (Jan 27 1978+)
    NvULV — [Ja 27 1978–Mr 1979]
Ref: files

Las Vegas Fun Times

The short-lived weekly *Las Vegas Fun Times* was begun on March 17, 1978, by Fun Times, Inc., with John Angus as managing editor. It apparently ceased in June.

Las Vegas Fun Times: (Mar 17 1978–c. Jun 23 1978)
    NvULV — Mr 17–Je 23 1978
Ref: files

Vegas Gay Times

The *Vegas Gay Times,* started in June of 1978, is a nonprofit monthly newsletter, "published by and for the gay community of Las Vegas in conjunction with the Human Rights Committee of the American Civil Liberties Union of Nevada."

Vegas Gay Times: (Jun 1978+)
    NvULV — Je 1978+
Ref: files

Backstage

The weekly *Backstage* was commenced by Ron Delpit on September 1,

1978, billed as "the hottest new publication in Las Vegas." It apparently suspended the following month.

Backstage: (Sep 1 1978–1978)
 NvULV — S 22 1978
Ref: files

Vida Nueva

Vida Nueva, "The Bilingual Magazine," was launched at Las Vegas as a bimonthly in April, 1979, by Librado and Rose Ramos, with Maria Merida as editor.

Vida Nueva: (Apr 1979+)
 NvULV — Ap 1979+
Ref: files

Frontline

Frontline, a "Weekly Newsletter for Professional Gamblers," began with the issue of April 6–12, 1979.

Frontline: (Apr 6–12 1979+)
 NvULV — Ap 6–12 1979+
Ref: files

The News

Larrie H. Schmidt and Jesse A. Morris launched this short-lived weekly on May 14, 1979.

The News: (May 14 1979–1979)
 NvULV — [1979]
Ref: files

Off the Strip

The free monthly *Off the Strip* was started in June, 1979, by Norma J. Engberg, editor and publisher.

Off the Strip: (Jun 1979+)
 Nv — Je 1979+
 NvULV — Je 1979+
Ref: files

Las Vegas West

On August 31, 1979, Cy Newman and Ralph Petillo of Galaxy Composition, Inc., commenced the black weekly, *Las Vegas West,* with Bob Palm as editor. It apparently ceased before the end of the year.

Las Vegas West: (Aug 31 1979–1979)
 NvULV — Ag 31 1979
Ref: files

◂❮ LATHROP WELLS ❯▸

Desert News

Irene Fowler started the monthly, mimeographed *Desert News* at Lathrop Wells in October, 1979, as a "community service."
Desert News: (Oct 1979+)
 NvHi — O 1979+
Ref: files

◂❮ LEWIS ❯▸

Lewis Herald

On November 23, 1881, E. T. George and Company commenced publication of the *Lewis Herald.* The paper was edited by George and issued weekly on Wednesdays, as a twenty-four-column sheet. George conducted the *Herald* ably, but with the decline of the camp it was forced to suspend on January 17, 1883. George returned to Battle Mountain, where he leased the *Messenger* for a time.
Lewis Herald: (Nov 23 1881–Jan 17 1883)
 No issues located.
Ref: RRR N 25, 26 1881; BMM F 24 1883

◂❮ LIDA ❯▸

Lida Enterprise

With the boom of Tonopah and Goldfield, interest was soon revived in the old camp of Lida. By the end of January, 1905, the town claimed four saloons, two stores, an assay office, a butcher shop, and three hundred hopeful inhabitants. And on April 14, it even boasted a newspaper, the *Enterprise.* Charles F. Spillman and Newman H. Mix were editors and proprietors, issuing the *Enterprise* as a Friday weekly. Early the following year the boom spread to neighboring Palmetto, and on February 23, 1906, Mix commenced the *Herald,* which was distributed at that camp but was undoubtedly printed at the *Enterprise* plant in Lida. The decline of Lida came quickly, however, and in mid-October of the same year, Mix suspended both papers, removing the plant to Blair, where he commenced the *Blair Press* on November 3.
Lida Enterprise: (Apr 14 1905–Oct 1906)
 No issues located.
Ref: PR Ap 28 1905; BMM My 13 1905; LCT Je 23 1906

⁓(LOGANDALE)⁓

Lower Taxes

In January of 1917, Charles MacKnight Sain commenced a quarterly magazine, *Lower Taxes,* at Logandale. The title might more appropriately have been *No Taxes,* since its principal goal was "to abolish all taxes except the inheritance tax," arguing that "the government should be run as a Big Business at a profit and pay dividends to its stockholders." Sain was sole owner, editor, and publisher, and issued the little eight-page magazine for over three years before he decided to enlarge its scope, if not its size, and change the name to the *Oak.*

Lower Taxes: (Jan 1917–c. Apr 1920)
   No issues located.
Ref: LO Jl 1920

The Oak

After three years of publishing *Lower Taxes,* Charles MacKnight Sain decided that he wanted to change the name of his little quarterly, and about the July issue of 1920, he rechristened it the *Oak.* He also widened its aims to include promotion of such schemes as building a billion-dollar railroad along the Colorado River and through the Grand Canyon. As a promotional gimmick to increase the number of subscribers to the magazine, he offered anyone who sent in five subscriptions — $10 — one sheep or the profits from the sale of such in May, 1921. How much longer the publication continued under this offer is unknown, but it probably suspended with the demise of the sheep in 1921.

The Oak: (c. Jul 1920–c. 1921)
   CU-BANC — Jl 1920
   film — Jl 1920
Ref: files

Sain's Weekly Letter

On November 12, 1926, Charles MacKnight Sain launched a new vehicle for the distribution of his wisdom, *Sain's Weekly Letter.* He persisted in it for at least four months.

Sain's Weekly Letter: (Nov 12 1926–c. Apr 29 1927)
   NvHi — N 12 1926, Ap 29 1927
Ref: files

Lake Mead Monitor

The weekly *Lake Mead Monitor,* a tabloid, began sometime in 1979. It was published by Bryant Robinson and had a series of editors, including Darrell Hallenbeck, Jack Walch, and Rex Jensen.

Lake Mead Monitor: (1979+)
  pub — 1979+
Ref: Jensen

⇜(LORENA)⇝

Lorena Miner

The *Miner* is said to have been a paper published by J. Holman Buck of Mina, in 1908, during the momentary existence of Lorena as a mining camp. It is possible, however, that this is confused with Buck's earlier *Lorena Ledge,* published in November of 1905, at a different camp of the same name in Mono County, California.

Lorena Miner: (c. 1908)
  No issues located.
Ref: Myrick

⇜(LOVELOCK)⇝

Nevada New Era

In the summer of 1892, Frank Francis quit as editor of the *Central Nevadan* at Battle Mountain, and with a press and material of his own, he arrived at Lovelock to give that town its first paper. He called his venture the *Nevada New Era,* issuing the first number on September 1, 1892, and extolling the prosperous future that awaited the ranchers of the valley. Francis was sole editor and proprietor of the paper and issued it every Thursday as a four-page, 15 by 22-inch weekly, dedicated to local interests, and selling for $4 a year. However, the new era of prosperity for Lovelock was still too far distant to bring financial support to a newspaper, and a disillusioned Francis suspended the paper in June of 1894, to move to the new camp of Kennedy. (See Kennedy, *Nevada New Era.*)

Nevada New Era: (Sep 1 1892–Jun 1894)
  pvt — O 21 1893; Je 2 1894
  film — O 21 1893; Je 2 1894
Ref: files; LA Je 29 1901

Lovelock Tribune

On May 21, 1898, the Lovelock *Tribune* was begun by the Lovelock Publishing Company, consisting of S. R. Young and George W. Peltier. Charles MacKnight Sain was editor and manager, issuing the paper as a four-page, six-column weekly at $3 a year, and on October 15, he bought Young's half interest. On October 31, 1903, H. C. Sommer bought the *Tribune,* and it changed hands frequently thereafter. Sommer sold in February of 1905, to J. R. Hunter, who, in turn, sold to Howard N. Cherry and partner Pearson on November 8, 1907. Cherry and George E. Riddle then took over for two weeks on April 24, 1908, followed by John S. Case and C. C. S. Wright on May 9. Case became sole editor and publisher on December 4 of that year. He enlarged the *Tribune* to a semiweekly on December 13, 1910, but, failing to enlarge its support, he was forced to suspend it on February 1, 1912.

Lovelock Tribune: (May 21 1898–Feb 1 1912)
   NvHi — 1904–12
   NvMus — Ag 30 1907
   NvU — [My 21 1898–F 1 1912]
   film — [My 21 1898–F 1 1912]
Ref: files; LRM F 1 1912

Lovelock Standard

The *Standard* was a weekly to be commenced at Lovelock, in April of 1900, by Professor W. L. Brandon, principal of the high school, and Homer T. Riddle, with the material of the defunct Elko *Nevada Silver Tidings*. If the paper did make its debut, it gave only a short performance and had suspended by September, when Riddle purchased the newly founded Lovelock *Argus*.

Lovelock Standard: (c. Apr 1900)
   No issues located.
Ref: GaN Ap 7 1900

The Argus

On May 5, 1900, Charles W. Patterson, formerly of the *Yerington Rustler*, published the first number of the Lovelock *Argus*. Patterson was sole editor and proprietor, issuing the paper as a four-page, Saturday weekly, at $2 a year. By September of 1900, Homer T. Riddle was editor and publisher. On August 16, 1902, C. H. McIntosh became editor, and on September 27, 1902, the Riddle brothers, Howard N. and Frank W., were listed as publishers. The *Argus* ran for nearly five years but finally suspended on January 27, 1905, to consolidate with the *Lovelock Tribune*.

The Argus: (May 1900–Jan 27 1905)
   NvHi — [O 4 1902–Ja 27 1905]
   NvU — [Ja 5 1901–D 23 1904]
   film — [Ja 5 1901–Ja 27 1905]
Ref: files; RG My 8 1900

Lovelock Review

Nearly a year after Howard W. Cherry suspended the *Review* at Vernon, he revived the name at Lovelock, where he commenced a new *Review* on August 21, 1908. Cherry was editor and publisher, and issued the *Review* as a Democratic Friday weekly. After little over two years Cherry suspended the *Review* on September 16, 1910. The plant then passed to Howard N. Riddle of the late Mazuma *Seven Troughs Miner*, who revived the *Review* on December 25, 1910. Five days later, on December 30, he suspended it, selling it and the *Miner* to the Lovelock Publishing Company, which merged the two to commence the *Lovelock Review-Miner* on January 6, 1911. (See *Lovelock Review-Miner.*)

Lovelock Review: (Aug 21 1908–Dec 30 1910)
   NvHi — Ag 21 1908–D 30 1910
   NvU — Ag 21 1908–D 30 1910
   film — Ag 21 1908–D 30 1910
Ref: files

Lovelock Review-Miner

Following the suspension of the Mazuma *Seven Troughs Miner* on October 1, 1910, the Lovelock Publishing Company purchased it and the *Lovelock Review,* and merged the two plants to found the weekly *Lovelock Review-Miner* on January 6, 1911. On February 9, 1912, the company hired John S. Chase as editor. He was replaced on February 7, 1913, by J. S. Brooks, who quit after thirteen weeks. W. W. Parke became editor on March 13, 1914, continuing as such until July 18, 1919, when the paper was purchased by Charles H. Keith and Harold Hale of the *Elko Independent.* Keith became sole editor and proprietor on October 10, 1919, but he sold the paper four years later to W. C. Black, who took over on July 6, 1923.

On January 16, 1931, in the depths of the Depression, Paul K. Gardner of Edgewood, Iowa, and Donald E. Morrison of Greenville, Michigan, bought out Black. On September 1, 1933, Gardner became sole editor and proprietor, continuing as such for a third of a century until about 1966, after which the management again went through many changes. Tony Payton and Tom Dickerson of the Gardnerville *Record-Courier* bought the paper, hiring Garrett M. Stack as editor about 1966. Stack was followed a year later by J. Ray Carlson, and about 1970, Michael Payton replaced Tony as copublisher and became editor. In April, 1971, Joseph and Carol Marshall became editors and publishers. After Joseph Marshall's death in August, 1975, Carol Marshall remained as editor and publisher. Since remarried as Carol Marshall Pringle, she continued the *Review-Miner,* "the Only Newspaper that has faith in, cares for and exclusively covers the news of Pershing County," as an independent, Thursday weekly.

Lovelock Review-Miner: (Jan 6 1911+)
   pub — Ja 6 1911+
   CHi — Ag 13–20 1915; Ja 7 1916
   NvHi — [1911–24] 1927+
   NvMus — D 16, 30 1932–Ja 6 1933
   NvU — Ja 6–13 1911; 1912+
   film — [Ja 6 1911+]
Ref: files

Northern Nevada Weekly Mine Review

The *Northern Nevada Weekly Mine Review* was begun at Lovelock as a

one-page weekly mining journal, early in June of 1915, by the Western Mining News Bureau, consisting of Chester Raymond Bunker and F. E. Becker. It flourished for barely seven months before suspending on December 29, 1915, to be absorbed into the *Lovelock Review-Miner*.
Northern Nevada Weekly Mine Review: (Jun 1915–Dec 29 1915)
    NvHi — N 17 1915
    NvU — [Ag 11–D 29 1915]
    film — [Ag 11–D 29 1915]
Ref: files; LRM Ja 7 1916

Nevada Legionnaire

The *Nevada Legionnaire,* published by the American Legion Department of Nevada, began as a monthly at Lovelock about September of 1932. Paul K. Gardner of the *Review-Miner* was editor and printer. Aside from a momentary lapse to a quarterly from September, 1938, to August, 1939, its history was relatively uneventful. Finally, after eighteen years, Gardner lost the printing contract to Carl Shelly of the *Sparks Tribune,* and Gardner printed his last issue at Lovelock in September of 1950. (See Sparks, *Nevada Legionnaire.*)
Nevada Legionnaire: (c. Sep 1932–Sep 1950)
    NvHi — Ja 28, Mr 25 1946
    NvU — [1934–50]
    film — [S 18 1934–S 1950]
Ref: files

~(LUCKY BOY)~

Luckyboy Mining Record (Walker Lake Mining Record)

The mining boom at Lucky Boy in the fall of 1908 spurred J. Holman Buck of the Mina *Western Nevada Miner* to commence the semiweekly *Walker Lake Mining Record* for the camp about December 22, 1908. The following year, on June 10, Grover T. Russell and George T. Russell bought the paper, changing its name to the *Luckyboy Mining Record* and reducing it to a weekly. The boom was over by the fall and *The Mining Record* folded on September 17, 1909.
Luckyboy Mining Record: (c. Dec 22 1908–Sep 17 1909)
    NvHi — Je 10–S 17 1909
    NvU — Je 10–S 10 1909
    film — Je 10–S 17 1909
Ref: files

Hawthorne–Lucky Boy News

In the spring of 1909, a second newspaper was commenced to exploit the Lucky Boy boom. On April 17, Irwin G. Lewis of the Carson City *Appeal* staff issued the first number of the *Hawthorne–Lucky Boy News* from the *Appeal* plant at Carson City, over a hundred miles from Lucky Boy. Lewis was sole editor and proprietor, issuing the paper as a four-page, illustrated weekly. Immediately after publishing the initial number, a press was shipped to Lucky Boy. The following month the plant was purchased by W. W. Booth, who commenced the *Hawthorne–Lucky Boy Post* at Hawthorne.

Hawthorne–Lucky Boy News: (Apr 17 1909–c. Apr 25 1909)
   NvMus — Ap 25 1909
   film — Ap 25 1909
Ref: files

Hawthorne–Lucky Boy Post

(See Hawthorne, *Hawthorne–Lucky Boy Post*)

MANHATTAN

Manhattan Mail

Lester W. Haworth founded the *Manhattan Mail* on January 10, 1906, under the firm name of Haworth, Anderson and Co. Haworth was editor, and issued the paper every Wednesday as a twelve-page weekly, at $5 a year. The *Mail* was printed on an old Washington hand press that traced its history back half a century, having previously done service on the *Belmont Courier,* the Carson City *Register, Appeal* and *Independent,* and before that, the Marysville, California, *Appeal.* In 1907, Haworth became sole proprietor, but by January of 1909, he had leased the paper to Frank F. Garside.

   Garside, serving as editor, held the lease for nearly two years before quitting to establish his own paper, the *Manhattan Post.* Roy R. Mighels then purchased the *Mail,* becoming sole editor and proprietor on October 22, 1910. Mighels got a job in the state printer's office, and on January 28, 1911, he sold the *Mail* to Newman H. Mix. Four months later Mix fell seriously ill in Tonopah and the paper was forced to suspend on June 24, 1911.

Manhattan Mail: (Jan 10 1906–Jun 24 1911)
  NvHi — My 16, Je 21 1906; Je 12 1907; Jl 7 1909–Je 24 1911
  NvU — [1909–11]
  film — [My 16 1909–Je 24 1911]
Ref: files; TB F 17 1906

Manhattan News

On January 27, 1906, less than three weeks after the founding of the *Mail*, T. J. Cullen commenced a rival paper, the *Manhattan News*. R. Leslie Smaill was editor, but he severed his connections with the paper on May 20. William McClure Gotwaldt held the editorship for two months, from September 2 to November 4. The *News* was issued every Sunday as a twelve-page weekly at $5 a year. The early numbers were printed by the *Tonopah Sun* until the plant of the defunct *Lida Enterprise* was moved to Manhattan. Cullen, too, eventually tired of the paper, selling it to H. A. McCraney on January 13, 1907. McCraney continued the *News* until July 7, 1907, when he suspended it to take the editorship of the new rival, the *Manhattan Times*.

Manhattan News: (Jan 27 1906–Jul 7 1907)
   NvHi — My 27 1906
   NvU — Ap 7–D 30 1906; Ja 13–Jl 7 1907
   film — Ap 7–D 30 1906; Ja 13–Jl 7 1907
Ref: files; TM Ja 27 1906; WPN F 1 1906

Manhattan Times

George S. Graves and Co. began the weekly *Manhattan Times* on July 6, 1907. H. A. McCraney suspended his *Manhattan News* to become its editor, and three months later he bought out Graves. The *Times* proved even less successful than the *News*, and on December 7, 1907, it was forced to suspend.

Manhattan Times: (Jul 6 1907–Dec 7 1907)
   NvU — Jl 13–D 7 1907
   film — Jl 13–D 7 1907
Ref: files

Manhattan Post

Following his termination of the lease on the *Manhattan Mail*, Frank F. Garside purchased a printing plant and commenced a rival paper, the *Manhattan Post*, on October 15, 1910. Garside was sole editor and proprietor, issuing the paper every Saturday as a four-page, 15 by 22-inch weekly, at $3.50 a year. The *Post*'s rates were much cheaper than those of the *Mail*, so many of the *Mail*'s former patrons defected, and in less than a year, the *Mail* suspended. Garside added Fred L. Miner as mining editor, on February 10, 1912. But with the decline in mining activities he finally suspended the *Post* on May 30, 1914, and moved to Tonopah, where he founded the *Daily Times* the following year.

Manhattan Post: (Oct 15 1910–May 30 1914)
   C — Ja 20 1912
   NvHi — [O 15 1910–My 30 1914]
   NvTC — Ap 1911–D 1912

NvU — [Ja 6 1912–My 30 1914]
film — [O 15 1910–My 30 1914]
Ref: files

The Knocker

Shortly before Labor Day of 1911, *The Knocker* made its brief but comic debut in Manhattan, as "the Highest Priced Newspaper in the World — $1 Per Copy." John T. Field, editor of the mimeographed sheet, modestly proclaimed it "a newly discovered Literary Gem, so Illiterate, so Crude It's Good! A Freak Creation." He further advised readers "If you 'Knock' buy the KNOCKER, Buy THE POST and get the News."

The Knocker: (c. Sep 1911)
   NvHi — S 1911
   film — S 1911
Ref: files

Manhattan Magnet

For nearly three years following the suspension of the *Post*, Manhattan was without a newspaper, until March 23, 1917, when William McClure Gotwaldt founded the *Manhattan Magnet.* Gotwaldt was sole editor and publisher, issuing the paper every Friday as a four-page, six-column, weekly, at $5 a year. The *Magnet* was well received and ran for over five years, until its suspension on September 30, 1922.

Manhattan Magnet: (Mar 23 1917–Sep 30 1922)
   CHi — My 25, D 22 1917; Ja 26 1918
   NvHi — Mr 30 1918–S 30 1922
   NvTC — Mr 23 1917–S 30 1922
   NvU — Jl 27 1917–Jl 6 1918
   film — [My 25 1917–S 30 1922]
Ref: files

MASON

Mason Valley News

Following the suspension of the *Rawhide News,* Clyde C. Emerson moved the plant to the new farming town of Mason. There, with aid from the Mason Townsite Company, he formed the Emerson Publishing Company, with himself as managing editor, and began the *Mason Valley News* on March 19, 1909. Mason failed to develop to his expectations, however, and on November 28, 1914, he published his last issue there, moving the plant to Yerington, where he resumed two weeks later. (See Yerington, *Mason Valley News.*)

Mason Valley News: (Mar 19 1909–Nov 28 1914)
   pub — Mr 19; My 7 1909–N 28 1914
   NvHi — O 29, D 31 1909; Mr 4, Ap 8–15, Je 24, Ag 5 1910–N 28 1914
   film — [Mr 19 1909–N 28 1914]
Ref: files

MAZUMA

Mazuma Herald

Following his suspension of the Seven Troughs district's first newspaper, the *Vernon Miner,* Howard N. Riddle moved the plant to the rival camp of Mazuma. There, with C. E. Peters, he started a new paper, the *Mazuma Herald,* in late July of 1907. This venture fared no better than the first, however, and the *Herald* suspended on November 21, the plant passing to new owners who brought out the *Mazuma World* the following week. Riddle still seemed determined to run a successful paper in Mazuma, however, and he tried again with the *Seven Troughs District News* the following year.

Mazuma Herald: (Jul 1907–Nov 21 1907)
   pvt — N 21 1907 (2nd page only)
Ref: NMN Jl 27 1907; LT Ag 16 1907; LRM F 9 1912

Mazuma World

Following the suspension of the *Mazuma Herald,* a new hopeful, McNeely, purchased the plant to commence the *Mazuma World* on November 28, 1907. Ed Murrish, the editor, wryly advised his readers, "If you have any criticisms to offer, kindly mail them to our New York office." But the *World* soon faded, apparently suspending the following spring.

Mazuma World: (Nov 28 1907–c. Mar 1908)
   pvt — N 28 1907; F 20 1908
Ref: files

Seven Troughs District News

On September 19, 1908, Howard N. Riddle issued the first number of the *Seven Troughs District News,* in an effort to revive a newspaper at the camp of Mazuma. Riddle was sole editor and proprietor, and published the paper every Saturday, as a four-page, six-column weekly, at $4 a year. The *News* flourished only briefly, however. Riddle bought the *Seven Troughs Miner* at the rival camp of Vernon, and on January 30, 1909, he absorbed the *News* into the *Miner.*

Seven Troughs District News: (Sep 19 1908–Jan 16 1909)
  NvHi — N 7 1908
  NvLR — S 19–D 5 1908
  NvU — S 19 1908–Ja 16 1909
  film — S 19 1908–Ja 16 1909
Ref: files

Seven Troughs Miner

Early in 1909, Howard N. Riddle of the Mazuma *Seven Troughs District News* purchased the rival Vernon *Seven Troughs Miner* from Ray Harris and moved it to Mazuma, where he merged it with his own paper on January

30, under the cumbersome title of *Seven Troughs Miner and Seven Troughs District News*. On March 20, he wisely trimmed the title back to the *Seven Troughs Miner*. As editor and proprietor Riddle issued the *Miner* every Saturday, as a four-page, 15 by 22-inch weekly. The Seven Troughs district boom was on the decline, however, and on October 1, 1910, Riddle suspended the *Miner*, selling the plant to Howard W. Cherry of the *Lovelock Review*, who combined the plant with his own to commence the *Lovelock Review-Miner*. (See *Lovelock Review-Miner*.)

Seven Troughs Miner: (Jan 30 1909–Oct 1 1910)
  NvHi — Ja–N 1909; Ag 27 1910
  NvLR — Ja 30 1909–O 1 1910
  NvU — Ja 30 1909–O 1 1910
  film — Ja 30 1909–O 1 1910
Ref: files

~(McGILL)~

Copper Ore

The *Copper Ore* was founded at McGill, some thirteen miles northeast of Ely, on February 11, 1909, by Austin Jackson. The paper was published every Thursday, as a four-page, 15 by 22-inch weekly. H. S. Godcharles served as editor until his drowning in November, 1909. Thereafter the editorship and proprietorship changed hands many times. Chet R. Graves took up the pen on November 4, and John D. Kenny replaced him as editor on April 7, 1910, holding the position for only two months. Jackson sold the paper to Joseph S. Jordan, who became editor and proprietor on January 5, 1911. Jordan, in turn, sold it to Nate W. Fay of the *White Pine News*, who took over on April 25, 1912, but disposed of the *Copper Ore* to D. M. McDonald on February 5, 1914, in order to give his full attention to the *News* again. McDonald went broke with the paper still on his hands and was forced to close down on June 11, 1914.

Copper Ore: (Feb 11 1909–Jun 11 1914)
  NvHi — O 14 1909–Je 11 1914
  NvU — [F 11 1909–Je 11 1914]
  film — [F 11 1909–Je 11 1914]
Ref: files

~(METROPOLIS)~

Metropolis Chronicle

On September 15, 1911, the Metropolis Chronicle Publishing Company, a subsidiary of the Pacific Reclamation Company, commenced the *Chronicle* as a booster paper to promote the sale of the latter company's land at Metropolis, twelve miles northwest of Wells. The *Chronicle* was issued semimonthly, on the first and fifteenth, as an eight-page, 15 by 22-inch sheet, selling at $2 a year. The agricultural "boom" of Metropolis was nurtured for two years by the *Chronicle,* while the promoters unloaded their property. The bubble finally burst and the paper suspended on December 15, 1913.

Metropolis Chronicle: (Sep 15 1911–Dec 15 1913)
   NvHi — O 1 1911–Ap 1 1913
   NvU — [S 15 1911–D 15 1913]
   film — [S 15 1911–D 15 1913]
Ref: files; Shepperson 50–51

Gold Circle Miner

On March 14, 1908, Mark W. Musgrove tried another comeback with the commencement of the *Gold Circle Miner* at the new boom camp of Gold Circle, soon known as Midas, some forty miles northwest of Golconda. The *Miner* was issued weekly at 10¢ a copy, by the Gold Circle Publishing Company, with Musgrove as editor. After a few months roughing it, however, Musgrove had had enough of the vicissitudes of mining camp life. He closed down the *Miner* and headed for the city lights of Reno, where he started an equally ill-fated journal, the *Mining Digest.*

Gold Circle Miner: (Mar 14 1908–c. May 1908)
   NvHi — Ap 11 1908
   film — Ap 11 1908
Ref: files

Gold Circle News

Within about a month of the suspension of Midas' first paper, the *Gold Circle Miner,* Frank L. Reber attempted to issue a second, starting the *Gold Circle News* on June 13, 1908. Reber was editor and manager for the Gold Circle News Publishing Company, which issued the paper every Saturday, as an eight-page weekly, at $4 a year. Like the *Miner,* the *News* failed to enlist sufficient support, and Reber was soon forced to suspend, probably sometime that fall.

Gold Circle News: (Jun 13 1908–c. Oct 1908)
   NvHi — S 26 1908
   film — S 26 1908
Ref: files

Gold Circle Porcupine

The *Gold Circle Porcupine,* an ephemeral little sheet, mimeographed on old ledger paper, was begun at Midas in May of 1914, by F. J. Benneson, one of the local merchants. Benneson, "assisted by an able corps of mining and society experts," was editor and published the *Porcupine* for probably no more than a few numbers.

Gold Circle Porcupine: (May 13 1914–c. May 1914)
   NvHi — My 20 1914
   film — My 20 1914
Ref: files; CO My 30 1914

⌒⨳(MILLERS)⨳⌒

Millers Booster

On October 2, 1907, only a few months after the suspension of his satellite sheet, the *Blair Booster*, W. W. Booth of the *Tonopah Bonanza* revived the name in a new weekly at the "thriving little railroad and mill town" of Millers, fifteen miles west of Tonopah. The *Booster* fared no better at Millers than at Blair, and the following spring Booth moved the plant and the name on to Bovard.

Millers Booster: (Oct 2 1907–c. 1908)
   pvt — N 14 1907
Ref: files; TB O 2 1907; LT Je 28 1907

⌒⨳(MINA)⨳⌒

Western Nevada Miner

Following the suspension of the *Aurora Borealis*, J. Holman Buck moved a portion of the *Bodie Evening Miner* plant to Mina, where he commenced the *Western Nevada Miner* on July 4, 1907. Buck was sole editor and proprietor, issuing the paper every Saturday, as a four-page, independent weekly. The *Miner* flourished and later served as the parent to many of Buck's short-lived journals, established at neighboring boom camps. Finally, after nearly a quarter century, ill health forced Buck's retirement and a temporary suspension of the paper, on December 10, 1927.

Buck soon sold the paper to Fred W. Egelston, who revived it on March 3, 1928. Later that year Egelston purchased the rival *Mineral County News*, and combined the plant with the *Miner*, saddling the paper with the cumbersome title of *Western Nevada Miner & Mineral County News*, beginning on November 2. Despite the burden of its new name, the paper held on for two years before the nationwide depression forced its suspension on December 12, 1930.

Western Nevada Miner: (Jul 4 1907–Dec 12 1930)
   CHi — Je 28 1913; D 12 1914; Mr 27, Ap 24, Je 12, Ag 14, D 18 1915
   NvHi — [S 19 1908–Jl 24, Ag 7 1909–D 12 1930]
   NvU — [1909–30]
   film — [S 19 1908–D 12 1930]
Ref: files

Mineral County News

The *Mineral County News* was a brief venture commenced at Mina about September 7, 1928, and suspended about October 26. Its editor and publisher are unknown, but its plant was purchased by the *Western Nevada Miner.* (See Mina, *Western Nevada Miner.)*

Mineral County News: (c. Sep 7 1928–c. Oct 26 1928)
  No issues located.
Ref: WNM N 2 1928

⸺(MINDEN)⸺

Minden Times

On June 12, 1936, A. E. and V. E. Haines founded the *Times* at Minden. A. E. Haines was editor, while his wife, V. E. Haines, was owner and publisher. They issued the paper every Friday, as a four-page, six-column, independent weekly. Following A. E. Haines's departure in May of 1937, his wife struggled on with the paper until Christmas of 1942, when she finally suspended it, not, "for lack of business but rather for the lack of competent help."

Minden Times: (Jun 12 1936–Dec 25 1942)
  NvMC — [Je 12 1936–42]
  film — [Je 19 1936–D 25 1942]
Ref: files

The Nevada Magazine

The *Nevada Magazine* was a monthly journal begun in July, 1945, by Clarence C. Crossley, editor and president of the Nevada Printing and Publishing Company. It was devoted principally to state news and flourished for three and one-half years, suspending in February of 1949.

The Nevada Magazine: (Jul 1945–Feb 1949)
  CU — Jl 1945–D 1948
  CU-BANC — Jl 1945–F 1949
  DLC — (Jl 1946–Je 1947)
  NvHi — Jl 1945–F 1949
  NvU — Jl 1947–F 1949
Ref: files

⸺(MONARCH)⸺

Monarch Tribune

Lester W. Haworth of the *Manhattan Mail* issued the first number of the *Tribune* on August 18, 1906, for the new camp of Monarch, some thirty-five miles northeast of Manhattan. Haworth was editor and manager and published the *Tribune* every Saturday, as a four-page, six-column weekly, at $5 a year. About September, when it was learned that Monarch's principal backer had absconded with nearly all the development company's money, the boom instantly collapsed and the *Tribune* suspended.

Monarch Tribune: (Aug 18 1906–c. Sep 1906)
  pvt — Ag 18, S 15 1906
  NvHi — Ag 25 1906
  film — Ag 25 1906
Ref: files

⁓{ MOTTSVILLE }⁓

Mottsville Star

The *Mottsville Star* was an amateur manuscript paper begun on May 1, 1879, by Miss Nancy Hill and her friends. Neighboring editors found it a spicy little sheet, but the novelty apparently wore off after the second or third issue.

Mottsville Star: (May 1 1879–c. May 1879)
  No issues located.
Ref: CVN My 2, 9 1879

⁓{ MOUNTAIN CITY }⁓

Weekly 6 Shooter

In September of 1869, the *Cheyenne Leader* announced that Mountain City, Nevada, "not to be behind other ambitious mining camps in that section of the State is about to have a newspaper . . . to be known by the somewhat novel but expressive title of *Weekly 6 Shooter.*" Whether it ever appeared is unknown.

Weekly 6 Shooter: (c. Sep 1869)
  No issues located.
Ref: CL S 27 1869

Mountain City Times

After the suspension of the *Gold Creek News* in December of 1897, Charles MacKnight Sain removed the plant to Mountain City. Here, in partnership with R. M. Woodward and Charles H. Keith, he began publication of the *Mountain City Times* on January 21, 1898. Sain was editor and manager and Keith was assistant. The *Times* was a four-page, six-column, 15 by 22-inch weekly, which sold for $5 a year. Sain used the paper to continue the serialized version of his novel, *Tom Davis in Heaven,* which he had started in the *Gold Creek News.* The *Times* ran for less than five months and suspended on May 13, 1898, when Sain left for Lovelock to become editor of the *Tribune.*

Mountain City Times: (Jan 21 1898–May 13 1898)
   NvU — Ja 21–Mr 25, Ap 8–22, My 13 1898
   film — [Ja 21–My 13 1898]
Ref: files

Mountain City Mail

During a brief revival of mining activity at Mountain City, on May 19, 1938, Clayton F. and Clinton A. Darrah founded the *Mountain City Mail.* Clayton Darrah served as editor, issuing the paper as an independent Thursday weekly, eventually building up a subscription of over 400. On February 23, 1939, however, the Darrahs suspended the paper "to enter the publishing business in Reno."

Mountain City Mail: (May 19 1938–Feb 23 1939)
   NvU — [N 17 1938–F 23 1939]
   film — [N 17 1938–F 23 1939]
Ref: files

~(NATIONAL)~

National Miner

In the summer of 1910, Frank L. Reber, formerly of the Midas *Gold Circle News,* arrived in the booming tent camp of National, some sixty miles north of Winnemucca. There, on July 22, 1910, he commenced the *National Miner.* Reber was sole editor and publisher, and issued the paper every Friday, as a four-page, 15 by 22-inch, Democratic weekly, at $4 a year. National prospered for several years, supporting the *Miner* until September 26, 1913.

National Miner: (Jul 22 1910–Sep 26 1913)
   NvU — [D 9 1910–S 26 1913]
   film — [D 9 1910–S 26 1913]
Ref: files

~(NELSON)~

Eldorado Canyon Miner

During the World War I revival of mining activity at Eldorado Canyon, H. H. Johnson brought a printing press to the camp, and on February 9, 1917, he commenced the *Eldorado Canyon Miner.* Johnson was editor and business manager of the Eldorado Canyon Miner Company, which issued the paper every Friday, as a four-page, six-column weekly. Eldorado Canyon's population was not sufficient to support a paper, however, and the *Miner* was forced to suspend publication after about three months.

Eldorado Canyon Miner: (Feb 9 1917–c. May 1917)
  CHi — Ap 20 1917
  film — Ap 20 1917
Ref: files

∽⊰(NIXON)⊱∾

Firewheel (Pyramid Lake News)

In October, 1972, Carole Wright and Katha Wight started a semimonthly newspaper for the Pyramid Lake Indian Reservation. The first issue was called the *Pyramid Lake News,* "for lack of a better name," but suggestions for a new name were requested, and the second issue appeared as *Firewheel.* It seems to have flickered out the following January.

Firewheel: (Oct 1972–c. Jan 1973)
  NvHi — O, N 30, D 15 1972; Ja 1973
Ref: files

∽⊰(NORTH LAS VEGAS)⊱∾

North Las Vegas News

The weekly *North Las Vegas News* was founded on September 22, 1949, by Joseph A. McLain as editor and publisher. After six months, however, he sold the paper to Richard King, who briefly changed its name to the *Sun,* from March 23, 1950, to January 11, 1951. In 1952, Charles Catt and Warren Stanley became copublishers. They lasted two years, selling on June 30, 1954, to Merrill Inch, who, in turn, soon sold it to the Bonanza Printers, S. F. (Scoop) Garside and Ray Germain. Finally, in July, 1955, it was purchased by Hank Greenspun's Las Vegas Sun, Inc., and was issued by him with Deke Hougate, Jr., as editor until March 25, 1959, when Liz McClain became editor. The *News* lasted until November 4, 1959, when it was suspended to combine with the *North Las Vegas Valley Times.* (See *North Las Vegas Sun.*)

North Las Vegas News: (Sep 22 1949–Mar 16 1950; Jan 18 1951–Nov 4 1959)
  NvU — [Jl 1951–N 4 1959]
  film — [Jl 5 1951–N 4 1959]
Ref: files

North Las Vegas Sun

On March 23, 1950, Richard King, having bought the *North Las Vegas News,* brought it out under a new name, the *North Las Vegas Sun.* It doubtless would have continued as such had it not soon been outshone by the *Las Vegas Sun* started by Hank Greenspun on July 1 of the same year.

Thus King finally dropped the name on January 11, 1951, to resume as the *North Las Vegas News*. (See *North Las Vegas News*.)
North Las Vegas Sun: (Mar 23 1950–Jan 11 1951)
   Nv — Mr 23 1950–Ja 11 1951
   film — Mr 23 1950–Ja 11 1951
Ref: files

Las Vegas Family Shopper

On March 13, 1958, the *Las Vegas Family Shopper*, an eight-page, five-column, free-distribution, Thursday weekly, was begun at North Las Vegas by the Family Shopper, publishers. The paper was devoted principally to advertising and special sales, claiming to be the "first of its kind in southern Nevada." It apparently suspended early in 1959.
Las Vegas Family Shopper: (Mar 13 1958–c. Mar 1959)
   pvt — Mr 13 1958
Ref: files; Averett

Nevada Times (Nevada Mobile Home Times)

The monthly *Nevada Mobile Home Times* was begun in North Las Vegas in August of 1958, by Pauline T. Dewey. In January of 1972, she renamed it the *Nevada Times*, to broaden its base.
Nevada Times: (Aug 1958+)
   Nv — Je 1967+
Ref: files

North Las Vegas Valley Times

On March 26, 1959, Adam Yacenda commenced the semiweekly *North Las Vegas Valley Times*. He waged an aggressive campaign against the seemingly well-established *News*, and forced its capitulation within the year. Thereafter the *Valley Times* prospered. Robert L. Brown, forming the Las Vegas Valley Publishing Company, purchased the paper on November 1, 1973, and expanded it to a daily in April of 1975.
North Las Vegas Valley Times: (Mar 26 1959+)
   film — 1959–66
Ref: files

Bullseye

The *Bullseye* was a weekly paper begun at North Las Vegas by Robert L. Brown of the Las Vegas Valley Publishing Company, on January 4, 1974, for the personnel of Nellis Air Force Base.
Bullseye: (Jan 4 1974+)
   film — Ja 4 1974+
Ref: files

OLINGHOUSE

Olinghouse Miner

In May of 1905, Mark W. Musgrove, after an interlude as a mining promoter in California, attempted a comeback in the Nevada newspaper business, and started the *Olinghouse Miner* at the fledgling camp of Olinghouse in Washoe county. The camp soon died, however, and Musgrove returned to the coast for a time.

Olinghouse Miner: (May 1905–1905)
  No issues located.
Ref: RG My 31 1905; PR Je 9 1905

ORO CITY

Oro City Times

In January, 1907, during the brief activity at Oro City, eleven miles south of Hawthorne, Joel Stimson commenced the *Oro City Times,* with Robert L. Lewis as editor and William E. Steinick as manager. The boom collapsed that summer, and the *Times* suspended.

Oro City Times: (Jan 1907–1907)
  No issues located.
Ref: Polk 1907–8; IR Ja 31 1907

OROVADA

Orovada Weekly Journal

I. J. Studebaker founded the weekly *Journal* at Orovada, forty miles north of Winnemucca, on September 5, 1924. As editor and owner, Studebaker devoted the *Journal,* "to the up-building of Northern Humboldt County," issuing it as a four-page, four-column paper every Friday, for $1.50 a year. The *Journal* lasted exactly one year, suspending publication after its fifty-second number on August 28, 1925, with Studebaker explaining, "Other pressing business matters make this step imperative."

Orovada Weekly Journal: (Sep 5 1924–Aug 28 1925)
  NvHi — S 5 1924–Ag 28 1925
  film — S 5 1924–Ag 28 1925
Ref: files

OSCEOLA

Osceola Nugget

The *Nugget* was started about May of 1903 during a brief revival of the old camp of Osceola in White Pine County. Its editor and publisher are unkown.

Osceola Nugget: (c. May 1903–1903)
   No issues located.
Ref: NSJ Je 5 1903

⁓(OVERTON)⁓

Moapa Valley Herald

The weekly *Moapa Valley Herald* was launched at Overton on Christmas Day, 1975, by Lee Bishop, with Noreen Bishop as editor. They found an enthusiastic readership and they even attracted a rival, the *Lake Mead Monitor*.

Moapa Valley Herald: (Dec 25 1975+)
   pub — D 25 1975+
Ref: Jensen

Lake Mead Monitor

The success of the *Moapa Valley Herald* prompted Darrell Hallenbeck to start a rival weekly, the *Lake Mead Monitor,* on October 4, 1979.

Lake Mead Monitor: (Oct 4 1979+)
   pub — O 4 1979+
Ref: Jensen

⁓(PACKARD)⁓
(See ROCHESTER)

⁓(PAHRUMP)⁓

Pahrump Valley Times

The *Pahrump Valley Times* was begun on December 23, 1971, as an occasional sheet promoting the land boom in southern Nye County. Milt Bozanic was editor and publisher with a post office box at the Charlotte Inn. The paper was printed in Las Vegas. The success of the Pahrump boom justified establishing the *Times* as a regular weekly paper on September 17, 1976.

Pahrump Valley Times: (Dec 23 1971+)
   pub — D 1971+
   film — D 1971+
Ref: files

Pahrump Valley Star

On May 5, 1972, Kathy Ledford Hall commenced a rival occasional sheet, the *Pahrump Valley Star,* which became the valley's first regular weekly on July 31, 1975. Editor-publisher Hall cornered a large share of the local advertising and expanded the *Star* from a tabloid to a "standard size" paper on November 8, 1979.

Pahrump Valley Star: (May 5 1972+)
  pub — 1972+
Ref: files

Desert Living

Pahrump's quarterly *Desert Living,* proclaiming itself, "the Home Magazine of the Southwest," was begun in the summer of 1979, by Fred S. Cook at The Printery, "Next Door to the Laundromat."
Desert Living: (Summer 1979+)
  NvULV — 1979+
Ref: files

Pahrump Tribune

The continuing Pahrump boom prompted the establishment of another rival paper, the twice-monthly *Pahrump Tribune,* on October 17, 1979. Ken Bouton was editor, Denny Lynch general manager, and Doalco, Inc., was the publisher.
Pahrump Tribune: (Oct 17 1979+)
  Nv — Oct 24 1979+
Ref: files

⁓(PALMETTO)⁓

Palmetto Herald

During the boom at Lida, the neighboring camp of Palmetto shared in the prosperity and on February 23, 1906, Newman H. Mix of the *Lida Enterprise* began the *Palmetto Herald.* Mix was editor and publisher. Printing the *Herald* at the *Enterprise* plant in Lida, he issued it every Wednesday as a four-page, six-column weekly, at 10¢ a copy or $5 a year. Both papers flourished only briefly. In July the *Herald* was absorbed into the *Enterprise,* and by the middle of October, the latter was suspended. Its plant was removed to Blair, where Mix commenced the *Press* on November 3, 1906.
Palmetto Herald: (Feb 23 1906–Jul 1906)
  NvHi — Mr 9–16, Je 1 1906
  film — Mr 9–16, Je 1 1906
Ref: files; LCT Jl 28 1906

⁓(PARADISE)⁓

Paradise Reporter

In March of 1879, J. J. Hill and Co., of the Winnemucca *Silver State,* purchased new material in San Francisco, to start a newspaper in the town of Paradise, forty miles north of Winnemucca. On May 10, he issued the first number of the *Paradise Reporter,* a sprightly Democratic weekly that sold for $4 a year. After three months Hill decided he was going broke trying to make money in Paradise, so he sold the paper to H. H. Crenshaw and Co., on August 30. By the following spring Crenshaw, too, found it "an elephant of enormous proportions," and "retired, like his predecessor, covered with glory but without a quarter." Thus on April 10, 1880, the editorship passed to H. Warren, a young man from Bakersfield, California, who was a former correspondent for the San Francisco *Chronicle* and *Call* and the *Stockton Herald.*

Warren soon saw the elephant as well, and in June he warned his readers:

> Two men have been busted out trying to run this paper on wind. With examples of our predecessors staring us in the face we shall make no further experiment of the wind process. If the people want a paper they must support it; if they won't do this then we shall be compelled to close the shebang. We have to buy paper and pay a printer and we can't do this on nothing.

The warning fell unheeded, however, and with the close of the political campaign Warren announced that he had "concluded that the only way to make money out of the *Reporter* is to close the shebang. It is not for any lack of appreciation, it is because there is no money in it, and it may be truthfully said of this paper that it died in order that its owners might live.'

Paradise Reporter: (May 10 1879–Nov 20 1880)
   CU-BANC — My 17–Ag 30 1879; [Ap 10–O 9 1880]
   film — My 17–Ag 30 1879; [Ap 10–O 9 1880]
Ref: files; RRR N 20 1880; GHN N 23 1880; BMM Je 5 1880

Paradise Sunshine

The *Paradise Sunshine* was begun in October of 1905, with C. G. Lucas as editor. It was published monthly, "in the Interest of Christ's Kingdom," by the Religious Newspaper Company of Chesaning, Michigan. It finally dimmed sometime after May of 1906.

Paradise Sunshine: (Oct 1905–c. May 1906)
  NvHi — My 1906
  film — My 1906
Ref: files

~(PINE GROVE)~

Pine Grove News

The *Pine Grove News* was an ephemeral weekly issued in the latter part of 1868, at the new camp of Pine Grove, some twenty-five miles north of Aurora. Nothing is known of its editor or publisher, but it is quite possible that it was printed on the old Ames press following suspension of the Aurora *Esmeralda Union* on October 3, 1868, and prior to the purchase of the press by Chalfant and Parker in the spring of 1870.

Pine Grove News: (c. 1868)
  No issues located.
Ref: Murbarger

~({ PIOCHE }~

Lincoln County Record (Pioche Record)

The pioneer paper of Lincoln County was begun at Pioche, in the Ely Mining District, on September 17, 1870, as the *Ely Record.* W. H. Pitchford and Co. issued it weekly from a canvas tent. Pat Holland bought the paper on October 8, and Robert W. Simpson became his partner the following week. The office was destroyed by the fire that swept the town in September of 1871, but, like the town, it was quickly rebuilt. Simpson retired from the paper on April 11, 1872, and Frank Kenyon became a silent partner and assumed the editorship. Three days later the *Record* was enlarged to a triweekly, but Holland and Kenyon disagreed on the politics of the paper, and Holland became sole proprietor on August 16.

A month later, on September 17, he increased the paper to a daily, as the *Pioche Record.* During the election campaign that year, the *Record* was a strong Democratic advocate, with A. D. Jones as editor. At the same time Kenyon, in partnership with William B. Taylor, commenced a rival Republican paper, the *Pioche Review,* which sparred with the *Record* until the election, when Kenyon left and the *Review* folded. Taylor then became part owner of the *Record,* adding the old *Review* plant to it. However, George G. Berry, Taylor's creditor, promptly took over his interest and disposed of it to John Booth on January 28, 1873. Booth quit six months later, leaving Holland sole proprietor once again.

On December 24, 1875, Holland went bankrupt. The Record Publishing Company, which was formed by his creditors, ran the paper for the next decade under the successive editorship of John Croyland, J. F. O. Holoran, George Gorman, and H. W. Turner. They also reduced it to a triweekly on September 17, 1876, and finally to a weekly on January 6, 1877. T. J. Osborne purchased the paper on February 25, 1888, and ran it until January 11, 1890, when he leased it to H. E. Freudenthal for the rest of the year. Osborne then resumed as publisher until November 5, 1891, when the Record Publishing Company took over, with Osborne as manager. On December 6, 1894, the plant was leased to Eugene Goodrich for a year but reverted again to the Record Company. James Pettee became editor and manager for the company on January 4, 1899, but quit on August 31.

Early the following year, on February 27, 1900, the *Record* suspended publication. It slept for four months before H. E. Freudenthal revived it on

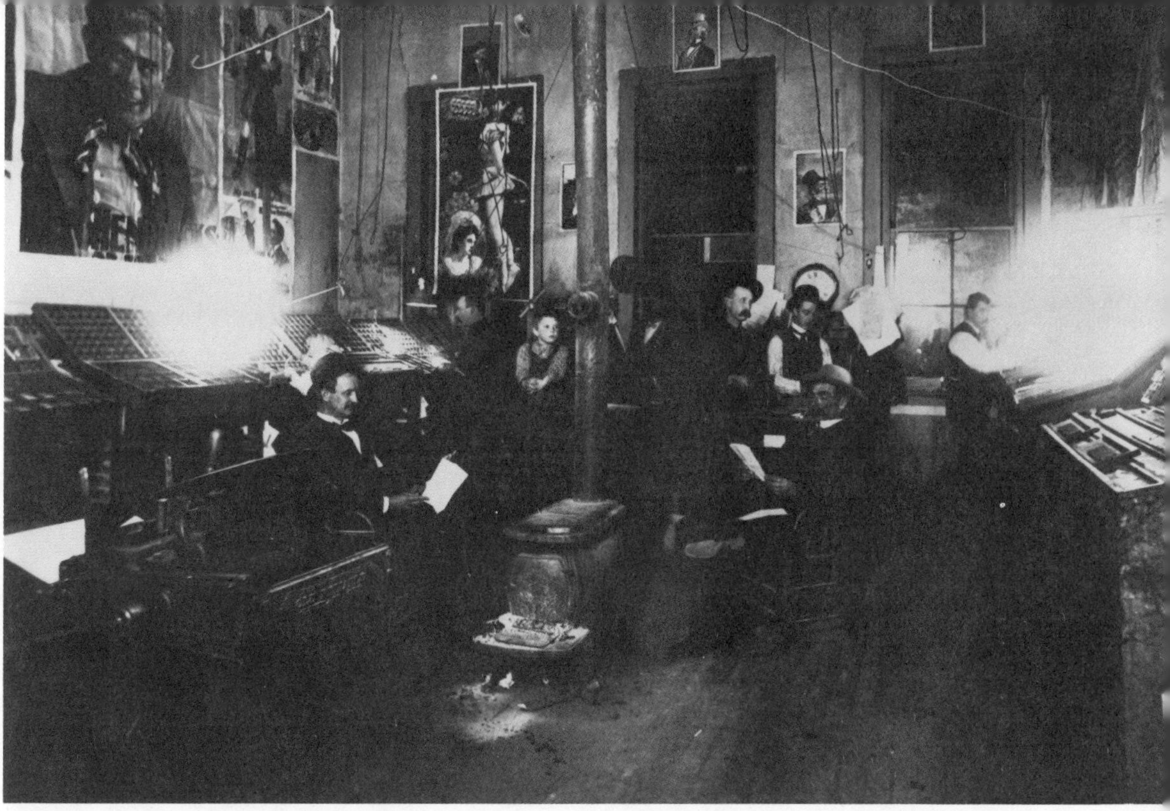

Composing room of the *Territorial Enterprise* circa 1895. *(Nevada Historical Society)*

Territorial Enterprise.

VOL. 1. CARSON VALLEY, UTAH TERRITORY, SATURDAY, JANUARY 1, 1859. NO. 3.

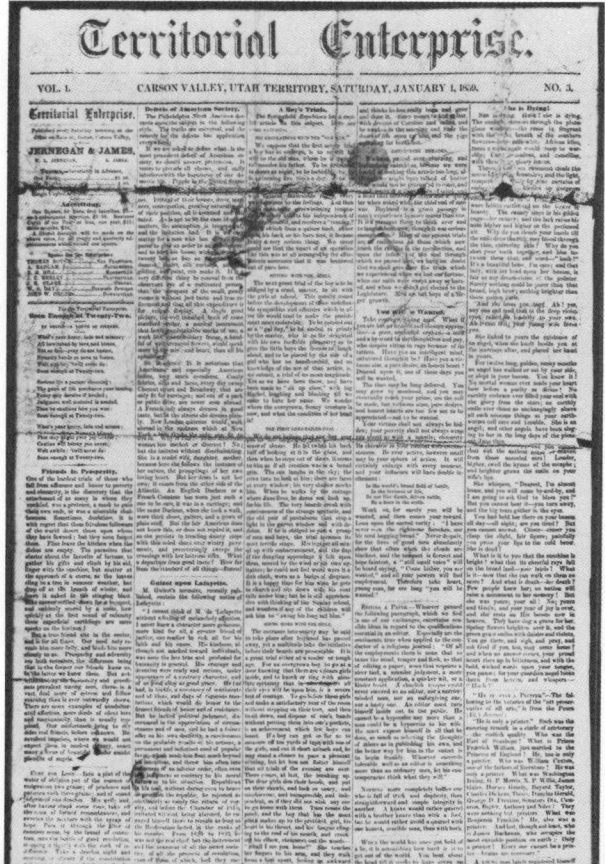

Earliest known copy of the *Territorial Enterprise* still in existence. January 1, 1859. (*Special Collections, Library, University of Nevada, Reno*)

"Local Reporters of the daily newspapers of Virginia and Gold Hill, Nevada, Dec. 10th, 1865." William Gillespie, Charles Parker, Dan De Quille, Robert Lowery, Alf Doten. *(Special Collections, Library, University of Nevada, Reno)*

Office of the *Rawhide Rustler* circa 1908. *(Courtesy of Gil Schmidtmann)*

Reese River Reveille, Austin, circa 1863. *(Nevada Historical Society)*

Tonopah Bonanza, the first frame building in Tonopah. (*Nevada Historical Society*)

The Eureka Sentinel circa 1940. (*Nevada Historical Society*)

Round Mountain Nugget circa 1906. (*George Barnett Collection, Nevada Historical Society*)

Hawthorne News circa 1936. *(Nevada Historical Society)*

Office of the *Gold Hill News* in 1880. (*Special Collections, Library, University of Nevada, Reno*)

Office of the *Nevada State Journal*, Reno, circa 1900. (*Nevada Historical Society*)

Office of the *Caliente Express* circa 1905.
(*Special Collections, Library, University of Nevada, Reno*)

Granite Times, April 17, 1908. $5 per copy. *(Nevada Historical Society)*

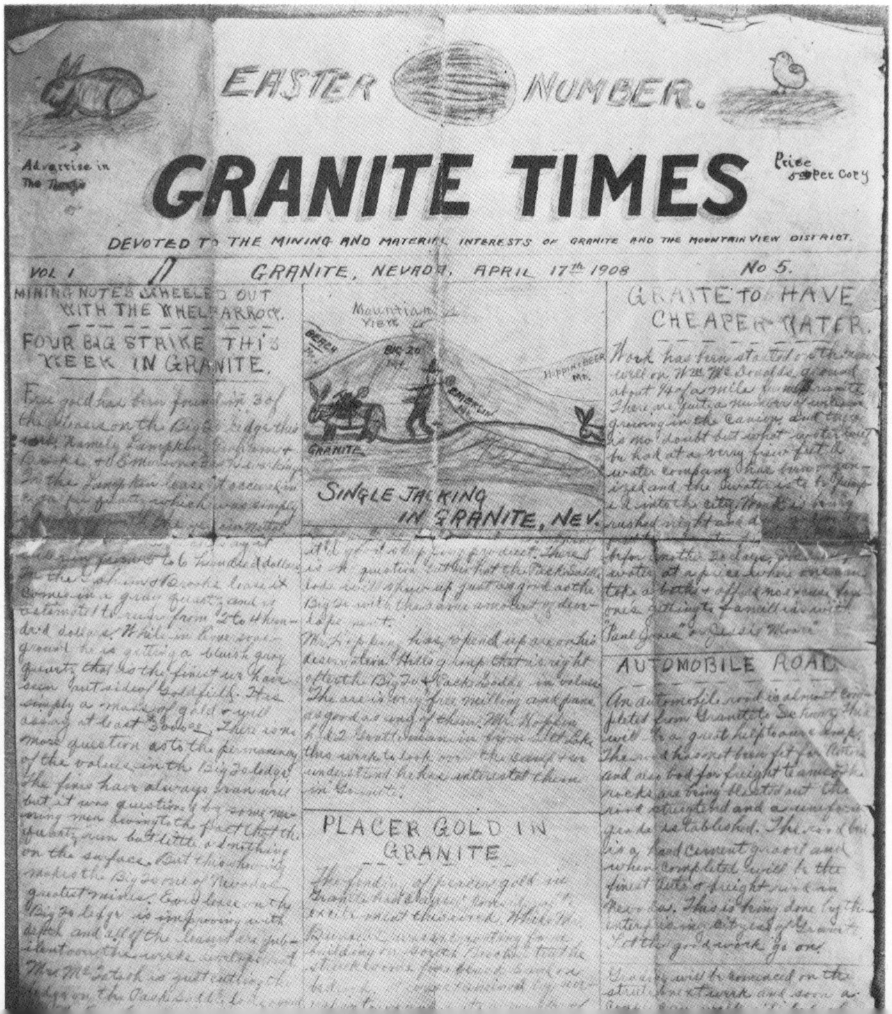

June 29, announcing, "Unlike most papers it does not start out with the intention of running first in the interest of the public, but will be run in the interest of the Proprietor and what he can make out of it." He apparently didn't make enough, for on September 11, 1903, he leased it to C. W. Garrison for two years and then to Eugene Goodrich and William E. Orr. The paper's name was changed to the *Lincoln County Record* on July 6, 1900. Finally, on December 26, 1908, Lewis H. Beason took over the Record Publishing Company, changed the name back to the *Pioche Record,* and ran it for nearly a decade before selling to Oliver R. Nation on February 8, 1918. Nation sold out the following year to A. A. Sherman, who, in turn, sold to E. L. Nores and F. E. Brown on September 10, 1920.

Nores, becoming president of the company, ran the paper for nearly forty years, reviving the name *Lincoln County Record* from June 2, 1925, through February 18, 1932, and then changing it back again to the *Pioche Record.* He and Brown served briefly as editors before hiring a succession of others: W. J. Campbell, S. D. Perry, Philip J. Dolan, Uther Jones, James Bardwell, and Walter Lage. On July 28, 1932, Nores again took over the editorship, continuing until he retired in September, 1958. A new string of editors then held the post: O. Burt Pace, Hollis H. Estill, James Justice and John Thomas. In June, 1968, the paper again became the *Lincoln County Record,* and in 1973, Thomas L. Clay became the majority shareholder in the Record Publishing Company. By the following year Clay was the corporate owner, publisher, and editor. He held these titles until his death on November 16, 1979.

Lincoln County Record: (Sep 17 1870+)
    CU-BANC — D 7, 17 1871; S 15, 17, 22, 25–N 9, 30, D 18 1872–Ja 30, F 1–14, 16–Mr 30 1873; F 5 1881; F 11, Mr 25–Je 17, Jl 1, 29 1882; [Mr 9–Ap 20 1889]
    ICHi — S 23 1876
    NvCH — 1928+
    NvHi — [Ja 10 1875+]
    NvPC — 1870+
    NvU — S 17 1872–5; Ja 3 1885–D 22 1888; 1947; 1949+
    film — [S 17 1872+]
Ref: files, Angel 307

Pioche Review

In September of 1872, following Frank Kenyon's split with Pat Holland of the *Pioche Record,* Kenyon and William B. Taylor of the *Elko Independent* moved the material of the old *Elko Chronicle* to Pioche. Here, on September 22, they commenced publication of an opposition daily, the *Pioche Review.* The new paper carried on a bitter war with the *Record* during the political campaign, but suspended, as was originally planned, after the election. Kenyon left Pioche but Taylor remained to become a part owner of the *Record,* incorporating the *Review* material into that office.

Pioche Review: (Sep 23 1872–Nov 9 1872)
  CU-BANC — S 23–N 9 1872
  film — S 23–N 9 1872
Ref: files, Angel 307

Pioche World

The *Pioche World,* a "monthly journal devoted to the best interests of its publishers," made its debut on March 23, 1874. It was a pint-sized newspaper burlesque claiming "J. Wilkins Micawber, Jr." as its proprietor and editor.

Pioche World: (Mar 23 1874)
  No issues located.
Ref: GHN Mr 30 1874

Pioche Journal

The *Pioche Journal* was first issued as a triweekly on December 15, 1874, by O. K. Wescott and Frank Wyatt. On March 1, 1875, A. D. Jones and James D. Murray purchased the establishment, enlarging the paper to a daily. They continued the paper until September 14 that year, when Murray became sole proprietor. On May 3, 1876, the entire office was destroyed by fire, but publication resumed briefly, only to suspend on June 7.

Pioche Journal: (Dec 15 1874–Jun 7 1876)
  CU-BANC — [Ap 6 1875–Ap 30 1876]
  film — [Ap 6 1875–Ap 30 1876]
Ref: files; Angel 308; GHN Je 13 1876

Local News

Soon after the *Pioche Journal* was burned out, Mark W. Musgrove decided to start a new daily rival to the *Record,* and on June 13, 1876, he issued the first number of the *Local News.* He found that, fire or no fire, Pioche could no longer feed two papers, and the *News* closed down about July 18.

Local News: (Jun 13 1876–c. Jul 18 1876)
  No issues located.
Ref: PR Je 14, Jl 19 1876

Pioche Boomlet

On July 13, 1888, Charley Thompson issued the first number of the *Pioche Boomlet.* It was a small amateur sheet that promised to appear monthly but probably never appeared again.

Pioche Boomlet: (Jul 1888)
  No issues located.
Ref: PR Jl 21 1888

The Memorandum

The *Memorandum* was a diminutive journal which flourished briefly at Pioche during the summer of 1891. Nothing is known of its personnel, and the only attention it seems to have attracted was a result of its issuance as a multicolored sheet on July 4. It was issued as a weekly and probably survived no more than a few weeks.

The Memorandum: (c. Jul 1891)
  No issues located.
Ref: PR Jl 9 1891

The Lode

Following the suspension of the *Ferguson Lode* at Delamar, N. P. Dooley removed the plant to Pioche, where he revived the *Lode* on March 11, 1893. The *Lode* was published every Saturday, as a four-page, six-column weekly, selling for $5 a year. After more than a year at Pioche, Dooley decided to move the *Lode* back to the Ferguson Mining District. On June 9, 1894, he suspended the *Lode* at Pioche, and nine days later, he revived the paper at Helene, then renamed Delamar. (See Delamar, *De Lamar Lode.*)

The Lode: (Mar 11 1893–Jun 9 1894)
  NvHi — [Mr 11 1893–Je 9 1894]
  film — [Mr 11 1893–Je 9 1894]
Ref: files

Local Messenger

On June 7, 1898, the Messenger Publishing Company issued the first number of the *Local Messenger* at Pioche. N. P. Dooley was manager of the paper and published it every Tuesday, as a four-page, five-column weekly, which sold for $2.50 a year. The paper was a poorly printed sheet, containing two pages of locals and two inside pages of patented, preprinted material. On May 23, 1899, Dooley suspended the *Messenger* at Pioche and leased the plant to A. Clifford, who revived the paper at Delamar the following June 3. (See Delamar, *Local Messenger.*)

Local Messenger: (Jun 7 1898–May 23 1899)
  NvHi — [Je 14 1898–My 23 1899]
  NvU — [Je 7–D 27 1898]
  film — [Je 7 1898–My 23 1899]
Ref: files

Pioche Times

The *Pioche Times* was a short-lived campaign paper, founded about July of 1902, by an aspiring U. S. Senatorial candidate. It was intended to run only until the election and hence probably suspended that fall.

Pioche Times: (Jul 1902–c. Nov 1902)
  No issues located.
Ref: PR Jl 6 1902

Chronicle

On January 15, 1910, Charles Lee Horsley commenced the weekly Pioche *Chronicle.* Horsley was editor and issued the paper as a six-page, independent, Friday weekly, at $2.50 a year. Pioche was unable to support two papers, however, and the *Chronicle* was forced to suspend by the following year.

Chronicle: (Jan 15 1910–c. 1911)
  No issues located.
Ref: LVA Ja 15 1910; Myrick

Lincoln County Independent

The *Lincoln County Independent* was begun at Pioche on August 18, 1938, by Uther Jones. Jones was editor and publisher, issuing the paper as a Thursday weekly, at $2 a year. The *Independent* succeeded in holding its own against the *Pioche Record* for three years, but finally succumbed on October 30, 1941, announcing simply, "After three years and three months of publishing the *Lincoln County Independent* we are bidding our friends in Pioche Goodbye."

Lincoln County Independent: (Aug 18 1938–Oct 30 1941)
  NvU — [Ag 18 1938–O 30 1941]
  film — [Ag 18 1938–O 30 1941]
Ref: files

Pioche People's Press

The *Pioche People's Press* was an undated one-issue campaign paper, put out just before the election in 1944, as a "political advertisement on behalf of Vail Pittman for Senator."

Pioche People's Press: (c. Nov 1944)
  NvU — undated issue
  film — undated issue
Ref: files

Slipstream

Slipstream was a curious little weekly begun at Pioche about January 23, 1946, by Richard "Nighthawk" Nores, who described it as "slipstream from the nighthawk . . . the only dingbat sheet published in the state of Nevada." It persisted for seven months.

Slipstream: (c. Jan 23 1946–c. Jul 1946)
  NvU — Je 12, 26, Jl 10 1946
  film — Je 12, 26, Jl 10 1946
Ref: files

PIONEER

Pioneer Topics

Following the discovery of rich ore in the Pioneer mine, eight miles north of Rhyolite, a camp grew rapidly at the site. On February 17, 1909, Theodore Lowe of the *Columbia Topics* commenced the weekly *Topics* at Pioneer. Lowe was editor and manager of the Pioneer Publishing Company, which issued the paper every Wednesday, as a four-page, six-column weekly. The day after the *Topics* first appeared, Earle R. Clemens of the nearby *Rhyolite Herald* began a rival paper, the *Pioneer Press* from the *Herald* press in Rhyolite. A spirited feud developed between the two papers, with Lowe arguing indignantly that the *Topics* was "the first and only paper printed in Pioneer." As the competition for subscribers grew fiercer, Lowe tried to double his share by starting a third competitor, the daily *Times,* in July. But the boom at Pioneer collapsed before any of the contenders could enjoy a victory, and all three succumbed in July.

Pioneer Topics: (Feb 17 1909–Jul 1909)
   NvHi — [F 24–Jl 24 1909]
   film — [F 24–Jl 24 1909]
Ref: files; RH Jl 31 1909

Pioneer Press

On February 18, 1909, just one day after Lowe commenced his *Pioneer Topics,* Earle R. Clemens of the *Rhyolite Herald* began the rival *Pioneer Press.* The *Press* was edited and published by Clemens at the *Herald* plant in Rhyolite, as a four-page, Saturday weekly, selling at $5 a year. Clemens immediately became involved in a journalistic war with Lowe, who charged, "Clemens spends six days a week in Rhyolite and the Press office is a sign on a real estate office which is usually closed." Despite such charges the *Press* held on until both papers suspended when the Pioneer bubble burst in July.

Pioneer Press: (Feb 18 1909–Jul 1909)
   No issues located.
Ref: RH F 17, Jl 31 1909

Pioneer Market Letter

Early in 1909, the Goldfield brokerage firm of George F. von Polenz and Co. opened an office in the new camp of Pioneer and commenced the *Pioneer Market Letter.* It was a free sheet, promoting just those "few very safe investments which will pay big profits."

Pioneer Market Letter: (c. Feb 1909–1909)
   No issues located.
Ref: PT F 24 1909

Pioneer Times

On July 4, 1909, in the heat of the journalistic war between the Pioneer *Topics* and *Press,* T. Lowe of the *Topics* began the daily *Times* in a vain attempt to win new subscribers. It seems never to have gotten beyond its first number.

Pioneer Times: (Jul 4 1909)
   No issues located.
Ref: PT Jl 8 1909

(PITTMAN)

Pittman Key

The *Pittman Key,* an awful pun on the town's namesake, started at Pittman, now part of Henderson, in 1942. Its editor and publisher are unknown, and it probably suspended in 1943.

Pittman Key: (1942–c. 1943)
   No issues located.
Ref: Folkes 28

(POTOSI)

East of the Nevada; or the Miner's Voice from the Colorado

Although the Potosi mines had been worked for lead by the Mormons in 1856, it was not until 1860 that silver was discovered in the ore. Late that summer, Captain J. E. Stevens and members of the Colorado Mining Company established the camp of Potosi in what was then the northwestern tip of New Mexico Territory, five miles south of Mountain Springs on the San Bernardino and Salt Lake road. As word spread and the weather cooled the rush to Potosi began. A saloon to grace the new camp was soon enroute from Los Angeles, and close behind was J. A. Talbott, a former printer from Calaveras, who enjoyed a reputation as an Amazon explorer. He came just to see the new diggings, but when the camp had grown to boast thirteen buildings Talbott decided it was time to start a newspaper. Undaunted by the lack of a printing press he commenced a manuscript sheet to which he assigned the unwieldy title *East of the Nevada; or the Miner's Voice from the Colorado.*

He issued the first number on February 19, 1861, stating in his introductory:

> The manifold wants of our community rendering it necessary, owing to our isolated position, shut out from those sources of information and instruction that is as familiar as "household words" in a settled community, renders it necessary to have a vehicle of thought amongst us by which an interchange of intelligence should be disseminated, questions discussed, wit circulated, and those precious gems preserved, without which "this world would be a void." For this end, and under our peculiar circumstances, our sheet is issued.

The sheet was organized in the best newspaper tradition and contained more news than many printed sheets of the day. Among its items was a description of the principal mines of the district, a notice of a theater to be built by the local thespian group, and an account of the great commotion caused by the arrival of the U.S. Boundary Commission party, which had in its troupe three camels.

But the boom was brief, and the *Miner's Voice* probably ran for no more than a few issues. Even then its command of public favor was shared by an even shorter-lived rival sheet, *the Potosi Nix Cum Rouscht*. A few months later Talbott joined the rush to Holcomb Valley, and by October all work had stopped and the mines were abandoned.

East of the Nevada; or the Miner's Voice from the Colorado: (Feb 19 1861–1861)
　No issues located.
Ref: LAS Mr 9 1861

Potosi Nix Cum Rouscht

Not to be outdone by Talbott's *Miner's Voice,* Captain J. E. Stevens, president of the Colorado Mining Company and founder of Potosi, commenced his own manuscript sheet, with the enigmatic title *Potosi Nix Cum Rouscht,* in late February of 1861. Stevens listed himself only as the "Man about the Mill," and claimed that the paper was "printed" at Las Vegas station and "published" at Potosi. The *Nix* probably lasted only one issue before surrendering the field.

Potosi Nix Cum Rouscht: (Feb 1861)
　No issues located.
Ref: LAS Mr 9 1861

~(QUARTZ MOUNTAIN)~

Quartz Mountain Miner

When the town of Quartz Mountain came into being some eighty miles northwest of Tonopah, W. W. Booth of the *Tonopah Bonanza* commenced the *Quartz Mountain Miner* on June 16, 1926. Booth was editor and manager, with J. N. Floyd as assistant editor, occupying the office at Quartz Mountain. The *Miner* was printed every Wednesday, at the *Bonanza* plant in Tonopah, as a four-page, seven-column, $5-a-year weekly. Quartz Mountain began to decline the following year, however, and the *Miner* was suspended. The *Miner's* office at Quartz Mountain was later removed to Hawthorne to serve as the office for Booth's *News*.

Quartz Mountain Miner: (Jun 16 1926–c. 1927)
　NvHi — Je 16 1926
　film — Je 16 1926
Ref: files

⁓⁓(RAMSEY)⁓⁓

Ramsey Recorder

Ramsey boomed quickly following the discovery of gold eighteen miles northeast of Virginia City in the winter of 1905. The first town lots were sold in July of 1906, and on August 5, the weekly *Ramsey Recorder* was printed at Carson City by the Recorder Publishing Company with I. G. Lewis as editor and W. P. Harrington as manager. On January 6, 1907, Roy R. Mighels became editor, continuing the *Recorder* until the decline of the camp forced its suspension on November 8, 1908.

Ramsey Recorder: (Aug 5 1906–Nov 8 1908)
  NvHi — [Ag 5 1906–N 1 1908]
  NvU — [Ag 5 1906–N 8 1908]
  film — [Ag 5 1906–N 8 1908]
Ref: files

⁓⁓(RAWHIDE)⁓⁓

Rawhide Rustler

Rawhide was christened on February 15, 1907, when it was only a single tent, but it grew rapidly, aided by the sensational stories of its riches published in promoter George Graham Rice's *Nevada Mining News.* On October 24, 1907, J. Holman Buck of the Mina *Western Nevada Miner* issued the camp's first newspaper, the *Rawhide Rustler.* Buck spent a few days each week in Rawhide gathering news, and then returned to Mina to print the paper. Despite such cavalier management the paper prospered. But in January of 1908, when moves were afoot to commence rival papers, Buck sold the name and the office to W. W. Booth of the *Tonopah Bonanza,* who was financially better able to withstand competition. Booth installed William Stuart Webster, formerly of the *Dutch Creek News,* as editor, brought in a $5,000 printing plant, and began printing the *Rustler* in Rawhide on February 15. Across the lead of the paper Booth proudly boasted, "This paper is different from other newspapers and I thank the Gods of Verse and Prose that it IS different."

In April, Booth incorporated as the Rawhide Rustler Publishing Company, with himself as president. Webster resigned as editor on June 13, and Booth's son Chauncey managed the paper for a month that summer. The *Rustler* survived the devastating fire that leveled most of Rawhide on September 5, but finally succumbed as the camp waned the following spring. Booth suspended the paper on April 17, 1909, shipping the plant to Hawthorne, where he commenced a new paper, the *Herald,* the following week.

Rawhide Rustler: (Oct 24 1907–Apr 17 1909)
   NvHi — F 22 1908–Ap 17 1909
   NvU — [Ja 16 1908–Ap 17 1909]
   film — [Ja 16 1908–Ap 17 1909]
Ref: files; RPT Ap 23 1909

Rawhide Times

The weekly *Rawhide Times* made its debut on January 16, 1908. It was published by the Rawhide Times Publishing Company, with John G. McMurry as president, Eugene Grutt as secretary, and Harry Hedrick as editor. Within the next couple of weeks two more papers, the *News* and *Press,* appeared, so the following month the *Times'* owners joined with Mark H. Bryan and Margaret E. Loughrin of the daily *Press* and combined the two papers to form the *Press-Times* on February 21. There was talk of continuing the *Times* as the weekly edition of the daily, but if this was done it apparently didn't last long, for the daily itself was reduced to a weekly in July. (See *Rawhide Press-Times.*)

Rawhide Times: (Jan 16 1908–c. Mar 1908)
   pvt — Ja 16 1908
   film — Ja 16 1908
Ref: files; RDP F 20 1908

Rawhide News

Rawhide's third paper, the weekly *News,* was founded by Clyde C. Emerson of the *Fairview News* on January 25, 1908. After yet another paper started the following week, Emerson suspended his Fairview paper and moved his printing plant to Rawhide to devote his full attention to the new venture. To aid him in his struggle he hired Joseph S. Jordan as editor. The *News* plant was one of the first casualties of the big fire, but Emerson, undaunted, telegraphed to San Francisco for a new press and equipment that same afternoon. Rawhide declined rapidly after the fire, however, and Emerson was forced to close down the paper in February of 1909. Emerson moved the plant to the new town of Mason to start the *Mason Valley News.*

Rawhide News: (Jan 25 1908–Feb 1909)
   NvHi — Mr 7, Ag 1 1908
   film — Mr 7, Ag 1 1908
Ref: files; RPT S 11 1908, F 19 1909

Rawhide Daily Press

On February 1, 1908, Mark H. Bryan, who claimed to be the first male born in Virginia City, commenced publication of the first daily in Rawhide, the *Rawhide Daily Press.* Bryan served as editor and in partnership with Margaret E. Loughrin, issued the paper every evening except Sunday, for $10 a year. There just wasn't enough business to support four papers, however, so on February 21, they merged their paper with the *Times* to form the daily *Press-Times.* Bryan soon became sole proprietor of the new firm and continued it until January 20, 1911. (See *Rawhide Press-Times.*)

Rawhide Daily Press: (Feb 1 1908–Feb 20 1908)
   NvHi — [F 1–20 1908]
   film — [F 1–20 1908]
Ref: files

Rawhide Press-Times

On February 21, 1908, Mark H. Bryan and Margaret E. Loughrin of the *Rawhide Press* joined with John McMurry and others of the Rawhide *Times* and, merging the two plants, commenced the daily *Press-Times.* Harry Hedrick of the *Times* continued as editor and Bryan served as business manager. On July 7, Bryan discontinued the daily edition and reduced the paper to a weekly on Friday, July 17. On September 4, the Press Times Publishing Company became the publisher, with Bryan as editor and manager. The *Press-Times* escaped destruction in Rawhide's great fire and survived for nearly three years, with Bryan eventually becoming sole editor and proprietor. With the collapse of the Rawhide boom, Bryan finally suspended the paper on January 20, 1911.

Rawhide Press-Times: (Feb 21 1908–Jan 20 1911)
   pvt — Mr 2 1908
   NvHi — [Mr 7 1908–Ja 13 1911]
   NvU — [Mr 16 1908–N 4 1909]
   film — [Mr 7 1908–Ja 20 1911]
Ref: files; RDP F 20 1908

Telegraph Gossip

The Rawhide *Telegraph Gossip* was a triweekly issued by the Rawhide Securities Company about March of 1908. Its editor and duration are unknown.

Telegraph Gossip: (c. Mar 1908)
   No issues located.
Ref: Myrick

Rawhide Miner

The *Rawhide Miner,* begun on April 1, 1908, by the Rawhide Miner Publishing Company, offered "Food for Investors and Facts for Everybody," for 10¢ a copy, and claimed a circulation of 25,000! It was a stock promotion sheet that soon folded.

Rawhide Miner: (Apr 1 1908–c. 1908)
   NvHi — Ap 1 1908
   film — Ap 1 1908
Ref: files

RENO

Reno Crescent

With the decline of Washoe City, John C. Lewis suspended the *Eastern Slope* and removed the plant to the rapidly growing town of Reno, at that time only a few months old. On July 4, 1868, he commenced publication of a Republican weekly, the *Reno Crescent*. During the election campaign of that year he added *Daily* to the name of the paper from October 22 to November 12, but he still issued it only once a week. W. C. Lewis, his son, took over as editor on January 2, 1873. Finally, on March 21, 1874, the growth of Reno actually warranted enlarging the paper to a daily, and it continued as such until its suspension on June 16, 1875. J. C. Dow purchased the establishment, using the material to start the *Daily Nevada Democrat* two weeks later.

Reno Crescent: (Jul 4 1868–Jun 16 1875)
   C — O 10 1868
   CU-BANC — [Jl 11 1868–S 14 1872]; O 23 1873; Ap 21, My 8–9, 30 1874
   N — F 20 1869
   NvHi — [Jl 4 1868–Mr 26 1875]
   NvRW — Jl 1871–My 10 1874
   NvU — F 12–Je 16 1875
   film — [Jl 4 1868–Mr 26 1875]
Ref: files; Angel 328; McMurtrie 303-4

Nevada State Journal

The *Nevada State Journal* was begun at Reno on November 23, 1870, by J. G. Law, W. H. H. Fellows, and E. A. Littlefield, under the firm name of J. G. Law and Co. Littlefield was editor and Law associate editor, issuing the paper as a twenty-four-column weekly. On August 26, 1871, Littlefield sold his interest to his partners, and the following year, on June 22, C. C. Powning purchased Law's holdings and became editor. With the rising prosperity of the paper, Fellows and Powning enlarged the *Journal* to a semiweekly on February 5, 1873. It was continued as such until March 31, 1874, when both a daily and a weekly were started. On the following September 5, Powning, who had entered the office as a "devil," purchased Fellows's interest and became sole editor and proprietor.

Powning continued the *Journal* until January 3, 1891, when it passed to the firm of E. D. Kelley and C. H. Stoddard. On February 2, 1892, Judge William Webster purchased Stoddard's interest, and the firm of Kelly and Webster managed the paper until November 26, 1898. At that time, Webster became sole proprietor under the firm name of William Webster and Son, hiring John H. Dennis as chief editor and Thomas Smith as local editor and reporter. They conducted the paper until July 1, 1901, when it was leased by Ernest L. Bingham. Merrill A. Teague, editor of George Graham

Rice's *Nevada Mining News,* leased the *Journal* on July 2, 1907, and became editor and general manager, apparently to help further some of Rice's mining schemes. George Kilborn took over the lease in September, however, and on February 27, 1908, he bought the paper, which he retained for over a decade until his death.

Kilborn hired a succession of editors to manage the paper for him, starting with D. E. W. Williamson in February of 1908, P. L. Bryant the following October, G. H. Beebe in March of 1909, A. R. Arbukle that July, and many others. After his death, his widow finally sold the paper, on August 1, 1922, to Governor Emmet D. Boyle, who became president of Nevada State Journal, Inc., with Homer Mooney as editor. Boyle died in January of 1926, and his widow, Vida M. Boyle, sold a majority of the stock to Governor James G. Scrugham on December 1, 1926. F. W. McKechic, Jr., became publisher on November 28, 1931. He was followed by Texan McHenry Tichenor on February 13, 1938.

Ownership of the major Reno dailies was consolidated by Merritt C. Speidel, who bought the *Reno Evening Gazette* and the *Nevada State Journal* on November 1, 1939. Joseph F. McDonald served as editor for the Speidel Newspapers, Inc., the corporate owner of Reno Newspapers, Inc., from 1939 until 1957. He was followed by Paul A. Leonard. In 1968, Speidel Newspapers, Inc., selected Richard J. Schuster as publisher, and he continued in this position until his resignation in 1975. Ronald Einstoss succeeded him, and upon his death in 1977, Warren L. Lerude was named publisher by Speidel Newspapers, which had merged with the Gannett Co., Inc., on May 11, 1977.

Nevada State Journal (weekly): (Nov 23 1870–c. 1902)
    C — D 10 1870–My 11, 25, Je 8–15, Jl 6–27, Ag 10–N 30, D 28 1872–Ja 18, F 5–Je 21 1873
    CHi — Ap 20, Je 15 1895; Je 5 1897
    CU-BANC — 1870–Mr 25, Ap 11 1874–D 1880; Ja–Je 1886; O 19 1889; Ja 1, My 31 1890
    DLC — 1872–D 13 1873
    ICHi — Ag 12 1876
    Nv — 1870–S 3 1871
    NvHi — N 23 1870; [1874–1902]
    NvRW — 1870–Mr 25 1874
    NvU — 1870–2
    film — [N 23 1870–D 26 1891]

Nevada State Journal (daily): (Mar 31 1874+)
    C — S 26 1890
    CHi — Ja 3, S 20 1874; Ap 17, My 14, 16 1895
    CoU — 1903; S 1906–My 1910
    CU-BANC — N 18 1876–8; F 1879–80; My 4, N 11 1882; Ja 18 1883; 1886–7; Ja 1–21, 24–25, 27, 29–31, F 25 1888; Ag 25 1889; S 27 1890; Mr 4–5 1896
    DLC — Jl 1893–1902
    ICHi — S 27 1876
    KHi — Jl 28 1912; Ap 18 1920; F 11, My 5 1922
    Nv — F 1875+
    NvR — Jl 29 1929+

NvRW — Mr 26 1874+
NvU — 1874+
WaPS — My 21–27 1917; Ap 7 1919; Mr 30 1929
  film — Mr 31 1874+
Ref: files; Angel 329; DNN 1970/71

Daily Nevada Democrat

Following the suspension of the *Reno Crescent,* J. C. Dow purchased the establishment to found the *Daily Nevada Democrat* on June 30, 1875. Dow issued the paper for only a few months and then sold the plant to Henry Mitchell. He quickly ran into debt and apparently suspended the paper in September, but as a contemporary noted, "It died game." The material was later purchased by H. A. Waldo and Co., to publish the *Reno Daily Record.*
Daily Nevada Democrat: (Jun 30 1875–Sep 1875)
  NvU — Je 30–Ag 26 1875
  film — Je 30–Ag 26 1875
Ref: files; Angel 329, GHN Jl 1 1875

Reno Evening Gazette

The firm of John F. Alexander and Edward W. Hayden commenced publication of the *Reno Evening Gazette* on March 28, 1876, from a small office on Commercial Street, near the Depot Hotel. John F. Alexander was only twenty-three years old, a recent graduate of the University of California when he started the *Gazette.* The paper prospered, and in 1877, the establishment was moved to a large brick building west of the plaza. On April 14 of that year, an eight-page weekly was added to the daily. The partnership between Alexander and Hayden was dissolved on September 2, 1878, and Alexander became sole proprietor. He enlarged both papers, but, on November 19, he sold them to Robert L. Fulton and William F. Edwards. Edwards retired on May 31, 1879, leaving Fulton to continue the *Gazette* alone. In the early 1880's, "Lying Jim" Townsend came down from the Sierra to liven the paper as local editor. During the time that Townsend was on the staff of the *Gazette,* his tall tales made the paper one of the most popular in the state.

On February 1, 1887, Fulton sold the paper to the firm of C. S. Preble and C. S. Young, who were joined on January 3, 1888, by John M. Dormer. On September 20, 1887, they purchased the defunct *Sagebrush Stockman,* renaming the weekly edition the *Weekly Gazette and Stockman.* The weekly continued under this head until its suspension about October, 1903. Allen C. Bragg purchased the paper on October 1, 1888, and took in A. O. Porter as a partner on June 1, 1889. This partnership ended with Porter's death early in April, 1891, and Bragg again became sole editor and proprietor. On July 1, 1893, the property was incorporated under the name of the Gazette Publishing Company, with William E. Sharon and A. H. Manning becoming part-owners. Bragg remained as editor until October 13, 1903, when Charles A. Norcross replaced him.

Oscar R. Morgan bought control of the paper on November 11, 1904, assumed the editorship, and held it for over a decade. When Morgan retired, on August 18, 1915, he sold to Samuel Platt, George L. Sanford, and Graham Sanford, under the name of the Reno Evening Gazette Company. David E. W. Williamson served as editor until 1929, when co-owner Graham Sanford took over the chair. Three years later, Graham and Leigh Sanford became the sole publishers. They sold the paper on September 30, 1939, to the newspaper chain of Merritt C. Speidel and Associates. Speidel also bought the rival daily *Nevada State Journal* and formed Reno Newspapers, Inc., to publish both the Republican evening *Gazette* and the Democratic morning *Journal.*

Joseph F. McDonald served as editor of both papers until 1957, when John Sanford became the *Gazette* editor and Paul A. Leonard the *Journal* editor. In 1968, Richard J. Schuster was named publisher for both newspapers, a post he held for seven years, until 1975, when he announced his resignation. Ronald Einstoss was named to succeed him and continued until his death in 1977. Warren L. Lerude was then named publisher by Speidel Newspapers, Inc., which had merged with the Gannett Company on May 11, 1977.

Reno Evening Gazette: (Mar 28 1876+)
    C — S 22 1881; Jl 8 1904+
    CHi — D 31 1878; Je 18 1891; Je 10 1892; S 21 1893; O 25 1894; Je 7 1895
    CU-BANC — Ap 25 1877–Ap 1883; Mr 7, Je 20–Jl 18, S 1887; Ja 3 1888–D 30 1891; Ja 30, Mr 2 1896
    KHi — Je 1917; Je 21 1919
    MWA — N 12–15, 22–23 1935
    NvHi — D 14 1877+
    NvR — [1929–33]; 34+
    NvRW — My 15 1876+
    NvU — Mr 1880+
    film — Mr 28 1876+
Weekly Gazette (and Stockman): (Apr 14 1877–c. Oct 1903)
    CU-BANC — Ap 14 1877–D 26 1878; Mr 6 1879–D 30 1880
    DLC — My 1900–2
    NvHi — Ap 14 1877–S 24 1885; D 20 1888–O 18 1900
Ref: files; Angel 329–30; Doten 2169; Ayer; DNN

Nevada State Fair Herald

The *Nevada State Fair Herald* was a twenty-four-column, free daily, issued briefly at the Reno Fair Grounds in October of 1877, by C. C. Powning of the *Nevada State Journal*. It was revived again in October 1881 by two *Gazette* printers, Pueschel and Harris, and in October of 1885 by L. Eugene Lee.

Nevada State Fair Herald: (Oct 1877; Oct 1881; Oct 1885)
    No issues located.
Ref: NSJ O 4 1877; RG O 10 1881, O 14 1885

Daily Evening Record

The first number of the *Reno Daily Record* was issued on Monday, August 5, 1878, by H. A. Waldo, W. W. Ellis, and B. M. Barney, under the firm name of H. A. Waldo and Co. It was published on the material of the former *Nevada Democrat,* and consisted of four pages of five columns each. The paper changed hands—and names—rapidly. On October 4, Waldo retired, leaving Barney and Ellis proprietors of the *Daily Record.* They brought in E. F. Reed as business manager, and on the following day the Record Publishing Company appeared as owner. This firm held control for scarcely a month, until S. F. Hoole became sole editor and proprietor on November 1. Hoole altered the name to *Daily Evening Record* on November 6, but soon realized the futility of the venture and suspended the *Record* on November 18. He then removed the material to the new camp of Bodie, in Mono County, California, where he started the *Morning News* early the following March.

Daily Evening Record: (Aug 5 1878–Nov 18 1878)
   NvU — [Ag 5–N 18 1878]
   film — [Ag 5–N 18 1878]
Ref: files; Angel 329

Reno Annual Advertiser

The *Reno Annual Advertiser* was begun on December 25, 1878, by Fulton and Edwards, publisher of the Reno *Gazette.* It was intended to be issued every Christmas, as a free distribution advertising sheet, but only one number was ever issued. The paper contained four pages of seven columns each and was published in the Reno *Gazette* office.

Reno Annual Advertiser: (Dec 25 1878)
   NvHi — D 25 1878
   film — D 25 1878
Ref: files

The Plaindealer

Henry Hardy Hogan began publication of the weekly Reno *Plaindealer* on March 28, 1881. The paper, containing eight pages of four columns each, was edited and published by Hogan as a strong advocate of the National Greenback Party. After the election in 1882, Hogan temporarily suspended the paper from November 25 until the following May 5. With the coming of the next election, the *Plaindealer* was enlarged to a semiweekly on September 7, 1884, and increased to a daily on October 7. It was issued as a daily until the election and then suspended again on November 22, 1884, this time for eleven years. (See Reno, *The Plaindealer,* 1895.)

The Plaindealer: (Mar 28 1881–Nov 1884)
   CU-BANC — Mr 28 1881–Nov 1883
   NvHi — [1881–4]
   NvRW — Mr 28 1881–O 31 1884
   NvU — Mr–D 1881; Jl–S 1882; My 1883–S 1884

film — Mr 28 1881–N 22 1884
Ref: files

Reno Times

The *Reno Times* was begun on January 16, 1882, by the firm of H. A. Waldo and T. V. Julien. They issued the *Times* every afternoon, except Sunday, as a four-page, four-column daily, which sold for $5 a year or one bit a week. The paper was not able to compete successfully and suspended publication on September 13, 1882.

Reno Times: (Jan 16 1882–Sep 13 1882)
   NvHi — Ja 16–S13 1882
   NvRW — Ja 16–S 13 1882
   film — Ja 16–S 13 1882
Ref: files

Reno Bazaar

L. Eugene Lee commenced the eight-page, amateur monthly, the *Reno Bazaar,* in December of 1882. Lee offered the paper at an annual subscription rate of 50¢, but it is doubtful that it lasted nearly that long.

Reno Bazaar: (Dec 1882–c. 1883)
   film — D 1882
Ref: files

Reno Democrat

Reno again lacked a Democratic paper until December 17, 1883, when Robert Glen established the *Reno Democrat.* The paper was issued from his office in the Plaindealer Building every Wednesday, as a four-page, six-column weekly, with the motto: "Where Liberty Dwells There is My Country." On January 7, 1884, J. B. Whitehead joined Glen as editor and proprietor, and this firm managed the paper until the following May 3. Fred W. Hagerman bought Glen's interest, and Hagerman and Whitehead continued the *Democrat* until after the election of 1884, when the paper was suspended.

Reno Democrat: (Dec 17 1883–Nov 1884)
   NvU — D 17 1883–Ag 2 1884
   film — D 17 1883–Ag 2 1884
Ref: files

Daily Morning Star

The *Daily Morning Star* was a diminutive paper started on October 20, 1884, by Runnels and Lee. W. H. Runnels soon retired, and the Lee brothers, William T. and L. Eugene, carried it on until mid-January of 1885, when L. E. Lee retired from the venture to attend business college in San Francisco. The *Star* apparently suspended a short time later, but William T. Lee reentered the publishing business again in 1892, with the founding of the *Carson Press*.

Daily Morning Star: (Oct 20 1884–c. Feb 1885)
   NvHi — O 21 1884
   film — O 21 1884
Ref: files; Myrick

Sagebrush Stockman

The weekly *Sagebrush Stockman* was founded in Reno in 1886, by the firm of Sayre and Vance, but D. L. Sayre soon sold out to George W. Bloor. The paper was devoted solely to livestock news and the interests of Nevada ranchmen. It contained four pages, 24 by 36 inches, and sold for $3 a year. Bloor and Vance were unable to make a financial success of the establishment and sold the plant to the Reno *Gazette* in September of 1887.
Sagebrush Stockman: (c. 1886–S 1887)
  No issues located.
Ref: REG S 15 1887, Ap 28 1890

The Free Lance

In the summer of 1889, Rev. C. H. Gardner moved the press of his defunct Genoa *Nevada Prohibitionist* to Reno. There he launched a new weekly, *The Free Press,* on September 4 and ran it until January of 1891 when Frank Sisson took the helm. It was on the rocks soon afterward.
The Free Lance: (Sep 4 1889–c. Feb 1891)
  No issues located.
Ref: GeC Jl 26, S 13 1889, Ja 23 1891

The Snowbound

In January of 1890, a paralyzing and prolonged snowstorm struck the northern and central portions of Nevada, blocking the passes in the Sierra, isolating communities, and killing countless thousands of cattle. For three weeks during the height of this great blizzard, 600 passengers on the Southern Pacific Railroad were stranded at Reno. Among these passengers was George T. McCully, who sought to relieve the anxious weeks of waiting by printing a newspaper for his fellow passengers.

On January 31, 1890, he published the first number of the *Snowbound,* "issued every week-day afternoon by S. P. Prisoner in Car No. 36, blockaded at Reno, Nevada." McCully issued his paper as a four-page daily, selling for 25¢ a copy. The outside pages were printed in blue ink, while the inside pages were written in pencil on manila paper. The venture was doubtless short-lived, and may not have survived beyond the first number.
The Snowbound: (Jan 31 1890–c. Feb 1890)
  CHi — Ja 31 1890
  CSmH — Ja 31 1890
  CU-BANC — Ja 31 1890

NvHi — Ja 31 1890 (facsimile)
film — Ja 31 1890
Ref: files

Cyclone Occasional

The *Cyclone Occasional,* issued at Reno on May 23, 1891, by Louis Stevenson, was printed on both sides of a single sheet, with one side news and the other ads. Its publisher apparently never found the occasion for a second issue.

Cyclone Occasional: (May 23 1891)
    NvU — My 23 1891
    film — My 23 1891
Ref: files; Doten, 1793

The Plaindealer

Eleven years after the second suspension of the Reno *Plaindealer,* Henry H. Hogan resurrected the paper under the same name on December 14, 1895. Hogan was sole editor and proprietor, and issued the paper as a four-page, five-column weekly, advocating this time the Populist party and selling for $2.50 per year. The paper prospered and on October 8, 1898, in preparation for the coming election, it was enlarged to a semiweekly and the subscription price was reduced to $1 per year. Hogan continued the *Plaindealer* as a semiweekly until December 31, 1898, when, owing to poor health, he was forced to suspend publication. This suspension did not last so long as the first two, however, and on May 6, 1899, the *Plaindealer* was again revived as a weekly, with the Plaindealer Publishing Company listed as proprietor. R. R. Crawford was business manager and H. H. Hogan was unofficially still editor. On October 28, 1899, Crawford purchased the plant and suspended the *Plaindealer* for the last time, to begin publication of the *Reno Ledger* on November 6. (See *Reno Ledger.*)

Plaindealer: (Dec 14 1895–Oct 28 1899)
    NvHi — D 14 1895–O 28 1899
    NvRW — D 14 1895–O 28 1899
    film — D 14 1895–O 28 1899
Ref: files

The Daily Nevada Tribune

On April 5, 1896, E. J. Parkinson suspended the *Daily Nevada Tribune* at Carson City, after twenty-four years of publication, and sold an interest in the plant to Charles A. Norcross. The following week Norcross removed it to Reno, where they hoped to continue with renewed prosperity. On April 22, 1896, they revived the *Tribune* as an independent, morning daily. Reno already had two dailies and three weeklies, which were well entrenched, however, and the new rival for public favor met an early defeat, suspending again on July 15, 1896.

The Daily Nevada Tribune: (Apr 22 1896–Jul 15 1896)
   NvRW — Ap 22–Jl 15 1896
   NvU — Ap 22–Jl 15 1896
   film — Ap 22–Jl 15 1896
Ref: files; Doten 1916–7, 1925

Nevada Citizen

The *Nevada Citizen,* a monthly suffrage organ, was commenced in Reno in March, 1897, "to promote the advancement of women in the ethics of civil government, ordained in the Declaration of Independence and established in the Constitution of the United States of America." Frances A. Williamson and her daughter, Mary L. Williamson, were the editors, issuing it at least until December.

Nevada Citizen: (Mar 1897–c. Dec 1897)
   CU-BANC — D 1897
   NvU — Je 1897
   film — Je, D 1897
Ref: files

Reno Ledger

On October 28, 1899, R. R. Crawford purchased the plant of the Reno *Plaindealer,* and the following week, on November 6, he began publication of the *Reno Ledger.* Crawford was sole editor and proprietor, and issued the *Ledger* every Monday, as a four-page, five-column, 13 by 20-inch weekly, selling at $1.50 a year. Confident in the future of the venture, Crawford enlarged the paper to a semiweekly on June 6, 1900. W. L. Brandon was added as business manager, and he increased the subscription price to $2.50 a year. However, on November 17, following the election, the paper was reduced to a weekly and Brandon was dropped from the staff. On December 1, 1900, the paper passed into the hands of the Ledger Publishing Company, with Crawford continuing as editor. The firm managed the *Ledger* until October 31, 1903, when the plant was sold to John L. Considine. He ran it for one more year before its final suspension in November of 1904.

Reno Ledger: (Nov 6 1899–Nov 1904)
   NvRW — N 6 1899–O 31 1903
   NvU — 1900–2
   film — N 6 1899–O 31 1903
Ref: files; PR N 18 1904

Pandora

Pandora was a small illustrated weekly issued at Reno in October, 1900, by Copeland, Lary *et al.,* as a Democratic campaign paper supporting Francis G. Newlands.

Pandora: (Oct 1900)
  No issues located.
Ref: Doten 2084

Mining and Industrial Review (Nevada Miner)

In the summer of 1902, when he began his unsuccessful campaign for Nevada's congressional seat, Clarence D. Van Duzer suspended the semi-monthly *Nevada Miner* at Golconda and, removing the plant to Reno, revived the paper under the same name on September 15, 1902. Van Duzer continued as editor, and Fred J. Cole as business manager. With the commencement of the second volume in March, 1903, the name was changed to the *Mining and Industrial Review,* which suspended a short time later.

Mining and Industrial Review: (Sep 15 1902–1903)
  NvU — S 15 1902
  film — S 15 1902
Ref: files; NSJ Mr 27 1903

Evening Telegram

In early April of 1903, the daily *Evening Telegram* began its brief career, published by Sackett Cornell, formerly of the *Tonopah Miner* staff, Mark H. Bryan, and J. X. Bryan. It was a bright paper with a good supply of advertisers and a claimed circulation of 1000. But it came to an end early in July, when Cornell "lit out" with all the money.

Evening Telegram: (Apr 1903–c. Jul 1903)
  Nv — Ap 9, 23, Je 25 1903
  NvHi — Je 24 1903
  film — Ap 9, 23, Je 24–25 1903
Ref: files; LA Ap 11, Jl 18 1903

Nevada Observer

On January 2, 1904, three printers, Allen C. Bragg, William Stuart Webster, and Nate W. Roff, founded the *Nevada Observer* at Reno, under the firm name of Nevada Observer Publishing Company. From their office in the upstairs of the Observer Building at 12–16 West 3rd Street, they issued the paper every Saturday, as a four-page, three-column, 10¢-a-copy weekly. In November of 1904, Bragg left to become editor of the Winnemucca *Silver State,* and about December of 1906, Webster retired from the firm to commence the *Dutch Creek News* at the new camp on Walker Lake. The following year, the *Nevada Observer* suspended publication.

Nevada Observer: (Jan 2 1904–c. 1907)
  NvHi — Ja 2, Je 18, S 3 1904; F 4–18 1905
  NvMus — [F 20 1904–Mr 18 1905]; N 18 1907
  film — [Ja 2 1904–Mr 18 1905]; N 18 1907
Ref: files

The Star

The Reno *Star* was a short-lived endeavor begun on February 4, 1904. It attracted attention only by its demise in June, when a sympathetic editor happened to notice that it had "dropped out of the constellation of sagebrush journalism."

The Star: (Feb 4 1904–Jun 1904)
   pvt–F 11 1904
   film–F 11 1904
Ref: files; TM Je 18 1904

Amateur Outlook

In May of 1904, D. M. McDonald, a student at the University of Nevada, commenced the monthly *Amateur Outlook,* "devoted to the upbuilding of the United Amateur Press Association." McDonald was both editor and printer, and Henry G. Wehking of St. Louis was associate editor. The paper flourished at Reno for only two months before McDonald went to Ely for the summer. After two months issued there, McDonald returned to the University and got off one final issue in September, before he became editor-in-chief of the school paper, the *Student Record.* (See Ely, *Amateur Outlook.*)

Amateur Outlook: (May–Jun, Sep 1904)
   No issues located.
Ref: AO Jl, Ag 1904

Progressive West

Mrs. M. M. Garwood commenced the monthly *Progressive West* at Reno in June of 1905. She was editor and publisher, issuing the journal as a sixty-page monthly "devoted to the interests of a Greater Nevada." The magazine flourished for a time during the southern Nevada mining boom, and in March of 1906, Mrs. Garwood formed the Progressive West Publishing Company, with herself as president and William M. Gotwaldt of the Carson City *News* as vice president and editor. Gotwaldt gave up the editorship in December of 1906, however, and was replaced by Hugh A. R. Ramsey for one month before publication lapsed. A brief effort to revive the magazine was made in March of 1907, by Henry L. Brooke, who took over the management and editorship and brought it out "in new dress." But it was suspended again soon after.

Progressive West: (Jun 1905–c. Mar 1907)
   CSmH — [1905–6]
   NN — [1905–7]
   NvHi — [1905–6]
   NvU — Je 1905–D 1906; Mr 1907
Ref: files

Reno Federation

A little over a year after the suspension of his *Reno Ledger,* R. R. Crawford again entered the journalistic field with the commencement of the *Reno Federation* on March 7, 1906. He sought a broad audience, devoting it "to the interest of the merchant, farmer, miner, mechanic, laborer and business man," but he failed to win sufficient support from any of them, and the *Federation* apparently failed within the year.

Reno Federation: (May 7 1906–1906)
  No issues located.
Ref: NF Mr 9 1906

Reno Call

The *Reno Call* was a short-lived affair which flourished in the fall of 1906, under the guidance of Frank Jenkins, but nothing more is known of its career.

Reno Call: (1906)
  No issues located.
Ref: LCT O 13 1906

Nevada Mining Investor

The *Nevada Mining Investor* was a semimonthly promotional journal, begun at Reno on October 15, 1906, by the Investor Publishing Co., with B. M. Barndollar as business manager and Charles A. Norcross as editor. In the first issue, Clarence S. King was listed as associate editor. It ran to 36 pages, sold for 10¢ a copy, and claimed to be "the only mining magazine published in the Sage Brush State." It survived on advertising from mining promoters for seven months before it succumbed in June of 1907.

Nevada Mining Investor: (Oct 15 1906–Jun 15 1907)
  NvU — [O 15 1906–Je 15 1907]
  film — [O 15 1906–Je 15 1907]
Ref: files

Nevada Mining Market Outlook

The *Nevada Mining Market Outlook* was a free distribution sheet issued weekly in late 1906, and early 1907, by the Andy Hampel Brokerage Company of Reno. It promised to keep prospective investors "in touch with the REAL NEVADA MINES."

Nevada Mining Market Outlook: (1906–1907)
  No issues located.
Ref: NMI Ja 15 1907

Carnival News

To promote their annual fair, the ladies of St. Thomas Aquinas Catholic Church issued the *Carnival News* in December of 1906. It proved so successful that they revived the practice the following year, but under a new name, the *Lantern.* (See Reno, *Lantern.*)

Carnival News: (Dec 1906)
   No issues located.
Ref: L D 10 1907

Nevada Mining News

On April 27, 1907, Jacob S. Herzig, under the alias of George Graham Rice, creator of the notorious Goldfield Nevada Mining News Bureau, founded the weekly *Nevada Mining News.* He issued the paper every Saturday, as an eight-page, 14 by 22-inch weekly. Rice chose Merrill A. Teague as editor, for his ability to "write more about nothing than any man I ever met before." Teague did just that until July 27, 1907, when he leased the *Nevada State Journal* and became its editor-in-chief. Rice took over the editorial duties himself, with the aid of Sam C. Dunham as mining editor. The *News* puffed Rice's mining promotions in southern Nevada to its 28,000 readers nationwide for nearly two years, until March 4, 1909, when, to keep pace with his expanding financial schemes, Rice renamed the paper the *Mining Financial News.* (See Reno, *Mining Financial News.*)

Nevada Mining News: (Apr 27 1907–Feb 25 1909)
   pvt—Jl 27, O 23 1907
   NvHi — F 18 1909
   NvU — D 5 1907–F 25 1909
   film — Jl 27, O 23, D 5, 19 1907–F 25 1909
Ref: files; Rice 196, 199

The Reveille

The first number of the *Reveille* was issued on July 13, 1907, by James F. Haley and John L. Considine of the Reveille Publishing Company at 125 Center Street. Haley was business manger, and Considine was editor, publishing the paper as a sixteen-page, five-column, Democratic weekly, at $3 a year. The *Reveille* prospered, running until April 5, 1910, when Douglass Shelor bought Haley's interest and changed the name to the *Nevada Weekly.* (See *Reno Nevada Weekly.*)

The Reveille: (Jul 13 1907–Apr 5 1910)
   NvHi — Ap 28 1908; Jl 20 1909–Ap 5 1910
   NvU — Mr 6 1908–Ap 5 1910
   film — Mr 6 1908–Ap 5 1910
Ref: files

Fortnightly Market Review

About August 19, 1907, the Nat C. Goodwin Company of Reno, another George Graham Rice front, commenced the *Fortnightly Market Review* to push the company's promotions. It probably suspended sometime the following year.

Fortnightly Market Review: (c. Aug 19 1907–1908)
   No issues located.
Ref: NMN Mr 12 1908

Corriere di Nevada

Nevada's first Italian newspaper, the *Corriere di Nevada,* was founded by M. Paggi at Sparks, on February 2, 1907, with Francisco M. Moracci as editor. Later that same year Paggi moved the plant to Reno, where he became both editor and proprietor, and continued the paper as a four-page, 18 by 24-inch, Saturday weekly. The *Corriere* survived only a short time and was probably suspended the following year. Moracci then purchased the plant and started a new paper, the *Italian-French Colony,* on September 12, 1908. (See Reno, *Italian-French Colony.*)

Corriere di Nevada: (1907–c. 1908)
  No issues located.
Ref: Myrick

Lantern

The *Lantern* first appeared on December 10, 1907, replacing the previous *Carnival News,* to advertise the annual Feast of Lanterns fair of the St. Thomas Aquinas Catholic Church. Its first editors were John L. Considine of the Reno *Reveille,* and P. D. Cronin. It was issued only for the duration of the fair for the first several years. Mrs. Theodore Martinez served as editor during its appearance in 1910, from November 2 to 7. Then Rev. Thomas M. Tubman assumed the editorship, making the *Lantern* the "Official Organ of St. Thomas Aquinas Parish." He also issued special editions on Christmas, Easter, and other occasions, until its final suspension with the issue of April 8, 1928.

Lantern: (Dec 10 1907–Apr 8 1928)
  NvHi — O 1912; Ap 4 1920; N 1922; Ap 8 1928
  NvU — D 10 1907; N 2–7 1910; Je 1, O 28, N 1 1912; D 25 1919;
  Ja 8, Ap 16 1922; Ap 20 1924; Ap 8 1928
  film — [D 10 1907–Ap 8 1928]
Ref: files

Hot Stuph

Hot Stuph was a curious little magazine served up at Reno in January, 1908, by A. L. Smith. Its readers quickly cooled to it, and the magazine was apparently abandoned within a short time.

Hot Stuph: (Jan 1908–c. 1908)
  No issues located.
Ref: TB Ja 4 1908; BMHCN Ja 2 1908

Daily American

On May 15, 1908, the Reno American Publishing Company commenced the *Daily American* from their offices in the Odd Fellows' Building. Mel A. Bley was managing editor and Fred E. Brown was business manager. They issued the *American* every afternoon except Sunday, as a four-page, seven-column daily, at 40¢ a month. The paper floundered briefly and finally suspended about July 25 of the same year.

Daily American: (May 15 1908–c. Jul 25 1908)
   NvHi — Jl 13, 15, 22, 25 1908
   NvU — Jl 2 1908
   film — Jl 2, 13, 15, 22, 25 1908
Ref: files

Reno Record

The *Reno Record* was a nonpartisan Saturday weekly, founded in 1908, by Levy and Shipaugh, publishers. Leo S. Levy was editor during its brief career, which terminated the same year.

Reno Record: (1908)
   No issues located.
Ref: Myrick

Italian-French Colony

Following the suspension of the Reno *Corriere di Nevada,* Francisco M. Moracci bought the press and material and commenced a new paper, the weekly *Italian-French Colony.* Even though it was "the only Italian paper between Sacramento and Salt Lake," it suspended about February 20, 1909.

Italian-French Colony: (Sep 12 1908–c. Feb 20 1909)
   NvU — [N 14 1908–F 20 1909]
   film — [N 14 1908–F 20 1909]
Ref: files; NF S 14 1908

Mining Digest

After his second unsuccessful return to mining camp journalism at Midas, Mark W. Musgrove headed for Reno, where, on December 1, 1908, he started the semimonthly *Mining Digest.* He promised that the paper would be "ultra-conservative in its criticism of mining securities." But perhaps because of his own questionable record, he found few followers, and apparently he never issued a second number.

Mining Digest: (Dec 1 1908)
   NvU — D 1 1908
   film — D 1 1908
Ref: files

Nevada Churchman

The *Nevada Churchman* was begun as a quarterly at Reno, in December of 1908. The Rev. Charles H. Powell was editor, the Rev. A. Lester Hazlett was business manager, and the paper was printed at the *Nevada State Journal* office. When Powell moved to Redding, California, the following spring, Hazlett unofficially took over the editorship until the Rev. George C. Hunting of Ely assumed the post in October, 1910. The following January, the *Churchman* was increased to a monthly, the editorial office was moved to Ely, and from March to December the printing was done at the *White Pine News* office in East Ely. Then, in January of 1912, the Rev.

Lloyd B. Thomas of Carson City became editor, and the printing was transferred back to the *Nevada State Journal* at Reno. The paper was finally forced to suspend with its issue of December, 1912, however, because, Thomas complained, "Our Nevada Church people have not backed the paper with subscriptions," of 50¢ per year.

Nevada Churchman: (Dec 1908–Dec 1912)
   NN — [1908–9]
   NNG — D 1908–D 1912
   film — D 1908–D 1912
Ref: files

Nevada-California Miner

The *Nevada-California Miner* was a bimonthly mining journal established at Reno in January of 1909, by J. Herbert Welch, formerly of the *Wonder Mining News*. The *Miner* contained news of all of the Nevada camps and many adjacent California camps, but failed to win equally broad support and apparently suspended after only a few issues.

Nevada-California Miner: (Jan 1909–1909)
   No issues located.
Ref: TM Ja 9 1909

Mining Financial News

On March 4, 1909, George Graham Rice renamed his *Nevada Mining News* the *Mining Financial News,* to cover his expanding promotional schemes. Three months later, on May 27, 1909, he and Merrill A. Teague, who had returned as editor, suspended the paper at Reno and moved it to New York City, where most of his credulous subscribers resided.

Mining Financial News: (Mar 4 1909–May 27 1909)
   NvU — Mr 4–My 27 1909
   film — Mr 4–My 27 1909
Ref: files; Rice 291–7

Nevada Mines and Farms

In 1909, the daily Reno *Nevada State Journal* commenced a weekly edition under the name of *Nevada Mines and Farms*. The paper was issued every Tuesday, dedicated, as the title suggests, to the mining and agricultural interests of the state. It prospered for several years, but was ultimately suspended on August 19, 1913.

Nevada Mines and Farms: (1909–Aug 19 1913)
   NvU — [D 26 1911–D 31 1912]
   film — [D 26 1911–D 31 1912]
Ref: files

Reno Whooperup

Reno Whooperup was a humorous promotional sheet, "published when the sign is right," by the Overland Trust and Realty Company. The paper was printed in red ink by the Reno Printing Company at 21 East Second Street, as a six-page, six-column sheet selling for two bits a copy. The proceeds were donated to the Salvation Army. With DeWitt C. Turner as editor, A. A. Hibbard as manager, and Charles H. Curtis as advertising manager, *Whooperup* flourished from 1909, to sometime about 1910.

Reno Whooperup: (1909–c. 1910)
  NvHi — My 1 1909; Ja 20 1910
  film — My 1 1909; Ja 20 1910
Ref: files

Reno Industrial Journal

The *Reno Industrial Journal* was begun as a monthly in March, 1910, by the Reno Industrial Association, with John Niemeyer as business manager. The following month, it was optimistically increased to a biweekly, and the month after that it apparently folded.

Reno Industrial Journal: (Mar 1910–c. May 1910)
  NvHi — Mr, Ap 8, My 9 1910
Ref: files

Reno Nevada Weekly

In April of 1910, Douglass Shelor bought out J. F. Haley's half interest in the *Reveille* and renamed it the *Reno Nevada Weekly,* beginning on April 12. The new *Weekly,* a "journal of Society, Music, Drama, Sports, Mining and Politics," was issued every Saturday by the Reno Reveille Publishing Company, as a six-page, 8 by 11-inch sheet, selling for $2 a year. Douglass Shelor served as business manager, while John L. Considine, who had served as editor on the *Reveille,* continued in that post until November 19, 1910, when Shelor bought his interest and became sole owner. In less than two months, however, on January 14, 1911, Shelor also sold out, to E. Kirman Kirk and Eric Reay Mackay. In their hands the paper died two months later, on March 11.

Reno Nevada Weekly: (Apr 12 1910–Mar 11 1911)
  NvU — Ap 12 1910–Mr 11 1911
  film — Ap 12 1910–Mr 11 1911
Ref: files

Voice of the People

The *Voice of the People* was begun at Reno as a Socialist campaign paper on October 10, 1910. It was issued irregularly by the Socialist Party of Nevada, with A. Grant Miller, a prominent Reno attorney, serving as editor. The *Voice* continued intermittently for nearly eight months after the election before it was stilled on June 22, 1911.

Voice of the People: (Oct 10 1910–Jun 22 1911)
  NvU — [O 10 1910–Je 22 1911]
  film — [O 10 1910–Je 22 1911]
Ref: files

Nevada Mining News

The *Nevada Mining News* was a biweekly commenced about January of 1911, by the mining promotion firm of G. S. Johnson Company. The *News* was a letter-size, eight-page, three-column sheet with free distribution. It continued for many years but probably suspended about the latter part of 1916.

Nevada Mining News: (c. Jan 1911–c. 1916)
   CHi — Ja 26–Mr 3, Jl 15 1916
Ref: files

Truth

In January of 1911, J. A. "Buck" Buchanan, fresh from serving as Tasker Oddie's right-hand man in the latter's successful gubernatorial campaign, commenced a newspaper at Reno modestly named *Truth*. It was devoted to social, political, and mining affairs, and his chums predicted it would become "one of the leading weekly papers in the West." It apparently folded within the month.

Truth: (Jan 1911)
  No issues located.
Ref: WPN Ja 22 1911

Nevada Bugle

On June 29, 1912, W. T. McNeil commenced the first number of the *Nevada Bugle,* which touted itself as "a Progressive Weekly Paper for Progressive People; Clean, Wholesome and Entertaining." McNeil was sole editor and proprietor, issuing the *Bugle* every Saturday, at 10¢ a copy or $3 a year. Evidently the market for clean, wholesome papers was rather limited, for the *Bugle* suspended with its seventh number on August 10, 1912. McNeil eventually moved on to Carlin, where two years later he commenced a similar paper, the *Western Home Builder.*

Nevada Bugle: (Jun 29 1912–Aug 10 1912)
  NvHi — Je 29 1912
  NvU — [Je 29–Ag 10 1912]
  film — [Je 29–Ag 10 1912]
Ref: files

New West

Despite claims that "it was a moral, if not a physical, impossibility to print a real magazine in Nevada," Edward Nelson Buck boldly launched the *New West* at Reno in October, 1912. He dedicated the magazine to the upbuilding of the intermountain states, and modeled the first issue after the popular *Sunset,* with a wide range of articles and some poems of his own. Buck quickly found that, even if it wasn't impossible to *print* a real magazine in Nevada, it was apparently impossible to support one — for he never issued another number.

New West: (Oct 1912)
   NvHi — O 1912
   NvU — O 1912
Ref: files

Nevada News Letter and Advertiser

Boyd Moore founded the *Nevada News Letter and Advertiser* on February 14, 1914. Moore was editor and publisher, issuing the magazine devoted to "state news and comment" every Saturday, on letter-size paper, at $3.50 a year. The magazine was well received and grew rapidly, soon enlarging to 10½ by 13½ inches, and containing as many as sixty pages per issue, complete with multicolored illustrations. About 1916, the Nevada News Letter Publishing Company was organized to publish the magazine, with Boyd as editor. This firm prospered for over a decade before its final suspension about June 25, 1927.

Nevada News Letter and Advertiser: (Feb 14 1914–c. Jun 25 1927)
   CSmH — Ja 10 1920; Ap 5 1924; Je 25 1927 (special issues)
   CU — F 18 1922; Je 25 1927
   KHi — Ja 1–10 1916; Je 21 1919
   NvHi — N 21 1914–D 30 1922; [Ja 6 1923–Je 25 1927]
   Nv — 1915
   NvU — 1915, 1919–20
Ref: files

Nevada Rockroller

The *Nevada Rockroller,* with its slogan, "out for the man," was a colorful sheet, begun on June 27, 1914, by Colonel Carl Young, as the "Official Organ Of The Union League Non-Partisan Club, Commonly Known As The 'Rockrollers'." Young was manager and publisher, and issued the *Rockroller* every Wednesday and Saturday as an independent semiweekly, on a single sheet of gaudy rose paper. Its life, though brilliant, was brief, and it was suspended in less than three months, on September 16, 1914.

Nevada Rockroller: (Jun 27 1914–Sep 16 1914)
   NvHi — Jl 22 1914
   NvU — Je 27–S 16 1914
   film — Je 27–S 16 1914
Ref: files

Nevada Socialist

In August of 1914, the State Executive Committee of the Socialist Party of Nevada commenced a monthly campaign paper, the *Nevada Socialist,* with the banner "Out for the People." State Secretary Thomas M. Fagan was editor, and issued the paper as a four-page, five-column sheet, at 5¢ a copy. The *Socialist* was continued as a monthly until October, when it became a biweekly, running as such until its suspension after the election. It was revived in name two years later. (See Reno, *Nevada Socialist* 1916.)

Nevada Socialist: (Aug 1914–c. Nov 1914)
   NvHi — S–O 26 1914
   NvU — [1914]
   film — S–O 26 1914
Ref: files

Nevada Democrat

The *Nevada Democrat* was founded as a weekly campaign paper on October 10, 1914, by the Democratic Central Committee, with Acting Governor Denver S. Dickerson as editor. The early issues of the paper were printed by the *Nevada State Journal.* The paper suspended after the election, but was revived on December 25, 1914, by the Nevada Democrat Publishing Company, under the auspices of the state Democratic Executive Committee. The "press of official duties" caused Dickerson to resign on April 9, 1915, and Homer Mooney became editor. The paper continued until September 3.

Nevada Democrat: (Oct 10 1914–Nov 1914; Dec 25 1914–Sep 3 1915)
   NvHi — O 16–27 1914
   NvU — O 10 1914–S 3 1915
   film — O 10 1914–S 3 1915
Ref: files

Reno Amusements

The Nevada Press Company started the weekly *Reno Amusements,* the city's first entertainment guide, on February 1, 1915. But they were ahead of the times and it apparently folded the same month.

Reno Amusements: (Feb 1, 1915–c. Feb 22 1915)
   NvHi — F 1, 15–22 1915
Ref: files

Western Miner

On May 3, 1915, Fred L. Miner issued the first number of the *Western Miner.* The paper, devoted solely to mining interests, was issued every Tuesday as a 7½ by 10½-inch weekly, selling for $3.50 a year, with Miner as sole editor and publisher. About June 30, 1916, the *Miner* was suspended, remaining dead for nearly three years, until April 30, 1919, when it briefly reappeared with the announcement that since Nevada had "come back," the *Miner* would also. In 1915–6, the *Miner* was a strong booster for the camp of Rochester, and upon its revival in 1919, it heaped its praises upon Divide City, south of Tonopah. But with the collapse of the Divide boom that summer, it was suspended again on June 30. Miner revived it one last time, as a biweekly, on March 15, 1927, to cash in on the Weepah boom. When the latter collapsed, the *Miner* folded for keeps on May 10, 1927.

Western Miner: (May 3 1915–Jun 30 1916; Apr 30–Jun 16 1919; Mar 15–May 10 1927)
   pvt — My 3–Jl 13, Ag 10 1915–Je 30 1916; Ap 30–Je 16 1919

NvU — My 3 1915–Je 30 1916; [Ap 30–Je 16 1919]; Mr 15–My 10 1927
film — My 3 1915–Je 30 1916; Ap 30–Je 16 1919; Mr 15–My 10 1927
Ref: files

Bollettino del Nevada

Nevada's third Italian newspaper, *Bollettino del Nevada,* was established at Reno on June 12, 1915, by John Granata and Company. Granata served as editor and publisher, issuing the paper as an independent Saturday weekly. The paper received the full support of the Italian population, prospering for over a quarter of a century, but "a causa di condizioni crate dalla guerra," the *Bollettino* finally suspended publication in the latter part of World War II, on May 26, 1944.

Bollettino del Nevada: (Jun 12 1915–May 26 1944)
  NvHi — [1926–35]
  NvU — [1915–9; 1927–44]
  film — [Je 19 1915–9; 1927–My 26 1944]
Ref: files

Nevada Federationist

The *Nevada Federationist* was begun as a labor weekly on September 17, 1915. It was published by Eugene Donovan, at $1 a year, until March 7, 1917, when the Reno Central Labor Council and the Washoe County Building Council became the publishers, installing C. W. Farrington as editor. He was soon replaced by C. W. Flodin, who quit in a heated dispute over ownership of the paper on November 14, and started a rival *Nevada Federationist.* The Labor Council then hired John W. Brooks as editor, and he kept the post until 1919. William D. McNair followed him as editor and manager, and in his hands the paper was suspended. (See Reno, *Nevada Federationist* 1917.)

Nevada Federationist: (Sep 17 1915–c. Jun 1919)
  CHi — Ap 25 1917
  NvHi — Je 5 1919
  NvU — 1915; 1917–9
  film — [1915–9]
Ref: files

Western Financier

The *Western Financier* was a monthly financial journal, which moved to Reno from San Francisco in February of 1916. Its editor, publisher, and duration are unknown.

Western Financier: (Feb 1916–c. 1916)
  No issues located.
Ref: Myrick

Nevada Socialist

On July 1, 1916, the Nevada Socialist Publishing Association, with A. B.

Riggle as chairman and J. T. Taylor as editor, revived the *Nevada Socialist* as a monthly paper with a revised slogan, "Out For The Workers." Though the publishers intended to establish "a permanent Socialist paper," it appears that lack of support after the election forced its suspension, making the issue of November 1 its last.

Nevada Socialist: (Jul 1 1916–Nov 1 1916)
   NvHi — Jl 1–Ag 1 1916
   NvU — Jl 1–N 1 1916
   film — Jl 1–N 1 1916
Ref: files

The Nevadan

On October 17, 1916, Al H. Martin commenced the Reno *Nevadan,* "a Statewide Publication Independent in Everything," from offices in Suite 32 of the Reno Gazette Building. Martin was editor and Frank MacBride was business manager. The paper was issued every Tuesday, as an eight-page, six-column weekly, which sold for $2 a year. Its career was brief, however, and it apparently suspended on October 31, 1916.

The Nevadan: (Oct 17 1916–Oct 31 1916)
   NvHi — O 24 1916
   NvU — O 17, 31 1916
   film — O 17–31 1916
Ref: files

Nevada Home Builder

Following his suspension of the *Nevada Bugle,* W. T. McNeil drifted to Carlin, where he founded the *Western Home Builder* on June 6, 1914. After two years, however, he decided to return to Reno. Suspending the paper at Carlin on November 23, 1916, he removed the plant to Reno, where he revived the paper as the *Nevada Home Builder* on January 19, 1917. W. T. McNeil was both editor and publisher, while Lee D. McNeil served as assistant editor. The *Home Builder* was issued as a four-page, six-column, independent Republican weekly, at $3 a year. On January 24, 1919, S. H. Freeman became part-owner and business manager, but within a few months the McNeils were again sole owners. The paper flourished for nearly five years, but was finally suspended in 1921 when McNeil reorganized the plant to commence the *Nevada Searchlight* on December 22. (See Reno, *Nevada Searchlight.*)

Nevada Home Builder: (Jan 19 1917–c. Dec 1921)
   NvHi — Ja 18, F 8, Je 4, N 1 1918; F 7, Ag 1, S 26 1919
   NvU — [O 19 1917–Ja 1 1919]
   film — [O 19 1917–S 26 1919]
Ref: files

Nevada Federationist

This *Nevada Federationist,* begun by C. W. Flodin with "volume 2, number 41," on November 21, 1917, was the second paper of the same name.

When C. W. Flodin took the editorship of the Labor Council's original *Nevada Federationist,* in April of 1917, he wanted control of the paper, but the Council opposed him and he quit in anger to start a rival. For three weeks Flodin issued his paper, claiming, "I am the GENUINE *Nevada Federationist,* I am the real thing." He finally gave up the fight and renamed his paper the *Nevada Observer* on December 12. (See Reno, *Nevada Observer.*)

Nevada Federationist: (Nov 21 1917–Dec 5 1917)
    NvU — [N 21–D 5 1917]
    film — [N 21–D 5 1917]
Ref: files

Nevada Observer

On December 12, 1917, C. W. Flodin changed the name of his *Nevada Federationist* to the *Nevada Observer.* Flodin was sole editor and publisher, issuing the *Observer* every Wednesday, as a Republican weekly, at $1.50 a year, from his offices at 234 North Virginia Street. This endeavor was short-lived, however, apparently suspending about May 15, 1918.

Nevada Observer: (Dec 12 1917–c. May 15 1918)
    CHi — Ja 23 1918
    NvHi — Ja 16 1918
    NvU — D 12 1917–My 15 1918
    film — D 12 1917–My 15 1918
Ref: files

The Fighting Mechanic

The *Fighting Mechanic* was issued during the latter part of World War I by the University of Nevada Training Detachment. It was founded on July 6, 1918, with Sergeant F. H. Walker as editor, Sergeant J. T. Fox as business manager, and Corporal R. W. Swick as secretary and treasurer. They issued the paper every Saturday, as a four-page, three-column sheet, selling for 5¢ a copy. About September 1, Sergeant R. H. Conley became editor, aided a month later by Sergeant O. C. Little as assistant editor. The paper ended with the war in November

The Fighting Mechanic: (Jul 6 1918–Nov 1918)
    NvHi — Ag 10, S 7–14, N 2 1918
    film — Ag 10, S 7–14, N 2 1918
Ref: files

Nevadan

The *Nevadan,* "a Magazine for the Home," appeared in Reno in September, 1918. Although its stated goal was to provide monthly coverage of events locally and abroad, its only issue was devoted entirely to the election laws and candidates for the primary election on September 3.

Nevadan: (Sep 1918)
    NvHi — S 1918
    NvU — S 1918
Ref: files

Nevada Mining Press

On December 10, 1918, Charles F. Spillman issued the first number of the *Nevada Mining Press* as a semimonthly mining magazine. Under Spillman's guidance as editor and proprietor, the journal prospered for many years. On September 9, 1921, Spillman increased the issue to a weekly, to keep "its readers in closer touch with events." As such it continued until its suspension on May 22, 1931.

Nevada Mining Press: (Dec 10 1918–May 22 1931)
   DGS — D 10 1918–9 (1920–Ag 1921)
   NvHi — [S 9 1921–My 22 1931]
   NvU — [S 1921–31]
   film — [S 9 1921–My 22 1931]
Ref: files

Nevada Stockgrower

The monthly *Nevada Stockgrower* was commenced in October, 1919, by the Nevada Livestock Association, with Vernon Metcalf as editor. It continued until 1933.

Nevada Stockgrower: (Oct 1919–1933)
   NvU — (1919–33)
   NvULV — (1919–32)
Ref: files

Nevada Topics and Advertiser

The *Nevada Topics and Advertiser,* begun at Reno on February 13, 1920, was a short-lived, catchall, weekly magazine, "devoted to topics, advertisements of the leading business houses, amusements, livestock, oil and mining companies, and professional men." Its editor was Ray E. Cooper and J. W. Stauffer was business manager.

Nevada Topics and Advertiser: (Feb 13 1920–1920)
   NvU — F 13 1920
Ref: files

Elks Show Message

The *Elks Show Message* was a single-issue paper, published on May 11, 1921, to promote Reno Elks Club festivities.

Elks Show Message: (May 11 1921)
   NvMus — My 11 1921
   film — My 11 1921
Ref: files

Theatre Herald

The *Theatre Herald* was begun on October 4, 1921, as the house organ of T. and D. Jr. Enterprises, who operated the Majestic, Rialto, and Grand theaters in Reno. It started as a weekly, with J. J. Martin as business manager and Norman Ogilvie as editor, and hoped "to establish itself on a policy far broader." It appeared irregularly, averaging about twice a month, and neither Ogilvie nor his January replacement, Earle Snell, could make it more than the advertiser that it was. It apparently suspended publication about March 25, 1922.

Theatre Herald: (Oct 4 1921–c. Mar 25 1922)
   NvHi — O 4 1921–Mr 25 1922
   film — O 4 1921–Mr 25 1922
Ref: files

Nevada Searchlight

In 1921, W. T. McNeil suspended the *Nevada Home Builder* and, reorganizing the plant, commenced the *Nevada Searchlight* on December 22. McNeil endeavored to make the *Searchlight* a weekly paper of statewide circulation, "Devoted to the Development of Nevada's Boundless Resources, Its Wonderful Industrial Possibilities and the Building of the West." He issued the paper every Thursday, at $3 a year, serving as managing editor of the Nevada Searchlight Publishing Company, with his wife, Lois, as associate editor. The change of name seems not to have been a success, for the *Searchlight* burned out within a year.

Nevada Searchlight: (Dec 22 1921–c. 1922)
   pvt — Ja 5, S 14 1922
   NvHi — S 14 1922
   film — S 14 1922
Ref: files

Sagebrush Legionnaire

The bimonthly *Sagebrush Legionnaire* was begun at Reno on February 10, 1922, by the Darrell Dunkle Post No. 1 of the American Legion, with J. T. Nicholson as editor. On June 29, it became the official organ of the whole Nevada Department of the American Legion, under the editorship of William B. Hilbish, who had taken the post two weeks earlier. A few months later Dennis P. Cahill replaced Hilbish, but despite its broader audience the paper failed to gain sufficient support, and folded within the year.

Sagebrush Legionnaire: (Feb 10 1922–c. 1922)
   NvHi — [F 10–Ag 10 1922]
   NvU — Jl 27–Ag 24, O 26 1922
   film — [F 10–O 26 1922]
Ref: files

Intermountain Liberal (Nevada Liberal)

The *Nevada Liberal,* an anti-prohibition monthly, was founded at Reno on August 1, 1924, by the Nevada Division of the Association Against the Prohibition Amendment, Inc. Its publishers sought to expand its sphere of influence by renaming it the *Intermountain Liberal* on February 1, 1925. As such it continued the fight for repeal of the Eighteenth Amendment for six years, but was finally suspended in 1931, two years before the battle was won.

Intermountain Liberal: (Aug 1 1924–1931)
   NvHi — Ag 1, S 1, 22, O 1 1926
   NvU — [Ag 1924–O 27 1926]
   film — [Ag 1924–S 1925; Je–O 27 1926]
Ref: files

Nevada Voice

The *Nevada Voice,* "a paper published in the interest of Good Morals and Good Citizenship, Non-sectarian, Non-partisan and Independent," was founded in March of 1926. It was published monthly, as a four-page, four-column sheet, by the Nevada Good Laws Committee, with G. B. Blair as president, Fanny B. Patrick as secretary and Otis L. Linn as editor. The *Voice* was heard for over a year but finally fell silent in the latter part of 1927.

Nevada Voice: (Mar 1926–c. 1927)
   NvHi — Mr–Ap, O 1926; F–Ap 1927
   film — Mr–Ap, O 1926; F–Ap 1927
Ref: files

Tri-State Miner

The *Tri-State Miner,* an "Independent Mining Paper Covering the Pacific Slope States," started at Reno on June 9, 1926, and was issued every other Wednesday. Its editor and publisher were not listed.

Tri-State Miner: (Jul 9 1926–1926)
   pvt — S 29 1926
Ref: files

Western Mines and Markets

About January of 1927, the Arthur Thomas Company commenced a promotional journal, *Western Mines and Markets,* at Reno, with Fred L. Miner as editor. Failing to attract sufficient readership, it folded three months later, just before the Weepah boom, when its editor became "absorbed" in a revival of his own phoenix-like *Western Miner* on March 15, 1927.

Western Mines and Markets: (c. Jan 1927–Mar 1927)
   No issues located.
Ref: WM Mr 15 1927

Nevada Review Monthly

Edward L. Clark commenced the *Nevada Review Monthly* at Reno in May, 1928. He proclaimed it "a Magazine for All ... conceived by Nevadans fired by a great belief and pride and made enthusiastic by a 'vision splendid' of the Nevada that may be." He filled it with good, local material, but did not succeed in attracting enough readers, and the *Review* apparently folded in September.

Nevada Review Monthly: (May 1928–c. Sep 1928)
    NvHi — My, Jl–S 1928
    NvU — My, Ag–S 1928
Ref: files

Reno News

The weekly *Reno News* was begun on November 27, 1930, by the Reno News Publishing Company, with Seth T. Bailey as editor. Subscriptions sold for $2.50 a year, but the paper may not have lasted past its first issue.

Reno News: (Nov 27 1930–c. 1930)
    NvHi — N 27 1930
    film — N 27 1930
Ref: files

Nevada State Builder

Doug H. Tandy commenced the weekly *Nevada State Builder* at Reno on April 24, 1931. He published it as "Labor's Official Publication" until its suspension on January 29, 1932. The plant was purchased by Ed M. Shirton and resurrected as the *Nevada Labor Record* four weeks later. (See Reno, *Nevada Labor Record.*)

Nevada State Builder: (Apr 24 1931–Jan 29 1932)
    NvHi — Je 12–19 1931
    NvU — [1931–2]
    film — [Ap 24 1931–Ja 29 1932]
Ref: files

Nevada Labor Record

On February 26, 1932, soon after the suspension of the *Nevada State Builder,* Ed M. Shirton revived the paper in spirit as the *Nevada Labor Record,* "pledged to the Principles and Policies of the American Federation of Labor." On January 20, 1933, it became the official bulletin of the Reno Building Trades Council with Shirton as editor, but it survived less than two years, and was suspended about September 22, 1933.

Nevada Labor Record: (Feb 26 1932–c. Sep 22 1933)
    NvHi — My 13–30 1932
    NvU — [Mr 4 1932–S 22 1933]
    film — [Mr 4 1932–S 22 1933]
Ref: files

Reno State Economist

The weekly *Reno State Economist* was commenced on April 14, 1932, by R. A. Hickey. It suspended before the end of the year.

Reno State Economist: (Apr 14 1932–1932)
    NvHi — Ap 14 1932
    film — Ap 14 1932
Ref: files

Nevada Register

The *Nevada Register* is a Catholic weekly magazine, begun at Reno on April 17, 1932. It is the local edition of the *National Catholic Register,* which has been published in Denver since 1905. The Most Reverend Thomas K. Gorman was the first editor and publisher.

Nevada Register: (Apr 17 1932+)
  pub — 1935+
  NvHi — [Ja 5 1947–D 31 1954]
  NvU — [1953–6]
  film — [1953–6]; 60+
Ref: files

News Advertiser

The *News Advertiser* was a weekly advertising sheet, begun on Friday, November 23, 1934. Its editor and publisher were not listed, and it apparently suspended after the close of its second volume, in November of 1936.

News Advertiser: (Nov 23 1934–c. Nov 1936)
  NvHi — Je 28 1935; O 23 1936
Ref: files

Nevada Veteran and Labor News

William Macura founded the *Nevada Veteran and Labor News* on June 14, 1935. Macura was sole editor and proprietor, issuing the paper every Friday at 139 North Virginia Street. The paper's life was brief, however, and its suspension seems to have come about the following October.

Nevada Veteran and Labor News: (Jun 14 1935–c. Oct 1935)
  NvHi — Je 14, S 1 1935
Ref: files

Desert, A Nevada Magazine

John Bott commenced *Desert, A Nevada Magazine* in April 1936, as a literary bimonthly. The second issue did not appear until July, and Emily Richards brought out the third and last issue for September-October.

Desert, A Nevada Magazine: (Apr 1936–Sep/Oct 1936)
  NvHi — Ap–O 1936
  NvU — Ap–O 1936
  NvULV — Ap–O 1936
Ref: files

Reno Life

In July 1936 Pat S. McCarthy issued the first number of *Reno Life,* a monthly magazine of music, arts, sports, and gossip. He probably never issued a second. Two years later, he ventured back into publishing with *Town Talk* to concentrate on night life, but fared no better.

Reno Life: (Jul 1936–c. 1936)
  NvHi — Jl 1936
Ref: files

Town Talk

The weekly *Town Talk,* edited and published by Pat S. McCarthy, made its appearance in the spring of 1938 to tell "Who's Who and What's What" about Reno night life.

Town Talk: (c. Spr 1938–c. 1938)
   NvHi — Je 6 1938
Ref: files

Nevada Independent

Doug H. Tandy founded the *Nevada Independent* from room 410 of the Clay-Peters Building on August 13, 1938. Tandy was both editor and publisher, issuing the paper every Saturday, as a four-page, eight-column weekly, at 5¢ a copy. The *Independent* had a brief career, however, suspending publication two months later, on October 15, 1938.

Nevada Independent: (Aug 13 1938–Oct 15 1938)
   NvU — [Ag 13–O 15 1938]
   film — [Ag 13–O 15 1938]
Ref: files

Mining Press

The *Mining Press* was begun at Reno on August 31, 1938, by R. L. Richie, editor and publisher, and it prospered for over a decade. It was published semimonthly until October, 1939, and monthly thereafter. In May, 1949, Richie finally gave up the editorship, hiring Harold V. Lankford, and in his hands it apparently died two months later.

Mining Press: (Aug 31 1938–c. Jul 1949)
   NvHi — Nov 15–30 1938; Ja 1947–My 1949
   NvU — [Ag 31 1938–Jl 1949]
   film — [Ag 31 1938–Jl 1949]
Ref: files

Shopping News

The *Shopping News* was a weekly advertising sheet begun at Reno on January 20, 1939. Its editor and proprietor are unknown, as is its exact duration. It did run to at least the end of 1947, and apparently merged with the *Reno Reminder* to become the *Shopping News Reminder.* (See Reno, *Shopping News Reminder.*)

Shopping News: (Jan 20 1939–c. 1948)
   NvHi — Ja 20–O 28 1939; [Je 6–N 14 1946; Ja 9–D 31 1947]
Ref: files

Here and Now

The monthly *Here and Now,* devoted to "the Interests and Opinions of Nevada's Young People," was started at Reno in March, 1940, by Here and Now Associates with Norman Towner as editor. It apparently lasted only three months.

Here and Now: (Mar 1940–c. May 1940)
   NvHi — Mr–My 1940
Ref: files

Nevada State Labor News

About May of 1941, Peter A. Burke and Paul E. Weaver, Sr., issued the first number of the semimonthly *Nevada State Labor News.* Burke served as editor, devoting the paper solely to labor interests. Weaver bought Burke's interest on December 19, 1947, becoming sole proprietor, and his son, Paul E. Weaver, Jr., became editor. Six months later, on June 25, J. J. "Joe" Cleary bought a half interest and took over the editorial chair. The *News* was expanded to a weekly on July 8. On June 23, 1949, Kevin Jones was hired as editor, and Cleary sold out to Weaver on October 6. The following year, Karl K. Karrasch replaced Jones as editor. Then, after ten years, Weaver, too, finally retired from the paper, selling it to Denver Dickerson, son of the former governor, on April 6, 1951. Dickerson shortened the name on November 2, 1951, to the *Nevada State News.* (See Reno, *Nevada State News.*)

Nevada State Labor News: (c. May 1941–Oct 26 1951)
   NvHi — [S 25 1942–N 10 1949]
   NvU — [S 13 1946–O 26 1951]
   film — [S 25 1942–O 26 1951]
Ref: files

The Pry

L. Perkins and V. Thorne started the gossipy, weekly *Pry* on November 16, 1942, under the banner "An Ounce of Mirth is Worth a Pound of Sorrow." It apparently failed two months later.

The Pry: (Nov 16 1942–c. Jan 11 1943)
   NvHi — N 23 1942; Ja 11 1943
Ref: files

Flyer

The *Flyer* was published by the *Nevada State Journal* for the personnel of the Reno Army Air Base, in an effort "to bring about a closer unity between the general public of Reno and the soldiers of the Air Base." It was a free weekly begun on January 9, 1943, with M/Sgt. C. A. Presley as managing editor. Over the next few years of its existence, the editorship passed in succession to Sgt. Fred Gailbraith, Fred Graff, William Dorsey, Sgt. Sam Sheplow, Sgt. James Lyman, Cpl. Elizabeth Everitt, and Cpl. Kit Crist. The end of the war brought an end to the *Flyer* on November 2, 1945.

Flyer: (Jan 9 1943–Nov 2 1945)
   NvHi — [Ja 9–D 31 1943; Ja–N 2 1945]
   film — [My 8–D 31 1943; Ja 6–N 2 1945]
Ref: files

Destinies

Wagon and Star Publishers of Los Angeles issued the small, undated literary quarterly *Destinies* at Reno, from 1943 to 1944, as an adjunct to the Destiny Editions Series of Contemporary Poets. Dion O'Donnol was the editor and Irene Bruce was managing co-editor.

Destinies: (1943–1944)
   DLC — 1943–4
   NvU — 1944
Ref: files

Reno Reminder

The *Reno Reminder* was an irregular advertising sheet begun about June of 1945. It was published by H. C. Daniel, with the motto "Reno Early Bird." By November, Pat O'Malley had become the publisher and Herb Glimpse had taken the editorial chair, adding a bit of local news. Its duration is unknown, but it was continued in spirit, at least, by the *Shopping News Reminder,* begun in 1949. (See Reno, *Shopping News Reminder.*)

Reno Reminder: (c. Jun 1945–1945)
   NvU — Je 29, Jl 10, Ag 25, N 25, D 20 1945
   film — Je 29, Jl 10, Ag 25, N 25, D 20 1945
Ref: files

Mountain Magic

Mountain Magic, the weekly "Picture Magazine of the World's Wonderland," was begun at Reno on December 24, 1947, by Robert A. Burns, publisher, and Fred S. Cook, editor. On February 3, 1948, Pat Harrison purchased controlling interest from Burns; the paper apparently suspended soon afterwards.

Mountain Magic: (Dec 24 1947–c. Mar 1948)
   NvHi — D 24 1947–Ja 17, F 3–17 1948
   NvU — D 24 1947–Mr 27 1948
Ref: files

Reno Reporter

The *Reno Reporter* was established by Milo P. Saling, on August 15, 1947, as an independent weekly. It had the questionable distinction of having the fastest turnover in editors of any newspaper in Nevada history. The first issue was edited by Brian Storm, and the second by Jeanette Roberts, after which Saling decided to edit it himself. On January 29, 1948, he hired Maurya Wogan, who held on as editor until May 19, 1949, when Lloyd A. Rogers took the job. He lasted only ten weeks.

At this point Saling began looking for a purchaser, and on September 22, 1949, Roy M. Avery and Norville W. Moyer became the new publishers, with Bill Gillis as editor. On December 15, Avery assumed the post of managing editor, assisted by Florence King Shettel as news editor. They guided the paper until March 2, 1950, when Avery changed the name to the *Nevada Independent and Reno Reporter.* (See Reno, *Nevada Independent and Reno Reporter.*)

Reno Reporter: (Aug 15 1947–Mar 2 1950)
   NvHi — [Ag 15 1947–Mr 2 1950]
   NvU — [Ag 22 1947–D 30 1948]
   film — [Ag 15 1947–Mr 2 1950]
Ref: files

CAPReno

CAPReno was a monthly published by the Reno Air squadron of the Civil Air Patrol, with Milo P. Saling as editor. It began in April of 1948, and probably folded a little over a year later.

CAPReno: (Apr 1948–c. Jun 1949)
   NvHi — [Ap 1948–Je 1949]
   film — [Ap 1948–Je 1949]
Ref: files

Nevada Hunting and Fishing

Frank McCulloch commenced an interesting and well-illustrated magazine, *Nevada Hunting and Fishing,* in October of 1948. McCulloch was editor, issuing the journal bimonthly at 423 North Virginia Street, adjacent to and possibly connected with the *Reno Reporter.* Unfortunately, its thirteenth issue of November, 1949, proved to be its last.

Nevada Hunting and Fishing: (Oct 1948–Nov 1949)
   pvt — [O 1948–N 1949]
   NvHi — Ja–F 1949
Ref: files

Shopping News Reminder

The *Shopping News Reminder* was an irregular advertiser published by Pat O'Malley and Rex Halloway. It most likely resulted from the merger of the *Shopping News* and the *Reminder,* sometime around 1949.

Shopping News Reminder: (c. 1949)
   NvHi — Je 2–9 1949
   film — Je 2–9 1949
Ref: files

Reno Fundial

The *Reno Fundial* was a pocket-sized entertainment guide begun about August of 1949. It was issued biweekly, for $1 a year, by Stewart and Caroline Walters and lithographed by the Silver State Press. The Walters sold it June, 1952, to Mark Curtis, who suspended it to commence *Reno Pace.* (See *Reno Pace.*)

Reno Fundial: (c. Aug 1949–Jun 1952)
   pvt — My 28, Je 11 1952
Ref: files

Nevada Independent and Reno Reporter

On March 9, 1950, Roy M. Avery and Norville W. Moyer rechristened their faltering *Reno Reporter* as the *Nevada Independent and Reno Reporter.* Avery continued as managing editor, but Herb Samuels was editor. He quit on June 8, leaving Avery to preside over the paper alone until its demise on June 29, 1950.

Nevada Independent and Reno Reporter: (Mar 9 1950–Jun 29 1950)
   NvHi — Mr 2–Je 29 1950
   film — Mr 2–Je 29 1950
Ref: files

Donner Trail Reporter

Kurt C. S. Mann of the M and N Publicity Company commenced the *Donner Trail Reporter* on March 24, 1950. It was published every two weeks, but folded after two months.

Donner Trail Reporter: (Mar 24 1950–May 24 1950)
   NvU — Mr 31, Ap 26–My 24 1950
Ref: files

Nevada State News

On November 2, 1951, soon after he purchased the weekly *Nevada State Labor News,* Denver Dickerson, hoping to increase its readership, decided to shorten its name to the *Nevada State News.* Dickerson's hopes apparently were not realized, however, for he sold the *News* on April 30, 1953, to Frank McCulloch, who sold it eight months later to Jock Taylor. The following year it passed to Wallie Warren, who, in turn, sold it in 1956, to Patricia and Merrill Inch. It apparently suspended the following year.

Nevada State News: (Nov 2 1951–c. 1957)
   NvU — [N 2 1951–N 22 1957]
   film — [N 2 1951–N 22 1957]
Ref: files

Reno This Week

On April 11, 1952, Ray Bohanan commenced a little entertainment magazine, *Reno This Week.* It was issued every Friday, at $3 a year, with Don Jones as editor-in-chief, and lithographed by the Reno Printing Co.

Reno This Week: (Apr 11 1952–c. 1952)
   pvt — My 30 1952
Ref: files

Nevada Beverage Index

The *Nevada Beverage Index* has been published monthly at Reno since 1952 by Cleveland B. Crudgington and the Nevada Publishing Company. Merna N. Wick was the first editor, followed by J. B. Davis, M. R. Williams, Dolly Waysom, and Lee M. Cargile. In the early 1970s it began publishing both a northern and a southern edition.

Nevada Beverage Index: (1952+)
  pub — 1952+
Ref: Ayer; Cargile

Reno Pace

In July of 1952, Mark Curtis, having suspended the weekly *Fundial,* commenced the monthly *Reno Pace,* "a Magazine of Reno Life and Living." It lasted just eight months.

Reno Pace: (Jul 1952–Feb 1953)
  NvHi — O 1952–F 1953
  NvU — N 1952–F 1953
Ref: files

Boots and Chutes

About January of 1954, the weekly *Boots and Chutes,* "a civilian enterprise in the interest of Stead Air Force Base," was commenced at Reno. No editor was listed, but it was printed in Reno until September 9, 1954, when the printing was transferred to the Western Printing and Publishing Company in neighboring Sparks. *Boots and Chutes* ran for over a year, but probably stopped in 1955.

Boots and Chutes: (c. Jan 1954–c. 1955)
  NvHi — [F 5–D 30 1954; Ja 6–Ap 15 1955]
  film — [F 5 1954–Ap 15 1955]
Ref: files

Friday

Friday appeared about 1954, possibly edited by W. K. Bixler. As its name indicated, it was issued weekly on Fridays. After a brief time it was transformed into the weekly *Independent.* (See Reno, *The Independent.*)

Friday: (c. 1954)
  No issues located.
Ref: Trego

The Independent

Following the suspension of the weekly *Friday,* W. K. Bixler commenced the Reno *Independent* early in 1955. It was issued on Mondays, with Bixler as publisher and Florence Coon as editor. It fared slightly better than its predecessor, lasting until November 10, 1958.

The Independent: (c. 1955–Nov 10 1958)
  NvU — F 27 1956–N 10 1958
  film — F 27 1956–N 10 1958
Ref: files

Vigilant Reporter

On August 15, 1957, the *Vigilant Reporter* began to cast a critical eye toward government programs, under the motto "Eternal Vigilance is the Price of Liberty." Elizabeth Stone was the editor of the first issue, but because of illness, E. Norman Johnson replaced her the following week. D. J. McDonald took over publication of the paper from the Vigilant Publishing Company on September 19, but the paper apparently failed two weeks later.

Vigilant Reporter: (Aug 15 1957–c. Oct 4 1957)
   film — Ag 22–O 4 1957
Ref: files

Sierra Magazine

The *Sierra Magazine* was commenced in January of 1959, by W. K. Bixler and Max Dodge of the former *Independent,* at 150 North Virginia Street. It was issued monthly and contained much interesting material, but it ceased publication after March of 1961.

Sierra Magazine: (Jan 1959–Mar 1961)
   NvHi — Ja 1959–Mr 1961
   NvU — Ja 1959–N 1960
Ref: files

Flight Times

The Carson City *Nevada Appeal* published *Flight Times,* an unofficial weekly newspaper for the personnel at Stead Air Force Base, from January, 1959, to late 1963.

Flight Times: (Jan 1959–c. 1963)
   NvHi — O 18 1963
Ref: files

The Sentinel

Ruth Giles Jones, a former reporter for the *Sparks Tribune,* began *The Sentinel* at Reno in July, 1959. She issued it monthly for sixteen years as an advocate of equal rights for blacks.

The Sentinel: (Jul 1959–c. 1975)
   NvHi — Ag, D 1971; Ap 1973; S 1975
   NvU — [Jl 1959–Ap 1973]
Ref: files; RG D 20 1977

Reno News

The Nevada State AFL-CIO commenced the weekly *Reno News* on July 23, 1959, during the strike of the Newspaper Guild against the Reno newspapers. The *News* continued for over two months before its suspension on September 17, 1959.

Reno News: (Jul 23 1959–Sep 17 1959)
   NvU — Jl 23–S 17 1959
   film — Jl 23–S 17 1959
Ref: files

Action

In July of 1960, the Reno Chamber of Commerce commenced a monthly newsletter, *Action*. It was suspended about 1971, but resumed as a bimonthly in 1977.

Action: (Jul 1960–c. 1971; 1977+)
  NvHi — 1977–My 1979
  film — [D 1960–O 1971]
Ref: files

Washoe County Citizen

On October 24, 1960, Clayton Darrah commenced the *Washoe County Citizen* to serve both Reno and Sparks. Darrah was sole editor and proprietor, issuing the paper every Monday. Failing to gain sufficient support, he was forced to suspend the paper on June 22, 1961.

Washoe County Citizen: (Oct 24 1960–Jun 22 1961)
  NvU — O 24 1960–Je 22 1961
  film — O 24 1960–Je 22 1961
Ref: files

KOLO Times

On November 30, 1961, the radio and television station KOLO commenced a weekly advertising sheet, the *KOLO Times*. Its career was brief.

KOLO Times: (Nov 30 1961–c. 1961)
  Nv — N 30 1961
  NvU — N 30 1961
Ref: files

Cupid's Destiny

Cupid's Destiny, an itinerant matrimonial quarterly apparently begun in 1937, first appeared in Reno about 1961, with Ralph Kelly as editor and publisher. Three years later, V. H. Raney of Phoenix took the publication there for a few years, after which R. J. Williams brought it back to Reno around 1966.

Cupid's Destiny: (c. 1961–c. 1977)
  Nv — Ja—O 1967; Jl 1976–Ja 1977
Ref: Ayer

Nevada Veterans' Journal

In the spring of 1962, John H. MacDonald began the monthly *Nevada Veterans' Journal* at Reno, as the new official organ of the Nevada Division of the American Legion. It flourished for nearly five years until March, 1966, when Ira N. Jacobson of the *Tonopah Times-Bonanza and Goldfield News* took over its publication at Tonopah. (See Tonopah, *Nevada Veterans' Journal*.)

Nevada Veterans' Journal: (Spring 1962–Mar 1966)
   NvU — [1965–6]
   film — [Ap 1963–6]
Ref: files

Native Nevadan (Newsletter)

The Inter-Tribal Council of Nevada began the monthly *Newsletter* at Reno in March of 1964, and renamed it the *Native Nevadan* in May of 1965. It was printed by the Sparks Publishing Company, and has had a number of editors, including Carole Wright, Bob Shaw, and Elmer D. Miller.

Native Nevadan: (Mar 1964+)
   CLU — 1970
   NvHi — Ag–N 1965; F–O 1966; 1972–Ap 1973; N 1974–Mr, My–D 1975+
   NvU — [My 1965+]
   film — Mr 1964–D 1974
Ref: files

Northern Nevada Labor News

In 1964, Glenn C. Vaux, publisher of the *Southern Nevada Labor News* at Las Vegas, commenced the monthly *Northern Nevada Labor News* at Reno, as the official organ of the Building and Construction Trades Council of Northern Nevada. It suspended publication in October 1979.

Northern Nevada Labor News: (1964–Oct 1979)
   Nv — F 1969–O 1979
   NvHi — Ap–Je 1972
   NvU — Ag 1972–O 1979
Ref: files

Camels Coming

Camels Coming was an illustrated poetry magazine begun at Albuquerque, New Mexico, by Richard Morris in August, 1965. It was moved to Reno the following month. There it remained until 1968, issued "whenever we have enough money to pay the printer." Morris later moved to San Francisco and revived the magazine there in 1972.

Camels Coming: (Sep 1965–1968)
   NvU — S 1965–8
   NvULV — S 1965–8
Ref: files

The Citizen

On December 15, 1965, the small weekly *Citizen* was begun at Reno by Allan Prell, editor and publisher. It had a short, erratic career. In less than two months it suspended and lay moribund for three months before Prell resurrected it in May of 1966. It struggled on for another four months before it vanished forever about August 30, 1966.

The Citizen: (Dec 15 1965–c. Jan 1966; May 1966–c. Aug 30 1966)
   NvU — [D 15 1965–Ag 30 1966]
   film — [D 15 1965–Ag 30 1966]
Ref: files

Many Smokes

Many Smokes, a quarterly "dedicated to Universal Indian Brotherhood," was begun by Sun Bear at Reno in January, 1966. It flourished there through winter 1974 when Sun Bear moved it to Klamath Falls, Oregon.

Many Smokes: (Jan 1966–c. 1974)
   Nv — [Jl 1966–74]
   NvHi — Ja 1966–O 1968
   NvU — Ja 1966–1974
Ref: files

The Camels Hump

In 1966, in between issues of *Camels Coming,* Richard Morris published *The Camels Hump,* an undated poetry newsletter.

The Camels Hump: (1966)
   NvU — 1966 (4 issues)
Ref: files

View Magazine

The monthly *View Magazine,* edited and published by Charles A. Dromiack, was apparently started in March, 1966, and lasted a little over a year.

View Magazine: (c. Mar 1966–c. Mar 1967)
   NvHi — Mr 1967
Ref: files

Air Age News

On March 14, 1967, the semimonthly *Air Age News* moved from Gardnerville to Stead Airport in Reno. With that issue Bill Thorpe quit as editor, to be succeeded the following month by E. G. Covington. The *News* survived barely a year at Reno and moved to Sparks to publish its last issue on March 26, 1968. (See Gardnerville, *Air Age News* and Sparks, *Air Age News.*)

Air Age News: (Mar 14 1967–Mar 12 1968)
   Nv — Mr 14 1967–Mr 12 1968
   film — Mr 14 1967–Mr 12 1968
Ref: files

Home and the Range

In January, 1968, the Builders Association of Northern Nevada began publishing *Home and the Range,* a monthly magazine aimed at fostering "better public understanding of the construction industry." It appears to have lasted about six months.

Home and the Range: (Jan 1968–c. Jul 1968)
 film — F–My, Jl 1968
Ref: files

Love

Love, a free-distribution, biweekly "underground newspaper," was commenced at Reno on May 10, 1968, by Robert Swetlik, editor and publisher. Unable to support the paper "solely by donations," Swetlik began charging 15¢ an issue in June. Even then it was a losing proposition, and *Love* seems to have died on October 31.

Love: (May 10 1968–c. Oct 31 1968)
 NvU — My 10–O 31 1968
Ref: files

West Coast Poetry Review

The quarterly *West Coast Poetry Review* began in the summer of 1971 and apparently ceased in 1977. W. M. Ransom and J. Glaser were the editors in Reno, subscriptions were collected through a Virginia City post office box and it was actually printed in Seattle, Washington.

West Coast Poetry Review: (Summer 1971–c. 1977)
 NvHi — Summer 1971–77
 NvU — Summer 1971–Winter 1974
Ref: files

Showtime

Aaron Ging started *Showtime* in 1971, as a free, biweekly "Visitor and Convention Guide."

Showtime: (1971+)
 NvU — Ap 23 1976+
Ref: files

Nevada Mobile Home News

Nevada Mobile Home News was a short-lived, free monthly, started at Reno in March, 1973, by Showtime International, Inc. It was edited by John Cronan.

Nevada Mobile Home News: (Mar 1973–c. May 1973)
 Nv — Mr, My 1973
Ref: files

Impact

In April of 1973, the Reno Community Environmental Association started a monthly, *Impact,* with William Fine as editor. It was changed to a quarterly that summer and continued as such until its demise in November of 1979.

Impact: (Apr 1973–Nov 1979)
 NvHi — Ap 1973–N 1979

NvU — AP 1973–Ap 1976
Ref: files

Our Town

Our Town was an ambitious 96-page quarterly launched in January of 1974, by the Real Resources Group, with Russell R. Goebel as publisher and Caroline J. Hadley as editor. It ended with the third number in July.
Our Town: (Jan 1974–Jul 1974)
   NvHi — Ja–Jl 1974
   NvU — Ja–Jl 1974
Ref: files

Fun and Gaming

Fun and Gaming, published twice a month by Phil Olsson, was a free-distribution entertainment advertiser that started about February of 1974 and apparently folded the following year.
Fun and Gaming: (c. Feb 1974–c. Apr 1975)
   NvHi — Ap 16 1975
Ref: files

Northern Nevada Shopping News

Tom Gibbons launched the bimonthly *Northern Nevada Shopping News* at Reno in July, 1974, but it died within a few months.
Northern Nevada Shopping News: (Jul 1974–c. Sep 1974)
   Nv — Jl–S 8 1974
Ref: files

Silver Circle Mobile Home News

Robert J. Armstrong edited and published the *Silver Circle Mobile Home News* every two months during its brief life from February to June of 1975.
Silver Circle Mobile Home News: (Feb 1975–Jun 1975)
   NvHi — F–Je 1975
Ref: files

The Nevada Outdoor Adventure

The Nevada Outdoor Adventure, a free recreational monthly, was launched in Reno in May of 1975 by Tod Bedrosian with Arline Fisher as editor.
The Nevada Outdoor Adventure: (May 1975+)
   NvHi — Je–N 1976
   NvU — My 1975+
Ref: files

The Nevada Sage

The Nevada Sage began in May of 1975 as a monthly "devoted to the interest of Nevada Senior Citizens." The first issue was funded by the

Reno Senior Citizen Center; the second by the Community Services Agency; and finally by Nevada Sage, Inc. In October, 1977, Odis Doyle became publisher; he continues to publish it as an independent newspaper for senior citizens.

The Nevada Sage: (May 1975+)
    Nv — [My 1975+]
    NvHi — [My 1975–6]; 1977; [1978+]
    NvU — [My 1975+]
Ref: files

Nevada Profiles

Thomas A. Gibbons launched the semimonthly *Profiles* on April 28, 1976, changed the name to *Nevada Profiles* in July, and sold it to Michael A. Wright in August. It died in Wright's hands in September.

Nevada Profiles: (Apr 28 1976–Sep 28 1976)
    NvHi — Ap 28–S 28 1976
Ref: files

Reno Magazine

Reno Magazine, the city's "first newsmagazine," was started in tabliod form on May 17, 1976, by John M. McWade, editor and publisher. McWade planned to issue the magazine biweekly, but he barely managed to get it out once a month, and it ceased with its seventh number on November 8, 1976.

Reno Magazine: (May 17 1976–Nov 8 1976)
    NvHi — My 17–N 8 1976
    NvU — My 17–N 8 1976
Ref: files

Northern Nevada Home

The *Northern Nevada Home,* a free, biweekly "crusade for Morality," was started by Jim Dykes on September 3, 1976, and ended on September 17.

Northern Nevada Home: (Sep 3 1976–Sep 17 1976)
    NvHi — S 17 1976
    NvU — S 3 1976
Ref: files

The Sierra Scene

The Sierra Scene, a free monthly "guide for recreation and entertainment," was started in November, 1976, by the Comstock Publishing Company and the Nevada Outdoor Adventure, with Larry Stallings and Tod Bedrosian as co-publishers. It apparently suspended within the year.

The Sierra Scene: (Nov 1976–c. Dec 1976)
    NvHi — N 1976
Ref: files

Cathouse News

T and L Enterprises put out the *Cathouse News* from February to March of 1977. Terri Bennett edited this curious monthly devoted to that oldest profession.

Cathouse News: (Feb 1977–Mar 1977)
   NvHi — F 1977
   NvU — Mr 1977
Ref: files

Western Wildlife

Western Wildlife, a monthly devoted to "hunting, fishing, conservation and outdoor recreation" was started at Reno in February, 1977, by Bill Platt and Don Landeck as publishers and Platt as editor. Landeck dropped out after four months and the paper apparently folded after a year.

Western Wildlife: (Feb 1977–c. Jan 1978)
   NvHi — [Ap 1977–Ja 1978]
   NvU — [F 1977–Ja 1978]
Ref: files

Nevada Horse Life

Nevada Horse Life, edited and published by Maxine Zimmerman, began as a quarterly in March, 1977, and grew to a bimonthly in May, 1979.

Nevada Horse Life: (Mar 1977+)
   Nv — Mr 1977+
   NvHi — Mr 1977+
   NvU — Mr 1977+
Ref: files

Discover Magazine

Discover Magazine, a monthly publication, began in Reno in December, 1977, as "the advisor, guide and promoter for businesses and visitors." Joane Lang was publisher and Janie E. Young was editor until it ceased in August, 1978.

Discover Magazine: (Dec 1977–Aug 1978)
   Nv — D 1977–Ag 1978
   NvHi — Ja, Ap–My 1978
   NvU — D 1977–Ag 1978
Ref: files; Young

The Green Sheet (Green Felt News)

In March, 1978, Dale and Peggy Walker commenced the monthly *Green Felt News* at Reno, as the "Exclusive Publication for All Hotel and Casino Employees." In December, they changed the name to the *Green Sheet,* but in February, 1979, it folded.

The Green Sheet: (Mar 1978–Feb 1979)
   NvHi — O 1978

NvU — Mr 1978–F 1979
Ref: files

Key Magazine

Key Magazine, a local entertainment and visitor's guide, began publishing in Reno in October, 1978. It is issued twice a month by the Levin Publishing Company with Janie Young as managing editor.

Key Magazine: (Oct 1978+)
   pub — O 1978+
Ref: Young

Nevadian

The *Nevadian* was begun at Reno in January, 1979, by Harry Copeland, with Gary Jesch as editor. It was distributed free, as a monthly supplement in over a dozen newspapers throughout the state.

Nevadian: (Jan 1979+)
   NvHi — Ja 1979+
   NvU — Mr 1979+
Ref: files

Arcadian

The *Arcadian,* "the Sierra Nevada's Competitive City Sports News Weekly," was launched in Reno on February 13, 1979, by Phillip M. Rulon with Michael S. Graham as editor. It apparently folded the following month.

Arcadian: (Feb 13 1979–c. Mar 1979)
   NvU — [F 13–Mr 7 1979]
Ref: files

Reno Magazine

Reno Magazine was resurrected as an attractive, slick news and feature monthly in March of 1979, by the Jonsson Communication Corporation, with Kenneth A. Jonsson as publisher, Jan Latimer as editor, and John M. McWade of the defunct original *Reno Magazine* as art director. The magazine failed, however, to attract sufficient advertising from Reno businesses.

Reno Magazine: (Mar 1979+)
Nv — Mr 1979+
NvHi — Mr 1979+
NvU — Mr 1979+
Ref: files

The Local Picture

The *Local Picture* was a weekly entertainment guide begun at Reno by Showtime on August 11, 1979, to provide "an alternative to the Listerine-like (Hated, but used twice a day) papers that have held a monopoly in the area until now."

The Local Picture: (Aug 11, 1979+)
   pvt — Ag 11 1979
   NvHi — Ag 25 1979+
Ref: files

⇜❮ RHYOLITE ❯⇝

Rhyolite Herald

On May 5, 1905, barely a month after Frank P. Mannix and C. W. Nicklin commenced their rival *Bullfrog Miners* at Bullfrog and Beatty, Earle R. Clemens and Guy T. Keene began a third competitor, the *Herald,* at Rhyolite. The *Herald* grew rapidly with the development of Rhyolite, which became the district's principal camp. By 1909, the *Herald* boasted a circulation of 10,000, and was available at newsstands throughout the nation, in Los Angeles, San Francisco, Salt Lake City, San Antonio, Omaha, Chicago, and New York. Clemens, who served as editor, bought Keene's interest on May 6, 1908, and soon had the field all to himself. Two of his competitors folded within the year, and on September 25, 1909, he eliminated the last competition with the purchase and suspension of the *Bullfrog Miner.*

A few years later, however, on April 8, 1911, Clemens, too, sold out, to Frank F. Garside. He kept part of the plant, and took it to the farming community of Terra Bella, California, where he started the weekly *News* and settled down to stay. Garside published the paper as the Rhyolite Printing Company, and hired A. B. Gibson as editor. But Rhyolite was clearly on the decline, and after little over a year Garside suspended the *Herald* on June 22, 1912.

Rhyolite Herald: (May 5 1905–Jun 22 1912)
   CLM — F 8 1907
   NvHi — [My 5 1905–My 13 1911]
   NvU — [O 11 1907–Je 22 1912]
   film — [My 5 1905–Je 22 1912]
Ref: files; Ritter; Hensher; GT Ja 8 1921

Bullfrog Miner

In March of 1906, with the close of the first volume of the *Miner* at Bullfrog, Frank P. Mannix moved the plant to neighboring Rhyolite, commencing the first issue of the *Bullfrog Miner* there on March 30. There the paper prospered, although its dispute with the *Beatty Bullfrog Miner* continued until the latter's suspension in October of 1908. Mannix enjoyed sole title to the name for less than a year before he finally suspended the paper, on September 25, 1909, and sold the plant to his competitor, Earle Clemens of the *Herald.*

Bullfrog Miner: (Mar 30 1906–Sep 25 1909)
   NvHi — [Mr 30 1906–Ag 25 1909]
   NvU — [S 19 1908–S 25 1909]

film — [Mr 30 1906–S 25 1909]
Ref: files

Rhyolite Daily Bulletin

On September 23, 1907, John App, Richard H. Carr, and C. H. Petterson commenced the *Daily Rhyolite Bulletin* under the firm name of the Bulletin Company. The *Bulletin* was a four-page, three-column sheet, issued at 65¢ a month from offices on Colorado Street, near the southwest corner of Golden. The paper was well received and was published almost continuously for nearly two years, being suspended briefly from May 16 to September 7, 1908, while App was in Denver visiting his ill mother. Carr retired and H. F. Kane became editor on March 19, 1909. As a daily, the *Bulletin* was acutely sensitive to the financial health of the camp, hence it was the first to feel its wane, which resulted in suspension on June 8, 1909.

Rhyolite Daily Bulletin: (Sep 23 1907–Jun 8 1909)
   NvHi — [S 23 1907–D 31 1908]
   NvU — S 23 1907–Je 8 1909
   film — S 23 1907–Je 8 1909
Ref: files

Death Valley Magazine (Death Valley Prospector)

The *Death Valley Prospector* was an interesting and informative illustrated monthly magazine, begun at Rhyolite in November of 1907, by Paul de Laney. With its third number, in January, 1908, the magazine was renamed the *Death Valley Magazine,* and under this head it continued until October.

Death Valley Magazine: (Nov 1907–Oct 1908)
   DLC — D 1907–Jl, S 1908
   NvHi — N 1907–O 1908
   film — N 1907–O 1908
Ref: files

ROCHESTER

Rochester Miner

Rich lodes were discovered near Rochester in 1911, and by the beginning of 1913, a boom was in full swing. On January 22, 1913, the Lovelock Publishing Company, publishers of the nearby *Lovelock Review-Miner,* commenced the first number of the *Rochester Miner.* J. S. Brooks served as editor, issuing the paper every Wednesday. It was quite possibly printed at the *Review-Miner* office in Lovelock. On May 13, 1913, William McClure Gotwaldt assumed the editorial post and continued the *Miner* until its suspension on January 7, 1914.

Rochester Miner: (Jan 22 1913–Jan 7 1914)
   NvU — [Ja 22 1913–Ja 7 1914]

film — [Ja 22 1913–Ja 7 1914]
Ref: files

Rochester Journal

On February 2, 1913, scarcely a week after the *Lovelock Review-Miner* began issuing a paper for Rochester, the Reno *Nevada State Journal* also entered the field, launching the *Rochester Journal.* F. E. Becker served as editor of the *Journal,* working from his "temporary office" in Rochester's new St. Francis Hotel, whence he distributed his eight-page, seven-column weekly every Sunday, following its arrival by train and stage from Reno. Within two weeks the paper's issue was changed to Thursday, in order to scoop the *Miner,* and it ran as such until the following May 1.

Rochester Journal: (Feb 2 1913–May 1 1913)
 NvHi — F 2 1913
 NvU — F 20, 27, Mr 6, My 1 1913
 film — [F 2–My 1 1913]
Ref: files

Rochester Mining News

Within a week of the suspension of the *Rochester Journal* on May 1, 1913, a new paper, the *Rochester Mining News,* made its bid for public favor. It probably lasted no more than a few weeks.

Rochester Mining News: (c. May 1913)
 No issues located.
Ref: FE My 10 1913

Rochester Paycrack

Following the suspension of the *Miner,* Rochester was without a paper for more than two years, until June 8, 1916, when Joe T. Camp drifted in to commence the *Rochester Paycrack.* Camp, as always, was sole editor and proprietor, issuing the *Paycrack* every Friday, as a four-page, 13¼ by 9¾-inch, Democratic weekly, at $3 a year. In 1917, Camp suspended the *Paycrack,* renaming it the *Rochester-Packard Miner.* (See *Rochester-Packard Miner.*)

Rochester Paycrack: (Jun 8 1916–1917)
 No issues located.
Ref: LRM Je 2 1916

Rochester-Packard Miner

Sometime in 1917, Joe T. Camp ceased publication of the *Rochester Paycrack* and renamed the sheet the *Rochester-Packard Miner,* to include the neighboring camp of Packard, two miles to the south. Under this new head the paper was continued as a four-page, 13¼ by 19¾-inch, Democratic weekly, issued every Saturday. With the post-World War I decline about 1919, the *Miner* was finally forced to suspend.

Rochester-Packard Miner: (1917–c. 1919)
   No issues located.
Ref: Myrick

⌒⊰(ROSEBUD)⊱⌒

Rosebud Mining News

Following the discovery of silver at Rosebud, fifty miles west of Winnemucca, the new camp grew quickly. By early 1907, Rosebud boasted a population of 800, and R. E. L. Windle, George M. Rose, and A. L. Brackett, publishers of the Winnemucca *Humboldt Star,* decided that the camp was ready for a newspaper. In February they commenced the weekly *Rosebud Mining News,* selling at $4 a year, and most probably printed at the *Star* plant in Winnemucca. Rosebud died on the vine, however, and the *Mining News* suspended within a short time.

Rosebud Mining News: (Feb 1907–c. Apr 1907)
   No issues located.
Ref: LT F 22 1907; TS Ap 3 1907; NMI My 1 1907; Polk 1907–8

⌒⊰(ROUND MOUNTAIN)⊱⌒

Nugget

Henry J. Bartlett and James Travers founded the *Round Mountain Nugget* at the new boom camp on June 2, 1906. They issued the paper every Saturday, as an eight-page, Democratic weekly. The first issues were printed in Tonopah. The paper became a good representative of the camp and soon gained a circulation of about two thousand. In 1907, Bartlett became sole editor and publisher, and on August 7, 1909, W. H. Bohannan replaced him. But the camp was on the decline and Bohannan sold out the following year to Edward N. Buck. He shortened the paper's title to the *Nugget,* but was forced to cease publication on October 23, 1910.

Nugget: (Jun 2 1906–Oct 23 1910)
   NvHi — Je 2 1906; Ap 20 1907; F 1 1908–Ap 2 23–O 23 1910
   NvU — Ja 4 1908–Ap 2 1910
   film — Je 2 1906; Ap 20 1907; F 1 1908–Ap 2, 23–O 23 1910
Ref: files; TS Je 1 1906

⌒⊰(RUBY HILL)⊱⌒

Ruby Hill Mining Report

Following his sale of the *Belleville Times* in April, 1878, Mark W. Musgrove served as mining reporter on the *Bodie Standard* for several months. In the fall of that year, he quit the *Standard* and brought material for a newspaper to Ruby Hill just two and one-half miles from Eureka. Here, he commenced publication of the *Ruby Hill Mining Report* on about October 10, 1978. Musgrove was sole editor and proprietor of the *Mining Report,* issuing it every Thursday as a large, twenty-eight-column weekly. Although the paper was well written, Ruby Hill was not yet able to support a newspaper, and it soon failed, probably in the summer of the following year. Musgrove then struck out for Salt Lake City, where he published the *Western Mining Gazetteer,* and eventually became involved in some rather questionable dealings before he finally returned to Nevada some thirty years later.

Ruby Hill Mining Report: (Oct 10 1878–c. 1879)
   NvHi — Ag 14 1879
   film — Ag 14 1879
Ref: files

Ruby Hill Mining News

With the continued development of the mines around Eureka, Ruby Hill prospered, and on April 24, 1880, James E. Anderson founded the *Ruby Hill Mining News.* This time the town was ready for a newspaper and the *News* was liberally patronized. Anderson was sole editor and proprietor, issuing the paper each Monday, as a four-page, seven-column, Republican weekly. The paper flourished and soon gained a circulation of about five hundred.

On October 3, 1881, Anderson sold the plant to Walter L. Marsden and George M. Payne, and went to Eureka, where he purchased the *Daily Leader.* Marsden became sole owner two months later. He ran the *Mining News* for about a year before he sold it to William J. Penrose and leased the *Leader* in November of 1882, after Anderson's death. Penrose, a twenty-six-year-old former miner from Cornwall, continued the *Mining News* as a strong union advocate until November 3, 1884, when he suspended the paper and moved the plant to Eureka to start the *Republican Press.*

Ruby Hill Mining News: (Apr 24 1880–Nov 3 1884)
   CU-BANC — Ap 24, O 30, D 11 1880–Ja 22, Ag 29 1881–Jl 1882
   NvU — [1883–N 3 1884]
   film — [Ap 24 1880–N 3 1884]
Ref: files

~(RUBY VALLEY)~

Ruby Valley News

The mimeographed *Ruby Valley News* was founded by Darlene Sharp in December of 1975, with Niki McQueary as editor. It is issued once a month, but "it depends on the weather, our machine and staff as to what day of the month it gets printed."

Ruby Valley News: (Dec 1975+)
   NvEHi — D 1975+
Ref: files

⁓(SAFFORD)⁓

Safford Express

In the spring of 1883, Lambert Molinelli, a real-estate broker and promoter from Eureka, decided to publish a newspaper to promote the new boom camp of Safford. Not wishing to risk the expense of purchasing a printing plant, however, he simply sent a bookkeeper to Safford to sign up advertisers and subscribers while he set up his editorial office at the nearby railroad junction of Palisade and had the paper printed at the *Sentinel* office in Eureka. There, on June 2, 1883, he printed the first number of the *Safford Express*, which was quickly carried by rail and stage to Safford for distribution. The paper was well received, despite the proprietor's lack of faith, but no press was ever set up at the new camp. On July 21, 1883, Molinelli retired from the establishment to go to Salt Lake City and W. W. Booth replaced him as editor. The boom at Safford ultimately proved to be short-lived and the paper undoubtedly suspended that same summer.

Safford Express: (Jun 2 1883–c. Aug 1883)
   pvt — Je 2–9 1883
   film — Je 2–9 1883
Ref: files; NeT Je 20 1883

⁓(SCHELLBOURNE)⁓

Schell Creek Prospect

In 1872, the mines of the Schell Creek Range gave great promise of wealth, and the town of Schellbourne grew into importance. The town soon demanded a newspaper, and together with his former partner, W. H. Pitchford, William J. Forbes of the *White Pine News* at Hamilton shipped a press and material to the camp. They issued the first number of the *Schell Creek Prospect* in July of 1872. The paper was a twenty-four-column weekly, which lasted as long as the boom, but no longer, and suspended in January of 1873. After the abandonment of the office, the building was removed, but the old press and material were left to the mercy of the elements. A portion of the material was later gathered together and removed to Battle Mountain, where it was used by Forbes to print *Measure for Measure*.

Schell Creek Prospect: (Jul 1872–Jan 1873)
   No issues located.
Ref: Angel 331; McMurtrie 304–5

⇜❦ SCHURZ ❧⇝

The Indian Call

The Indian Call was published at Schurz on the Walker River Indian Reservation in 1939. No editor or publisher was listed, but it appears to have been published by the Indian Mission of the Methodist Episcopal Church.

The Indian Call: (1939)
   NvHi — F 1 1939
Ref: files

Agai Dicutta Yuduan (Paiute)

The Walker River Paiute Tribe commenced a bimonthly paper at Schurz on September 8, 1975. Originally called the *Paiute,* it was renamed *Agai Dicutta Yuduan* on October 20. John Martin served as editor until its suspension on June 24, 1977.

Agai Dicutta Yuduan: (Sep 8 1975–Jun 24 1977)
   Nv — S 8 1975–D 23 1976
   film — S 8 1975–D 23 1976
Ref: files

News Notes

Six months after the suspension of *Agai Dicutta Yuduan,* the Walker River Paiute Tribe issued *News Notes* on December 12, 1977. This mimeographed monthly newsletter continued until February 8, 1979, when it was superseded by the monthly *Numa News.*

News Notes: (Dec 12 1977–Feb 8 1979)
   Nv — D 12 1977–F 8 1979
Ref: files

Neh-Muh News (Numa News)

On February 26, 1979, the Walker River Paiute Tribe replaced their *News Notes* with a new mimeographed monthly, *Numa News,* edited by Debbie West. This was renamed *Neh-Muh News* on June 8, and apparently folded on October 5.

Neh-Muh News: (Feb 26 1979–Oct 5 1979)
   Nv — F 26–My 11 1979
   NvU — [Mr 15–O 5 1979]
Ref: files

⇜❦ SEARCHLIGHT ❧⇝

Searchlight Bulletin (The Searchlight)

On June 13, 1902, H. A. Perkins issued the first number of the weekly *Searchlight* at the camp of the same name. Perkins was editor for the

Searchlight Publishing Company, which printed the paper every Friday, as an eight-page, independent sheet selling for $2.50 a year. The paper received the full support of the camp and prospered for over a decade. On October 26, 1906, Perkins changed the name to the *Searchlight Bulletin* and changed its politics to Republican. In 1912, Charles J. Carr replaced Perkins as editor, continuing the paper less than a year before its suspension on January 3, 1913.

Searchlight Bulletin: (Jun 13 1902–Jan 3 1913)
   CLCM — Je 13 1902
   NvHi — [Je 26 1903–D 27 1912]
   NvU — [O 11 1907–Ja 3 1913]
   film — [Je 26 1903–Ja 3 1913]
Ref: files; PR Je 27 1902

Searchlight News

J. B. Flanigan commenced the weekly *Searchlight News* on May 4, 1907. Unable to gain sufficient support or "promised capital," he suspended the *News* on August 30, 1907. He was determined to try again, however, and after rounding up new backing, he revived the paper that winter. In January of 1908, he expanded his shaky empire by establishing a second paper, the *Hart Enterprise,* at a new camp across the state line in California. This venture proved more successful than the *News,* and in April he suspended the latter, packed up the printing plant, and moved it to Hart. Perkins of the *Bulletin* bid the competition good riddance and dubbed its editor "Off again; Back again; Gone again-Flanagan." Two years later Flanagan was in fact off again, folding up the *Enterprise* at Hart to move to Parker, Arizona, where he started the *Post.*

Searchlight News: (May 4 1907–Aug 30 1907; 1907–c. Apr 1908)
   No issues located.
Ref: SB My 10, S 13 1907, F 1, Ap 10 1908, F 26, My 20 1910; Polk 1907–8

Searchlight Enterprise

On April 14, 1917, during the World War I revival of activity at Searchlight, George B. Corn founded the *Searchlight Enterprise.* Corn was both editor and publisher, issuing the paper every Saturday for $2.50 a year. The revival was not strong enough to support a paper, however, and the *Enterprise* suspended within a year.

Searchlight Enterprise: (Apr 14 1917–c. 1918)
   No issues located.
Ref: ECM Ap 20 1917

Searchlight Journal

On August 29, 1946, Howard E. Mildren began the weekly *Searchlight Journal.* Although he had it printed in Boulder City, Mildren edited and published it in Searchlight, with the help of his wife, Sinah, as circulation

manager, and Berta Silveira as local news editor. It lasted until May 14, 1947, succumbing when merchants started paying their advertising bills with bottles of wine and whiskey.
Searchlight Journal: (Aug 29 1946–May 14 1947)
   pvt — [Ag 29 1946–My 14 1947]
Ref: Mildren

Searchlight News-Bulletin

On October 30, 1951, A. J. McLain and Marc Wilkinson revived the names of Searchlight's two pioneer papers with the establishment of a new weekly, the *Searchlight News-Bulletin.* McLain was publisher at Searchlight, while Wilkinson printed the paper at Las Vegas. It seems to have survived only a short time, suspending publication before the end of the year.
Searchlight News-Bulletin: (Oct 30 1951–c. Dec 1951)
   No issues located.
Ref: Averett

~(SHERMANTOWN)~

White Pine Evening Telegram

In the spring of 1869, three camps, Hamilton, Treasure City, and Shermantown, were rivals for dominance of the rich mines of Treasure Hill. Hamilton and Treasure City each had a newspaper to aid its fight for supremacy, and it was necessary that Shermantown, too, should have an organ. On June 2, 1869, Edward F. McElwain and U. E. Allen took up the cause of Shermantown in their first number of the *White Pine Evening Telegram.* They issued the paper daily, except Sunday, as a four-page, six-column sheet, selling for $16 a year or 75¢ a week. In less than six weeks, on July 13, Allen gave up the fight, but McElwain was determined to make the paper last. Three dailies were too many for the population of Treasure Hill, however, and the *Telegram,* being the youngest, was the first to fail. That fall McElwain conceded defeat.
White Pine Evening Telegram: (Jun 2 1869–c. Sep 1869)
   CU-BANC — Je 2–14, 16–21, 23–Jl 10, 13–Ag 6, 9–13, 16–18 1869
   film — [Je 2–Ag 18 1869]
Ref: files; GHN My 27, Je 8 1869

Shermantown Reporter

The continued rivalry between the *White Pine News* at Treasure City and the *Inland Empire* at Hamilton — both large morning papers — finally prompted Forbes of the *News* to make an arrangement with Pat Holland, a former carrier of the *Inland Empire.* According to the agreement, Holland would ostensibly be the publisher of an evening paper, which would be circulated in Hamilton with the aim of reducing the circulation and advertising of the *Empire.* Thus, in the winter of 1869, Pat Holland commenced publication of the *Reporter* at nearby Shermantown, on the old press of the former Belmont *Mountain Champion.* Forbes handled the editorials and Fred Hart filled in the locals, but the paper proved only partly successful in its aim. As a result, Forbes moved the *News* to Hamilton in January of 1870, to do battle at close range. This was much more effective, and by April the *Empire* capitulated.

Forbes, who had let the *Reporter* lapse, sold the plant to Archibald Skillman and G. A. Brier, who had been the last editor of the *Empire.* They revived the paper on May 9, 1870, but just eight days later Brier dropped dead at the Wells Fargo office. Less than a month later, on June 12, Skillman suspended the paper, and removed the press and material to the new camp of Eureka, where he used it to found the *Sentinel*. The press was a nomadic one, a small Washington, which was already ancient when Joseph Eckley first brought it to Nevada to issue the *Nye County News* at Ione.

Shermantown Reporter: (c. Dec 1869–c. Jan 1870; May 9–Jun 12 1870)
   No issues located.
Ref: Angel 330; McMurtrie 305; Jackson 158–9

SILVER BOW

Silver Bow Standard

On August 5, 1905, the *Silver Bow Standard* made its bow at the short-lived camp, some fifty miles east of Tonopah. Its editor and publisher, R. Leslie Smaill, formerly of the *Fallon Standard,* was an enthusiastic inveterate promoter, who sold the first paper off the press at auction for $7. The following January 6, he pulled off a much grander stunt, printing the front page headline of the *Standard* in a brilliant mixture of yellow ink and gold dust that assayed $80,000 a ton! This effort may have bankrupted him, as the paper folded soon after, and Smaill took a job as editor of the new *Manhattan News.*

Silver Bow Standard: (Aug 5 1905–c. Jan 1906)
   pvt — S 2 1905
   NvHi — Ja 6 1906
   film — Ja 6 1906
Ref: files; TS Ag 2, 9 1905; VC Ja 16 1906

SILVER CITY

Washoe Times

The third newspaper to be published in Nevada, the second on the Comstock, and the first in Lyon County was the *Washoe Times,* issued at Silver

City, while that camp still rivaled Virginia City for supremacy on the Lode. The *Times* was a Saturday weekly, begun on March 16, 1861, by William L. Card, editor, and a former San Francisco printer, R. P. Locke. John Lewis of the Carson City *Silver Age,* an old-timer of four months, wished that the newcomer might have "the most complete success, and that *that Card* may prove to be a trump, as the printing business is, financially speaking, powerful *trick-y,* unless a proper *lead* is made." The *Territorial Enterprise* apparently over-trumped, however, and the *Times* capitulated in September of 1861, surrendering with it the hopes of Silver City. Thirteen years passed before a paper was revived at Silver City, but only thirteen months passed before the name of the *Washoe Times* was resurrected by other parties in a paper at Washoe City.

Washoe Times: (Mar 16 1861–Sep 1861)
  No issues located.
Ref: SFAC Mr 23 1861

Lyon County Times

For eight years after the suspension of the Dayton *Sentinel,* Lyon County was without a newspaper. On July 4, 1874, Frank A. Kenyon revived a paper in the county with the issuance of the *Lyon County Times* at Silver City. Kenyon was sole editor and proprietor and issued the paper as a triweekly of twenty-four columns, nearly two-thirds of which were filled with advertising. On April 6, 1875, Harry J. Norton became associate editor and retained the position until January 4, 1877. The size of the paper was enlarged several times, and on March 4, 1876, it was increased to a daily. After three months, however, the daily proved to have been an overexpansion, and on June 9, the *Times* was again reduced to a triweekly. On January 8, 1877, it was further reduced to a semiweekly.

Finally, on July 6, 1878, Kenyon sold the plant to T. E. Picotte and sailed to Guatemala. He died en route. Picotte ran the paper for more than a year before selling it to John M. Campbell on May 15, 1880. It soon became evident that the town would no longer support a paper, and on December 11, 1880, Campbell suspended the *Times* at Silver City. He moved the press and material to Dayton, where he revived the *Lyon County Times* as a weekly on December 18. (See Dayton, *Lyon County Times.*)

Lyon County Times: (Jul 4 1874–Dec 11 1880)
  CU-BANC — Jl 9 1874–Mr 2, 4–Je 7, 9 1876–Ja 8, 13 1877–D 6 1879; Ja 17, Mr 6, 17, Ap 17–D 11 1880
  NvHi — [1875–80]
  film — [Jl 9 1874–D 11 1880]
Ref: files; Angel 308

Mining Reporter

On March 9, 1876, the Reporter Publishing Company issued the first number of the daily *Mining Reporter* at Silver City. Harry J. Norton and Alex Scrimgeour, former local editor of the *Gold Hill News,* were joint editors, and D. S. Stanley was business manager. The paper did not receive the support its publishers anticipated, however. On May 3, Scrimgeour left and Norton became sole editor and publisher. Six days later he reduced the paper to a triweekly. Even this move failed to make the paper solvent; by early June it was reduced to a weekly, and on August 6, it was suspended. (See Silver City, *Reporter.*)

Mining Reporter: (Mar 9 1876–Aug 6 1876)
   CU-BANC — Ap 22–My 28, Je 25–Ag 6 1876
   film — Ap 22–My 28, Je 25–Ag 6 1876
Ref: files; Angel 309

Reporter

Seven weeks after the suspension of his *Mining Reporter,* Harry J. Norton succeeded in rounding up enough money from local Democrats to make a fresh start with a new *Reporter.* He began again with vol. 1, no. 1 on September 28, 1876. After the election he was again without support, and was finally forced to suspend the paper on December 5.

Reporter: (Sep 28 1876–Dec 5 1876)
   CU-BANC — O 5–8, N 2–5, 12–D 5 1876
   film — O 5–8, N 2–5, 12–D 5 1876
Ref: files

SILVER PEAK

Silver Peak Post

With the revival of activity at the old camp of Silver Peak in 1906, W. W. Booth of the *Tonopah Bonanza* dispatched A. A. Blum to the district to gather news, and on June 6, they commenced the *Silver Peak Post.* Printed at Tonopah and "devoted to the masses," the *Post* was issued every Wednesday, as a four-page, six-column weekly, selling at $5 a year. In the fall of 1906, however, Silver Peak was overshadowed by a new townsite at Blair. Newman Mix started a rival paper, the *Blair Press,* there, and in January of 1907, Booth shipped a press and equipment to Blair to print the *Post.* As the competition with Mix grew heated, Booth tried changing the name to the *Blair Booster* on March 13, but despite all his efforts the paper soon failed. (See *Blair Booster.*)

Silver Peak Post: (Jun 6 1906–c. Mar 6 1907)
   pvt — D 26 1906–Mr 6 1907
   NvHi — Je 6 1906
   film — Je 6 1906
Ref: files

~({ SKOOKUM })~

Skookum Times

In early April of 1908, Lester S. Haworth of the *Manhattan Mail* issued the first number of the *Skookum Times* to help boost the hopeful new camp between the Shoshone and Toiyabe ranges in southern Lander County. Skookum's boom was brief, however, and Haworth undoubtedly never bothered moving a press to the camp.

Skookum Times: (Apr 4 1908–1908)
  No issues located.
Ref: TB Ap 8 1908; RH Ap 22 1908

~({ SPARKS (HARRIMAN) })~

Harriman Herald

H. W. Patton founded the *Harriman Herald* at the railroad town of Sparks, then known as Harriman, on January 16, 1904. Patton was sole editor and publisher, issuing the *Herald* every Saturday as an eight-page, six-column, Democratic weekly, from his office in Ferguson and Willi's store on Harriman Avenue. On July 20 William McClure Gotwaldt purchased the plant and suspended the *Herald* to begin the *Sparks Headlight* on July 30. (See *Sparks Headlight.*)

Harriman Herald: (Jan 16 1904–Jul 1904)
  NvHi — F 13, Mr 26 1904
  film — F 13, Mr 26 1904
Ref: files; RG Jl 21 1904

Sparks Headlight

On July 30, 1904, following his suspension of the *Harriman Herald,* William McClure Gotwaldt, formerly city editor of the Reno *Gazette,* used the *Herald* plant to commence the *Sparks Headlight.* Gotwaldt was sole editor and publisher, and issued the paper every Wednesday and Saturday, as a semiweekly much the same size as the former *Herald.* Gotwaldt sold out to the Headlight Publishing Company, who, with H. M. Standerwick as editor, continued publishing the paper until sometime the following year.

Sparks Headlight: (Jul 30 1904–1905)
  NvHi — Ja 21 1905
  film — Ja 21 1905
Ref: files; RG Jl 21, 30 1904

Sparks Dispatch

With the removal of the railroad shops from Wadsworth to Sparks, Nicholas A. Hummel suspended the *Wadsworth Dispatch* and moved the plant to Sparks. On January 18, 1905, he revived the paper as the *Sparks Dispatch.*

Hummel was editor and owner of the Dispatch Publishing Company, and Joseph J. Jackson was manager. They issued the paper every Wednesday and Saturday, as a four-page, Republican semiweekly. The *Dispatch* ran until the end of the year, when the plant was purchased by Louis Purcell to commence the *Nevada Forum*.

Sparks Dispatch: (Jan 18 1905–Dec 27 1905)
   NvU — Ja 21–D 27 1905
   film — Ja 21–D 27 1905
Ref: files; NF Ja 8 1906

The Forum (Nevada Forum)

Louis Purcell, as the Forum Publishing Company, purchased the *Sparks Dispatch* plant and established the *Nevada Forum* at Sparks on January 8, 1906. Purcell served as editor, issuing the paper every Monday, Wednesday, and Friday, as a six-page, independent triweekly. On July 12, 1909, the plant was purchased by A. Grant Miller of the Union Printing and Publishing Company, and the following month he shortened the title to *The Forum*. On December 1, the paper was enlarged to a daily and it continued as such until its suspension about April 27, 1910.

The Forum: (Jan 8 1906–c. Apr 27 1910)
   pvt — [Ja 8–D 1906]
   CU-BANC — F 15 1910
   NvHi — [Ja 3–Ap 27 1910]
   NvU — [Ja 12 1906–Mr 30 1910]
   film — [Ja 8 1906–Ap 27 1910]
Ref: files

Corriere di Nevada

Nevada's first Italian newspaper, *Corriere di Nevada,* was founded at Sparks on February 2, 1907, by M. Paggi. Paggi, living in Reno, was manager and publisher, while Francisco M. Moracci served as editor. The paper was issued at Sparks every Saturday, as a four-page, 18 by 24-inch weekly. Later the same year the paper was moved to Reno, where it was suspended the following year. (See Reno, *Corriere di Nevada*.)

Corriere di Nevada: (Feb 2 1907–c. 1907)
  No issues located.
Ref: GR F 9 1907

Nevada Methodist

The *Nevada Methodist* was begun at Sparks in September, 1907, by the Nevada Methodist Publishing Company, with Rev. E. E. Robbins as editor. It was to be issued monthly, but may not have survived to its second month.

Nevada Methodist: (Sep 1907–c. 1907)
   NvU — S 1907
   film — S 1907
Ref: files

Headlight

The *Headlight* was revived, in name at least, in August and September of 1908, to promote and advertise the Sparks Fair.

Headlight: (Aug 1908–Sep 1908)
  No issues located.
Ref: NF Ag 31 1908

The Magnet

On December 4, 1909, the Socialist Publishing Company of Sparks commenced *The Magnet,* with W. H. Burton as editor, "for the purpose of advocating the principles of the International Socialist Movement." It apparently failed to attract sufficient support to enable it to survive more than a few months.

The Magnet: (Dec 4 1909–c. Feb 5 1910)
  NvU — F 5 1910
  film — F 5 1910
Ref: files

Sparks Tribune

Following the suspension of the *Nevada Forum,* about April of 1910, Sparks was without a newspaper for nearly four months until the establishment of the *Sparks Tribune* by P. H. Mulcahy and his sons, Howard and Edwin C., on August 20, 1910. Under the name of The Tribune Publishing Company, P. H. Mulcahy was editor and Howard was business manager. They issued the four-page paper every Monday, Wednesday, and Friday. The *Tribune* prospered under the Mulcahys's management, and they ran the *Tribune* until P. H. Mulcahy's death in the fall of 1922, when it passed to Edwin C. Mulcahy and Joseph J. Jackson, Jr., who continued it for many years.

On January 9, 1934, it was reduced to a Tuesday and Friday semiweekly. In 1950, the *Tribune* was purchased by Mr. and Mrs. Carl Shelly, who published it for nine years. They reduced it to a weekly on February 1, 1951. Starting in June, 1958, the *Tribune* experienced frequent changes in editors and owners. George R. Lill became editor and publisher that year, and issued both the *Tribune* and the Gerlach *Valley Press* from the plant before he sold to Elizabeth Erlich in August, 1961. She was editor and proprietor for only seven months before selling the paper to Ira N. Jacobson, who added it to his growing stable of newspapers. Jacobson first hired William J. Henley as editor, but Henley was quickly replaced by Jock Taylor.

In December, 1962, the *Tribune* was sold again, this time to Jack M. Carpenter. He, too, had a series of editors: Jock Taylor, Chuck Thomas, Lloyd Leonard, and D. L. Woodward, Jr. Carpenter found ownership of the *Tribune* trying, and in 1965, he sold it to Stan and Matie Barker. In July, 1969, they sold it to Don Woodward, triggering another parade of editors:

Madlen Mendive, Jan Overpeck, Mike Cuno, and Janis Higginbotham. In April, 1978, James McClatchy became publisher with Woodward, and by the end of 1979, Marilyn Herlihy Leary was editor.

Sparks Tribune: (Aug 20 1910+)
   pub — 1910+
   CHi — F 12 1914; Ja 28 1918
   NvHi — [1910–24; 1927–34; 1936–8; 1940–9]
   NvU — [S 1 1910–49]
   film — [S 1 1910–1949] 1950+
Ref: files

Saturday Reporter

The weekly *Saturday Reporter,* "devoted particularly to the city of Sparks," was begun on October 30, 1915, by the Sierra Press, with Randolph Billington as editor. It failed to break the *Tribune's* monopoly, and probably failed before the end of the year.

Saturday Reporter: (Oct 30 1915–c. 1915)
   NvHi — N 20 1915 and supplement
   film — N 20 1915 and supplement
Ref: files

Nevada Legionnaire

After eighteen years at Lovelock, the *Nevada Legionnaire* moved to Sparks in October of 1950, when Carl Shelly of the *Sparks Tribune* took over the printing, and he and Bruce Shelly became editors. It continued in Sparks for eight more years as the official monthly of the American Legion, Department of Nevada. (See Lovelock, *Nevada Legionnaire.*)

Nevada Legionnaire: (Oct 1950–c. Feb 1958)
   NvU — [1950–8]
   film — [1950–8]
Ref: files

Nevada Sportsman

Russ Keeney started the weekly *Nevada Sportsman* at Sparks about March 2, 1956. Mike Schon was its first editor, but the post changed hands rapidly in the next year and one-half before the paper folded.

Nevada Sportsman: (c. Mar 2 1956–c. Sep 6 1957)
   Nv — [Mr 23 1956–S 6 1957]
   film — [Mr 23 1956–S 6 1957]
Ref: files

Sparks Advertiser

The *Sparks Advertiser* was a weekly begun on August 29, 1958, by the Guardian Printing Company, with Clayton Darrah as editor. It folded on October 10.

Sparks Advertiser: (Aug 29 1958–Oct 10 1958)
   Nv — [Ag 29–O 10 1958]

film — [Ag 29–O 10 1958]
Ref: files

Nevada Federal Journal

The short-lived monthly *Nevada Federal Journal,* published "in the interest of civilian and military personnel residing in the state of Nevada," was begun in August of 1964, by the NVJ Corporation of Sparks. Jack Barnes was editor and John H. MacDonald was publisher.

Nevada Federal Journal: (Aug 1964–c. Sep 1964)
   film — S 1964
Ref: files

Nevada State Public Observer

Eva Nance started the monthly *Nevada State Public Observer,* a "Statewide Newspaper . . . Dedicated to Better Government," in December of 1964. It carried news from state, county, and city offices, as well as recipes, but may not have survived past the first number.

Nevada State Public Observer: (Dec 1964–c. 1964)
   Nv — D 1964
   film — D 1964
Ref: files

Hearth and Home

Hearth and Home, a semimonthly, business and real estate paper, was begun at Sparks in July, 1966, by the Nevada Printing Company, with Jack J. Wendell as editor.

Hearth and Home: (Jul 1966–c. Oct 28 1966)
   film — Jl 29–O 28 1966
Ref: files

Air Age News

After an itinerant career of two years, the *Air Age News* came to Sparks to die. There, on March 26, 1968, E. G. Covington put out the final issue. (See Gardnerville, *Air Age News* and Reno, *Air Age News.*)

Air Age News: (Mar 26 1968)
   Nv — Mr 26 1968
   film — Mr 26 1968
Ref: files

Big Nickel

The *Big Nickel* is published by the Sparks Tribune, Inc., in Sparks. An advertiser only, it is distributed at no cost through local stores or at a subscription of $1 per month. It began in 1968, and is called the *Big Nickel* because the ads sell for a nickel a word.

Big Nickel: (1968+)
  pub — Two most recent years
Ref: pub

Key

Key, a fortnightly entertainment guide, was started at Sparks on March 6, 1971, by West Publishing, Inc., with Walter L. West, Jr., president and publisher. It lasted about six issues.

Key: (Mar 6 1971–c. May 1971)
  NvHi — Mr 6 1971
Ref: files; Young

Nevada Rancher

The monthly *Nevada Rancher,* begun at Sparks in May, 1971, by Alex Jay, is the official publication for the Nevada Cattlemen's Association and the Nevada Land Action Association.

Nevada Rancher: (May 1971+)
  Nv — My 1971+
  NvU — My 1971+
  film — My 1971+
Ref: files

Valley Green Sheet

James F. "Bud" Gallagher commenced the weekly *Valley Green Sheet* on November 8, 1972, promising "News with Integrity." The paper apparently failed within the year.

Valley Green Sheet: (Nov 8 1972–c. Dec 20 1972)
  film — N 8 1972–D 20 1972
Ref: files

Sierra Shopper

The *Sierra Shopper* was issued at Sparks from November 23, 1976, to about May 10, 1977, by Edward C. Sweeney of American Model Publications, Inc.

Sierra Shopper: (Nov 23 1976–c. May 10 1977)
  Nv — F 8 1977
  NvHi — N 23 1976–My 10 1977
Ref: files

~(STATE LINE (CLARK COUNTY))~

Mining News

W. J. Campbell started the *Mining News* at the fleeting boom camp of State Line, on the Nevada-Utah border, in September of 1902. It was a weekly that grew weaker, doubtless failing before the end of the year.

Mining News: (Sep 1902–c. 1902)
  No issues located.
Ref: TM O 3 1902

State Line Oracle

The *Oracle* was a second short-lived paper, which flourished momentarily at State Line about April of 1903, under the hand of a Mr. Stevenson.

State Line Oracle: (c. Apr 1903)
  No issues located.
Ref: DL My 5 1903

STATELINE (DOUGLAS COUNTY)

Tahoe Chronicle

(See Carson City, *Carson Chronicle*)

STEWART

Indian Advance

The *Indian Advance* was a monthly journal begun on September 1, 1899, by the Carson Indian School at Stewart, three miles south of Carson City. May Longenbaugh was manager of the paper, but the mechanical work was done by the pupils. E. Brown, a graduate of the Indian school at Carlisle, Pennsylvania, served as editor.

Indian Advance: (Sep 1 1899–Sep 1903)
  NvHi — [1901–3]
  NvMus — Mr 1903
  NvU — S 1 1899
  film — [S 1 1899–S 1903]
Ref: files; RG My 7 1900

New Indian

In November of 1902, the Carson Indian School commenced a second monthly, the *New Indian.* It was a four-page paper, containing local news, stories, and advertisements, and was published for several years.

New Indian: (Nov 1902–c. 1907)
   NvHi — Jl 1904
   NvMus — Ja 1903
   film — Ja 1903, Jl 1904
Ref: files; Polk 1907–8

Nevada American

The *Nevada American,* printed by the students at the Carson Indian School, began about November 15, 1913. It was a neatly printed, illustrated weekly, issued every Saturday during the school term, but apparently lasted for only two terms.

Nevada American: (c. Nov 15 1913–c. May 1915)
   NvHi — My 1 1915
   NvMus — Ap 4 1914
   film — Ap 4 1914
Ref: files

(SUN VALLEY)

Valley Outlook

The semiweekly *Valley Outlook* was started at Sun Valley, northeast of Reno, on December 4, 1972, by B. G. Weide and Happ Arnold, publishers. It was "Tailored to the Needs of the Valley People," but those needs were not sufficient to support the paper, and it folded the following summer.

Valley Outlook: (Dec 4 1972–c. Jul 1973)
   film — D 18 1972–Jl 12 1973
Ref: files

(SUTRO)

Sutro Independent

The weekly *Sutro Independent* was launched on July 1, 1875, in the new town of Sutro at the mouth of Adolph Sutro's tunnel, then being run to tap the Comstock Lode. T. E. Picotte edited and published the paper, and Adolph Sutro financed it in return for its advocacy of his political and financial interests. On November 11, 1876, Frank B. Mercer, formerly of the Oakland, California, *Daily Tribune,* succeeded Picotte as publisher. He continued the *Independent* until its temporary suspension on March 1, 1879. This suspension resulted from the cessation of work on the tunnel pending negotiations between the tunnel company and the Comstock mine owners.

On April 21, 1879, publication of the *Independent* was resumed by J. P. Cosgrove and James McAfee. On May 29, they enlarged it to a semi-weekly, but when Cosgrove retired from the firm on the following August 11, to take a teaching position in San Francisco, it was reduced to a weekly again. Two weeks later, Frank Mercer again purchased an interest in the paper and, in partnership with McAfee, continued it until November 17, when McAfee withdrew. Mercer remained as sole editor and proprietor, as well as typographer, pressman, devil, and carrier, until the final suspension of the *Independent* on November 29, 1880.

Sutro Independent: (Jul 1 1875–Mar 1 1879; Apr 21 1879–Nov 29 1880)
   C-S — Ap 21 1879–N 29 1880
   CU-BANC — O 16–N 20 1875; Mr 18–O 21, D 1876; Jl 7–21, Ag 4 1877; Je 29, [Jl 13–D 7, 28 1878]; Ja 4–Mr 1, [Ap 21–N 22 1880]
   ICHi — Je 24 1876
   NvU — [S 25 1875–N 29 1880]
   film — [S 25 1875–N 29 1880]
Ref: files; Angel 309; Doten 2241

~(TAYLOR)~

White Pine Reflex

About early June of 1884, Robert W. Simpson suspended the *Reflex* at Ward and removed the press and material to the promising new camp of Taylor. There, on June 21, 1884, he revived the paper as the *White Pine Reflex,* issuing it as a four-page weekly, at a subscription price of $7.50 per year. Simpson continued the paper at Taylor until August 12, 1885, when he announced, "This will be our parting shot if we 'fall straddle mit der fence, both legs on one side', otherwise we will give Taylor a paper fourteen columns on both sides." He fell straddle, and W. L. Davis of the *White Pine News* purchased the plant, suspending the *Reflex.*

White Pine Reflex: (Jun 21 1884–Aug 12 1885)
   NvELC — [Je 21 1884–Ag 12 1885]
   film — [Je 21 1884–Ag 12 1885]
Ref: files

White Pine News

As the prosperity of Cherry Creek waned, W. L. Davis induced Robert W. Simpson to sell the *White Pine Reflex* at Taylor. Davis then suspended the *News* at Cherry Creek and, combining the two plants, began publishing the *White Pine News* at Taylor on August 22, 1885. While at Taylor, the *News* was continued as a four-page, five-column weekly, selling for $5 a year. In 1887, the county courthouse at Hamilton was destroyed by fire and the county seat was moved to the new camp of Ely. The following year, on September 8, 1888, Davis suspended the *News* at Taylor and removed the plant to Ely, where he again revived the *News.* (See Ely, *White Pine News.*)

White Pine News: (Aug 22 1885–Sep 8 1888)
   NvELC — Ag 22 1885–S 8 1888
   NvHi — [1886–8]
   NvMus — F 13 1886
   NvU — Ag 1885–D 31 1887
   film — Ag 22 1885–S 8 1888
Ref: files

～{ TENABO }～

Bullion District Miner

On July 23, 1907, T. J. McParlin and Co. launched the Bullion Mining District's first and only paper, a weekly, noting, "To get proper recognition, a Nevada mining camp must have a paper of its own ... the *Bullion District Miner* is the result." The paper was probably published in Tenabo, the largest camp in the district, but apparently not wishing to slight the rival camp of Lander, the publishers simply put the Bullion Mining District on the dateline.

Bullion District Miner: (Jul 23 1907–c. 1907)
   NvU — Jl 23 1907
   film — Jl 23 1907
Ref: files; CSMI Ag 12 1907

～{ TOBAR }～

Eye-Opener

Attorney Frank W. Spear planned to publish the *Eye-Opener* at Tobar, fifteen miles southeast of Wells, on July 1, 1912. Whether it ever made its appearance, however, is unknown.

Eye-Opener: (Jul 1 1912?)
   No issues located.
Ref: RRR Je 12 1915

Tobar Times

On July 22, 1916, A. L. Colvert founded the weekly *Tobar Times.* Colvert was sole editor and publisher, issuing the paper every Saturday, from his office at 240 Broadway. The paper apparently suspended sometime later the same year.

Tobar Times: (Jul 22 1916–c. 1916)
   NvHi — Jl 27 1916
Ref: files

TONOPAH (BUTLER)

Tonopah Bonanza

Scarcely a year after its discovery, the booming camp of Tonopah boasted a population of over one thousand and demanded a newspaper. Tasker Oddie called a mass meeting to raise funds for a printing plant, and William W. Booth, the only printer in camp, was elected to run the establishment. At a total cost of about $600, he got together a job press, a stone, and two cases of type. On Saturday, June 15, 1901, Booth issued the first number of the weekly *Bonanza* from "Butler, Nevada," as the camp's post office was identified. The *Bonanza*'s office was a twelve by fourteen-foot shack, which Booth bought in Candelaria and shipped in pieces to Tonopah. Type was so scarce that a canvas was spread on the floor to catch any stray pieces. At first Booth served only as editor and manager for the Tonopah Publishing Company, but soon he purchased the plant and became sole proprietor.

In March of 1905, the camp's mailing address became Tonopah, and the *Bonanza* changed its dateline on March 11. The *Bonanza* grew rapidly with the development of the district and on March 10, 1906, Booth added a daily edition. On December 25, 1909, the weekly edition was suspended. The daily, however, continued under Booth's management for nearly a quarter-century. It was finally suspended on November 16, 1929, when the plant was purchased by Frank Garside of the *Tonopah Daily Times* to form the daily *Times-Bonanza*. (See *Tonopah Times-Bonanza*.)

Tonopah Bonanza (weekly): (Jun 15 1901–Dec 25 1909)
  pvt — D 20 1902; F 7, My 2, 16 1903; Ja 9, Jl 23 1904
  NvMus — [Je 22 1901–D 24 1904]; O 11 1908
  NvTC — Je 15 1901–D 25 1909
  NvU — [Je 15 1901–D 25 1909]
  film — [Je 15 1901–D 25 1909]

Tonopah Bonanza (daily): (Mar 10 1906–Nov 16 1929)
  CHi — Ag 8, D 19, 30 1914; Ja 30, F 10, Mr 11, 26, My 4, N 3, D 15 1915; Ja 29–30 1918
  NvFC — O 1 1904
  NvHi — Mr 10 1906; Jl 13, S 12 1907–O 6 1918; 1928–N 15 1929
  NvTC — Mr 10 1906–N 15 1929
  NvU — [F 1907–O 1918]
  film — [Mr 10 1906–N 16 1929]
Ref: files

Tonopah Miner

On June 20, 1902, C. J. McDivitt and T. H. Eckles founded the *Tonopah Miner* to share in the prosperity of the new boom, but they sold quickly to Sam C. Dunham and T. D. Van Devort, who took over on August 15, 1902. Dunham, a part-time poet, served as editor, and Van Devort as business manager, issuing the *Miner* at $5 a year. On February 27, 1903,

James Morris purchased Van Devort's interest, becoming part owner with Dunham. In October, 1907, Dunham retired from the firm, and Morris became editor for the Tonopah Miner Publishing Company. Morris continued as editor until October 12, 1912, when he was replaced by a series of editors, beginning with W. J. Stoneham, who was replaced by James O'Brien on November 28, 1914, followed by W. C. Lamb on October 9, 1915, followed in turn by P. C. Fisler on April 8, 1916. The *Miner* prospered for nearly two decades, until November 5, 1921, when the gradual decline of the camp finally forced its suspension.

Tonopah Miner: (Jun 20 1902–Nov 5 1921)
    pvt — N 28–D 5 1902; F 4, 25–Mr 4 1905
    CHi — D 19 1914; Mr 20, Ap 10 1915; My 26 1917
    CSmH — Je 26, Jl 3 1902
    NN — Je 25 1910–3
    NvFC — Ja 2 1904
    NvHi — Mr 10 1906; [Ja 18 1908–My 28 1921]
    NvTC — 1904–N 5 1921
    NvU — [Je 26 1902–N 5 1921]
    film — [Je 26 1902–N 5 1921]
Ref: files

Tonopah Sun

On May 11, 1904, Lindley C. Branson brought out Tonopah's third paper, the weekly *Sun*. At first he had only a small job press that could print no more than one page at a time. The press work, all done by foot power, assisted only by a typesetter and an apprentice, took three days. But Branson's enthusiasm made the *Sun* shine, and won him a wide readership. With the arrival of a linotype machine and power press, he commenced the camp's first daily edition on January 10, 1905. The following month, on February 1, Branson further expanded his sphere of influence with the establishment of the daily *Goldfield Sun*. By the end of his first year, he had two printing plants worth over $10,000, and twenty men on the payroll. Branson remained sole editor and publisher, although he hired W. M. Gotwaldt as city editor and A. B. Gibson as business manager from April 11 to May 19, 1905, and Lester W. Haworth served as manager from July 6, 1905, to August 18, 1906. On January 27, 1906, the weekly edition was renamed the *Saturday Mining Edition of the Tonopah Sun*.

When the boom years ended, Branson finally sold out, on February 13, 1910, and the *Sun* began to go down. W. H. Bohannan and W. H. Fording became the publishers and served respectively as editor and manager. They took in a third partner, Edwin J. Bennett, on April 7, but were unable to give the paper new fire. On May 7, they suspended the weekly and daily editions to issue it only biweekly. The fast sinking *Sun* passed to the Sun Publishing Company on June 22 and finally set on July 16, 1910. (See Goldfield, *The Goldfield Sun*.)

Tonopah Sun (weekly): (May 11 1904–May 7 1910)
  CSmH — My 11, 25, Je 19, Jl 20 1904
  NvU — [Ja 27 1906–My 7 1910]
  film — My 11–Jl 20 1904; [Ja 27 1906–My 7 1910]
Tonopah Sun (daily): (Jan 10 1905–May 7 1910)
  CSmH — Je 2, D 30 1905
  NvHi — [Ja 10 1905–Ap 29], My 2 1907–My 7 1910
  NvTC — [Jl 1906–10]
  NvU — [Jl 1905–My 7 1910]
  film — [Ja 10 1905–My 7 1910]
Tonopah Sun (biweekly): (May 11 1910–Jul 16 1910)
  NvHi — My 11–Jl 16 1910
  NvU — My 11–Jl 16 1910
  film — My 11–Jl 16 1910
Ref: files

Tonopah Nevadan

The *Tonopah Nevadan* was founded as a Democratic campaign paper on October 8, 1912. The paper was printed each night at the weekly *Miner* plant, by the Tonopah Nevadan, Inc., with no editor listed. It suspended publication on June 5, 1913.

Tonopah Nevadan: (Oct 8 1912–Jun 5 1913)
  NvHi — [O 8 1912–D 31 1912]
  NvU — 1912
  film — [O 8–D 31 1912]
Ref: files

Tonopah Daily Times

On December 1, 1915, Frank F. Garside issued the first number of the *Tonopah Daily Times.* Garside was sole editor and owner, publishing the paper every morning except Monday, as a four-page, six-column, independent daily, selling at $11 a year. The *Times* shared the World War I mining prosperity at Tonopah and continued until November 15, 1929, when Garside purchased the daily *Bonanza* plant from Booth, merging the two to form the *Tonopah Times-Bonanza* on the following day. As such it was still published in 1979. (See *Tonopah Times-Bonanza.*)

Tonopah Daily Times: (Dec 1 1915–Nov 15 1929)
  pub — D 1 1915–N 15 1929
  CHi — F 11, 13 1916
  NvHi — [1919–29]
  NvMUS — F 23 1917, My 27 1922
  NvTC — 1916–N 15 1929
  NvU — [1917–29]
  film — D 2 1916–21; 1923–9
Ref: files

The Net

The *Net*, "a Great Net of Mercy Drawn Through an Ocean of Unspeakable Pain," was begun at Tonopah about July, 1918. It was published by the Nye County Chapter of the American Red Cross and was probably suspended at the end of the First World War.

The Net: (c. Jul 1918–c. Nov 1918)
   NvHi — S 1918
Ref: files

Tonopah Mining Reporter

On August 27, 1921, W. W. Booth of the Tonopah daily *Bonanza* started the weekly *Tonopah Mining Reporter* to provide a synopsis of the district mining news for outside investors and speculators. It was issued every Friday as a four-page, seven-column paper, at $5 a year. The *Reporter* flourished with the *Bonanza* until the stock market crash in 1929, when Booth suspended both papers and sold the plant to Frank Garside of the *Times*. Garside combined the *Reporter* with his weekly *Nevada Mining Record* to form the burdensome *Nevada Mining Record & Reporter*. (See Tonopah, *Nevada Mining Record & Reporter*.)

Tonopah Mining Reporter: (Aug 27 1921–Nov 16 1929)
   NvHi — S 7 1921; S 9 1922
   NvU — [Ag 27 1921–N 16 1929]
   film — [Ag 27 1921–N 16 1929]
Ref: files

Nevada Mining Record

Following the suspension of his *Gilbert Record,* printed at the *Daily Times* office in Tonopah, Frank F. Garside changed the name, and began the *Nevada Mining Record* the following week, on May 15, 1926. Garside was sole editor and publisher, issuing the mining paper every Saturday, for $3.50 a year, in competition with W. W. Booth's *Tonopah Mining Reporter*. In 1929, Garside purchased Booth's *Reporter*. Combining it with the *Record,* he commenced the *Nevada Mining Record & Reporter*. (See Tonopah, *Nevada Mining Record & Reporter*.)

Nevada Mining Record: (May 15 1926–Nov 16 1929)
   NvHi — [1927–9]
   NvU — [My 15 1926–N 16 1929]
   film — [My 15 1926–N 16 1929]
Ref: files

Tonopah Times-Bonanza

On November 16, 1929, the day following his purchase of W. W. Booth's daily *Tonopah Bonanza,* Frank F. Garside merged it with his *Times* to form the daily *Tonopah Times-Bonanza*. Garside served as both editor and publisher until February 4, 1933, when Clyde R. Terrell took over the editorial chair. Terrell was followed by E. N. Richardson on October 15, 1934, and he, in turn, was replaced by Ray and Virginia Germain on January 17, 1935. They remained until February 2, 1945, when Clyde Terrell bought the paper, becoming sole editor and proprietor. Garside had reduced the *Times-Bonanza* from a daily to a weekly on April 2, 1943.

Starting about 1950, S. W. Terrell was listed as acting editor and publisher. Two years later, Mr. and Mrs. Robert A. Crandall of the *Goldfield News* bought the paper. On January 4, 1957, they merged both papers as the *Tonopah Times-Bonanza and Goldfield News.* Mr. and Mrs. Ira N. Jacobson purchased the paper in 1958, and in February, 1961, they added the *Eureka Sentinel* to their holdings. Soon after, Gerald A. Roberts was made editor of the Central Nevada Newspapers combine, which was subsequently expanded to include the monthly *Nevada Democratic Record* and the *Nevada Veterans' Journal.* In March, 1975, William G. Roberts became publisher and editor, with Gerald A. Roberts continuing as general manager.

Tonopah Times-Bonanza: (Nov 16 1929+)
  pub — N 16 1929+
  NvHi — [N 16 1929+]
  NvU — [N 16 1929+]
  film — [N 16 1929+]
Ref: files

Nevada Mining Record & Reporter

After the stock market crash of 1929, Frank Garside purchased W. W. Booth's weekly *Tonopah Mining Reporter* and combined it with his own weekly *Record,* to begin the *Nevada Mining Record & Reporter* on November 23, 1929. Under the lengthy weight of its new banner, the paper struggled on into the deepening depression. Finally, on May 14, 1932, Garside announced its suspension, "until such time that business conditions warrant its resumption."

Nevada Mining Record & Reporter: (Nov 23 1929–May 14 1932)
  NvHi — [N 23 1929–My 14 1932]
  NvU — [N 23 1929–My 14 1932]
  film — [N 23 1929–My 14 1932]
Ref: files

Bombing and Gunnery Range

Bombing and Gunnery Range was a weekly newspaper begun about September 12, 1942, for the servicemen at the Tonopah Air Base. It was printed by the *Tonopah Times-Bonanza* and apparently ran at least until 1943.

Bombing and Gunnery Range: (Sep 12 1942–c. 1943)
  film — Ja 23 1943
Ref: files

Nevada Democratic Record (Nevada Record)

In April, 1962, Ira N. Jacobson further expanded his journalistic empire with the establishment of the monthly *Nevada Record,* renamed the *Nevada Democratic Record* in May of 1963. It is printed at his *Tonopah Times-Bonanza and Goldfield News* plant, and Gerald A. Roberts serves as its editor.

Nevada Democratic Record: (Apr 1962+)
  NvHi — Ap 1966; Jl 1969
  NvU — Ap 1962; [1963–6]
  film — Ap 1962+
Ref: files

Nevada Veterans' Journal

The monthly *Nevada Veterans' Journal* is the latest addition to Ira N. Jacobson's newspaper combine. It was begun in Reno in 1962, but was moved to Tonopah in April, 1966. It is printed at the *Tonopah Times-Bonanza and Goldfield News* plant, with Gerald A. Roberts as editor.

Nevada Veterans' Journal: (Apr 1966+)
  NvU — [1966–8]
  film — Ap 1966+
Ref: files

~(TRANSVAAL)~

Transvaal Miner

After the new camp of Transvaal sprang up in the Bullfrog Mining District, T. G. Nicklin of the *Beatty Bullfrog Miner* enlarged his empire with the addition of the *Transvaal Miner* on April 14, 1906. Nicklin was sole editor and proprietor, printing the paper at Beatty every Saturday, as a twelve-page, four-column weekly, at $3 a year. Transvaal collapsed almost immediately, however, and the *Miner* was suspended within a month.

Transvaal Miner: (Apr 14 1906–c. May 1906)
  NvHi — Ap 14 1906
  film — Ap 14 1906
Ref: files

Transvaal Tribune

In April of 1906, just a few days after T. G. Nicklin commenced the *Transvaal Miner,* his rival, Earle R. Clemens of the *Rhyolite Herald,* took up the challenge and began a competitor, the *Transvaal Tribune.* The two papers fought briefly for dominance, but the townsite boom collapsed before the victor could be determined, and both folded within a month.

Transvaal Tribune: (Apr 1906–c. May 1906)
  No issues located.
Ref: RH Ap 20 1906

~{ TREASURE CITY }~

White Pine Gazette

In the winter of 1868, Tallman H. Rolfe brought a press and material to Treasure City in the White Pine District and founded the region's first newspaper, the *White Pine Gazette*. Rolfe, a pioneer printer who had worked on the *California Star* in 1848, was editor and publisher, and issued the *Gazette* as a weekly. Although the prospects of the district seemed good, Rolfe suspended the *Gazette* after a very short time, turning the field over to the *White Pine News*, which was begun in December of that year.

White Pine Gazette: (c. Dec 1868)
  No issues located.
Ref: Myrick

White Pine News

The suspension of the *Silver Bend Reporter* at Belmont in the summer of 1868 resulted from the departure of its proprietor, M. D. Fairchild, to the new bonanzas of White Pine. That winter, the press and material passed into the hands of W. H. Pitchford and Robert W. Simpson, who, also attracted by the new mines, removed the plant to Treasure City. There, atop nine-thousand-foot Treasure Hill, they commenced publication of the *White Pine News* on December 26, 1868, as a twenty-four-column independent weekly. Myron Angel, formerly of the *Reese River Reveille*, became editor of the paper on March 20, 1869. In February of the same year, it had been enlarged to a triweekly, which ran only two months before being increased to a daily on April 19.

Simpson soon sold his interest, and Pitchford became sole proprietor on April 24, 1869. He, in turn, soon sold to William J. Forbes. Forbes was formerly of the Virginia City *Trespass*, but had come to White Pine to run a saloon. He maintained that of twenty men, nineteen would patronize the saloon and only one the newspaper, and that he was going for the crowd. However, he soon took up his old vocation again. On May 10, 1869, Forbes assumed the proprietorship, in partnership with John I. Ginn. Ginn retired on June 19, leaving Forbes as sole editor and proprietor. But Forbes was unable to go it alone and on August 16, the proprietorship passed to the Daily News Company, in which he was joined by Ginn and Pitchford, to whom he was still in debt. At the end of that month, the *News* was reduced to a triweekly, and to a weekly on October 9. Under Forbes the *News* engaged in a bitter battle with the *Inland Empire* at nearby Hamilton. To better combat the *Empire*, Forbes finally suspended the *News* at Treasure City on January 8, 1870. He moved the plant to Hamilton, where he revived the *News* the following week. (See Hamilton, *White Pine News*.)

White Pine News: (Dec 26 1868–Jan 8 1870)
   C—Mr 6 1869
   CU-BANC — [D 26 1868–Ja 8 1870]
   NvHi — F 27 1869
   WHi — Je 15 1869
   film — [D 26 1868–Ja 8 1870]
Ref: files; Angel 330; McMurtrie 306

~(TUSCARORA)~

Tuscarora Times

Early in 1877, E. A. Littlefield of the *Elko Post* shipped an extra press and material to the new camp of Tuscarora. Here, on March 24, he commenced publication of the *Tuscarora Times.* The paper was issued each Saturday, as a four-page, Republican weekly, at a subscription rate of $5 a year. The *Times* prospered, but the dual proprietorship proved to be too great a burden on Littlefield. Thus, in the fall of that year, he sold the *Times* to John H. Dennis and Oscar L. C. Fairchild. With Dennis as editor, they continued the paper as a weekly until the end of 1877, when they merged with the Tuscarora *Mining Review* to form the daily *Times-Review.* (See *Tuscarora Times-Review.*)

Tuscarora Times: (Mar 24 1877–Dec 1877)
   CU-BANC — Mr 24, Ap 21, My 5, 19–Je 23, S 25–D 1877
   film — Mr 24, Ap 21, My 5, 19–Je 23, S 25–D 1877
Ref: files

Mining Review

Two months after the founding of the *Times* at Tuscarora, C. C. S. Wright arrived with material to start a competitor. On May 23, 1877, he issued the first number of the *Mining Review.* Wright was sole editor and proprietor and published the paper as a four-page semiweekly, at $10 a year. The paper flourished and was soon enlarged to a daily, but Wright and his rivals soon concluded that Tuscarora was "too small for two journals," and they agreed to consolidate. On December 30, 1877, Wright suspended the *Review* and combined the plant with that of the *Times* to publish the daily *Times-Review.* (See *Tuscarora Times-Review.*)

Mining Review: (May 23 1877–Dec 30 1877)
   CU-BANC — O 24, 31–D 30 1877
   film — O 24, 31–D 30 1877
Ref: files; Angel 294

Tuscarora Times-Review

On January 3, 1878, the weekly *Tuscarora Times* and the daily *Mining Review* were merged to form the daily *Times-Review,* under the management of O. L. C. Fairchild and John H. Dennis of the *Times*. Dennis was editor and issued the paper every morning, except Monday. On August 18, 1881, Fairchild became sole editor and proprietor, and two months later, on October 29, he cut the paper back from a daily to a weekly. Fairchild continued the paper for fourteen years, with Dennis briefly rejoining him as co-owner from July 30, 1883, to September 14, 1886.

Finally, Fairchild suspended the paper on October 5, 1895, and it lay dormant until June 15, 1897, when the Bingham Brothers, C. E. and E. L., leased the plant and resurrected the *Times-Review* as a triweekly. On November 20, 1900, T. C. Plunkett and his son, W. D., took the lease. They ran it until July 18, 1903, when T. C. Plunkett retired. His son tried to continue alone, but after a lapse in publication from October 20 to November 21, he reduced it to a weekly, and then finally laid it permanently to rest on December 26, 1903.

Tuscarora Times-Review: (Jan 3 1878–Oct 5 1895; Jun 15 1897–Dec 26 1903)
   CSmH — O 21, N 29, D 23 1902
   CU-BANC — Ja 10 1878–Jl 31 1882; Ag 27, O 12 1889; Ja 6–7, 9–11 1890
   MWA — Je 18 1878 O
   NvHi — [1882–3]; o 14 1887; Ag–S 1892; Ap 4 1901
   NvMus — Je 18 1885; F 13 1886
   NvU — S 1880–O 1895; 1897–1903
   film — [Ja 3 1878–D 26 1903]
Ref: files

Mining News

The daily *Mining News* was begun at Tuscarora in January of 1883, in an attempt to break the monopoly of the *Times-Review*. The paper was edited by Harry Fontecilla of the News Publishing Company, and was issued every morning, except Monday, as a four-page, 18 by 24-inch sheet, at a subscription price of $10 a year. The position of the *Times-Review* was too strong to be usurped, however, and the *Mining News* was forced to capitulate on July 29 of the same year.

Mining News: (Jan 1883–Jul 29 1883)
   No issues located.
Ref: SS Jl 30 1883; TTR Ag 6 1883

Tuscarora Mining News

On August 17, 1907, D. G. McKenna made a brief attempt to revive a newspaper at the old camp of Tuscarora, with the founding of the *Tuscarora Mining News*. McKenna published the paper every Friday, as a four-page, $3-a-year weekly. After about six months, however, it became apparent that Tuscarora's boom days were past and the *Mining News* closed down.

Tuscarora Mining News: (Aug 17 1907–c. 1908)
  NvHi — S 21, O 26, D 7 1907
  film — S 21, O 26, D 7 1907
Ref: files

Business Talks

Business Talks, "Distributed FREE All Over This Country," was published by the Mail Order Printery of Tuscarora, as an "advertising medium for our stationery printing and the bargains we are able to offer." The publishers also promised, "so far as our limited space will permit, to publish all important local happenings." They issued the paper irregularly for only a few months, starting about September of 1908.

Business Talks: (c. Sep 1908–c. Nov 1908)
   NvHi — O 30–N 21 1908
   film — O 30–N 21 1908
Ref: files

⤳(TYBO)⤳

Tybo Sun

The town of Tybo came into being in 1874, and had a population of nearly one thousand when John C. Ragsdale started the *Tybo Sun* on May 19, 1877. Ragsdale was sole editor and proprietor and issued the paper as a Republican weekly. After four months Ragsdale was succeeded by William B. Taylor, who, in turn, sold the establishment to Charles Garrett on March 29, 1879. He maintained the paper for several months until it passed to D. M. Brannan, in whose hands it died in March of 1880. The plant was afterwards removed to Bristol to found the *Times* in 1881.

Tybo Sun: (May 19 1877–Mar 1880)
   CU-BANC — S 15 1877–Mr 30, Ap 13–Jl 27, Ag 10–S 14, 28–N 9, 23 1878–Ja 18, F 8, Mr 1–8, 22–Je 7, 21, Jl 5–Ag 9, S 6 1879
   NvHi — D 28 1878 (copy)
   NvMus — S 13 1879
   film — [S 15 1877–S 13 1879]
Ref: files; Angel 311

⤳(UNIONVILLE)⤳

Humboldt Register

The first paper in Humboldt County was started at Unionville on May 2, 1863, by William J. Forbes and Charles L. Perkins. Forbes had hauled the press across the Sierra from Downieville with an ox team, and the citizens of Unionville celebrated its arrival with a thirty-gun salute from an anvil and nine cheers, after which they paraded through town, led by a single cornet. The *Humboldt Register* was only a small weekly, but its editorial matter soon made it one of the leading papers in the territory. Forbes's editorial quips, under his nom de plume of "Semblins," were widely copied.

With the twelfth number, on July 18, Forbes became sole proprietor and continued as such until February 2, 1867, when he sold the paper to Judge

George G. Berry, Henry C. Street, and McKaskia S. Bonnifield. The following week, C. L. Perkins and Bonnifield assumed the editorship, announcing that, with the change in editors, the *Register* had met with a change of heart, becoming a Democratic journal. Bonnifield retired from the paper on October 12 of the same year, to turn his attention to politics. On February 6, 1869, the paper was sold to the militantly anti-Chinese Workingman's Protective Union, which changed its name to the *Humboldt Register and Workingman's Advocate*. (See Unionville, *Humboldt Register and Workingman's Advocate*.)

Humboldt Register: (May 2 1863–Feb 6 1869)
   C — O 10 1868
   CLU — Ap 29 1865–Mr 31, Ap 14–21 1866
   CU-BANC — My 2 1863–F 6 1869
   DLC — D 26 1863 (supp)
   NvHi — [Mr 5, Ap 30 1864–Ap 21 1866]
   NvMus — [My 2 1863–F 6 1869]
   NvWC — Ap 29 1865
   film — [My 2 1863–F 6 1869]
Ref: files; Angel 301–2; Doten 2249

Humboldt Register and Workingman's Advocate

On February 13, 1869, the Workingman's Protective Union took control of Unionville's only paper, changing its name to the *Humboldt Register and Workingman's Advocate*. The Protective Union, which had driven the Chinese from the camp by mob action the previous month, sought to make the paper the spokesman for the anti-Chinese movement throughout Nevada. William S. Bonnifield, former editor McKaskia's brother and a former miner, became the new editor, announcing, "It is a long and dangerous leap from the pick to the pen but we have determined to try the experiment, though we shall not pretend to indulge in brilliant rhetorical flourishes or labored dissertations on abstract questions." As his own words betrayed, he was already enamored with rhetorical flourishes, and when his editorial career came to a close some months later, he went into law with his brother. Within six years he became district court judge for Humboldt County.

On April 24, E. D. Kelley and Company became the publishers, but the editorial policy was unchanged. After the Central Pacific Railroad bypassed Unionville, however, the town declined rapidly and on May 29, 1869, the *Register* suspended publication. Kelley removed the material to the new railroad town of Elko, where he started the *Independent* in mid-July, but after five months he decided to return to Humboldt County. In late October, Kelley sold the *Independent* and went to Winnemucca. There, in partnership with McKaskia Bonnifield, Kelley revived the name of the old *Humboldt Register* in a weekly paper, which they began on October 30, 1869. (See Winnemucca, *Humboldt Register*.)

Humboldt Register and Workingman's Advocate: (Feb 13 1869–May 29 1869)
   CU-BANC — F 13–My 29 1869
   NvMus — F 13–My 29 1869
   film — F 13–My 29 1869
Ref: files

Silver State

Early in 1870, almost a year after the suspension of the *Humboldt Register,* John C. Fall, a prominent local mine owner and merchant, purchased a press and material to revive a paper at Unionville. Fall arranged for H. A. Waldo to publish the paper, and on March 22, 1870, Waldo issued the first number of the weekly *Silver State.* Waldo was succeeded in August of that year by John I. Ginn, who, in turn, was relieved by John Booth on January 7, 1871. The following year, on February 17, the paper again changed hands, this time passing to R. L. Tilden.

In his opening number Tilden explained that he had left the county in 1864, when everyone was leaving, that now he had come back, when everyone was returning, and that he intended to remain as long as Unionville prospered. Tilden increased the paper to semiweekly on August 28, 1872, for the election campaign, but sold it after the election, on November 23, to J. J. Hill and Company, who cut it back to a weekly. John Hill bought out his partners, becoming sole editor and proprietor on July 26, 1873. In 1874, Peter Myers joined Hill, and on September 3, 1874, they suspended the *Silver State* at Unionville and removed it to Winnemucca, where they continued the *Silver State* the following week. (See Winnemucca, *Silver State.*)

Silver State: (Mar 22 1870–Sep 3 1874)
   CU-BANC — Mr 22 1870; Ag 5 1871–S 3 1874
   NvWC — [Mr 22 1870–S 3 1874]
   film — Mr 22 1870; [Ag 5 1871–S 3 1874]
Ref: files; Angel 303

Mining Topics

The monthly *Mining Topics,* published at Unionville and Sacramento, was founded in 1921, by the Mining Topics Publishing Company, with Bert F. Hews as editor. Billing itself as the "Official Publication of the Department of Mines and Mining of the Sacramento Chamber of Commerce," the *Topics* sold for 20¢ a copy. Although the masthead stated that it was issued monthly, it appeared more frequently. In September of 1925, it changed its places of publication to San Francisco and Unionville, but it was suspended in less than a year, in August, 1926.

Mining Topics: (Sep 17 1921–Aug 1926)
   pvt — Jl 13 1922
   NvHi — D 6 1921; Jl 13, 27 1922
   film — D 6 1921; Jl 13 1922
Ref: files

VERNON

Vernon Miner

The camp of Vernon grew rapidly with the boom of the Seven Troughs Mining District, and on January 4, 1907, J. R. Hunter began the camp's first paper, the *Vernon Miner*. Hunter was sole editor and proprietor, issuing the paper every Friday from his *Lovelock Tribune* plant, as a six-page, six-column weekly, at $4 a year. Before the *Miner* was two months old, Hunter sold it to Boericke and Howard N. Riddle, in whose hands it apparently folded about April. Riddle then moved the plant to rival Mazuma, where he commenced the *Herald*.

Vernon Miner: (Jan 4 1907–c. Apr 1907)
  NvHi — Mr 1 1907
  film — Mr 1 1907
Ref: files; LT Ja 4 1907

Vernon Review

On June 29, 1907, about two months after the suspension of the *Vernon Miner*, Howard W. Cherry revived a paper at Vernon with the establishment of the *Vernon Review*. Cherry was sole editor and publisher, issuing the *Review* every Thursday as a Democratic weekly. The camp was not yet able to support a paper, and the *Review* was suspended on October 12. Two months later, Ray Harris used the plant to commence the *Seven Troughs Miner*, and the following year Cherry revived the name in the new *Review* at Lovelock.

Vernon Review: (Jun 29 1907–Oct 12 1907)
  NvMus — Ag 31 1907
  NvU — [Je 29–O 12 1907]
  film — [Je 29–O 12 1907]
Ref: files

Seven Troughs Miner

Less than two months after the suspension of the *Vernon Review*, on December 7, 1907, Ray D. Harris took over the plant for a new weekly, the *Seven Troughs Miner*. The *Miner* continued the serial of the *Review*, and was issued every Saturday, as a four-page, 15 by 22-inch, independent weekly. Harris was sole editor and proprietor. By then the camp was finally able to support a paper, and the *Miner* prospered. Its success soon drew competition from Howard N. Riddle, who started the rival *News*, at Mazuma. The competition proved too much for Harris, and he sold the *Miner* to Riddle in January of 1909. The latter merged both papers on January 23, as the *Seven Troughs Miner and Seven Troughs District News*. The following week he moved the newspaper to Mazuma. (See Mazuma, *Seven Troughs Miner*.)

Seven Troughs Miner: (Dec 7 1907–Jan 23 1909)
   CHi — [1908]
   Nv — 1908
   NvHi — [Jl 25 1908–Ja 23 1909]
   NvLR — D 7 1907–Ja 23 1909
   NvU — N 1908–Ja 23 1909
   film — D 7 1907–Ja 23 1909
Ref: files

VIRGINIA CITY

Territorial Enterprise

The *Territorial Enterprise* was Nevada's first, and for many years its most influential, newspaper. Almost every prominent early Nevada journalist served on its staff at some time during his career, and much color was added to its pages by the emerging talents of young Samuel Clemens, the steady William Wright (Dan De Quille), a member of its staff for nearly thirty years, and the erratic James W. E. "Lying Jim" Townsend.

The *Enterprise* was founded by William L. Jernegan and Alfred James on December 18, 1858, at Genoa, then the county seat of Carson County, Utah Territory. James sold his interest in the paper to Jonathan Williams in August of 1859, and three months later the proprietors moved it to Carson City. Jernegan defaulted in July of 1860, and Williams became sole editor and proprietor.

In October of 1860, Williams moved the *Enterprise* once again, this time to the center of the mining rush — Virginia City — where the paper resumed on November 3. I. B. Wollard soon bought an interest in the paper, but he promptly sold it for $1,000, to Joseph T. Goodman and Denis E. McCarthy, who became partners with Williams on March 2, 1861. William Wright, who joined the staff as local and mining editor later that year, recalled the cramped quarters they shared in the small frame office at the corner of A street and Sutton Avenue:

> The building was a one-story frame with a shed addition on the north side. In the main structure were the cases of the compositors, the table at which all the writing, local and editorial, was done, and the old Washington hand-press on which the papers were worked off.
> The shed addition was used as a kitchen (an old Chinaman called "Joe" doing the cooking) and eating-room, and ranged on the sides were sleeping bunks, one above another in ship shape. Here all hands ate at a long table, and here nearly all slept. This arrangement continued until it was broken up by the slovenliness and filthiness of old "Joe," the cook. All hands then scattered, each man finding for himself an eating and sleeping place.
> At that time J. T. Goodman was editor-in-chief — in fact did all the work except the local. News and letters came overland from the East by pony

express. We then had only a few printers. Among those I remember were Pitney Taylor, Henry Deane and Dick James. George A. Thurston did the presswork, assisted by a boy named Noyes as "devil," and by outsiders who were brought in to "pull the press" at times.

As the town boomed, the *Enterprise* was enlarged to a daily on September 24, 1861, and it was soon clearing between $6,000 and $10,000 a month. Early the following year the office moved to larger quarters, on North C Street between Sutton and Union. At the same time Dennis Driscoll bought Williams's interest. Williams drifted about Nevada for many years, ultimately committing suicide at Pioche in January of 1876. It was while the *Enterprise* was published on North C Street that Samuel Clemens, who had been contributing letters to the paper from Aurora under the name of "Josh," first joined the staff as a local reporter. In August of 1863, the paper moved into the stately new two-story brick Enterprise Building, on South C Street between Union and Taylor, that still stands. Driscoll sold his interest in the paper to Goodman and McCarthy on October 28, 1863, and McCarthy, in turn, sold out to Goodman on September 15, 1865. McCarthy had made a "snug fortune" for a man still in his early twenties. Heady with success, he journeyed to San Francisco to parlay it into millions on the stock exchange, but within four months he had "lost his last dollar." He came back to Virginia City to start all over again as foreman in what had been his own job printing office only a few months earlier.

The *Enterprise* prospered under Goodman, who remained sole proprietor until February of 1874. At that time the *Enterprise* was a larger paper than any published in San Francisco, and it won national attention. But its power attracted the powerful, and Goodman finally sold it on February 10, 1874, to William Sharon, who was preparing to wage campaign for the U.S. Senate. Sharon organized the Enterprise Publishing Company, hiring Rollin M. Daggett as managing editor, assisted by Judge Charles C. Goodwin. Sharon took his Senate seat in 1875, and Daggett won Nevada's congressional seat in 1878. Goodwin remained as editor until 1880, when he was succeeded by Fred Hart, who was followed in a few weeks by Colonel Henry G. Shaw.

By then Virginia City was on the decline, taking the *Enterprise* with it. Jesse Taggert replaced Shaw as editor on September 28, 1886, and he leased the paper on the following May 26. On April 3, 1888, Shaw transferred the lease to John M. Campbell, who was also unable to make a success of it. Finally, on January 16, 1893, Campbell closed down the *Enterprise.* The paper was dead for nearly a year, until December 3, when John E. McKinnon revived it, with George R. Paynter as editor. Paynter quit in November of 1894, and was succeeded as editor by Fred J. Norris. In partnership with Frank A. Blake, the chief printer, Norris took over the lease on August 13, 1896. Blake subsequently became sole lessee on November 15, 1898, and ran the *Enterprise* through the turn of the century mining boom. He finally suspended the grand old rag on May 30, 1916, to merge it with the rival *Chronicle*.

Territorial Enterprise: (Nov 3 1860–Jan 16 1893; Dec 3 1893–May 30 1916)
    pvt — Mr 31 1863; S 27 1881; Jl 24 1885; Je 23 1888
    C — Mr 24 1865; O 30 1868; Mr 7, Ap 6, O 26, N 21 1882; O 3 1888
    CHi — Ap 11 1877; O 23 1879; My 31 1881
    CLM — Ag 7 1878
    CPom — Mr 7, Ap 6, O 26, N 21 1882
    CSfWF-H — Ag 12 1898
    CSmH — Ja 23 1867; Ag 20 1879; N 30 1912
    CU-BANC — Ap 3 1863; [1867]; Ja 10 1868–78; Je 1879–80; [F 10 1881–D 1882]; Ja 27, N 2 1883; [1884–1900]
    DLC — Jl 1874–Jl 18 1882; 1889–92
    DNA — Jl 20, N 17 1861
    ICHi — Ag 5 1876
    MnHi — [1879]
    MWA — Ap 6 1865; S 6 1879
    NcD — F 4–Je 25 1879
    NHi — My 6 1873
    NvFC — Ap 6 1865
    NvGM–Ja 1 1859
    NvHi — Ja 10 1863; Mr 18, Ap 8, 9, 12–15, 18, Jl 6 1865; Mr 9, S 14, 16, O 14, N 8, 18 1866; N 3 1868; Mr 2, N 5 1869; Ap 9, 10, Je 18 1870; [1871–4]; F 1 1876–Je 30 1880; F 26 1885; Je 9, Jl 14, S 3–N 22 1892; D 3 1893–F 28 1895; F 24 1900; My 20 1902; [1903–16]
    NvMus — N 22 1865
    NvU — [Ap 1866–1916]
    film — Jl 20, N 17 1861; Ja 10, Mr 31, Ap 3 1863; [Ap 6 1865–My 30 1916]
Ref: files; Angel 317–20; Doten 1640, 1670, 1877, 1926; SFE Ja 22 1893; Beebe

Virginia Daily Union

In the spring of 1862, the Carson City *Silver Age* passed into the hands of the Age Association, consisting of John Church, Sam S. Glessner, and James L. Laird. These gentlemen soon became dissatisfied with the prospects of Carson City and suspended the *Silver Age* in the winter of that year. Within two days they removed the plant to Virginia City, where, on November 4, 1862, they commenced publication of the *Virginia Daily Union*. The paper, edited by Munroe Thompson, was staunchly Republican in politics and gave the *Territorial Enterprise* stiff competition. But with the collapse of the speculative boom it fell on hard times, and on May 30, 1865, was purchased by O. E. Jones and Co.

This new firm was also an association of printers, consisting of Orlando E. Jones, Timothy L. Ham, E. Armand, A. P. Church, James Conley, Jake H. Bain, and James T. Huling. The *Union* continued as a Republican journal, with Thompson as chief editor, H. Pitney Taylor as associate editor, and Alf Doten as local editor, until October 17, 1865. On that date

Bain, Ham, and Huling withdrew, the editorial staff quit, and the paper became a Democratic organ. Orlando Jones assumed the editorship and Robert E. Lowery was local reporter. Then, on November 12, 1866, the former publishers, John Church and S. A. Glessner, again became proprietors, although they sold the paper to William J. Forbes in less than three months, on January 22, 1867. On the following February 5, Forbes suspended the *Union.* He used the material to begin the *Trespass* two days later.

Virginia Daily Union: (Nov 4 1862–Feb 5 1867)
  pvt — D 10 1863; F 13 1864
  C — Mr 19, Ap 18–19, 21–22, Je 25, Jl 9, 16 1865
  CSfWF-H — S 20 1864
  CSmH — Je 25 1865
  CU-BANC — Ja 1, 3, 5 1864–F 5 1867
  NvHi — Ja 21, S 27 1863; Mr 16, Ap 18 1865
  NvU — O 2 1864–O 21 1865
  film — Ja 21, S 27, D 5, 10 1863; [Ja 1 1864–F 5 1867]
Ref: files; Angel 322–3; Doten 2231

Virginia Evening Bulletin

In the spring of 1863, Thomas B. Valentine, the San Francisco publisher, furnished material and money to start a paper in Virginia City. Howard P. Taylor and Richard A. James each purchased a one-third interest in the establishment on credit, and the firm name became H. P. Taylor and Co. On July 6, 1863, they commenced publication of the *Virginia Evening Bulletin.* The paper was a thirty-two-column Republican daily, measuring 24 by 36 inches, and selling at a subscription price of $16 a year. F. B. Haswell soon purchased Valentine's interest, and on November 21 of that year Taylor sold out to Charles A. Parker. These gentlemen managed the paper until the following February 20, when Haswell withdrew from the firm after an argument over who should be supported as candidate for mayor. At this time Virginia City was overrun with newspapers — five dailies and several weeklies all vying for public favor. This competition proved too great, and after less than a year of publication, the *Bulletin* succumbed on May 17, 1864.

Virginia Evening Bulletin: (Jul 6 1863–May 17 1864)
  CHi — O 14, N 28, 30, D 4 1863
  CU-BANC — Ap 29 1864
  NvU — Jl 1–11, 14–21, 23–N 3, 5 1863–F 29, Ap 1–My 16 1864
  film — [Jl 6 1863–My 16 1864]
Ref: files; Angel 323; GHN My 18 1864

Democratic Standard

In the summer of 1863, O. E. F. Hastings and J. F. Linthicum raised $3,000 by subscription from the Democrats of Virginia City, for the purpose of starting a Democratic newspaper. On August 10, 1863, they issued the first number of the daily *Democratic Standard.* Linthicum, who was formerly the editor of the *Marysville Express* in California, held the editorial post. However, Union sentiment was strong in Virginia City, and the Copperhead venture failed to gain much support. After only two months of publication the *Standard* suspended on October 17. The equipment was purchased by John K. Lovejoy to commence the *Old Piute* the following spring.

Democratic Standard: (Aug 10 1863–Oct 17 1863)
   No issues located.
Ref: Angel 323; HR O 24 1863

The Occidental

Nevada's first literary journal, the weekly *Occidental,* was started at Virginia City on March 6, 1864. Thomas Fitch, whom Mark Twain described as "a felicitous skirmisher with a pen," was both editor and proprietor, issuing the paper every Sunday at No. 4 Myers' and Daggett's Building, on the west side of B Street between Union and Sutton Avenues. The *Occidental* contained the literary endeavors of all the aspiring Washoe journalists. In *Roughing It,* Twain gives an entertaining, if imaginative, sketch of a serialized novel that they wrote for the *Occidental.* But despite its eloquence, the paper was forced to suspend with its third or fourth number.

The Occidental: (Mar 6 1864–Mar 27 1864)
   No issues located.
Ref: Angel 323; Rogers

Nevada Pionier

The first foreign language newspaper in Nevada was the *Nevada Pionier,* founded at Virginia City on March 31, 1864. Jacob F. Hahnlen, who had previously started the first German newspaper in California, the San Francisco *Staats-Zeitung* in 1852, was sole editor and proprietor of the *Pionier.* He issued it as a German semiweekly, Democratic in politics, at a subscription price of $9 a year. The Democratic party had offered Hahnlen $500 if he would make the *Pionier* a Democratic organ, but he received only $ 100 of this amount. After less than seven months, the paper was forced to suspend from lack of support, on October 22, 1864.

Nevada Pionier: (Mar 31 1864–Oct 22 1864)
   No issues located.
Ref: Angel 325

The Daily Old Piute

In the spring of 1864, John K. Lovejoy sold his interest in the *Old Pah Utah* at Washoe City and moved to Virginia City. There, purchasing the defunct *Democratic Standard* material, he and D. B. Woolf commenced publication of the *Daily Old Piute* on April 18 of the same year. The paper was issued evenings, except Sunday, as a Republican journal. Lovejoy held the editor's post, William M. Gillespie was associate editor, F. C. Farington was local editor, and Woolf was business manager.

Lovejoy was an eccentric genius, who never missed an opportunity to make a pun with an acid twist. In repartee he had no superior in the territory, and those who assailed him always withdrew in defeat. However, this talent only made enemies for him, and did not build the support that the paper needed to survive. Unable to maintain the paper, he sold the firm to Travis Rhodes on September 8, 1864, and retired to his ranch near Verdi. Rhodes changed the politics of the *Piute* to support the Democratic Party in the fall election, and continued it a few months after the election, suspending publication on January 8, 1865.

The Daily Old Piute: (Apr 18 1864–Jan 8 1865)
   CSmH — My 14, Ag 25, 27, 1864
   CU-BANC — Je 18 1864
   film — My 14, Je 18, Ag 25, 27 1864
Ref: files; Angel 325

Washoe Stock Circular

On May 23, 1864, J. Wells Kelly and Co., publisher of Nevada's first business directories, commenced the daily *Washoe Stock Circular*. It was printed at the Union office daily, except Sunday, and contained four three-column pages of stock quotations. It sold for a subscription price of $1 a week, but only a true capitalist could afford the paper — even in Virginia City — and as a result the *Circular* soon failed from lack of support.

Washoe Stock Circular: (May 23 1864–c. Jun 1864)
   CU-BANC — My 25 1864
   film — My 25 1864
Ref: files

Daily Evening Washoe Herald

The beginning of July, 1864, saw four dailies being published in Virginia City, but Thomas Fitch and H. C. Bennett believed that there was still room for more. Thus, on July 1, they commenced publication of the *Washoe Herald*. Fitch was a brilliant and eloquent writer and Bennett was stubborn and aggressive to the point of belligerency. Together they produced a vigorous paper that crusaded loudly for reform and Republicanism. One of their first acts was to expose the blatant corruption of the judiciary. But the paper lasted little over a month, suspending August 8, 1864, unable to pay the printers their last two weeks' wages.

Daily Evening Washoe Herald: (Jul 1 1864–Aug 8 1864)
   CU-BANC — Jl 2 1864
   film — Jl 2 1864
Ref: files; Angel 325; RRR Ag 11 1864

The Daily Constitution

On October 26, 1864, the Constitution Association, consisting of printers John T. Barry, John I. Ginn, E. Armand, and William Woodburn, issued the first number of the *Daily Constitution.* C. H. Kungle was editor and William Woodburn acted as business manager in their offices at No. 27, North C Street. The paper was published every evening except Sunday, as a twenty-eight-column Democratic sheet, at 50¢ a week or $16 a year. The *Constitution* prospered for a time but soon suffered the fate of its contemporaries, and on January 2, 1865, it "passed in its checks."

The Daily Constitution: (Oct 26 1864–c. Jan 2 1865)
   CU-BANC — D 23 1864
   film — D 23 1864
Ref: files; McMurtrie 308

Nevada Staats Zeitung

On October 28, 1864, six days after the suspension of the *Nevada Pionier,* Dr. H. M. Bien started the second German newspaper, the *Nevada Staats Zeitung,* at Virginia City. Bien was sole editor and proprietor and issued the paper as a Republican weekly, "devoted to politics, literature and science." However, this paper had no better luck than its predecessor, and it ceased publication before the end of the year.

Nevada Staats Zeitung: (Oct 28 1864–c. Dec 1864)
   No issues located.
Ref: Angel 325; McMurtrie 308

Local Advertiser

By the spring of 1865, Virginia City had seen the establishment of eleven newspapers, only two of which had survived. Yet statistics teach no lessons, for on April 8, 1865, John P. Morrison began a new daily, the *Local Advertiser.* Morrison distributed the paper free throughout the town, hoping to support it on the business and theater advertising alone — with brief snatches of local news to attract readers. Apparently this quickly proved unsatisfactory, for within the week the *Advertiser* suspended to make way for a subscription daily, the *Two O'clock News.* (See Virginia City, *Two O'clock News.*)

Local Advertiser: (Apr 8 1865–c. Apr 14 1865)
   No issues located.
Ref: Angel 325, McMurtrie 308

Two O'clock News

On April 17, 1865, following his suspension of the free *Local Advertiser,* John P. Morrison launched Virginia City's thirteenth newspaper, the *Two O'clock News,* in black-border mourning for the recent assassination of Lincoln. The paper soon suffered the fate which superstition might suggest and suspended within the month.

Two O'clock News: (Apr 17 1865–c. Apr 1865)
   No issues located.
Ref: Angel 325; McMurtrie 308

Deutsche Union

Not discouraged by the failure of his *Nevada Pionier,* Jacob F. Hahnlen tried once more to publish a German newspaper in Virginia City. On October 16, 1866, he issued the first number of the weekly *Deutsche Union.* It was neutral in politics and had an equally neutral effect in gaining supporters, which resulted in its suspension within the year.

Deutsche Union: (Oct 16 1866–c. Dec 1866)
   No issues located.
Ref: Angel 326; McMurtrie 308

The Daily Trespass

Two weeks after his purchase of the Virginia City *Union,* William J. Forbes suspended the paper. On the following day, February 6, 1867, he commenced publication of the *Daily Trespass.* Forbes was sole editor and proprietor of the paper and issued it every evening except Sunday, from his office on Taylor Street between B and C Streets. The *Trespass* was a twenty-eight-column Democratic sheet, which sold at a subscription price of $16 a year. Although the paper was well written, it was not destined to endure. On October 3, 1868, Forbes suspended the paper in disgust and retired from the newspaper business to open a saloon in the new White Pine District. The material was purchased by the Nevada Democratic Printing Company, which used it to issue the short-lived *Safeguard.* In 1869, the plant was removed to White Pine to print the *Inland Empire.*

The Daily Trespass: (Feb 6 1867–Oct 3 1868)
   pvt — Jl 1 1867
   CHi — O 11 1867
   CU-BANC — [F 6 1867–O 3 1868]
   film — [F 6 1867–O 3 1868]
Ref: files

The Daily Safeguard

William J. Forbes suspended the *Trespass* on October 3, 1868, and retired from the newspaper business for a time to open a saloon in White Pine. The establishment was purchased for $8,000 by the Nevada Democratic Printing Company, which commenced publication of the *Daily Safeguard* on October 5, at Virginia City. John I. Ginn and Robert E. Lowery edited the paper, conducting it as a strong Democratic advocate during the political campaign of that year. The *Safeguard* lasted only three months after the end of the campaign, suspending on February 1 of the following year. The press and material were purchased by James J. Ayers and Charles A. V. Putnam, who moved it to Hamilton to issue the *Inland Empire* in March, 1869.

The Daily Safeguard: (Oct 5 1868–Feb 1 1869)
  C — O 26 1868
  CU-BANC — O 5–10, 12, 14–23, 26 1868–F 1 1869
  film — [O 5 1868–F 1 1869]
Ref: files; Angel 323; TE F 2 1869

City Review

In December of 1868, the *Territorial Enterprise* launched a war of extermination against its only competitor, the *Safeguard.* The *Safeguard* had been started as a campaign paper in the fall of that year, by the Nevada Democratic Association; but instead of suspending it after the election, its owners chose to continue its publication — much to the financial distress of the *Enterprise.* Thus on December 9, the publishers of the *Enterprise* set up a free daily, the *City Review.* Its titular head was Pat Holland, who had formerly been a pressman on the *Safeguard* but had been fired after the election. The *Review* was modeled after the San Francisco *Dramatic Chronicle* — containing in addition to its regular business ads, the opera review and spicy local items.

Six hundred copies were issued each day and the paper apparently cut into the *Safeguard's* advertising rather severely — at least to the extent that the *Safeguard* denounced it as a "little scullion," and a "poor little wart," which was "in a state of rapid transition to cancer." In all it seems to have achieved its goal quite quickly, for although it was suspended on January 24, 1869, the *Safeguard* folded only eight days later. The press of the *Safeguard* was then shipped to White Pine to start the *Inland Empire.* Ironically, Pat Holland also migrated that way, to repeat the same shenanigans as titular head of the *Shermantown Reporter,* a sheet started by the *White Pine News* to kill the *Inland Empire.*

City Review: (Dec 9 1868–Jan 24 1869)
  No issues located.
Ref: Angel 323; CL Mr 23 1869

Virginia Evening Chronicle

After the prosperity of the mid-1860's, Virginia City suffered a short depression, during which the *Territorial Enterprise* was the sole paper on the Comstock. It held its monopoly for four years, until April 8, 1872, when Edwin F. Bean and John I. Ginn established the *Virginia Evening Chronicle.* The paper was issued daily, except Sunday, and contained twenty-two columns. On the following October 25, Ginn sold his interest in the paper to Bean and became local editor of the paper. H. C. Street became a partner on May 2, 1873, and the firm name was changed to Bean and Street. On July 14, William P. Pratt purchased Bean's interest, and Street sold out to Charles C. Stevenson on August 28. John I. Ginn retired as editor in May of 1874, to commence an opposing paper, the *Independent.* Stevenson retired from the firm on September 28, leaving Pratt as sole proprietor. The paper passed to the Chronicle Publishing Company on October 7, and on

November 9, R. D. Bogart became editor and manager. Six months later, on April 14, 1875, Bogart was succeeded by Sands W. Forman as editor and C. C. Carson as business manager.

Denis E. McCarthy purchased the establishment on May 24, 1875, becoming sole editor and proprietor. The *Chronicle* prospered under his guidance and on September 11, 1877, a weekly edition was added. It ran until about March 18, 1904. After McCarthy's death on December 23, 1885, his widow retained the paper, hiring as manager the temperamental John H. Coleman, who constantly quit and then returned. Coleman and four other employees of the paper, E. D. Blake, W. H. Kearns, J. Winfield Scott, and James H. Sullivan, leased the paper on April 13, 1896, and Coleman eventually became sole lessee.

After Coleman's death, John L. Considine became the editor on September 5, 1901. Then J. M. Davis, E. D. Blake, and W. P. Harrington took up the lease on September 19, 1903. Harrington dropped out the following year, leaving Davis and Blake, who served as editor, until September 3, 1909, when L. N. Clark, Jr., and Mrs. M. Davis took over the lease. They finally bought and closed down their old rival the *Territorial Enterprise* on May 30, 1916. But little over a decade later, on August 6, 1927, they reluctantly suspended the *Chronicle* as well, with an "Au Revoir, but not goodbye."

Virginia Evening Chronicle: (Apr 8 1872–Aug 6 1927)
  C — Ap 17 1874–Ap 2 1875; S 30 1876–Ap 6, O 12 1878–Ap 4 1879; Je 1 1880–O 7, 13, 23–25, N 29–D 1 1882; Ja 26 1907; Jl 29 1908; [Mr 7 1910–My 2 1912]; Jl 3 1913; Ap 21 1914; Ag 18 1915; Ja 12 1917; [My 1 1919–Ag 6 1927]
  CHi — Mr 19, 21, 25 1884; [Ap 25–N 30 1885]; S 6 1894
  CoU — 1901; 1906–My 1910
  CPom — [1881–2]
  CSfCP — Mr 1 1892
  CSfWF-H — O 30 1873
  CSmH — Jl 25 1872; My 5 1877
  CU-BANC — Ap 8, 11, 13–D 1872; F 1873–8; Mr 1879–80; [1881–4]; 1885; [86]; 87; [1888–1900]; Mr 18 1904
  DLC — Ap 8–O 7 1875
  MWA — My 4 1876
  NvHi — S 24 1888; S 22 1891; Ag 20–N 1892; My 19, D 4 1896; 1907–26
  NvU — [F 1875–1927]
  film — [Ap 8 1872–Ag 6 1927]
Ref: files; RG Ap 16 1896; Doten 1775, 1805, 1845–9, 1917, 2115, 2167, 2237

Footlight

The *Footlight* was established at Virginia City in 1872, by J. Croall and Co. Croall was a pressman on the *Evening Cronicle*, and *The Footlight* was printed in that plant. It was issued weekly as a theatrical advertising medium and contained the weekly program for Piper's Opera House. By 1875, John W. Plant and John A. Mahanny became publishers, but Plant soon retired from the firm and David L. Brown replaced him. Brown and

Mahanny published the *Footlight* from a small office in the rear of their bookstore on the corner of C and Taylor streets. The columns of the paper were spicily written, and the *Footlight* soon came to be regarded as "the *Punch* of Nevada."

About 1880, Mahanny retired from the firm and D. L. Brown became sole editor and proprietor. Brown removed the press and material to new offices at No. 63 South C Street and, suspending the weekly edition, commenced publication of the *Daily Evening Footlight* on March 15, 1881. The daily was issued every evening except Sunday, as a four-page, four-column, 10 by 13-inch sheet. It sold for $5 per year or one bit per week. Except for a two-year hiatus, from November 17, 1884, to October 12, 1886, the paper was continued by Brown until January 25, 1887, when he suspended the *Footlight* and, in partnership with Alfred Chartz, he began the *Evening Report*. (See Virginia City, *The Evening Report*.)

The Footlight: (c. 1872–Nov 17 1884; Oct 12 1886–Jan 25 1887)
   pvt — N 23 1886
   CHi — F 9 1877
   CU-BANC — Ja 19, 22–27, 29, F 8–10, 14–22 1881; N 23 1886
   NvHi — [N 8 1875–Ja 25 1887]
   NvU — S 10 1874 (extra); My 24 1883–N 17 1884; O 12–D 31 1886
   film — S 10 1874 (extra); [N 8 1875–Ja 25 1887]
Ref: files; McMurtrie 310

Pacific Coast Advertiser

The *Pacific Coast Advertiser* was an ephemeral advertising sheet issued at Virginia City in 1873. It left little impression on the times, and it passed with only a mention in Steiger's *Periodical Literature of the United States* for 1873.

Pacific Coast Advertiser: (c. 1873)
   No issues located.

Nevada Mining Review

At the end of November or the beginning of December, 1873, J. D. Bethel and Co. established the *Nevada Mining Review* at Virginia City. The paper was issued weekly and was dedicated to the mining interests of the entire state. It proved financially unsuccessful and folded probably before the end of December of the same year.

Nevada Mining Review: (c. Nov 1873–c. Dec 1873)
   No issues located.
Ref: ANR D 8 1873

The Daily Independent

On June 1, 1874, the *Daily Independent* was founded at Virginia City by the Independent Publishing Company, with J. D. Bethel as manager and John I. Ginn as editor. The paper was financed by Adolph Sutro and was issued for the sole purpose of promoting his senatorial campaign under the

Independent Party banner. It was not financially successful, however, and on December 4, Bethel was replaced as manager by J. C. Lewis. In January of the following year, the *Independent* was suspended. The following July, Sutro removed the plant to the town of Sutro in Lyon County, where he used it to publish the weekly *Sutro Independent* with T. E. Picotte as editor.

The Daily Independent: (Jun 1 1874–Jan 1875)
   C — O 31 1874 (supp)
   CHi — O 31 (supp), D 16, 18, 23 1874; Ja 5 1875
   CSmH — O 31 1874 (supp)
   CU-BANC — Jl 15–D 31 1874
   NNHi — O 31 1874 (supp)
   NvHi — O 31 1874
   film — Jl 15–D 31 1874; Ja 5 1875
Ref: files; Angel 328

Nevada Post

The *Nevada Post* was a Democratic campaign paper started on October 12, 1874. Its editor and publisher are unknown and it probably suspended publication shortly after the election on November 3.

Nevada Post: (Oct 12 1874–c. Nov 1874)
  No issues located.
Ref: VC O 13 1874

Nevada Staats-Zeitung

Louis Joachim commenced publication of a second German newspaper under the name of the *Nevada Staats-Zeitung,* at Virginia City on about March 20, 1875. The paper was issued weekly on Saturdays, with Joachim acting as both editor and publisher. The German population throughout the state gave the paper their full support, but their number still proved too small to sustain a newspaper. The *Nevada Staats-Zeitung* was forced to suspend, probably in December of 1875.

Nevada Staats-Zeitung: (c. Mar 20 1875–c. Dec 1875)
  No issues located.
Ref: ANR Mr 29 1875

Comstock Record

On September 15, 1876, four practical printers — Pat Holland, Robert Glen, H. H. Watts, and T. E. Regan — launched the *Daily Comstock Record* into the fray against the *Enterprise* and *Chronicle* at Virginia City. Unfortunately they hired Professor W. Frank Stewart as editor, and though they promised to support the "interests of the working classes," the good professor weighted down its pages with stultifying essays on "troglodytes" and "pre-Adamite" geology that stopped it dead within a week. The *Gold Hill News* wrote its obituary:

> The *Comstock Record* died last night. It was murdered. The boys saw that the jig was up. All hands got tight and amused themselves by pi-ing the

forms and smashing the material generally. The *Record* was just one week old. It is a pity that it did not live a little longer as it would have given Professor Stewart a chance to get away from the cave-dwellers and come down in the course of time to the bronze and iron ages, origin of species and other live topics.

Comstock Record: (Sep 15 1876–Sep 21 1876)
  No issues located.
Ref: GHN S 15, 22 1876; TE S 5, 16 1876

Stock Report

About January 23, 1877, James McAfee commenced publication of a daily stock market quotation sheet, the *Stock Report.* It was printed in the *Enterprise* job shop and appeared immediately after the board closed each day. Its success soon prompted competition in the form of the *Stock Ledger.* The following year McAfee sold the *Stock Report* to Charles H. Sproule and Co., who carried on the rivalry until September of 1878, when W. W. Carrigan purchased both sheets and suspended the *Report.*

Stock Report: (c. Jan 23 1877–Sep 1878)
  No issues located.
Ref: LCT Ja 24 1877; TE S 17 1878

Nevada Statesman

The *Nevada Statesman* was a short-lived weekly which made its appearance in Virginia City on April 9, 1877. It was originally to be called the *Virginia Weekly Messenger,* but its publishers changed the name at the last minute, apparently in the hope of attracting a broader readership. Ostensibly a Nevada paper, it was in fact published in Oakland by John F. Uhlhorn, and edited there by Calvin B. McDonald. Only Harry McCausland, its business manager, lived in Virginia City so he could sell the paper. The Comstock papers roundly condemned the whole business and the *Chronicle* chided, "If Messrs. Uhlhorn and McDonald want to be recognized as journalists of Nevada, they must move over here and learn something." It got no better reception among its potential patrons.

Nevada Statesman: (Apr 9 1877–c. Apr 1877)
  No issues located.
Ref: NT Mr 23 1877; GHN Mr 22, Ap 11 1877; RG Ap 10 1877

The Lariat

On August 27, 1877, Captain Jack Crawford — "The Poet Scout of the Black Hills" — issued the first and probably the only number of a four-page "literary" paper, *The Lariat.* The paper was printed in the *Virginia Evening Chronicle* job office and was stuffed with poems by Captain Jack. It was distributed free to advertise a benefit for Captain Jack, held in Virginia City on September 6, 1877.

The Lariat: (Aug 27 1877)
  CU-BANC — Ag 27 1877
  NvHi — Ag 27 1877

film — Ag 27 1877
Ref: files

Stock Ledger

Spurred by the success of the *Stock Report*, the Nevada Publishing Company, with Henry S. Moore as its titular head, established a competing daily market report, the *Stock Ledger*, on October 1, 1877. It was neatly printed on tinted paper, and the *Gold Hill News* praised it as "a beautiful as well as useful little sheet," noting that "it contains not only the quotations from the San Francisco markets, but a list of all the active mines, with their offices and officers, and the number of feet embraced in them; an assessment list, and the highest and lowest prices of stocks for the last six months." The *Ledger* seemingly outshone its rival in every way. It issued two editions a day, which were delivered by carriers anywhere in Virginia City, Gold Hill, and Silver City for 50¢ a week. In September of 1878, W. W. Carrigan bought out both the *Ledger* and the *Report*, continuing the *Ledger* from the *Footlight* office until sometime in 1879.

Stock Ledger: (Oct 1 1877–c. 1879)
   pvt — Numbers 40, 51, 63–64, 67–68, 83, Nov 1877
Ref: GHN S 28, O 17 1877; TE S 17 1878

The Stage

The *Daily Stage*, begun by R. S. Lawrence to challenge the *Footlight* at Virginia City on January 24, 1878, contained the official program of Piper's Opera House and occasional commentary of the current dramatic season. The paper was printed on the Lightning Steam Press of the *Virginia Evening Chronicle*, but the first editorial office was Lawrence's room in the International Hotel. The proprietorship, however, changed seasonally. Lawrence sold out on March 21, 1878, to Edward W. "Ned" Townsend and James B. Griffen. That summer Townsend sold his interest to John W. Plant and left Nevada to pursue a career as a novelist. Griffen then sold his interest to a printer named Halpin that fall. The following year they both sold out to Wells Drury, and he held the *Stage* until September 23, 1880, when it passed into the hands of James T. Huling and a partner, Shannon. They rang down the curtain on the *Stage* November 5, 1880, leaving only the *Footlight* shining.

The Stage: (Jan 24 1878–Nov 5 1880)
  CSmH — S 22–N 5 1880
  CU-BANC — Mr 18, 21, O 9 1878
  film — Mr 18, 21, O 9 1878; S 22–N 5 1880
Ref: files; Bishop 579

Rushlight

The Virginia City *Rushlight* was a short-lived theatrical paper begun in late September of 1878, in competition with the *Footlight* and the *Stage*. Its editor and publisher are unknown, and its appeal proved less than that of its competitors.

Rushlight: (Sep 1878–c. Oct 1878)
  No issues located.
Ref: RG O 1 1878

Nevada Monthly

The third magazine to be published in Nevada was the *Nevada Monthly,* begun at Virginia City in February of 1880. The editors described the magazine as a "Book of Reference and Information, Devoted to the Mining, Agricultural and Industrial Interests of the State and Literature." It was published in octavo, contained 68 pages, measured 6 by 9 inches, and sold for $2.50 a year or 25¢ a copy. The *Nevada Monthly* contained many interesting articles on Nevada, and the original works of such Nevada writers as Dan De Quille, Sam Davis and others. It was unable to sustain itself, however, and finally suspended publication about October of 1880.

Nevada Monthly: (Feb 1880–c. Oct 1880)
  CSmH — F, Je–S 1880
  CU-BANC — F–Ag, O 1880
  NvHi — F–Mr, My–Je, Ag 1880
  NvU — F, Ag 1880
Ref: files

The Occasional

William P. Pratt, the last editor of the *Gold Hill News,* launched a spicy little Democratic campaign sheet, *The Occasional,* at Virginia City in June of 1886. When Pratt, with a caustic pen, opposed the renomination bid of Democratic governor Jewett Adams, the governor started his own paper, the *Comstock Union.* Adams won the renomination but lost the general election.

The Occasional: (Jun 1886–c. Aug 1886)
  NvHi — Ag 19 1886
  film — Ag 19 1886
Ref: files; NSJ Je 16 1886; NeT Je 16 1886; RRR Je 19 1886

Comstock Union

Infuriated by the Democratic *Occasional*'s opposition to his renomination, Democratic Governor Jewett Adams issued his own paper, the *Comstock Union,* just before the primary election on August 11, 1886. He won the day but lost in the general election in November to Republican C. C. Stevenson.

Comstock Union: (c. Aug 10 1886)
  No issues located.
Ref: NeT Ag 10 1886; RRR Ag 11 1886; LCT Ag 11 1886; RG Ag 12 1886

The Evening Report

In late January, 1887, Alfred Chartz joined with David L. Brown of the Virginia City *Footlight,* and on February 2, they renamed it the *Evening Report.* Brown and Chartz issued the paper every evening except Sunday, as a four-page, six-column sheet, that sold for $5 a year or one bit a week. For the first three days the *Report* was published from the old *Footlight* office at No. 63 South C Street, but on February 5, the plant was moved to new offices at No. 51 South C. Chartz served as editor of the paper until September 23, 1887, when he retired from the firm, leaving Brown as sole proprietor.

On December 3, 1888, Brown suspended publication, but the *Report* remained dead for only a few years, until March 23, 1891, when the Report Publishing Company was organized with D. L. Brown as president, Frank S. Cox as treasurer, and John L. Considine as secretary. They apparently ran the paper for only a few months, before it died again, this time not to be resurrected until August 1, 1897. David Brown, Frank Cox, James Sullivan, John Considine, and John Mahoney then decided to try once more to "make a living for them selves out of it." This time they managed to keep the sheet alive for a number of years, but how well they fared is problematical. Considine finally quit on September 5, 1901, taking the lease on the rival *Virginia Evening Chronicle,* while its reporter, George Warren, replaced him as editor of the *Report.* The others apparently held on until the last and final suspension of the paper in May of 1904.

The Evening Report: (Feb 2 1887–Dec 3 1888; Mar 23–Aug 1891; Aug 31 1897–May 1904)
  CHi — Ag 25, 28–29 1888; S 1 1898
  CSfCP — O 31 1898
  CSfWF-H — Jl 23 1887
  CU-BANC — N 18 1887
  NvHi — Jl 30 1887; O 25 1898
  NvU — F 2 1887–N 30 1888; Ja 3 1898–D 15 1903
  film — [F 2 1887–D 15 1903]
Ref: files; Doten, 1655, 1718, 1964, 2115, 2167, 2256; TM My 28 1904

The Orphans' Appeal

In the first week of November of 1887, during their annual Orphans' Fair, the Virginia City Sisters of Charity published a little paper, *The Orphans' Appeal.* Its editor, Dollie A. McCone, filled it "full of local and general news" and it proved so successful that it was revived again each November for the next three years.

The Orphans' Appeal: (Nov 1887; Nov 1888; Nov 1889; Nov 1890)
  No issues located.
Ref: RG O 28, N 4 1887, O 31 1890; NSJ N 5 1887, N 1 1890

Republican Principles

During the election campaign of 1888, the State Central Committee of the Republican Party had William Sutherland of Virginia City print two undated issues of a campaign sheet called *Republican Principles.* The first, issued about October 19, 1888, was a one-foot-square affair, with three columns to the page. It consisted entirely of clippings from eastern papers with not one line from Sutherland's pen.

Republican Principles: (c. Oct 19 1888)
   NvHi — 2 issues in a scrapbook
   film — 2 issues in a scrapbook
Ref: files

Comstock Miner

On January 21, 1889, a Comstock printer, M. W. Sills, commenced a new weekly at Virginia City, with the plant of the old *Evening Report.* The *Comstock Miner* was unable to compete with two rival dailies, however, and it was forced to suspend in a short time.

Comstock Miner: (Jan 21 1889–c. 1889)
   No issues located.
Ref: EN Ja 26 1889; Doten 1723

Campaign Notes

Campaign Notes was a daily Republican campaign sheet issued in Virginia City by William Sutherland from October 8, to election day, November 6, 1900.

Campaign Notes: (Oct 8 1900–Nov 6 1900)
   NvHi — O 8 1900
   NvU — O 8–N 6 1900
   film — O 8–N 6 1900
Ref: files; Doten 2082

Monday Budget

H. P. Remington founded the weekly *Monday Budget* at Virginia City on December 24, 1917. Remington was sole editor and proprietor, issuing the paper for $2 a year. After slightly less than a year the paper suspended publication on November 4, 1918. Nine years later, after the suspension of the *Chronicle,* the *Budget* was revived for a few more years. (See Virginia City, *Monday Budget* 1927.)

Monday Budget: (Dec 24 1917–Nov 4 1918)
   NvHi — D 31 1917–N 4 1918
   NvU — D 24 1917–N 4 1918
   film — D 24 1917–N 4 1918
Ref: files

Monday Budget

Following the suspension of the *Virginia Evening Chronicle,* veteran Comstock printer James T. Huling revived a paper at Virginia City by resurrecting the former *Monday Budget* on August 29, 1927. The *Budget* was issued weekly by Huling until July 22, 1929, when Neida Adler took over the paper after Huling suffered a crippling fall. She bowed out the following week, and Vincent C. Nevin became editor and publisher. Nevin continued as such until the suspension of the paper on December 23, 1929.

Monday Budget: (Aug 29 1927–Dec 23 1929)
   C — Ag 29 1927–Ag 27, S 10 1928–Mr 18, Ap 1–My 20, Je 3–Jl 8, 22–Ag 26, S 8–O 14, D 9, 23 1929
   NvU — [Ag 29 1927–Jl 29 1929]
   film — [Ag 29 1927–D 23 1929]
Ref: files

Virginia City News

About 1930, Vincent C. Nevin started a new venture, the *Virginia City News,* from the old *Monday Budget* plant. Nevin ran it on county advertising for at least a decade before he sold it on April 9, 1943, to Doug H. Tandy. It changed hands rapidly thereafter. Tandy died later that year, and Wesley L. Davis, Jr., son of the former *White Pine News* publisher, purchased the paper on January 10, 1944. Davis was followed by Dixie Dixon on April 5, 1947, and she was succeeded by Peter and Linda Burke in September. They sold the *News* to Milo P. Saling and Aldo A. Perino in 1949. Saling became sole editor and publisher early in 1950, but sold to E. Frank Cooper in May. He hired Clarence C. (Spud) Crossley as editor, but the latter quit a year later to go to Alaska and the *News* was suspended on June 30, 1951. Lucius Beebe and Charles Clegg then purchased the plant, revitalized the format and content, and revived it as the *Territorial Enterprise and Virginia City News* on May 2, 1952. (See Virginia City, *Territorial Enterprise and Virginia City News.*)

Virginia City News: (c. 1930–Jun 30 1951)
   NvHi — 1941, 1943, 1945, 1947–51
   NvU — [1934]; 1936–51
   film — Ja 5–F 23 1934; [Mr 13 1936–Je 30 1951]
Ref: files; Ayer; DNN

Territorial Enterprise

On March 13, 1946, Helen Crawford Dorst issued the first number of a new *Territorial Enterprise* at Virginia City, reviving in name Nevada's pioneer journal. Helen Dorst was publisher, and Jock Taylor was editor. The paper was published irregularly from temporary offices in the old Virginia and Truckee Railroad station at Carson City. It sold for $2.50 a year. The venture proved to have been a few years premature, however, as popular interest in western revivals was not yet large enough to support it. The *Enterprise* suspended publication with its seventh issue, on June 12.

Territorial Enterprise: (Mar 13 1946–Jun 12 1946)
   CSmH — Mr 13, Ap 10 1946
   NvHi — Mr 13–Je 12 1946
   NvMus — Ap 24 1946
   film — Mr 13–Je 12 1946
Ref: files

Territorial Enterprise and Virginia City News

In the winter of 1951, Lucius Beebe and Charles Clegg bought the defunct Virginia City *News.* The following year they once again resurrected the name of the *Territorial Enterprise,* with the founding of a new paper, the *Territorial Enterprise and Virginia City News,* on May 2, 1952. With Beebe as publisher and Clegg as editor, the paper grew rapidly and soon boasted the largest circulation of any weekly in Nevada, although most of its subscribers were out of state. Beebe's journal was, in keeping with its banner, "A Weekly of the Western Frontier Literary Tradition," but after he sold it in 1960, the *Enterprise* passed lifelessly through several hands. It finally faded away on March 28, 1969. Only the name remained, to be adopted temporarily by the *Humboldt Bulletin.* (See Winnemucca, *Territorial Enterprise.*)

Territorial Enterprise and Virginia City News: (May 2 1952–Mar 28 1969)
    pub — My 2 1952–69
    C — My 2 1952–69
    NvHi — [Ja 20 1967–Mr 29 1968]
    NvU — My 2 1952–62
    WHi — Ag 31 1956
    film — My 2 1952–Mr 28 1969
Ref: files

Virginia City Times

The *Virginia City Times* was issued once a year, beginning in 1958, by the Lamp Post. It was edited by Effie Mona Mack and contained articles on the history of the Comstock.

Virginia City Times: (1958–c. 1961)
    film — 1958; 1961
Ref: files

Virginia City Chronicle

The *Virginia City Chronicle,* begun on April 13, 1962, by Bob Richards, was a resurrection in name, but not in spirit, of the paper that helped put the original *Territorial Enterprise* out of business. Richards may have hoped that history would repeat itself, but in this latter-day replay of the contest the resurrected *Territorial Enterprise* carried the day.

Virginia City Chronicle: (Apr 13 1962–c. Nov 9 1962)
    Nv — Ap 13–N 9 1962
    film — Ap 13–N 9 1962
Ref: files

Sun Mountain Sentinel

Mike Payette commenced the *Sun Mountain Sentinel* at Virginia City on January 1, 1964, "for the amusement and edification of the finest people on earth, the residents of Storey County, Nevada, and their many friends throughout the world." It was originally issued weekly, but was cut back to a monthly, and finally died about February, 1965.

Sun Mountain Sentinel: (Jan 1 1964–c. Feb 1965)
   NvHi — Ja 1–Ap 17, D 15 1964
   film — (Ja 1 1964–F 1965)
Ref: files

Virginia City Times Bonanza

Following the suspension of the *Territorial Enterprise,* its place was promptly filled by the weekly *Virginia City Times Bonanza,* which borrowed the name of Tonopah's great paper and began about July 11, 1969. Dick Copp was publisher and Clyde R. Rutledge was editor. It was one Virginia City newspaper that proudly proclaimed, "Mark Twain Didn't Do Nothing in Here." But it suspended on December 27, 1969, when the editor left for the winter. Although he promised to resurrect it in the spring, Rutledge started a new newspaper when he came back. (See *Virginia City Legend.*)

Virginia City Times Bonanza: (c. Jul 11 1969–Dec 27 1969)
   film — Ag 8–D 27 1969
Ref: files

Virginia City Legend

About August 17, 1970, Clyde R. Rutledge, former editor of the *Virginia City Times Bonanza,* commenced a new "Voice of the Comstock," the weekly *Virginia City Legend.* He seems to have suspended the paper temporarily that winter, but the following year it was resumed by Johnny Gunn, who kept it going until December 28, 1973.

Virginia City Legend: (c. Aug 17 1970–Dec 28 1973)
   NvHi — Ja 27 1972
   film — N 23 1970; Ag 15 1971–D 28 1973
Ref: files

Virginia City Crier

The *Crier,* a voice "for and of the forgotten ones ... the small miners and prospectors" was begun about July, 1974, by C. E. Pollock, editor and publisher. It was heard every other week until the fall of that year when it increased to a weekly and became the official publication of the Nevada Miners and Prospectors Association. It apparently fell silent the following year.

Virginia City Crier: (c. Jul 1974–c. May 1975)
   NvHi — Jl 8 [O 9 1974–My 21 1975]
Ref: files

We, The People

Richard L. Downing issued the monthly *We, The People* in Virginia City from April to December 1975. It was a congressional report and the newsletter of his We, The People Foundation.

We, The People: (Apr 1975–Dec 1975)
   Nv — Ap–D 1975
Ref: files

⟶(WABUSKA)⟵

Wabuska Mangler

The *Wabuska Mangler* was the mythical creation of Sam Davis, the editor of the Carson City *Appeal,* and it was never even proposed in reality. Its occasional appearance among the exchanges in the late 1880's however, warrants its mention here. Davis conjured its first issue on November 3, 1888, and laid it and its publisher, E. P. Lovejoy, to rest in 1891, but its story is best told by Wells Drury:

> The queerest of all the names chosen for newspapers in Nevada was possibly that of the Waubuska *Mangler.* The paper was supposed to have been published in Waubuska, in Lyon County, but as a matter of fact, it never had any existence outside the Carson *Appeal* office. There was never any paper published at Waubuska, but the *Appeal* imagined one and located it there. For some years the *Appeal* pretended to reprint savage editorials credited to the *Mangler,* whose editor it frequently took to task as "a disgrace to journalism."
>
> The controversies between the *Mangler* and its contemporaries were continued for years and with such a show of plausibility that some people to this day still regard the Waubuska *Mangler* as one of the liveliest sheets ever published in the arid West. When the *Appeal* got tired of keeping the fictitious newspaper before the public it announced that the editor, on account of ill-health, had closed up his office and gone east. It republished a valedictory containing these statements and supplemented it with a story that the publisher had really slid out between suns to avoid a grand jury indictment. Nothing more was heard of the spectral *Mangler* after that and the real cause of its suspension is still a matter of speculation.

Wabuska Mangler:
   Nonexistent.
Ref: CA My 3 1889, Ag 28 1891; Drury 185

##

Wadsworth Dispatch

The *Dispatch* was begun at the railroad town of Wadsworth on September 21, 1892, by the Dispatch Publishing Company, with attorney Nicholas A. Hummel, proprietor, and W. H. A. Pike, editor. It was issued semiweekly, as a four-page, four-column, 11 by 15-inch sheet, which sold at a subscription price of $3 a year. The paper was enlarged to twice its original size on October 5, 1892, but on September 30, 1904, it became a weekly. As such it continued until a bad fire and the removal of the railroad shops to Sparks forced its suspension on December 23, 1904. Hummel then removed the plant to Sparks, where he revived the paper as the *Sparks Dispatch*. (See *Sparks Dispatch*.)

Wadsworth Dispatch: (Sep 21 1892–Dec 23 1904)
   NvHi — 1892; F 2 1893; N 7 1900; 1902
   NvRW — S 21 1892–D 29 1903
   NvU — [1892–1904]
   film — [S 21 1892–D 23 1904]
Ref: files

The Dispatch

Following the suspension of the Fernley *Enterprise,* Joe T. Camp moved the press and material to nearby Wadsworth, where he resurrected the name of the *Dispatch* in late August of 1920. Wadsworth was still unable to support a paper, however, and Camp packed up and moved on later the same year.

The Dispatch: (Aug 1920–c. 1920)
   No issues located.
Ref: LVA S 4 1920

Nevadian Times

On July 22 1927, A. E. Haines revived a paper at Wadsworth with the establishment of the *Nevadian Times.* Haines was sole editor and proprietor, issuing the *Times* every Friday, as a $2.50-a-year, Republican weekly. After about four years Haines concluded that neighboring Fernley offered more promise, and in early 1931, he suspended the paper at Wadsworth and moved the plant to Fernley. He was quickly disenchanted with Fernley, however, and the *Nevadian Times* drifted on to Carson City. (See Fernley, *Nevadian Times,* Carson City, *Nevadian Times.*)

Nevadian Times: (Jul 22 1927–1931)
   NvU — D 16 1927
   film — D 16 1927
Ref: files

(WARD)

Ward Miner

By the fall of 1876, the rumored wealth of the Martin White and other mines had attracted over 1,500 people to the new camp of Ward. Among them was Mark W. Musgrove, who felt that the camp needed a newspaper. In mid-November of that year, Musgrove issued the first number of the semiweekly *Ward Miner* on a sheet of paper no larger than a letter. During the winter the paper prospered and in January of 1877, he enlarged the *Miner* to a triweekly.

With the arrival of spring, however, the illusion of rich mines melted with the snow and two-thirds of the population departed. Musgrove felt that doom was near and suspended the *Miner* early in April. He sold the establishment to Robert W. Simpson, who was a seasoned journalist and not so easily discouraged. Simpson used the material to publish the *Ward Reflex,* which he continued for nearly seven years. Musgrove was always too early or too late. In the following eighteen months, he founded and sold three newspapers, the *Battle Mountain Messenger,* the *Belleville Times* and the *Ruby Hill Mining Report.* (See *Ward Reflex.*)

Ward Miner: (c. Nov 15 1876–Apr 1877)
   CU-BANC — N 24, D 7–11 1876; Ja 15–18, 29–F 9, 16–26, Mr 5–9, 21, 29, Ap 1877
   NvElC — N 1876–Mr 1877
   film — [N 24 1876–Ap 1877]
Ref: files; Angel 331

Ward Reflex

Following the suspension of the *Ward Miner,* Robert W. Simpson purchased the plant and commenced publication of the *Ward Reflex* on April 19, 1877. Simpson was sole editor and proprietor, and issued the paper as a weekly of twenty columns, measuring 18 by 24 inches, at a subscription price of $7.50 a year. The *Reflex* was well received and from August 9 to September 30, 1877, it was issued as a semiweekly. The paper was then reduced to a weekly again and continued until May 17, 1884. That day Simpson suspended the paper at Ward and removed the plant to "the Promised Land," the new camp of Taylor, where he revived the paper as the *White Pine Reflex.* (See Taylor, *White Pine Reflex.*)

Ward Reflex: (Apr 19 1877–May 17 1884)
   CU-BANC — Ag 9 1877–Jl 26 1882
   NvElC — Ap 19 1877–My 1884
   NvMus — N 2 1878, O 26 1882
   film — [Ag 9 1877–My 17 1884]
Ref: files; Angel 331

WASHOE CITY

Washoe Times

The first number of the *Washoe Times* was issued at Washoe City by George W. Derickson on October 18, 1862. General James Allen was editor, and the paper was published as a twenty-four-column Republican weekly, at a subscription price of $5 per year. Misfortune attended those connected with the *Times.* On January 23, 1863, Derickson was shot and killed by H. F. Swayze. General Allen became proprietor on February 13, but died suddenly on October 31, while attending the first Nevada State Fair at Carson City. Publication of the *Times* was continued by B. F.

Derickson, administrator of Allen's estate, and Judge Charles C. Goodwin became editor. In a little over a month John K. Lovejoy purchased the ill-fated establishment, and on December 5, 1863, he suspended the *Times* to commence publication of the *Old Pah Utah* the following week.
Washoe Times: (Oct 18 1862–Dec 5 1863)
   CBiI — Ag 29 1863
   CU-BANC — F 28, Jl 11 1863
   NvHi — Ja 10, 24–31, S 19, N 7 1863
   film — Ja 10, 24–31, F 28, Jl 11, S 19, N 7 1863
Ref: files; Angel 328

Old Pah Utah

Following the suspension of the *Washoe Times,* John K. Lovejoy used the material to commence the weekly *Old Pah Utah* on December 12, 1863. The *Old Pah Utah* was a revival in spirit of the *Old Mountaineer,* which Lovejoy and E. F. McElwain had published in Quincy, California. Lovejoy was editor and proprietor of the paper and issued it as a lively sheet of twenty-four columns, measuring 21 by 28 inches, at $5 a year. The editorials and locals were spiced with a peculiar twist, which made them unpopular in more refined circles. The Lovejoy clan were also noted for being rabid abolitionists. One of Lovejoy's relatives, Owen, was killed in a famous incident in Alton, Illinois, because of his free soil sentiments. Early in 1864, William Gregory became a partner in the *Old Pah Utah.* On April 9, Lovejoy sold his remaining interests to E. B. Wilson, and moved to Virginia City to start the *Old Piute.* The new proprietors immediately suspended the *Old Pah Utah* to begin the *Washoe Weekly Star.*
Old Pah Utah: (Dec 12 1863–Apr 9 1864)
   CU-BANC — D 26 1863
   film — D 26 1863
Ref: files; Angel 328; HR Ap 30 1864

Washoe Weekly Star

After their purchase of the *Old Pah Utah,* William Gregory and E. B. Wilson suspended that paper and began publication of the *Washoe Weekly Star* on April 16, 1864. No change was made in the size or price of the paper, and it continued as a twenty-four-column weekly, selling for $5 a year. Wilson became sole proprietor on May 7, remaining as such until January 21, 1865. The establishment was then purchased by DeLashmutt and Co., who suspended the *Star* to commence the *Washoe Weekly Times.*
Washoe Weekly Star: (Apr 16 1864–Jan 21 1865)
   CU-BANC — N 19 1864; Ja 7 1865
   NvHi — Ag 27, D 31 1864
   film — Ag 27, N 19, D 31 1864; Ja 7 1865
Ref: files; Angel 328, HR Ap 30 1864

Washoe Weekly Times

The firm of DeLashmutt and Co. purchased the plant of the *Washoe Weekly Star* and suspended that paper to commence the *Washoe Weekly Times* the following week, on January 28, 1865. Van B. DeLashmutt, Joshua G. Laws, and Charles Spencer Clarke made up the publishing firm, with Clarke also serving as editor. On July 22, 1865, Laws retired from the firm and the establishment was sold to F. A. Prentice and Co. on August 26. John C. Lewis held two-thirds of the interest in the new firm, and with the change in management he replaced Clarke in the editorship. In the fall of 1865, Lewis went to California on business. In his absence Prentice admitted to legal demands made against the office, which resulted in seizure of the plant by the sheriff and the subsequent suspension of the paper on November 18, 1865.

Washoe Weekly Times: (Jan 28 1865–Nov 18 1865)
   CU-BANC — Ja 28–Mr 4, 18–25, Ap 8–Je 24, Jl 15–Ag 5, O 14, 28–N 4 1865
   NvU — S–O 1865
   film — [Ja 28–N 4 1865]
Ref: files; Angel 328

Eastern Slope

John C. Lewis returned from California to discover that his interest in the *Washoe Weekly Times* had been seized by the sheriff for liabilities against the office and that the paper had suspended. Determined to revive a paper at Washoe City, he purchased the material of the former Carson City *Post,* and on December 9, 1865, he began the *Eastern Slope.* Lewis issued the paper as a twenty-four-column weekly, for $5 a year, the same size and price as the former *Times.* The new paper was well received and continued through the prosperous period of Washoe City. With the decline of the town, however, Lewis suspended the *Eastern Slope* on June 27, 1868, and removed the plant to the newly founded rival town of Reno. Here, he used the material to establish the *Reno Crescent.* (See *Reno Crescent.*)

Eastern Slope: (Dec 9 1865–Jun 27 1868)
  CU-BANC — D 9 1865–Mr 31, Jl 7–Ag 25, S 15 1866–Je 1, 15–Jl 27, Ag 10
    1867–Ap 25, My 9–Je 13, 27 1868
  NvHi — D 9 1865–Je 27 1868
  NvU — Ap 1866–N 1867
  film — D 9 1865–Je 27 1868
Ref: files; Angel 328

Wells Index

About May of 1896, Phil S. Triplett commenced the weekly *Index* at Wells, on the Southern Pacific Railroad. The paper was not a financial success,

however, and was suspended three months later, in August. Five years later Triplett returned to Wells and purchased the *Nevada State Herald,* which he ran for many years.
Wells Index: (c. May 1896–Aug 1896)
   No issues located.
Ref: Myrick

Nevada State Herald

The *Nevada State Herald* was begun at Wells on March 19, 1897, by the Nevada State Herald Printing and Publishing Company, with George S. Ferguson and George R. Vardy as managers and editors. The paper was issued every Friday, as an eight-page, five-column weekly, selling for $2 a year. On November 12, 1897, Ferguson retired from the firm and Vardy became manager and editor. Vardy conducted the *Herald* until July 5, 1901, when Phil S. Triplett purchased the plant, to become editor and publisher. The Triplett family continued the paper for many years. After Phil Triplett's death in April of 1921, Frances and Charles J. Triplett took over the paper. The latter became sole owner and editor on December 15, 1926. From October 12, 1928, to May 24, 1929, William R. Keegan was briefly a co-owner. The national Depression finally killed the *Herald* in October of 1933.
Nevada State Herald: (Mar 19 1897–Oct 1933)
   NvEHi — [1902–8; 1913–8]
   NvHi — [1900–33]
   NvU — [1897–1933]
   film — [Mr 19 1897–Ap 14 1933]
Ref: files

Wells Progress

Ed M. Shirton revived a newspaper at Wells on June 26, 1936, with the establishment of the weekly *Wells Progress.* On August 9, 1940, Charles J. Triplett bought the paper, and continued it until about 1963, when his wife, Ola F. Triplett, became the publisher and his son, Charles J. "Bud" Triplett, Jr., assumed the editorship. About 1969, the latter became sole editor and proprietor, continuing as such until his death in 1976. In March, 1977, his widow, Rose Marie, sold the paper to the Elko *Free Press,* which, with a group of local residents, formed Wells Progress, Inc., with Roseanne Crago as editor. In 1978, Cathy Igoa became publisher for the corporation, and Marilyn Ranson became editor.
Wells Progress: (Jun 26 1936+)
   NvEHi — Je 26 1936+
   NvHi — Je 28 1940; Je 27 1941+
   NvU — [1937–67]
   film — Je 26 1936+
Ref: files

⚞ WHITE PLAINS ⚟

Churchill News

The first and only nineteenth-century newspaper published in Churchill County was the *Churchill News,* issued at White Plains, on the Central Pacific Railroad between the Carson and Humboldt Sinks. The *News* was begun on March 31, 1888, as a small occasional sheet. With tongue in cheek, its editor, P. W. Smith, claimed for it "the largest circulation of any newspaper in Churchill County." Unfortunately, however, the subscribing population of Churchill County was not large enough to support a newspaper, and the *News* was probably suspended within the year.

Churchill News: (Mar 31 1888–c. 1888)
  NvHi — Mr 31 1888
  film — Mr 31 1888
Ref: files

⚞ WHITNEY ⚟

Whitney News

The *Whitney News* was a short-lived sheet published during World War II at Whitney, eight miles southeast of Las Vegas. Its editor or publisher was a woman known as the "Mayor of St. Anne," and the paper was actually published in St. Anne, a shantytown just east of Whitney. No precise information is available about its staff or duration.

Whitney News: (c. 1942–1943)
  No issues located.
Ref: Averett

⚞ WINNEMUCCA ⚟

Winnemucca Argent

In May of 1868, John and Joseph Wasson purchased the plant of the defunct Aurora *Times* and shipped it to the promising new town of Winnemucca, on the Central Pacific Railroad. There, on July 23, they issued the first number of the *Winnemucca Argent.* It was published every Thursday as a Republican weekly, at a subscription price of $5 per year. Winnemucca was not yet able to support a newspaper, however, and the *Argent* was forced to suspend on November 21. The material was later taken to Silver City, Idaho, where it was used in publishing the *Tidal Wave.* John Wasson went to Tucson, Arizona, and purchased the *Tucson Citizen,* which he ran until 1877. While there he was also appointed surveyor general of the territory. Joseph Wasson drifted to Mono County, California, where he became a representative in the state legislature.

Winnemucca Argent: (Jul 23 1868–Nov 21 1868)
   pvt — S 17 1868
   CU-BANC — Jl 23–N 21 1868
   NvMus — S 24 1868
   NvU — Jl 23–N 21 1868
   film — Jl 23–N 21 1868
Ref: files; Angel 303; RC N 21, 28 1868

Humboldt National

Winnemucca was without a newspaper for nearly a year until James Anson Booth decided to try his luck. On August 14, 1869, he issued the first number of the *Humboldt National,* as a twenty-eight-column weekly. Booth soon saw that the paper would not survive, and on October 16, 1869 he disposed of it to Robert McBeth, in whose hands it promptly died.

Humboldt National: (Aug 14 1869–Oct 1869)
   pvt — [Ag 14–O 16 1869]
   film — [Ag 14–O 16 1869]
Ref: files; Angel 303

Humboldt Register

After the *Humboldt Register and Workingman's Advocate* suspended at Unionville, in May, 1869, E. D. Kelley took the material to the new railroad town of Elko, where he established the *Elko Independent.* When Elko failed to develop as rapidly as Kelley had hoped, he sold the *Independent* in October of the same year. He then returned to Winnemucca, where, in partnership with former editor McKaskia Bonnifield, he revived the old *Humboldt Register* as a weekly on October 30, 1869. On March 19, 1870, Robert McBeth bought the paper and Thomas V. Julien became editor. This arrangement lasted only until August 6, when John Robbins purchased the firm and assumed the editorial post.

Julien returned and bought the paper on May 4, 1872, in partnership with H. A. Waldo. But some four years later, on January 28, 1876, they sold the paper to Charles H. Stoddard, who enthusiastically added a daily edition to the weekly. Stoddard was unable to make a success of the paper, and on November 4 of the same year he suspended the daily, because, "Times are too hard and Winnemucca is too small." Five days later, he sold the weekly to H. A. Waldo and J. C. Ragsdale, who suspended it on December 1, and took the material to Eureka to found the *Republican.*

Humboldt Register (weekly): (Oct 30 1869–Dec 1 1876)
   CU-BANC — N 27 1869–Ag 6, 20 1870–D 1 1876
   MH — My 3 1873
   film — N 27 1869–Ag 6, 20 1870–D 1 1876
Humboldt Register (daily): (Jan 7 1876–Nov 4 1876)
   CU-BANC — My 29–O 30 1876
   NvU — [Ja 28–N 4 1876]
   Film — [Ja 28–N 4 1876]
Ref: files; Angel 302

The Silver State

On September 3, 1874, Peter Myers and John J. Hill suspended the *Silver State* at Unionville and removed the plant to Winnemucca. There they revived the paper under the same name on September 10. The *Silver State* was issued as a twenty-two-column weekly until October 7, 1874, when it was increased to a daily of twenty columns. E. D. Kelley served as editor, and on September 8, 1875, he replaced Myers as a partner in the firm of J. J. Hill and Co. This firm managed the paper until December 1, 1890, when the Silver State Publishing Company, owned by banker and later U.S. Senator George S. Nixon, assumed control, with George W. Rutherford as editor. On September 25, 1899, Nixon leased the paper to R. E. L. Windle and A. L. Brackett, and on November 17, 1902, he sold it to the Winnemucca Publishing Company, a group of local businessmen led by Thomas Nelson.

They hired William M. Gotwaldt as editor, and changed its name to the *Winnemucca Republican*. Windle and Brackett started a rival Democratic paper, the *Humboldt Standard*. Gotwaldt quit as editor on March 16, 1903, and the *Republican* had a rapid succession of editors during the next year and one-half: E. C. Bradshaw, Frank W. Roach, Frank G. Jenkins, and Lester Osborne. Finally, Allen C. Bragg became the editor on November 28, 1904, and changed the name back to the *Silver State*.

James E. Nugent succeeded Bragg on March 1, 1906, and was quickly followed by John S. Case, who leased the paper on June 22, 1906, with James Ezell. Howard N. Riddle took Ezell's interest in the lease on September 8, but sold to Case on December 13. On June 20, 1907, Case took in a new partner named Wright, who immediately reduced the daily to a semiweekly and renamed the paper the *Silver State News*, due to his notion that "*Silver State* in itself is hardly suitable for a newspaper."

After Case and Wright gave up the lease in July of 1908, Thomas Nelson and his associates exorcized *News* from the masthead, and on July 7, 1910 they increased the issue to triweekly. On April 2, 1912, they sold the paper to Edward R. Harroun, who ran it until his death on August 11, 1917. His widow, Genevieve, continued the paper until January 3, 1919, when C. D. Ayers and his son, W. H., bought it. They were partially burned out on September 13, 1921, and C. D. Ayers quit soon after, but his son kept the paper going. Although he reduced it to a weekly on January 4, 1923, he expanded it back to a semiweekly on December 4.

The Silver State Publishing Company took over the paper one year later. They increased it to a triweekly on April 18, 1925, and to a daily two days later. When they leased it to F. C. Stitser on June 6, however, he immediately cut it back to a triweekly, and it died in the hands of a receiver, Sheriff George H. Rose, on July 11, 1925.

The Silver State: (Sep 10 1874–Jul 11 1925)
  C — Jl 3–7 1876; O 31 1877; F 4 1879

CU-BANC — S 10 1874–Jl 28 1882; Je 29 1885; Ja 1 1886–D 31 1891
DLC — My 26 1877
NvHi — S 1–N 23 1892; D 9 1898; Mr–S 23 1899; S 7 1907–25
NvU — [F 1875–Jl 11 1925]
NvWH — 1876–1925
film — [S 10 1874–Jl 11 1925]
Ref: files; Angel 303; Doten 2249

Humboldt Mail

During the election campaign in August of 1886, John Church started the *Humboldt Mail* at Winnemucca. It probably suspended right after the election.

Humboldt Mail: (Aug 1886–1886)
  No issues located.
Ref: RG Ag 6 1886

People's Advocate

On May 17, 1898, David S. Truman, an attorney at Winnemucca, issued the first number of the *People's Advocate,* principally to support his campaign for Nevada's seat in Congress. Truman was sole editor and proprietor. He issued the paper daily, except Monday, as a four-page, five-column, 12 by 18-inch sheet, selling for $6 a year. Winnemucca was unable to support two dailies, however, and on August 19 of the same year the *Advocate* was reduced to a semiweekly, at $4 a year. Truman became discouraged with the prospects of his venture after losing the election, and on March 3, 1899, he leased the establishment to M. S. Riddle and Sons. When they failed to live up to the lease, Truman attached the plant, and on April 28, 1899, the *People's Advocate* suspended publication.

People's Advocate: (May 17 1898–Apr 28 1899)
  NvMus — [My 17 1898–Ap 18 1899]
  NvU — [My 19 1898–Ap 28 1899]
  film — [My 17 1898–Ap 28 1899]
Ref: files; RG Ap 28 1898, Mr 9 1899

The Nevada Magazine

The *Nevada Magazine* was an interesting journal begun at Winnemucca in August of 1899, by Van Duzer and Haley. Clarence D. Van Duzer, a recent graduate of the University of Nevada and the Golconda *News,* was editor, residing in Winnemucca. James F. Haley acted as business manager, with offices in Reno. The *Nevada Magazine* was a 5½ by 9-inch monthly of about a hundred pages, selling for 15¢ an issue or $1.25 a year. It proclaimed itself a "monthly magazine devoted to literature, current events, and the best interests of the state of Nevada." The magazine was well written and contained many contributions from early Nevada journalists and pioneers. Unfortunately, it was not a financial success and was forced to suspend with the sixth number, in January of 1900.

The Nevada Magazine: (Aug 1899–Jan 1900)
   pvt — S–O, D 1899
   CSmH — Ag–D 1899
   DLC — Ag–D 1899
   Nv — Ag–S, N–D 1899
   NvHi — Ag 1899–Ja 1900
   NvU — Ag–D 1899
Ref: files

Nevada News

In July of 1900, George B. Russell suspended the *News* at Golconda. Six weeks later, on August 23, 1900, in partnership with Merchant S. Riddle of the late *People's Advocate,* he revived the paper at Winnemucca as the *Nevada News.* Within a month Riddle sold out, leaving Russell as sole editor and publisher. He issued the paper as an eight-page semiweekly, at $3 a year. Six months later Russell, too, gave up, finally suspending the *News* on March 4, 1901.

Nevada News: (Aug 23 1900–Mar 4 1901)
   NvHi — Ja 3–Mr 4 1901
   NvU — [Ag 23 1900–Mr 4 1901]
   film — [Ag 23 1900–Mr 4 1901]
Ref: files

Winnemucca Republican

(See Winnemucca, *The Silver State*)

Humboldt Standard

In December of 1902, R. E. L. Windle and A. L. Brackett, former lessees of the *Silver State,* purchased a printing plant in San Francisco. On February 16, 1903, they commenced a rival Democratic daily, the *Humboldt Standard.* Winnemucca was unable to support two papers, however, and the *Standard* was forced to suspend on September 28 of the same year.

Humboldt Standard: (Feb 16 1903–Sep 28 1903)
   NvU — [F 16–S 28 1903]
   film — [F 16–S 28 1903]
Ref: files; NSJ D 19 1902; WD N 25 1902, F 23 1903

Humboldt Star

On January 11, 1906, three years after their first attempt to break the *Silver State's* monopoly, R. E. L. Windle and A. L. Brackett joined with a new partner, George M. Rose, to found the *Humboldt Star.* They were joint editors and publishers, issuing the paper as a Democratic weekly. Winnemucca was experiencing a new boom and the *Star* prospered. By 1907 it had become a triweekly. Rose eventually retired on December 9, 1912, but Windle and Brackett continued for another decade. Ill health forced

Windle to quit on June 7, 1922, and he sold his interest in the paper to Rollin Charles Stitser. Brackett and Stitser hired W. C. Black as editor. Brackett retired soon after and Stitser became sole proprietor on July 18, 1923. The *Star* remained in his family for nearly forty years.

When the rival *Silver State* folded, Stitser bought the paper and combined it with his own as the daily *Humboldt Star and Silver State* on August 1, 1925. The name was eventually trimmed back to the *Humboldt Star* about 1950. Stanley Bailey served as editor from July 6, 1923, to September 12, 1933. He was followed by Warren L. Moore, who was succeeded in turn by Marion Eakes. After Stitser's death on January 29, 1939, his wife, Avery, took over as publisher and hired Horace Smith as editor. He quit on July 16, 1942, and a series of editors followed rapidly: Pierce Egan, Robert H. Trego, Ernest T. Spencer, Maurya Wogan, William Friel, Jack Fleming, William Henley, Jr., A. E. Gerber, Winthrop Bowles, Robert J. Craigue, and Arthur J. Welter.

Finally, Peter R. Jenkins took the post about 1954. He remained until Mrs. Stitser sold the *Star* to Donald Reynolds in October of 1960, and Ken Hanson became editor. In the face of competition from the new *Humboldt Bulletin,* the *Star* was merged in November, 1962, with the *Battle Mountain Scout,* to form the *Humboldt Star and Battle Mountain Scout.* (See Winnemucca, *Humboldt Star and Battle Mountain Scout.*)

Humboldt Star: (Jan 11 1906–Nov 1962)
   pub — Ja 11 1906–N 1962
   CHi — My 13 1914; Mr 1, 10 1915; F 14, 28 1916
   NvHi — My 10 1906; F 1 1907; [F 3 1908–57]
   NvU — Je 7 1907–N 1962
   film — Ja 11 1906–N 1962
Ref: files

Silver State News

(See Winnemucca, *The Silver State*)

Humboldt Bulletin

On September 14, 1961, Peter R. Jenkins, former editor of the *Humboldt Star,* joined with Clayton Darrah to start a rival paper, the *Humboldt Bulletin.* Darrah was publisher and Jenkins editor, but the latter was soon hired back on the *Star* after its merger with the *Battle Mountain Scout.* Darrah, thus left as sole editor and publisher, carried on an aggressive battle for patronage with the *Star* for several years before he finally won in 1967. Two years later, when the Virginia City *Territorial Enterprise* succumbed, Darrah couldn't resist the opportunity to adopt the name, so he renamed his *Bulletin* the *Territorial Enterprise* on April 2, 1969. His infatuation with the name lasted less than a year, however, and he rechristened the paper the *Bulletin* on February 18, 1970. It died on May 3, 1972. (See Winnemucca, *Territorial Enterprise.*)

Humboldt Bulletin: (Sep 14 1961–Mar 26 1969; Feb 18 1970–May 3 1972)
  film — [S 14 1961–My 3 1972]
Ref: files

Humboldt Star and Battle Mountain Scout

Early in November of 1962, facing stiff competition from the *Humboldt Bulletin,* the Winnemucca *Humboldt Star* and the *Battle Mountain Scout* were merged under the cumbersome title of the *Humboldt Star and Battle Mountain Scout.* It was originally published weekly by the Southwest Publishing Company, with Stuart Robertson as editor. Glenn E. Maley became publisher the following year and hired Peter R. Jenkins away from the *Bulletin* as editor. Maley lasted only three months, selling in August, 1963, to Robert A. Davis. With Larry Hiatt as co-publisher, Davis lasted through February, 1965, when it was sold to William Fagan. Fagan was replaced that same year by Norman H. and Mary E. Butler. Fagan remained as editor for a short time, and was followed by Marian Rogan. The combined populations of Winnemucca and Battle Mountain couldn't support two papers, however, so Clayton Darrah of the *Humboldt Bulletin* bought the *Humboldt Star and Battle Mountain Scout* and suspended publication on October 6, 1967.

Humboldt Star and Battle Mountain Scout: (Nov 1962–Oct 6 1967)
  NvU — [1962–4]
  film — N 1962–O 6 1967
Ref: files

Nevada Mining Record

In February, 1966, Clayton Darrah of the *Humboldt Bulletin* launched the monthly *Nevada Mining Record,* with Robert H. Trego as editor, "in the belief that the newspaper will fill a need of the resurgent mining industry in this state." It didn't.

Nevada Mining Record: (Feb 1966–c. Mar 1966)
  Nv — F–Mr 1966
  NvU — F 1966
  film — F–Mr 1966
Ref: files

Territorial Enterprise

When the Virginia City *Territorial Enterprise* stopped publishing for the last time, on March 28, 1969, Clayton Darrah of the Winnemucca *Humboldt Bulletin* promptly adopted the time-honored name, bringing out his paper under the new banner of the *Territorial Enterprise* on April 2, 1969. In less than a year he had a change of heart, and on February 11, 1970, he issued his last *Enterprise,* to resume the *Bulletin* the following week. (See Winnemucca, *Humboldt Bulletin.*)

Territorial Enterprise: (Apr 2 1969–Feb 11 1970)
  film — Ap 2 1969–F 11 1970
Ref: files

Humboldt Sun

The weekly *Humboldt Sun* was begun at Winnemucca on January 19, 1972, by Cal Sunderland, with Mike Sunderland as editor. It was purchased in February, 1978, by Mark and June McMahon, who published it in 1979, with Chet Dinnell as editor and manager.

Humboldt Sun: (Jan 19 1972+)
  film—Ja 1972+
Ref: files

Winni Minimart

The *Winni Minimart,* a free weekly advertiser, was started about August 2, 1977, by Mark Keyser-Cooper of the Battle Mountain *Bugle.* It was put together in Battle Mountain and printed in Elko.

Winni Minimart: (Aug 2 1977+)
  NvHi–Ja 4 1978+
Ref: files

⁓{ WONDER }⁓

Wonder Mining News

The rich lodes at Wonder were discovered on April 7, 1906, and, in keeping with its name, a bustling camp stood on the site only four months later. On August 11, 1906, only four months and four days after the discovery, the *Wonder Mining News* made its debut. Clyde C. Emerson of the neighboring *Fairview News* was half owner of the Wonder Mining News Company, which listed as its president J. Herbert Welch. The *News* was published every Saturday, as a four-page, six-column weekly, at $5 a year. Despite its quick boom, Wonder was destined to prosper for a number of years, producing nearly six million dollars. The *Wonder Mining News* shared this prosperity.

    On November 29, 1906, Emerson sold his interest in the paper to Welch, and on January 2, 1909, Welch leased it to Fred W. Kettle and W. W. Ellis. But editor Ellis soon had to remind his patrons: "The mountain scenery is awe-inspiring, you may drink it in, and it will nourish your soul. But you cannot eat it; it will do little good for your stomach. We therefore, ask you, friends, brothers, fellow countrymen, to come through with the money for your subscriptions. . . . Would you have us toying for nourishment with the fibrous sagebrush?" They came through as best they could, but Fred Kettle had had enough. He departed for California on August 21, leaving Ellis sole editor and proprietor. He guided the paper through its waning years to its final suspension on November 18, 1912. The camp, however, had lived up to its name, surprising many who had expected it to be dead within six months.

Wonder Mining News: (Aug 11 1906–Nov 18 1912)
   NvHi — Ag 11, S 22 1906; Ja 25 1908–N 18 1912
   NvU — [D 28 1907–N 18 1912]
   film — [Ag 11 1906–N 18 1912]
Ref: files; FN D 1 1906

Wonder Miner

The *Wonder Miner* was a short-lived venture begun on March 7, 1907, by John L. Emerson. The printing plant had been shipped to Wonder the previous September by the deadbeat publisher of the *Fairview Miner,* E. B. Clark. But Clark skipped out, leaving it to his creditors, and they leased it to Emerson.

Wonder Miner: (Mar 7 1907–c. 1907)
   No issues located.
Ref: FN O 13 1906, Mr 2 1907; Polk 1907–8

American Enterprise

In 1908, the weekly *American Enterprise* briefly sought a share of Wonder's patronage, apparently heedless of the *Mining News'* difficulty in finding sustenance.

American Enterprise: (c. 1908)
   No issues located.
Ref: Folkes 16

YERINGTON (GREENFIELD)

Mason Valley Tidings

Following his suspension of the *Chloride Belt* at Candelaria, D. L. Sayre removed the press and material to the farming community of Greenfield. Here, on March 25, 1893, he commenced publication of the *Mason Valley Tidings.* The paper was issued every Saturday, as a four-page, six-column weekly, at an annual subscription price of $3. In early April of 1894, the citizens of Greenfield elected to rename the town Yerington, and on April 5, Sayre changed the dateline of his paper. Eventually, Sayre became discouraged with the slow growth of farming communities, and on November 29, 1894, he suspended the *Tidings.* Within a few months, Charles Patterson purchased the material to found the *Yerington Rustler* on February 28, 1895.

Mason Valley Tidings: (Mar 25 1893–Nov 29 1894)
   NvHi — O 11 1894
   NvU — [Mr 25 1893–N 29 1894]
   film — [Mr 25 1893–N 29 1894]
Ref: files

Yerington Rustler

Shortly after the suspension of the *Mason Valley Tidings* at Yerington,

Charles W. Patterson purchased the plant. On February 28, 1895, he issued the first number of the *Yerington Rustler*. Patterson was sole editor and proprietor, and published the paper as a four-page, six-column weekly. He temporarily suspended the paper during the summer of 1898, while he joined the Klondike rush and he revived it on his return in September. Shortly thereafter he was taken ill, and in February his wife assumed the management of the paper. She ran it for over a year until he recovered and resumed his duties on April 27, 1900. Within a month, however, on May 25, 1900, Patterson suspended the *Rustler* and moved the plant to Lovelock, where he started the *Argus*.

Yerington Rustler: (Feb 28 1895–May 25 1900)
   Nv — F 28 1895–Ap 28, N 26 1898–My 25 1900
   NvHi — N 21 1895
   film — [F 28 1895–My 25 1900]
Ref: files; SS S 5 1898

Lyon County Monitor

On June 8, 1900, J. B. Gallagher commenced the first number of the *Lyon County Monitor,* within weeks of the demise of the *Rustler*. Gallagher was proprietor of the Monitor Publishing Company, which issued the paper every Wednesday, as an independent weekly, with Ed Patterson as editor. In September of 1901, F. W. Fairbanks moved the old *Lyon County Times* to Yerington, and by the following March 7, the competition forced the suspension of the *Monitor*.

Lyon County Monitor: (Jun 8 1900–Mar 7 1902)
   NvU — Je 8 1900–Mr 7 1902
   film — Je 8 1900–Mr 7 1902
Ref: files

Yerington Times (Lyon County Times)

In July of 1901, Fred W. Fairbanks suspended the *Lyon County Times* at Dayton and removed the plant to Yerington, where he revived the paper under the same name on August 10. Fairbanks continued as sole editor and proprietor until August 24, 1907, when R. Leslie Smaill purchased the paper. He changed its name to the *Yerington Times* on September 21. Within the next few years the management passed in succession to A. B. Gray on May 23, to D. H. Dickason on September 5, to the Times Printing Company on July 31, 1909, and then to James F. O'Brien, founder of the *Goldfield News,* on May 7, 1910.

F. W. Fairbanks finally took over the paper again on April 1, 1911, but sold it on July 3, 1915, to Warren Hauser and Stanley Netherton. R. L. Waggoner bought Hauser's interest on May 19, 1917, and Netherton's on October 26, 1918. He, in turn, was bought out on August 16, 1919, by J. A. McCarthy, who at last brought stability to the paper. McCarthy ran the *Times* uninterrupted for over a decade, until its suspension on January 22,

1932, when he sold the plant to Frank S. Cox and Son of the *Mason Valley News.*

Yerington Times (Lyon County Times): (Aug 10 1901–Jan 22 1932)
   NvHi — [1901–31]
   NvU — [S 1901–D 1931]
   film — [Ag 10 1901–D 23 1931]
Ref: files

Lyon County Wasp

Charles E. Gardner commenced the *Wasp* at Yerington on September 3, 1912, during the election campaign. Gardner was the sole editor and publisher, issuing the paper every Thursday, as a four-page, four-column weekly, for $3 a year. The paper attempted to continue after the campaign but finally succumbed on February 27, 1913.

Lyon County Wasp: (Sep 3 1912–Feb 27 1913)
   NvHi — S 3 1912–F 27 1913
   NvU — S 3 1912–F 27 1913
   film — S 3 1912–F 27 1913
Ref: files

Mason Valley News

In November of 1914, Clyde C. Emerson moved his weekly *Mason Valley News* plant from Mason to Yerington, where he resumed publication on December 11, 1914. Emerson retired from the *News* five years later, leasing the paper to Wharton and McNeary on September 13, 1919, and then selling it three weeks later to Wharton and Cox. Frank S. Cox and his son, Walter J., bought out Wharton on January 19, 1924, and Walter became sole editor and publisher on July 24, 1936. He sold a half interest to Jack Carpenter on January 17, 1947. Fifteen years later, Robert Sanford bought Carpenter's interest, and in 1972, he became sole editor and publisher.

Mason Valley News: (Dec 11, 1914+)
   pub — D 11 1914+
   CHi — F 5 1915
   NvHi — [D 11 1914+]
   NvU — [Ag 1928+]
   film — [D 11 1914+]
Ref: files

Numu Ya Dua' (Numa Ya' – Dua')

The Yerington Paiute Tribe issued an illustrated biweekly newspaper, *Numa Ya'-Dua,* from about February of 1973, until about 1976. On September 14, 1979, they revived it as the weekly *Numu Ya Dua',* with John Kite Tieben as editor. It is printed by the *Lahontan Valley News* of Fallon.

Numu Ya Dua': (c. Feb 1973–c. 1976; Sep 14 1979+)
   NvHi — D 5 1975–Je 25 1976; S 14 1979+
   NvU — D 19 1975–Je 11 1976; S 14 1979+
Ref: files

The Border Newspapers

In addition to those papers published within the boundaries of the state of Nevada, a number of the papers published in neighboring states also devoted a portion of their coverage to the events of Nevada. This was particularly true at Placerville, California, where in the days prior to the establishment of the press in Nevada, the Placerville papers were almost the sole public voice for the settlers in western Utah. As mining developed in Nevada, parallel developments took place just across its borders in eastern California, southeastern Oregon, Idaho, Utah, and Arizona. The geographical and economic ties between these regions were reflected in the overlapping coverage of their newspapers. Sometimes these ties were more than casual. When the *Inyo Independent* was established in Inyo County, California, its editors specifically dedicated its coverage and support to the events and interests of both Inyo and Mono counties in California and Esmeralda County in Nevada.

To provide supplementary information on Nevada source material, this appendix lists those newspapers published prior to 1950 in some of the nearest of the bordering towns. Only the name, frequency, period of publication, and holdings are given here. Frequency is indicated by bm–bimonthly, bw-biweekly, d-daily, irr-irregular, m-monthly, q-quarterly, sm-semimonthly, sw-semiweekly, tw–triweekly, and w–weekly. For more detailed information the reader should consult the following press histories:

ARIZONA

"Newspapers and Periodicals of Arizona, 1859–1911," by Estelle Lutrell, *University of Arizona Bulletin*, vol. XX no. 3, July, 1949.

CALIFORNIA

"Southern California Newspapers, 1851–1876," by Muir Dawson, *Quar- terly of the Historical Society of Southern California*, March and June, 1950.

California Mining Town Newspapers, 1850–1880, a bibliography compiled by Helen S. Giffen, J. E. Reynolds, Van Nuys, 1954.

A History of California Newspapers, 1846–1858 by Edward C. Kemble. Reprinted From the Supplement to the Sacramento Union of December 25, 1858. Edited by Helen H. Bretnor. Los Gatos: Talisman Press, 1962.

OREGON

History of Oregon Newspapers, by George S. Turnbull, Binfords & Mort, Portland, 1939.

UTAH

Early Utah Journalism, by J. Cecil Alter, Utah State Historical Society, Salt Lake City, 1938.

Aside from geographical proximity, some papers and journals published at great distance from Nevada, but still sharing a proximity of interest, also gave good coverage to Nevada affairs. This was true of the San Francisco, Sacramento, Los Angeles, and San Bernardino papers, as well as those of Bakersfield, Havilah, Visalia, Downieville, and Quincy. Much valuable information on Nevada can also be found in the mining journals, such as the San Francisco *Mining & Scientific Press,* the Salt Lake *Mining Review,* and the Chicago *Mining & Engineering World;* in financial sheets, such as the Philadelphia *Profits* and the Colorado Springs *Mining Investor;* or in the Western Federation of Miners' journal, the Denver *Miner's Magazine,* or in such political papers as the *Silver Knight,* published at Washington, D.C., by Nevada Senator William Stewart. Further interesting items can be found in various magazines, of which the *Arrowhead Magazine,* published by the San Pedro, Los Angeles and Salt Lake Railroad, and *Desert Magazine,* published at Palm Desert, are good examples.

ARIZONA

MOHAVE COUNTY

CHLORIDE

Arizona Arrow, w (1901–1902)
  (moved from Kingman)
  AzTP — Jl 1902
Arizona Standard, w (Sep 1910–?)
  No issues located.
Chloride Herald, w (1916–Dec 6 1917)
  Az — D 1916–D 6 1917
Chloride Mining Review, w (1917–Apr 1917)
  (merged with the *Chloride Herald*)
  No issues located.

KINGMAN

Wallapai Tribune, w (1885–1887)
  No issues located.
Mohave County Miner, w (Jan 23 1887+)
  (moved from Mineral Park)
  Az — Ja 1897+
  AzTP — Ja 1887–8; Ap 27 1889–[92]–96; My 1929+
  AzU — N 1919–N 16 1923
  CU-BANC — [1888]–Je 1890
Mohave Daily Miner, d (Mar 1 1916–c. Aug 10 1917)
  Az — Mr 8 1916–Ag 10 1917

Our Mineral Wealth, w (1893–1919)
   (merged with *Mohave County Miner*)
   Az — S 4 1903–Ap 22 1904; Jl–D 1915
Arizona Educator, m (Oct 1897–c. 1898)
   (moved to Jerome)
   CLSM — O, D 1897
Arizona Arrow, w (1901)
   (moved to Chloride)
   No issues located.

MINERAL PARK
Wallapai Enterprise, w (Jun 1 1876–1876)
   AzTP — Je 1 1876
Mohave County Record, w (Mar 1880–?)
   No issues located.
Alta Arizona, w (Oct 15 1881–Aug 5 1882)
   AzTP — O 15 1881–Ag 5 1882
Mohave County Miner, w (Nov 1882–Jan 16 1887)
   (moved to Kingman)
   AzTP — Ja 27 1884–Ja 16 1887

OATMAN
Oatman Miner, w (Oct 21 1915–Mar 1 1916)
   (name changed to *Oatman News*)
   Az — O 21 1915–Mr 1 1916
   MWA — D 23 1915
Oatman News, w (Mar 8 1916–1917)
   (name changed to *Oatman Mining News*)
   Az — Mr 8 1916–17
   MWA — Ap 12 1916
Oatman Mining News, w (1917–c. 1926)
   Az — 1917–21

CALIFORNIA

ALPINE COUNTY

MARKLEEVILLE
Alpine Chronicle, w, d (Apr 23 1864–Aug 1867)
   (moved to Silver Mountain)
   pvt — Ap 23 1864; N 18 1865
   CU-BANC — Je 16 [O 13 1866–Ag 1867]
Alpine Signal, w (Jul 3 1878–c. Aug 22 1879)
   pvt — F 26 1879
   CU-BANC — [Jl 17–D 1878]–Ja 1, 15–Ag 22 1879
Alpine Argus, w (Jun 13 1884–Dec 25 1886)
   (moved from Monitor)
   pvt — My 22, D 25 1886
   CMrC — Je 13 1884–D 25 1886

MONITOR

Monitor Gazette, w (Jun 4 1864–May 26 1866)
 (followed by *Alpine Miner*)
 pvt — Ja 21, Mr 11 1865
 CMrC — Mr 18 1865
 CU-BANC — Je 4 1864–My 26 1866

Alpine Miner, w (Jun 2 1866–c. 1875)
 (follows *Monitor Gazette*)
 pvt — O 20 1866; Ja 12, Mr 16, My 25, Je 29 1867; Ja 11, Je 27, O 31 1868; Ja 2, F 20 1869
 CLU — O 22 1870
 CMrC — N 17 1866; My 30 1868
 CP — Je 27 1868
 CSmH — Ap 22, 1865; O 20 1866 [F 9–O 19 1867; Ja–N 1868] Ja 16 1869
 CU-BANC — Je 2 1866–D 1873; My 2–Jl 4, S 19 1874

Monitor Argus, w (Sep 15 1879–Jun 6 1884)
 (moved to Markleeville)
 pvt — N 29 1880; Jl 11 1881; Ja 30 1882; My 18, Ag 10, O 26 1883; Ja 4 1884
 CMrC — Mr 1 1880–Je 6 1884

SILVER MOUNTAIN

Silver Mountain Bulletin, w (Apr 30 1864–Nov 1864; May 6 1865–1867)
 CU-BANC — O 13, D 22 1866; Ja–My 18 1867

Alpine Chronicle, w (Sep 1867–Nov 23 1878)
 (moved from Markleeville in Aug 1867 and moved to Bodie, Mono County, in Nov 1878 as *Mono-Alpine Chronicle*)
 pvt — S 25 1875; Ag 11 1877
 C — O 24 1868; Ap 23 1870–D 21 1872
 CU-BANC — [S–D 1867]–Ag 7, S 25, O 1875–Ja 1, 15, F 5–Ap 8, 29, My 6, 20 1876–Ja 1877; Ja–O 19 1878

Silver Miner, w (Apr 25 1868–Jun 20 1868)
 CSmH — Je 20 1868

ELDORADO COUNTY

PLACERVILLE (to c. 1870)

El Dorado News, w (Dec 6 1851–Jun 3 1853)
 (moved from Coloma, name changed to *El Dorado Republican*)
 MWA — F 19–26, Mr 12, 26, My 21 1853

Placerville Appeal, w (Mar 3 1853–May 12 1853)
 No issues located.

Placerville Herald, w (Apr 30 1853–Nov 5 1853)
 C — Ap 30–N 5 1853
 MWA — My 21, Je 25, Ag 6–13 1853

El Dorado Republican, w (Jun 11 1853–Feb 17 1854)
 (merged with *Mountain Democrat*)
 MWA — Ag 6 1853

Mountain Democrat, sw, w (Feb 17 1854+)
 (sw Ag 22–D 29 1860)
 pub — 1861–[65–80]81+
 C — F 25 1854–68; Ap 30 1870–S 6 1884; Ja 25 1890–1900 [1904–36, 48–58]
 CL — Ja 6 1928
 CSmH — Ja 6 1928

CU-BANC — 1864–Je 1880; 1886–F 1, N 1 1890; Mr 3 1923; F 6 1925; Ag 3 1934
DLC — Ja 3 1857; Ap 27 1861; D 17 1864
P — My 27 1854

Placerville American, w (Jul 6 1855–Nov 1859)
NHi — F 2, Jl 19 1856

El Dorado County Times, w (Sep 1856–Nov 1856)
No issues located.

Empire County Argus, w (Aug 13 1857–Oct 1857)
(moved from Coloma; name changed to *Tri-Weekly Argus*)
No issues located.

Tri-Weekly Argus, tw (Oct 1857–Feb 6 1858)
(followed by *Tri-Weekly Index*)
No issues located.

El Dorado Republican, w (Aug 1857–Sep 1857)
No issues located.

Tri-Weekly Index, tw (Feb 13 1858–Jun 3 1858)
(followed by *Tri-Weekly Register*)
No issues located.

Tri-Weekly Register, tw (Jun 8 1858–Sep 1858)
No issues located.

Semi-Weekly Observer, sw (Feb 2 1859–Feb 4 1860)
No issues located.

Central Californian, sw (Aug 1860–c. 1860)
No issues located.

El Dorado Union, w, d (Jun 28 1861–Jul 20 1861)
No issues located.

Placerville News, w, tw, d (Aug 14 1861–Jan 5 1865)
CSmH — My 21–N 24 1864
CU-BANC — Ja 6 1865

Weekly Mirror, w (Jun 3 1865–1866)
CU-BANC — Jl 29 1865–Mr 10 1866
MWA — Ja 27 1866

Weekly Recorder, w (Aug 9 1865–c.Sep 26 1866)
CU-BANC — O 18 1865, Ag 1, 15–S 26 1886

Placerville Courier, w (Jun 9 1866–1867)
CU-BANC — Jl 28, O 13 1866–Ag 31 1867

El Dorado Republican, w (Jun 22 1871–1924)
C — 1901–23
CU-BANC — Je 27, Ag 3–10, 24, S 5–14, 28 1871–8; Mr–Jl 24, Ag 7, 21–O 16, 30 1879–80; Je 13, Jl 25, Ag 1 1889(90–1) S 19–O, N 14–21, D 5–12 1907

TAHOE VALLEY (AL TAHOE)

Lake Tahoe News, w (1947+)
C — 1961+

INYO COUNTY

BEND CITY

Owens River Herald, sm (c. Jun 15 1864–1864)
No issues located.

BIG PINE

Owens Valley Herald, w (Aug 28 1908–c. 1913)
  (published concurrently at Bishop)
  (See Bishop, *Owens Valley Herald*)

Big Pine Citizen, w (Dec 11 1913–Jun 24 1933)
  (merged with Lone Pine *Owens Valley Progress* to form Lone Pine *Owens Valley Progress-Citizen*)
  CI — [1914–5]–[29]–[33]
  CLU — Jl 11 1914–D 26 1931

BISHOP

Bishop Creek Times, w (Oct 29 1881–Jun 3 1882)
  pvt — F 25 1882
  CSmH — N 12 1881–Je 3 1882
  CU-BANC — O 29 1881–Je 3 1882

Inyo Register, w (Apr 4 1885+)
  pub — 1885+
  C — S 23 1909+
  CInI — [1914–5+]
  CLCM — [1891–1904]
  CSmH — [Ap 4 1885–D 27 1923]
  CU-BANC — F 28–Mr 14, Ag 29, S 12, O 31–N 14 1889; O 2 1890; Jl 22–D 23 1909; Ja–Jl 7 1910; Je–S 12 1912
  NvU — 1946–58

Inyo Index, w (1896)
  (moved from Independence)
  No issues located.

Inyo Magazine, sm (Jul 1908–Dec 1908)
  (name changed to *Sierra Magazine*)
  CIE — Jl–D 1908
  CU — Jl–D 1908

Owens Valley Herald, w, sw (Aug 28 1908–Dec 27 1927)
  (published concurrently at Big Pine)
  CI — [1914–5]–[19–20]–[23–4]–[27]
  CLU — S 12 1908–D 29 1911; N 1 1912–D 27 1927
  CU-BANC — Ap 16, 30–My 21, Je 4–11 1909

Sierra Magazine, m (Jan 1909–Feb 1909)
  (follows *Inyo Magazine*)
  CIE — Ja–F 1909
  CU — Ja–F 1909

CERRO GORDO

Bugle of Freedom, irr (Aug 20 1870–c. Aug 1870)
  No issues located.

DARWIN

Coso Mining News, w (Nov 6 1875–Sep 14 1878)
  CBiI — Mr 18, Ap 22, My 6 1876; F 24, Mr 24, Ap 21, My 26, Je 16, Ag 4, 18, S 8–15, N 10 1877
  CIE — Mr 31 1877 CSmH — [Mr 1876–N1877]
  CSmH — [Mr 1876–N 1877]
  CU-BANC — N 6–13 1875
  MWA — My 27–Je 3 1876

GREENWATER

Greenwater Times, w (Oct 23 1906–Jun 1908)
 NvHi — O 23, N 6 1906
Greenwater Miner, w (Dec 1906–Aug 1907)
 No issues located.
Death Valley Chuck-Walla, sm (Jan 1 1907–Jun 1907)
 pvt — My 15 1907
 CSmH — Ap 1 1907
 CU-BANC — Ja 1–Je 1907

INDEPENDENCE

Inyo Independent, w (Jul 9 1870+)
 C — Jl 9 1870–Je 14 1884; 1901+
 CInI — [1870–1916]17+
 CLCM — [1889–1900]
 CLU — [Jl 9 1870–N 26 1932]
 CU-BANC — Jl 16–N 21, D 26 1870; F 18 1871–Mr, My 20, Je 10, Jl 29, 1882;
  My 3 1884[87]–Jl, O 13 1888–[90]91; Jl 16 1909–Jl 22 1910; Je–S 13 1912;
  Ja 20 1923–Ja 1933
Inyo Lancet, w (Aug 19 1871–Sep 2 1871)
 CBiI — Ag 19–S 2 1871
The Medley, m (Feb 1874–c. 1874)
 No issues located.
Juvenile Weekly, w (Apr 1876–Jul 1876)
 No issues located.
Tarantula, w (Aug 12 1876–c. 1877; Apr 27 1878–Sep 14 1878)
 (follows *Juvenile Weekly;* suspended c. 1877 to Apr 1878)
 CBiI — O 21 1876
 CIE — F 24 1877
Owens Valley News-Letter, w (Jul 9 1881–Oct 29 1881)
 CBiI — Jl 9–O 29 1881
Inyo Index, w (Jul 27 1887–1896)
 (moved to Bishop)
 pvt — D 14 1887
 C — 1891–3
Eastern Californian, w (May 7 1910–c. Jun 1910)
 CIE — My 7–Je 18 1910

KEELER

Keeler Post, w (Feb 7 1909–c. Jul 1909)
 No issues located.

LEADFIELD

Leadfield Chronicle, w (Mar 1926)
 No issues located.

LEE

Lee Herald, w (Oct 15 1907–Feb 1908)
 No issues located.

LONE PINE

The Sorehead, w (Jul 23 1871–c. 1871)
 No issues located.

Mount Whitney Observer, w (1924–Dec 25 1931)
  CInI — [1924–6]
Owens Valley Progress, w (1932–Aug 24 1933)
  (merged with *Big Pine Citizen* to form Lone Pine, *Owens Valley Progress-Citizen*)
  CInI — 1932–Ag 24 1933
Owens Valley Progress-Citizen, w (Aug 31 1933+)
  CInI — Ag 31 1933+
Inyo Trails, q (Winter 1933–Spring 1934)
  DLC — 1933–4

MANZANAR
Manzanar Free Press, sw, tw (Apr 8 1942–Oct 19 1945)
  C — Ap–Jl 1942
  CIE — [Ap 11–Ag 12 1942] Mr 20 1943
  CLU — Ap 11 1942–O 19 1945
  DLC — Je 1942–S 1945
Manzanar Sentry, bm (May 18 1942–c. Jun 16 1942)
  CIE — My 18–Je 16 1942

PANAMINT
Panamint News, tw, w (Nov 26 1874–Oct 21 1875)
  (moved to Darwin as *Coso Mining News*)
  (tw — N 26 1874–Jl 8 1875)
  pvt — N 26 1874
  CBiI — N 28–D 1 1874; My 18 1875
  CU-BANC — F 23–Mr 9, 13, 18–23, 27, Ap 24, O 21 1875

POLETA
Weekly Horned Toad, w (c. 1890)
  CIE — Ap 25 1890

SKIDOO
Skidoo News, w (Dec 21 1906–Aug 1908)
  pvt — D 28 1906; Ap 25 1908
  CIE — Ja 25 1907; Ap 25 1908

KERN COUNTY

BORON
Enterprise, w (1950+)
  pub — 1950+
  CBak — 1954+

GARLOCK
Garlock News, w (c. Jan 1898–1898)
  No issues located.

JOHANNESBURG
California Rand, w (c. Feb 18 1898–c. 1898)
  No issues located.

MOJAVE
Mojave Tomahawk, w (Jan 1901–Jul 1901)
  (moved to Tehachapi)
  pvt — Ja–Jl 1901

Mojave Press, w (Aug 14 1914–1919)
   CB — 1914–Mr 21 1919
   CTeN — O 12 1917–S 1918
Mojave Record, w (May 23 1924–Jun 14 1929)
   (merged with *Randsburg Times* to form *Mojave-Randsburg Record-Times*)
   C — My 23 1924–Je 14 1929
   CB — F 1927–Je 14 1929
   CTeN — My 23 1924–Je 14 1929
Mojave-Randsburg Record-Times, w (Jun 21 1929–Dec 29 1932)
   (Je 21–S 18 1929 as *Mojave Record-Times*; merged with *Tehachapi News* to form *Techachapi News & Mojave-Randsburg Record-Times*)
   C — Je 21 1929–D 29 1932
   CBaK — Je 21 1929–D 29 1932
   CTeN — Je 21 1929–D 29 1932
Mojave Record, w (1937–c. 1952)
   No issues located.
Desert News, w (1938+)
   pub — 1938+
   CBak — 1954+

RANDSBURG

Randsburg Miner, w (1896–1916)
   (name changed to *Golden State Miner*)
   CBaK — Ap 28 1900–7; F 1912–5
Golden State Miner, w (1917–1918)
   (moved to Wickenburg, Arizona, as *Arizona State Miner*)
   No issues located.
Rand District News, w (Jun 7 1922–c. 1922)
   pvt — Je 14 1922
Southwest Mining Review, w (c. Mar 1923–c. 1923)
   No issues located
Randsburg Times, w (May 23 1924–May 24 1929)
   (merged with *Mojave Record* to form *Mojave-Randsburg Record-Times*)
   CBaK — 1925–7
   CTeN — My 23 1924–My 24 1929
Randsburg Times, w (1937–1951)
   (merged with Ridgecrest *Herald* to form *Times-Herald*)
   CU — 1946–50

RIDGECREST

Herald, w (1945–1951)
   (merged with *Randsburg Times* to form *Times-Herald*)
   pub — 1945–51

TRONA

Argonaut, w (1923–c. 1954)
   (bought by the San Bernardino *Sun*)
   No issues located.

LASSEN COUNTY

AMEDEE

Amedee Geyser, w (Mar 30 1892–c. 1893)
   pvt — Je 7 1893

BIEBER

Mountain Tribune, w (May 6 1881–Dec 31 1892)
  C — My 6 1881–D 31 1892
  CU-BANC — [1888]–Je 1889; Ja–F, Je 12–S, O 18, N 8 [D 1890–D 8 1891] Jl 23 1892

Big Valley Gazette, w (Jun 29 1893–1949)
  (merged with the Adin [Modoc Co.] *Argus* to form the Bieber *Argus-Gazette*)
  C — Je 29 1893–1949
  CSuLas — 1922–49

Northwestern News, w (Oct 15 1931–c. 1937)
  C — O 15 1931–7

Argus-Gazette, w (1948–1956)
  C — 1948–56

HERLONG (SIERRA ORDNANCE DEPOT)

The Challenge, w (Apr 1 1943+)
  pub — Ap 1 1943+
  CU — My 1943–Ap 14 1944
  NvHi — Ap 1–My 7 1943

SUSANVILLE

Sage Brush, w (Jul 1 1865–Dec 21 1872)
  (after Sep 5 1868 as *Lassen Sage Brush;* name changed to *Lassen Advocate*)
  C — D 19 1868
  CU-BANC — F 22 1868–[69]–71; F 10–D 21 1872

Lassen Advocate, w (Jan 1 1873+)
  pub — Ja 1875+
  C — Ja 1909+
  CLU — Ap 24 1884; Jl 23 1885; Jl 18 1889
  CSuLas — 1873+
  CU — [1931–5] 43+
  CU-BANC — Ja 1 1873–D 1880; S 20 1883–[85–Ap 1886]–Ja 5, Jl 12–D 1888; Je 27 1889–[90]91; Je 18 1907–Jl 8 1910

Lassen County Journal, w (Oct 21 1874–c. Nov 1875)
  CU-BANC — F 4, Ag 5–O 14 1875

Lassen Mail, w (1885–1940)
  CSuLas — Ja 1916–40
  CU-BANC — F 23 1912–[14]–40

MODOC COUNTY

ADIN

Adin Hawkeye, w (Sep 1878–Nov 19 1880)
  CU-BANC — Ag 8 1879–N 19 1880

Adin Argus, w (Aug 1881–1949)
  (merged with the Bieber [Lassen Co.] *Big Valley Gazette* to form the Bieber *Argus-Gazette*)
  C — Ag 1887–98
  CAltu — 1882–1947
  CLU — F 28, N 7 1889
  CU-BANC — [1888]–[91–92]

ALTURAS (DORRIS' BRIDGE)

Modoc Independent, w (Nov 7 1874–Aug 28 1890)
  (name changed to *Weekly Modoc*)
  CU-BANC — Ag 14 1875–[76–80] Ag 31 1882; O 18 1883–Je 25, S 10 1885[88]–Ag 28 1890

New Era, w (Apr 7 1888–Aug 12 1925)
  (merged with *Chronicle* to form *New Era-Chronicle,* 1889–Jl 30 1915)
  C — F 8 1901–Ag 12 1925
  CAltu — [1889–1925]
  CU-BANC — Ag 31–S 14, O 26–D 7, 28 1889–F 1, Ag 23, O–N 1 1890

Chronicle, w (c. 1888–1889)
  (merged with *New Era*)
  No issues located.

Alturas Herald, w (Jun 3 1890–c. 1896)
  CU-BANC — Jl–D 1891

Weekly Modoc, w (Sep 4 1890–Jan 1 1891)
  (formerly *Modoc Independent;* merged with *New Era*)
  CU-BANC — S 4 1890–Ja 1 1891

Alturas Plaindealer, w (1895–Dec 26 1934)
  (merged with the *Modoc County Times* to form *Alturas Plaindealer and Modoc County Times*)
  C — S 19 1913–D 26 1934
  CAltu — 1906–D 26 1934

Modoc Republican, w (1904–Jul 30 1915)
  (merged with *New Era-Chronicle* to form *New Era*)
  C — 1913–N 20 1914
  CAltu — [1906–15]

Modoc County Times, w (1928–Dec 27 1934)
  (merged with *Alturas Plaindealer* to form *Alturas Plaindealer and Modoc County Times*)
  C — Mr 26 1931–D 27 1934
  CAltu — 1928–D 27 1934

Alturas Plaindealer and Modoc County Times, w (Jan 2 1935–1952)
  C — Ja 2 1935–52
  CAltu — Ja 2 1935–52
  CU — 1936–46

Modoc County Record, w (1937+)
  (moved from Cedarville; as *Modoc County Record and Surprise Valley Record* 1937–49)
  pub — 1937+
  CAltu — 1937+

CEDARVILLE

Surprise Valley Record, w (1892–1937)
  (moved to Alturas as *Modoc County Record*)
  CAltu — 1906–37

Surprise Valley Journal, w (1950+)
  pub — 1950+
  CAlta — [1952–8]

FORT BIDWELL

Bidwell Herald, w (Nov 1 1876–Aug 25 1877)
  CU-BANC — N 1 1876–Je 20, Ag 25 1877

Bidwell Gold Nugget w (1906–1912)
    CAltu– 1907–12
Fort Bidwell News, w (1912–1917
    CAltu — 1912–17

MONO COUNTY

AURORA (county seat of Mono County until September 1863)
  (See Aurora, Esmeralda County, Nevada)

BENTON

Mono Messenger, w (Feb 1 1879–Apr 19 1879)
    CU-BANC — F 1–Mr 22, Ap 5–19 1879
Tri-Weekly Letter, tw (Jun 7 1879–Jul 1879)
    CIE — Je 12 1879
    CSmH — Je 7, 24, 28–Jl 1 1879
Bentonian, tw, sw, w (Aug 14 1879–Feb 1881)
  (tw — Ag 14–c. S 4 1879; sw — c. O 16 1879–F 7 1880)
    CIE — Ag 19 1879; Ap 19 1880
    CU-BANC — Ag 16, 21 1879; Ja 22, F 14, 28, Ap 19–26, S 29 1880

BODIE

Bodie Weekly Standard, w (Oct 10 1877–Jul 17 1880)
  (merged with *Bodie Weekly News* to form *Bodie Weekly Standard-News*)
    CU-BANC — N 7–D 26 1877; Ja 2–Mr 13, Ap 3, 17–D 11, 25 1878; Ja 4, 18–Ap 5 1879
Bodie Tri-Weekly Standard, tw (May 7 1878–Dec 7 1878)
  (followed by *Bodie Daily Standard*)
    CU-BANC — Jl 9–11, S 21 1878
Bodie Daily Standard, d (Dec 10 1878–Jul 20 1880)
  (merged with *Bodie Morning News* to form *Bodie Standard-News*)
    CU-BANC — D 10–17, 21–30 1878 [Ja 20–F 27, Mr 14, My 24, Je 12 1879–Jl 20 1880]
Mono-Alpine Chronicle, w (Nov 30 1878–May 3 1879)
  (moved from Silver Mountain, Alpine County; name changed to *Bodie Chronicle*)
    CMrC — N 30, D 21 1878
    CU-BANC — D 1878; F 15–22, Mr 8, My 3 1879
Bodie Morning News, d (Mar 8 1879–Jul 20 1880)
  (merged with *Bodie Daily Standard* to form *Bodie Standard-News*)
    CLU — My 16, N 13 1879; Mr 3, Ag 17, N 18 1880
    CU-BANC — [Mr 14 1879–Jl 20 1880]
Bodie Chronicle, w, d (May 10 1879–Oct 23 1880)
  (d — F 1–O 23 1880)
  (merged with *Bridgeport Union* to form *Bridgeport Chronicle-Union)*
    pvt — Jl 12, Ag 23, O 4, N 1–15 1879; Ap 2, S 11–18 1880
    CLU — [Ja 3–Ag 2 1880]
    CU-BANC — My 10, O 25–N 8, 22 1879–F 21, Ap 24–My 15, Je 5–O 23 1880
Bodie Union, d (Sep 1879–Dec 1879)
  No issues located.
Bodie Weekly News, w (Dec 14 1879–Jul 18 1880)
  (merged with *Bodie Weekly Standard* to form *Bodie Weekly Standard-News*)
    CU-BANC — D 21 1879

Bodie Daily Free Press, d (Sep 6 1879–Jul 9 1886)
    pvt — S 6 1879; Ap 1 1881
    CBrC — Ja 1881–D 1882
    CLU — Mr 10, 19 1880; Ja 1, Ap 6, 14, 28, Ag 18, O 7 1881; Ja 12, F 10, 25, Ag 1–4 1882, Ja 26 1884
    CU-BANC — N 3 1879–Ap 22 1883; Ja 26 1884

Daily Standard-News, d (Jul 21 1880–Dec 11 1880)
    (continuation of *Bodie Daily Standard* and *Bodie Morning News*)
    CU-BANC — Jl 21–22, 24–N 1, 3–24, 26–D 9, 11 1880

Weekly Standard-News, w (Jul 24 1880–c. Oct 1880)
    (continuation of *Bodie Weekly Standard* and *Bodie Weekly News*)
    CU-BANC — S 4–O 9 1880

Weekly Standard-News and Free Press, w (Dec 22 1880–Aug 2 1882)
    (revived as weekly edition of *Daily Free Press*)
    CLU — D 22 1880; Mr 16 1881; (Ja 4–Ag 2 1882)
    CU-BANC — D 22–29 1880; Mr 2, 16, 30–My 4, 18, Je 8–Jl 27, Ag 10–D 28 1881; Ja 4–Je 28, Jl 12–Ag 2 1882

Evening Standard-News, d (Jun 1 1881–Jun 14 1881)
    (revived by *Daily Free Press*)
    CU-BANC — Je 6–7, 9–10 1881

The Opinion, w (Jan 2 1882–Jan 23 1882)
    No issues located.

Bodie Evening Miner, d, w (May 8 1882–Dec 5 1896)
    (merged with *Bodie Mining Index* to form *Bodie Miner-Index*)
    pvt — Mr 18 1889; Jl 21 1890; Mr 30 1894
    CBiI — My 18 1882
    CSmH — N 11 1884; N 10–12, D 4–31 1885; F 26–Mr 18, Ap 21–29, N 10–19 1886
    CU-BANC — Ag 4 1890

Bodie Mining Index, w (Dec 20 1895–Dec 5 1896)
    (moved from Lundy)
    pvt — F 28 1896
    CHi — D 27 1895

Bodie Miner-Index, w (Dec 12 1896–c. 1908)
    (continuation of *Bodie Mining Index* and *Bodie Evening Miner;* name changed to *Bodie Miner* c. 1908)
    pvt — N 13 1897; S 3, O 15 1898; D 23 1905
    CSmH — Ja 23 1897
    CYoM — Ja 23 1897
    NvHi — D 2 1905

Bodie Miner, w (c. 1908–c. 1912)
    (formerly *Bodie Miner-Index*)
    NvHi — D 5–12 1908; Ja 2 1909–N 24 1910

BRIDGEPORT

Bridgeport Union, w (May 15 1880–Nov 1 1880)
    (merged with *Bodie Chronicle* to form *Bridgeport Chronicle-Union*)
    pvt — Jl 10 1880
    CU-BANC — Jl 3–10, 24–N 1 1880

Bridgeport Chronicle-Union, w (Nov 8 1880+)
    (d — Ap 23–26 1906)

(continuation of *Bridgeport Union* and *Bodie Chronicle*)
   pvt — D 4 1886; Ap 10 1897; D 6–13 1902; Ja 3–10 1903
   C — Jl 12 1890+
   CLU — (Ja 22–O 22 1881)
   CU-BANC — N 8 1880–D 17 1881; Mr 11 1882[Ja 20–Mr 1883]Jl 5 1884; F 28–Mr 7 1885; N 6 1886; Jl 7 1888–Mr 23, Ag 31, S 7–14 1889; Ja 4–18 1890; My 14 1892; O 1933+
   NvHi — Ap 23–26 1906
Mono County Relief, w (1886–Jul 1888)
   No issues located.

LORENA
Lorena Ledge, w (Nov 7 1905–c. Feb 10 1906)
   No issues located.

LUNDY
Homer Mining Index, w (Jun 12 1880–Nov 1 1884; Oct 13 1888–Oct 12 1895)
   (moved to Bodie as *Bodie Mining Index*)
   pvt — Ag 17 1889; N 11 1893
   CBiI — Ag 25 1894
   CLU — Ja 28–F 4, 18–25 1882, N 1 1884, F 1, Mr 1 1890
   CSmH — Mr 25, Je 10 1882; N 1 1884; Jl 1 1893
   CU-BANC — (Je 12 1880–My 21, Ag 20 1881–Jl 29 1882) Je 16, Jl 28, Ag 11, O 20–N 10, 24 1883; Ja 5–19, Mr 1–8, Ap 5–19, My 10–31, Jl 12, Ag 23, S 6–13, O 1 1884; Ja 13, F 24, Mr 24, Ap 7, My 19–Je 2, Jl 7, 21–28, Ag 4, O 13, N 3–10 1894
   MWA — N 1 1884; F 1, Mr 1 1890

MAMMOTH CITY
Lake Mining Review, w (May 24 1879–Oct 11 1879)
   (name changed to *Mammoth City Times*)
   CU-BANC — My 31, Ag 16–30, S 13–20 1879
Mammoth City Herald, sw, w (Jul 2 1879–c. Feb 12 1881)
   (sw — Jl 2 1879–Jl 24 1880)
   CBiI — D 31 1880
   CIE — Ap 17 1880
   CU-BANC — Jl 9, 19, 30, Ag 6–13, 20, 27, S 3–O 15, 22 1879–D 11 1880; Ja 1–F 12 1881
Mammoth City Times, sw (Oct 8 1879–Mar 6 1880)
   (formerly *Lake Mining Review*)
   CU-BANC — O 18–N 26, D 6–31 1879; Ja 7–F 7, 14–18, Mr 3 1880

MASONIC
Masonic Pioneer, w (Nov 8 1905–c. Feb 28 1906)
   pvt — N 8 1905: Ja 3, F 28 1906

MONTGOMERY CITY
Montgomery Pioneer, w (Nov 26 1864–c. Dec 1864)
   No issues located, but extensively quoted in *Bodie Daily Free Press,* Apr 13 1881

NEVADA COUNTY

MEADOW LAKE
Meadow Lake Sun, d, sw, w (Jun 6 1866–1867)
   (d — Je 6–Jl 1866; sw — Jl–N 1866)

C — Je 6, D 8 1866
CU-BANC — [1866–7]

TRUCKEE

Truckee Tribune, w, sw (Sep 19 1868–Mar 19 1870)
(sw — My 1869–Ja 1870)
C — D 19 1868
CU-BANC — S 19 1868–Mr 19 1870

Truckee Republican, tw, sw, w (Apr 30 1872–Jul 1933)
(merged with *Sierra Sun* to form *Sierra Sun & Truckee Republican*)
pub — Ja 1926–Jl 1933
C — [1901–23]
CLU — Ag 28 1880
CSto — D 1874–D 4 1875
CU-BANC — D 1874–[75–6]–[78]80; Ap 26 1882–Mr 12, Ap 19, Ag 30 1884;
N 25 1885 [86–Je 20 1888]
KHi — Ja 16 1889

Truckee News, tw (Dec 1884–c. 1885)
No issues located.

Sierra Sun, w (c. 1933–Jul 1933)
(merged with *Truckee Republican* to form *Sierra Sun & Truckee Republican*)
No issues located.

Sierra Sun & Truckee Republican, w (Aug 1933+)
pub — Ag 1933+

PLACER COUNTY

KINGS BEACH

Lake Tahoe Journal, w (1946–1954)
No issues located.

TAHOE CITY

Tahoe Tattler, d (Jul 9 1881–c. Jul 15 1882)
CSmH — [Jl 9 1881–F 18] Jl 15 1882
NvHi — Jl 11, 19, 20, 26, 27 1881

Tattler (c. Jl 20 1886)
No issues located.

Tahoe Tattler, w (c. Jun 1935–c. Aug 1941)
C — [Je 1935–Ag 1941]

SAN BERNARDINO COUNTY

BARSTOW

Barstow Printer, w (1910+)
(as *Barstow Printer-Review* after c. 1938)
pub — 1910+
C — 1943+
CLCM — Je 30 1911

CALICO

Calico Print, w (Jul 8 1882–c. Jun 1884; Feb 1886–Sep 1887)
(moved to Daggett and back)
CLCM — O 10 1886

CSfCP — Jl 8–Ag 1882
CU-BANC — O 21 1882

CRACKERJACK
Crackerjack News, w (May 1907–Mar 1908)
No issues located.

DAGGETT
Calico Print, w (c. Jul 1884–Feb 1886)
(moved from Calico and back)
CU-BANC — F 8–Je 7, 21–Jl 19 1885

HART
Hart Enterprise, w (Jan 1908–1909)
No issues located.

HESPERIA
Hesperia Herald, w (Dec 24 1887–c. 1888)
CLCM — D 24 1887; F 4 1888

NEEDLES
Our Bazoo, w (Sep 1 1888–Feb 9 1889)
(name changed to *Booth's Bazoo*)
CLCM — Ja 26 1889
Booth's Bazoo, w (Feb 16 1889–1890)
(follows *Our Bazoo*; name changed to *Needle's Eye*)
CLCM — [1889–90]
Needle's Eye, w (1891–c. 1914)
(follows *Booth's Bazoo*)
CLCM — [1891–3]
CU-BANC — Ja 1906–My 9 1914
Nugget, w (1912–1945)
No issues located.
Desert Star, w (1944+)
pub — 1944+

NIPTON
Tie-Up, irr (Mar 1907–Apr 1907)
No issues located.

ORO GRANDE
Mojave River Enterprise, w (1888–Feb 1889)
No issues located.
Kingdom of the Sun, irr (Dec 1912–1917, 1935)
CHi — 1915–6
CLU — 1916–7
CSd — 1915
CU-BANC — 1916
NN — 1935

SILVER LAKE
Silver Lake Miner, w (Apr 4 1908–Jun 1908)
No issues located.

TWENTYNINE PALMS
Desert Trail, w (1935+)
  pub — 1935+
Calico Print, bm (1945–Nov 1953)
  CU — 1945–53

VANDERBILT
Vanderbilt Shaft, w (Dec 1 1893–Aug 13 1894)
  No issues located.

VICTORVILLE
Victorville Hawkeye, w (1913–1913)
  (name changed to *Victor Valley News*)
  No issues located.
Victor Valley News, w (1913–1914)
  (merged with *Victor Valley Herald*)
  No issues located.
Victor Valley Herald, w (Aug 29 1913–1914)
  (merged with *Victor Valley News*)
  No issues located.
Victorville Valley News-Herald, w (1914–1957)
  CU-BANC — N 26, D 10 1915–F 1916
Victor Press, w (1937+)
  pub — 1937+
Corralings, m (1944–c. 1957)
  No issues located.

SIERRA COUNTY

LOYALTON
Loyaltonian, w (1902–c. 1910)
  No issues located.
Sierra Valley News, w (1912–1944)
  BMI — Ag 1926–My 1937; Ja 1940–S 1942
  CQCL — Ag 19 1926–44
  CU-BANC — 1927 (28–32)–44
Lumberworker, w (1939–1944)
  No issues located.
Loyalton Times, w (1940–c. 1943)
  BMI — F–O 1942
Sierra Booster, bw (1949+)
  pub — 1949+
  BMI — O 1949+

SIERRA VALLEY
Sierra Valley Leader, w (1882–c. 1894)
  CU-BANC — [1888] Ja 11–Mr 8, Ap 12–D 13, 27 1889–My 16, Ag 22–S 19, O 3, 31 1890; Ja 8–Je 3, S 2, 23–30, O 14, N 11–25, D 9 1892–Ja 6 1893
Mountain Mirror, w (Sep 10 1890–c. 1892)
  CU-BANC — S 10, O 29 1890
Sierra Valley Record, w (c. 1897–c. 1900)
  No issues located.

~(IDAHO)~
OWYHEE COUNTY

BRUNEAU

Owyhee Nugget, w (1889–c. 1937)
  (moved to Marsing)
  pub — 1889–1937

RUBY CITY

Owyhee Avalanche, w (Aug 19 1865–Aug 4 1866)
  (moved to Silver City)
  CU-BANC — [Ap 21–Ag 4 1866]
  Nv — S 1865–Ag 4 1866
  WHi — Ag 19 1865–Ag 4 1866

SILVER CITY

Owyhee Avalanche, w (Aug 1866–c. 1937)
  (moved from Ruby City)
  (Ap 29 1876–Ag 20 1897 as *Idaho Avalanche*)
  C — D 19 1868
  CU-BANC — Ag 1866–S 9 1882; 1887–Ja 10 1891; O 23 1893 [F 17–N 9 1894]
  DLC — D 24 1870; Ja 7, D 30 1871–S 1874; S 11, O 6 1880; Ja 25 1890
  WHi — Ag 1866–N 7 1868; F 26 1870–Ap 17, S 18 1875–Jl 1904

Idaho Daily Avalanche, d (Oct 17 1874–Apr 26 1876)
  CU-BANC — O 17, 19 1874; S 18, N 20, D 31 1875; Ja–Ap 1876
  WHi — O 17 1874–Ap 26 1876

Owyhee Bullion, w (c. Nov 14 1866–1867)
  CU-BANC — Ap 18 1867

Owyhee Tidal Wave, sw (c. Dec 11 1868–Feb 10 1870)
  (merged with *Owyhee Avalanche*)
  C — D 29 1868
  CU-BANC — Ja 15–19 1869
  WHi — D 15 1868–F 10 1870

~(OREGON)~
LAKE COUNTY

LAKEVIEW

State Line Herald, w (Sep 1878–c. 1883)
  (merged with the *Lake County Examiner*)
  CU-BANC — [Mr 22 1879–S, D 1880] Mr 18 1882
  Or — N 18 1878

Lake County Examiner, w (1879+)
  (after 1954 as *Lake County Examiner-Tribune*)
  CU-BANC — N 17 1883; Je 21–Ag 23, S 6, 20–O, N 8, 22–D 1884; My 23 1885;
    D 18 1886; Ap 28 1887; Mr 7–21, Je 13, Jl 11, Ag 29–S 19, O 24–31, N
    21–D 5 1889; Ja 2–9, Ag 21, O 2–16 1890; F 22 1894
  OrHi — Jl 27 1893–N 21 1901; Ag 14 1902–S 29 1904 [1908–10] 1924 –30, 36
    –42, 45–7, 53–4
  OrU — Jl 27 1893–1954

Lake County Rustler, w (1895–Oct 17 1901)
  (name changed to *Lakeview Herald*)
  OrU — [F 7–O 17 1901]
Lakeview Register, w (1898–1899)
  No issues located.
Lakeview Herald, w (Oct 24 1901–1915)
  (formerly *Lake County Rustler:* merged with *Lake County Examiner*)
  OrHi — Ja 27 1910–Ja 28 1913
  OrU — [1901–S 23 1913]
Lake County Review, w (c. 1913)
  OrU — [1913]
Lake County Tribune, sw, w (Apr 12 1928–Apr 25 1940)
  (merged with *Lake County Examiner* to form *Lake County Examiner-Tribune*)
  OrU — Ap 1928–Ap 1940

∼⁂(UTAH)⁂∼
TOOELE COUNTY

GOLD HILL
Gold Hill Standard, w (1916–1919)
  No issues located.

IBAPAH
Deep Creek News, w (1914–1916)
  No issues located.

WASHINGTON COUNTY

ST. GEORGE
Our Dixie Times, w (Jan 22 1868–Apr 22 1868)
  (name changed to *Rio Virgin Times*)
  CU-BANC — Ja 22–Ap 22 1868
  UStGD — Ja 22–Ap 22 1868
Mineral Cactus, w (Feb 25 1868–Nov 24 1870)
  CU-BANC — My 12–N 24 1870
  UStgD — [Mr 1868–Je 19 1869]
Rio Virgin Times, w (May 13 1868–Nov 24 1869)
  (formerly *Our Dixie Times*)
  CU-BANC — My 13 1868–Mr 1869
  UStgD — My 13 1868–N 24 1869
St. George Juvenile, sm (Dec 15 1868–c. 1869)
  (revived as the *St. George Enterprise*)
  No issues located.
Utah Pomologist, m (Apr 1 1870–c. Jan 1877)
  (as *Utah Pomologist & Gardener;* Jan 1872–1876)
  UStgD — [Ap 1 1870–F 1876]
St. George Enterprise, m (Nov 1871–Aug 14 1874)
  CU-BANC — Ap–My, Jl, N–D 1872; My, D 1873; Ja–F, Jl 1874
The Union, sm, irr (Jun 14 1878–Nov 2 1878; Nov 12 1880–Feb 1887; Feb 1896–May 19 1898) (as *Union Footlight,* c. 1892–1895)
  UStgD — [Je 14–N 2 1878; N 12 1880–F 1887; F 1896–My 19 1898]

The Evening Telegram, d (Apr 8 1879–c. May 1879)
   UStgD — [Ap 8–My 1879]
Southern Utah Star, w (Jul 20 1895–c. Aug 1895)
   UStgD — Jl 20 1895
Washington County News, w (Jun 18 1898–Jul 28 1900; Jun 30 1908+)
   pub — Je 30 1908+
   UHi — Je 18 1898–Jl 28 1900
   UmC — Ja 30 1908+
Dixie Falcon, w (Sep 22 1900–c. 1900)
   UStgD — S 22 1900
Dixie Advocate, w (Sep 6 1901–Nov 1906)
   (moved to Virgin City)
   pvt — [S 13 1901–N 6 1906]

SILVER REEF

Silver Reef Echo, d, w (Feb 24 1877–c. Oct 1878)
   (early issues as *Utah Pomologist & Silver Reef Echo*)
   USlGS — F 24 1877
Silver Reef Miner, tw, sw, w (Oct 1878–c. Feb 1883)
   (tw — O 1878–c. 1879; F 18–Ap 3 1882; sw — c. 1879–F 7 1880)
   CU-BANC — [Ap 12 1879–F 1883]
   UStgD — [Mr 17–O 28 1882]
Southern Utah Times, w (1886–1887)
   No issues located.

VIRGIN CITY

Dixie Advocate, w (1907–1908)
   UStgD — Ap 2 1908
Virgin Valley Enterprise, w (1908)
   No issues located.

Bibliography

American Newspaper Reporter. George P. Rowell and Co.

Angel, Myron, ed. *History of Nevada.* Oakland, Calif.: Thompson & West, 1881.

Ayer Press, comp. *Ayer Directory of Publications.* Bala Cynwyd, Penn.: Ayer Press, 1869–.

Bancroft, Hubert Howe. *Nevada, Colorado and Wyoming.* San Francisco: The History Company, 1889.

Beebe, Lucius, *Comstock Commotion: The Story of the Territorial Enterprise.* Stanford: Stanford University Press, 1954.

Bishop, D. M., & Company. *Bishop's Directory of Virginia City, Gold Hill, Silver City, Carson City and Reno.* San Francisco: B. C. Vandall, 1878.

Bulletin of Bibliography. Boston: F. W. Faxon, 1897–.

Davis, Samuel P., ed. *The History of Nevada.* Reno, Los Angeles: Elms Publishing Co., 1913.

De Quille, Dan [William Wright]. *History of the Big Bonanza.* Hartford, Conn.: American Publishing Company; San Francisco: A. L. Bancroft & Co., 1877.

Directory of Nevada Newspapers. Carson City: Nevada State Press Association, biennial publication.

Doten, Alfred R. *The Journals of Alfred Doten, 1849–1903.* Reno: University of Nevada Press, 1973.

Drury, Wells. *An Editor on the Comstock Lode.* New York: Farrar and Rinehart, 1936.

Folkes, John G. *Nevada's Newspapers: A Bibliography. A Compilation of Nevada History, 1854–1964.* Reno: University of Nevada Press, 1964.

Greenspun, Herman M. *Where I Stand.* New York: McKay, 1966.

Gregory, Winifred, ed. *American Newspapers 1821–1936, A Union List of Files Available in the United States and Canada.* New York: H. H. Wilson Co., 1937.

Hazlett, Fanny G., and Gertrude Hazlett Randall. "Historical Sketch and Reminiscences of Dayton, Nevada." Nevada Historical Society Papers, 1921–1922.

Hensher, Alan. "Earle Clemens and the Rhyolite Herald." *Historical Society of Southern California Quarterly* 49 (1967): 311–325.

Inventory of County Archives of Nevada. Reno: Nevada Historical Records Survey Project, 1941.

Jackson, William Turrentine. *Treasure Hill: Portrait of a Silver Mining Camp.* Tucson: University of Arizona Press, 1963.

Lillard, Richard G. "Studies in Washoe Journalism & Humor." Part II of Ph.D. diss., State University of Iowa, April, 1943.

Lingenfelter, Richard E. *The Newspapers of Nevada, 1858–1958; A History and Bibliography.* San Francisco: John Howell Books, 1964.

McMurtrie, Douglas C. *A Bibliography of Nevada Newspapers, 1858 to 1875 Inclusive.* Mainz: Gutenberg-Jahrbuch, 1935.

Pacific States Newspaper Directory. San Francisco: Palmer and Rey, 1886.

Polk, R. L., & Co. *Nevada State Gazetteer and Business Directory, 1907–1908.* Salt Lake City: R. L. Polk & Co., 1907.

Rice, George Graham. *My Adventures With Your Money.* Boston: R. G. Badger, 1913.

Ritter, Betsy [Mrs. Earl R. Clemens]. *Life in the Ghost City of Rhyolite, Nevada.* 1939. Reprint. Morongo Valley, Calif.: Sagebrush Press, 1982.

Rogers, Franklin R. "Washoe's First Literary Journal." *California Historical Society Quarterly* 36 (1957): 365–370.

Rowell, George P., ed. *Rowell's American Newspaper Directory.* New York: G. P. Rowell & Co., 1869–1908.

Shepperson, Wilbur S. *Retreat to Nevada: A Socialist Colony of World War I.* Reno: University of Nevada Press, 1966.

Twain, Mark. *Roughing It.* Berkeley: University of California Press, 1972.

Wren, Thomas. *A History of the State of Nevada.* New York: Lewis Publishing Company, 1904.

Various Nevada and Pacific Coast business directories for the years 1858 to 1900.

INDEX

Aalbu, R. M., 117
Abraham, T. W., 56, 57, 58, 59
Action (Reno), 210
Adams, Jewett, 267
Adams, Paul, 117
Adams, Si, 43
Adler, Neida, 269
Advance (Las Vegas), 125
Advertiser (Ione), 121
Advocate (Austin). See *People's Advocate*, 10
Advocate (Dayton). See *Dayton Advocate*, 60
Africa, L. V., 130
Agai Dicutta Yuduan (Schurz), 224
Age (Boulder City). See *Boulder City Age*, 22
Age (Las Vegas). See *Las Vegas Age*, 126
Air Age News (Gardnerville), 89
Air Age News (Reno), 212
Air Age News (Sparks), 234
Alexander, John F., 177
Allen, George B., 38, 39, 40
Allen, James, 275, 276
Allen, Samuel J., 87
Allen, U. E., 226
Amateur Outlook (Ely), 71
Amateur Outlook (Reno), 185
Ambrose, Kenneth, 52
American Enterprise (Wonder), 287
Ames, J. Judson, 2, 3, 5
Amusements (Reno). See *Reno Amusements*, 194
Anderson,——, 148
Anderson, George M., 44
Anderson, James E., 78, 222
Angel, Myron, 7, 246
Angus, John, 140
App, John, 219
Arbukle, A. R., 176
Arcadian (Reno), 217
Argent (Winnemucca). See *Winnemucca Argent*, 279
Argonaut (Elko). See *Daily Argonaut*, 68
Argus (Las Vegas), 127
Argus (Lovelock), 145
Armand, E., 255, 259
Armour, James R., 49
Armstrong, Robert J., 214
Arnhold,——, 56
Arnold, Happ, 237
Arnst, Dick, 133
Ashcraft, Alta, 20
Aston, M. B., 107
Atchison, Mary, 100
Aurora Borealis, 7
Aurora Daily Times. See *Aurora Weekly Times*, 4
Aurora Star, 6

Aurora Times. See *Aurora Weekly Times*, 4
Aurora Weekly Times, 4
Austin Holiday Review, 10
Austin Republican, 9
Austin Sun, 11
Avard, John W., 5
Avery, Roy M., 205, 207
Ayers, C. D., 281
Ayers, J. J., 33
Ayers, James J., 111, 112, 260
Ayers, W. H., 281

Backstage (Las Vegas), 140
Bagley, H. P., 72
Bailey, Seth T., 201
Bailey, Stanley, 284
Bain, Jake H., 255, 256
Balling, Ruth, 58
Ballot Box (Fallon), 82
Bardwell, James, 165
Barker, Matie, 232
Barker, Stan, 232
Barnard, Olaf G., 63
Barndollar, B. M., 186
Barnes, H. M., 19
Barnes, Jack, 234
Barnes, William W., 55, 56
Barney, Benjamin M., 53, 179
Barrett, J., 35
Barry, John T., 259
Bartlett, Dorothy, 48
Bartlett, George A., 48
Bartlett, Henry J., 221
Bartlett, Margaret, 48
Bartlett, Roland C., 135, 137
Basic Bombardier (Henderson), 118
Bates, Joseph B., 130
Battle Mountain Bugle, 15
Battle Mountain Herald, 14
Battle Mountain Herald and Central Nevadan, 14
Battle Mountain Messenger, 12
Battle Mountain Scout, 14
Baughman, S. Dee, 84
Bean, Edwin F., 261
Bearss, A. C., 121, 122
Beason, Lewis H., 165
Beat of the Boulevard (Las Vegas), 136
Beatty Bulletin, 16
Beatty Bullfrog Miner, 16
Beatty Newsbits, 16
Becker,——, 104
Becker, F. E., 147, 220
Beckwith, L. F., 33
Bedrosian, Tod, 214, 215
Bee (Carson City). See *Daily Bee*, 42

Bee Hive (Las Vegas), 139
Beebe, G. H., 176
Beebe, Lucius, 270, 271
Bell, Charles R., 134
Bellehelen Record, 17
Belleville Times, 17
Belmont Courier, 20
Benneson, F. J., 153
Bennett, Edwin J., 241
Bennett, H. C., 258
Bennett, Terri, 216
Berry, George G., 64, 65, 164, 250
Best, Robert D., 139, 140
Bethel, J. D., 263, 264
Bettersworth, A. P., 81, 82
Betty O'Neal Concentrator, 20
Bien, H. M., 259
Bierce, Ambrose, 46
Biersmith, L. M., 13
Big Job–Basic Magnesium Newsletter (Henderson). See *Basic Bombardier,* 118
Bigler, John, 5
Big Nickel (Sparks), 234
Billington, Randolph, 233
Bingham, C. E., 81, 248
Bingham, Ernest L., 81, 175, 248
Bingham, L. H., 81
Bishop, Lee, 161
Bishop, Noreen, 161
Bixler, W. K., 208, 209
Black, W. C., 146, 284
Black, William C., 81
Blair, G. B., 200
Blair Booster, 21
Blair Press, 21
Blake, E. D., 262
Blake, Frank A., 254
Blake, L. J., 35
Bland, Gladwin, 108
Bley, Mel A., 188
Bloor, George W., 98, 99, 181
Blossom, J. A., 13
Blossom, R. C., 13
Blum, A. A., 229
Boericke,——, 252
Bogart, R. D., 262
Bohanan, Ray, 207
Bohannan, W. H., 221, 241
Bollettino del Nevada (Reno), 195
Bombing and Gunnery Range (Tonopah), 244
Bonanza (Butler). See *Tonopah Bonanza,* 240
Bonanza (Grantsville). See *Grantsville Bonanza,* 111
Bonanza (Tonopah). See *Tonopah Bonanza,* 240
Bonelli, Leonard, 123
Bonnifield, McKaskia S., 250, 280
Bonnifield, William S., 250
Booher, W. W., 65
Boomlet (Pioche). See *Pioche Boomlet,* 166
Booster (Blair). See *Blair Booster,* 21
Booster (Bovard). See *Bovard Booster,* 23

Booster (Millers). See *Millers Booster,* 154
Booth, Chauncey, 172
Booth, James Anson, 280
Booth, John, 8, 9, 20, 37, 121, 122, 164, 251
Booth, Mrs. John, 8
Booth, Kenneth, 70
Booth, Newton, 33
Booth, William W., 9, 10, 21, 23, 29, 63, 115, 116, 148, 154, 171, 172, 223, 229, 240, 242, 243, 244
Boots and Chutes (Reno), 208
Borax Miner (Columbus), 55
Borealis. See *Aurora Borealis,* 7
Borghi, Dick, 52
Bott, John, 202
Boulder City Age, 22
Boulder City Journal, 21
Boulder City News, 22
Boulder City Reminder, 22
Boulder Dam Challenge, 22
Boulder Dam Informer, 23
Bouton, Ken, 23, 162
Bovard Booster, 23
Bowler, P. M., Jr., 115
Bowles, Winthrop, 284
Boyle, Emmet D., 176
Boyle, Vida M., 176
Bozanic, Milt, 139, 161
Brackett, A. L., 15, 221, 281, 283, 284
Bradley, Dave, 136
Bradley, Lewis R., 33
Bradshaw, E. C., 281
Bragg, Allen C., 177, 184, 281
Brandi, C. F., 51
Brandi, Pauline, 51
Brandon, W. L., 145, 183
Brann, R. W., 22
Brannan, D. M., 17, 24, 249
Branson, Lindley C., 1, 69, 103, 109, 241
Bray, R. E., 83
Bridge, Charles, 15
Brier, G. A., 74, 112, 227
Bristol Times, 24
Brooke, Henry L., 185
Brooks, E. R., 7
Brooks, J. S., 146, 219
Brooks, John W., 195
Brown, Alfred, 14
Brown, David L., 262, 263, 268
Brown, E., 236
Brown, Edwin B., 15, 36, 50
Brown, F. E., 165
Brown, Fred E., 188
Brown, James, 26, 58, 125
Brown, Robert L., 128, 139, 159
Brown, Sam, 74
Bruce, Irene, 205
Bryan, J. X., 184
Bryan, Mark H., 173, 174, 184
Bryant, P. L., 176
Buchanan, J. A., 192
Buck, Edward N., 221
Buck, Edward Nelson, 192

Buck, J. Holman, 1, 7, 63, 110, 144, 147, 154, 172
Buckner, Amos O., 36
Bugbee, Frank Eugene, 110, 125
Bugle (Battle Mountain). See *Battle Mountain Bugle,* 15
Bugle (Genoa), 93
Bugle (Junctionville), 123
Bugle (Reno). See *Nevada Bugle,* 192
Bulletin (Beatty). See *Beatty Bulletin,* 16
Bulletin (Hawthorne). See *Walker Lake Bulletin,* 114
Bulletin (Las Vegas), 127
Bulletin (Rhyolite). See *Rhyolite Daily Bulletin,* 219
Bulletin (Searchlight). See *Searchlight Bulletin,* 224
Bulletin (Virginia City). See *Virginia Evening Bulletin,* 256
Bulletin (Winnemucca). See *Humboldt Bulletin,* 284
Bullfrog Miner (Beatty). See *Beatty Bullfrog Miner,* 16
Bullfrog Miner (Bullfrog), 24
Bullfrog Miner (Rhyolite), 218
Bullion District Miner (Tenabo), 239
Bullseye (North Las Vegas), 159
Bunker, Chester Raymond, 147
Bunning, Chuck, 30
Bunning, Jan, 30
Buntin, W. H., 22
Burgess, Samuel E., 84
Burke, Linda, 270
Burke, Peter, 270
Burke, Peter A., 204
Burnell, J. M., 103, 105
Burns, Robert A., 205
Burt, Raymond F., 14
Burton, W. H., 232
Busick, Bill, 129
Business Talks (Tuscarora), 249
Butler. See Tonopah
Butler, Mary E., 285
Butler, Norman H., 84, 285
Butler, T. J., 65, 66

Cabaret Magazine (Las Vegas), 137
Cahill, Dennis P., 199
Cahlan, Al E., 21, 127, 128, 131
Caliente Express, 25
Caliente Herald, 27
Caliente Lode-Express, 26
Caliente News, 27
Caliente Progress, 25
Caliente Record, 27
Call (Reno). See *Reno Call,* 186
Calwell, G. W., 33
Camels Coming (Reno), 211
Camels Hump (Reno), 212
Camp, Joe T., 30, 85, 93, 94, 96, 220, 274
Camp, Sol, 102
Campaign Notes (Virginia City), 269
Campbell, John M., 59, 114, 228, 254
Campbell, Robert, 134
Campbell, W. J., 165, 235
Campbell, Wilkes J., 62
Canfield, Charles L., 77, 78
CAPReno, 206
Captain Jim, 74
Card, William L., 228
Cargile, Lee M., 208
Carlin Courier, 30
Carlisle, Boynton, 92
Carlson, J. Ray, 146
Carney, P. J., 109
Carnival News (Reno), 186
Carpenter, George A., 8
Carpenter, Jack, 289
Carpenter, Jack M., 232
Carpenter, R. E., 49
Carr, Charles J., 225
Carr, Richard H., 219
Carrara Miner, 31
Carrara Obelisk, 31
Carrigan, W. W., 265, 266
Carson Appeal. See *Nevada Appeal,* 35
Carson Boys, 43
Carson Chronicle, 49
Carson City Chronicle. See *Carson Chronicle,* 49
Carson City Enlightener, 48
Carson City Gazoot. See *Karson Sity Gazoot,* 48
Carson City News (1891–1930), 44
Carson City News (1961), 51
Carson Daily Appeal. See *Nevada Appeal,* 35
Carson Daily Independent, 33
Carson Evening Gazette, 48
Carson Free Lance, 42
Carson Post, 43
Carson Press, 45
Carson Review and Advertiser, 51
Carson-Tahoe Chronicle. See *Carson Chronicle,* 49
Carson Times (1880–81), 40
Carson Times (1977), 52
Carson Valley Farmer (Genoa), 91
Carson Valley News (Genoa), 91
Carson Weekly, 47
Carson, C. C., 262
Carter, Eliza, 22
Carter, Marvin E., 22
Carter, Robert E., 22
Carville, Edward P., 73
Cary, William J., Jr., 81, 82, 83, 84, 86
Casamayou, Andrew, 8, 20
Casamayou, Mrs. Andrew, 20
Case, John S., 145, 281
Casino Post (Las Vegas), 139
Cassidy, George W., 74, 75, 112
Cathouse News (Reno), 216
Catt, Charles, 158
Caudle, George, 84
Cauley, Roy, 73
Celebration Gazetteer (Carson City), 46
Central Nevadan (Battle Mountain), 13

Chafey News, 52
Chalfant, Pleasant A., 3, 5, 164
Chapin, N. H., 71
Chartz, Alfred, 77, 263, 268
Chase, John S., 146
Chatelle, Ray J., 8
Chavez, Bob, 134
Cherry, Howard N., 144
Cherry, Howard W., 145, 152, 252
Cherry Creek Independent. See *Independent* (Cherry Creek), 53
Cherry Creek Miner, 54
Childs, E. H., 57
Chloride Belt (Candelaria), 29
Chronicle (Carson City). See *Carson Chronicle,* 49
Chronicle (Elko). See *Elko Chronicle,* 65
Chronicle (Goldfield). See *Goldfield Chronicle,* 106
Chronicle (Metropolis). See *Metropolis Chronicle,* 152
Chronicle (Pioche), 168
Chronicle (Virginia City, 1872–1927). See *Virginia Evening Chronicle,* 261
Chronicle (Virginia City, 1962). See *Virginia City Chronicle,* 271
Church, A. P., 255
Church, John, 32, 33, 255, 256, 282
Churchill County Courier (Fallon), 84
Churchill County Standard. See *Fallon Standard,* 81
Churchill News (White Plains), 279
Citizen (Fallon). See *Fallon Citizen,* 84
Citizen (Reno), 211
City Review (Virginia City), 261
Clark County Review. See *Las Vegas Review,* 126
Clark, E. B., 80, 119, 287
Clark, Edward L., 200
Clark, Edwin J., 67
Clark, Hugh, 73
Clark, L. N., Jr., 262
Clark, S. F., 10
Clarke, Charles Spencer, 277
Clarois Review, 54
Clay, Thomas L., 165
Clayton, Hal, 74
Clearly, William P., 21
Cleary, J. J., 204
Clegg, Charles, 270, 271
Clemens, Earle R., 16, 119, 120, 169, 218, 245
Clemens, Samuel (Mark Twain), 74, 99, 253, 254, 257
Clifford, A., 62, 167
Cloudburst (Las Vegas), 129
Cloverdale Budget, 54
Clyde, E. T., 36, 45
Cockrell, N. W., 20
Colburn,——, 102
Cole, Fred J., 95, 184
Coleman, John H., 262
Collins, Mrs. W. E., 73
Columbia Topics, 55

Colvert, A. L., 239
Commonwealth (Carlin), 29
Commonwealth (Deeth), 60
Como Sentinel, 56
Comstock Miner (Virginia City), 269
Comstock Record (Virginia City), 264
Comstock Union (Virginia City), 267
Concentrator (Betty O'Neal). See *Betty O'Neal Concentrator,* 20
Conley, James, 255
Conley, R. H., 197
Connell, W. F., 26
Connella, J. W., 72
Connors, J. W., 116, 117
Considine, John L., 54, 183, 187, 188, 191, 262, 268
Contact Miner, 57
Cook, Fred S., 117, 162, 205
Cook, John S., 105, 106
Cooke, Jane, 22
Coon, Florence, 208
Cooper, B. F., 59
Cooper, E. Frank, 270
Cooper, Ray E., 198
Co-operative Colonist (Fallon), 83
Copeland,——, 183
Copeland, Harry, 85, 217
Copp, Dick, 272
Copper Ore (McGill), 152
Copperfield. See Acme
Corbett, W. L., 43
Corkhill, Charles C., 126, 127
Corkhill, May, 127
Corn, George B., 225
Cornell, Sackett, 184
Corriere di Nevada (Reno), 188
Corriere di Nevada (Sparks), 231
Cortez, E. B., 131
Cortez, Jack, 131
Cosgrove, J. P., 237
Coulter, Charles C., 107
Courier (Belmont). See *Belmont Courier,* 20
Courier (Carlin). See *Carlin Courier,* 30
Courier (Gardnerville), 87
Courier (Genoa). See *Genoa Weekly Courier,* 92
Covington, E. Gorton, 36, 73, 212, 234
Cowan, Billy, 43
Cox, Frank S., 268, 289
Cox, Walter J., 86, 289
Cradlebaugh, John H., 92
Crago, Roseanne, 278
Craigue, Robert J., 284
Crain, C. S., 64
Crandall, Robert A., 16, 101, 244
Crandall, Mrs. Robert A., 244
Crawford, Israel, 33, 34
Crawford, Jack, 265
Crawford, R. R., 182, 183, 185
Crenshaw, H. H., 163
Crescent (Reno). See *Reno Crescent,* 175
Cresent Times, 58
Crier (Virginia City). See *Virginia City Crier,* 272

Crist, Kit, 204
Critchell, Don, 79
Critchell, Linda, 79
Critchlow, Jno. Q., 53
Croall, J., 262
Cronan, John, 137, 138, 213
Cronin, P. D., 188
Cross,——, 56
Crossette, John D., 70, 71
Crossley, Clarence C., 155, 270
Croyland, John, 164
Crudgington, Cleveland B., 207
Cullen, T. J., 149
Cuno, Mike, 233
Cupel (Eureka), 76
Cupid's Destiny (Reno), 210
Curry, John J., 6
Curtis, Charles H., 191
Curtis, Mark, 206, 208
Cyclone Occasional (Reno), 182

Daggett, Rollin M., 254
Daily American (Reno), 188
Daily Appeal (Carson City). See *Nevada Appeal*, 35
Daily Argonaut (Elko), 68
Daily Bee (Carson City), 42
Daily Constitution (Virginia City), 259
Daily Evening Herald (Carson City), 39
Daily Evening Record (Reno), 179
Daily Evening Washoe Herald (Virginia City), 258
Daily Independent (Virginia City), 263
Daily Index (Carson City), 41
Daily Lode (Delamar). See *De Lamar Lode*, 61
Daily Morning Message (Gold Hill), 98
Daily Morning Post (Carson City), 34
Daily Morning Star (Reno), 180
Daily Nevada Democrat (Reno), 177
Daily Nevada Tribune (Carson City), 37
Daily Nevada Tribune (Reno), 182
Daily News (Goldfield). See *Goldfield News*, 101
Daily Old Piute (Virginia City), 257
Daily Safeguard (Virginia City), 260
Daily Stage (Virginia City). See *Stage*, 266
Daily State Register (Carson City), 37
Daily Trespass (Virginia City), 260
Daily Union (Virginia City). See *Virginia Daily Union*, 255
Dalby, Allan K., 82
Dalton, T. H., 8
Daly,——, 104
Dam Informer. See *Boulder Dam Informer*, 23
Daniel, H. C., 205
Darrah, Clayton, 51, 157, 210, 233, 284, 285
Darrah, Clinton A., 157
David, W. M., 46
Davis, George T., Jr., 44, 45
Davis, J. B., 207

Davis, J. C., 64
Davis, J. M., 262
Davis, Jefferson, 35
Davis, Mrs. M., 262
Davis, Robert A., 285
Davis, Sam P., 35, 38, 267, 273
Davis, W. L., 54, 70, 238
Davis, Walter H., 12
Davis, Wesley L., Jr., 36, 49, 270
Day, C. E., 21
Dayton Advocate, 60
De Groot, Henry, 31, 120
De La Mar Roaster (Delamar), 62
De Lamar Lode, 61
De Quille, Dan (William Wright), 253, 267
Deane, Henry, 254
Dearing, David, 139
Death Valley Magazine (Rhyolite), 219
Death Valley Prospector. See *Death Valley Magazine*, 219
Decker, E. H., 70
Deeth Tidings, 60
DeLashmutt, Van B., 276
Delpit, Ron, 140
Dement, James A., 73
Demers, Fran, 138
Democrat (Austin), 9
Democrat (Las Vegas), 138
Democrat (Reno). See *Reno Democrat*, 180
Democratic News (Las Vegas), 137
Democratic Standard (Virginia City), 256
Dennis, John H., 8, 12, 13, 75, 175, 247, 248
Denton, J. A., 25
Derby, Lieutenant (John Phoenix, Squibob), 2, 3, 5
Derickson, B. F., 276
Derickson, George W., 275
Desert, A Nevada Magazine (Reno), 202
Desert Living (Pahrump), 162
Desert News (Carson City), 51
Desert News (Lathrop Wells), 142
Desert Rat Review (Boulder City), 23
Desert Roundup (Fallon), 85
Desert Scorpion (Camp Sibert), 28
Desert Sun (Las Vegas), 129
Destinies (Reno), 205
Deutsche Union (Virginia City), 260
Dewey, Pauline T., 159
DeYoung, M. H., 46
DiCarlo, Gary D., 135
Dial, Benjamin, 71
Dickason, D. H., 288
Dickerson, Denver S., 49, 70, 72, 194, 204, 207
Dickerson, Tom, 88, 146
Digilio, Don, 128
Digles, Joe, 128
Dilkes, Gene, 15
Dinnell, Chet, 286
Discover Magazine (Reno), 216
Dispatch (Sparks). See *Sparks Dispatch*, 230
Dispatch (Wadsworth, 1892–1904). See

Wadsworth Dispatch (1892–1904), 273
Dispatch (Wadsworth, 1920), 274
Divide City Times, 62
Divison, Jay, 124
Dixon, Dixie, 270
Dixon, Randy, 120
Dodge, Max, 209
Doherty, Charles S., 129
Doherty, Florence S., 110
Doherty, Frank A., 110
Dolan, Philip J., 27, 165
Dolan, William, 50
Dollarhide, Vienna, 9
Donald, Samuel, 20, 111
Donner Trail Reporter (Reno), 207
Donoghue, Arthur Kenneth, 52
Donoghue Letter (Carson City), 52
Donovan, Eugene, 195
Dooley, N. P., 61, 62, 167
Dormer, John M., 6, 17, 28, 177
Dorothy, Dorothy, 16
Dorsey, F. M., 106
Dorsey, William, 204
Dorst, Helen Crawford, 270
Doten, Alf, 8, 56, 57, 97, 98, 255
Dougan, Michael, 120
Douglas County Banner (Genoa), 91
Douglas County Silverite (Gardnerville), 87
Dow, Amos H., 101
Dow, J. C., 34, 175, 177
Downing, Richard L., 272
Doyle, Odis, 215
Draper, Robert E., 4
Driscoll, Dennis, 254
Dromiack, Charles A., 212
Drury, Wells, 28, 39, 41, 42, 76, 97, 266, 273
Duck Valley News, 62
Duluth Tribune, 63
Dungan, Jesse H., 92
Dunham, Sam C., 187, 240, 241
Dunn, H. C., 38, 44
Dunn, H. William, 25
Dunn, Horace A., 106, 107
Dupuis, Edwin T., 44
Dutch Creek News, 63
Dykes, Jim, 215

Eagle (Fallon). See *Fallon Eagle*, 82
Eagle-Standard (Fallon). See *Fallon Eagle-Standard*, 84
Eakes, Marion, 284
Earth (Las Vegas), 137
East of the Nevada; or the Miner's Voice from the Colorado (Potosi), 170
Eastern Slope (Washoe City), 277
Eckles, T. H., 240
Eckley, Joseph E., 19, 120, 121, 227
Edes, George A., 33
Edwards, William F., 177, 179
Egan, Pierce, 284
Egelston, Fred W., 154
Eggleston, C. V., 83

Eichelroth, W. E., 4
Einstoss, Ronald, 176, 178
Eldorado Canyon Miner (Nelson), 157
Elko Chronicle, 65
Elko Enterprise, 69
Elko Free Press. See *Free Press*, 67
Elko Independent, 64
Elko Leader, 66
Elko Post, 66
Elks Show Message (Reno), 198
Ellendale Lode, 70
Ellendale Star, 69
Elliott, Fred, 112
Elliott,——, 102
Elliott, C. H., 102
Elliott, Fred, 6, 74, 75
Elliott, L. L., 70
Ellis, Adrian C., 35
Ellis, G. Harold, 96
Ellis, George, 128
Ellis, W. W., 8, 179, 286
Ellsworth,——, 13
Ely Daily Times, 73
Ely Mining Expositor, 72
Ely Post, 73
Ely Record, 71
Emerson, Clyde C., 80, 81, 82, 150, 173, 286, 289
Emerson, John H., 119, 287
Empire City Globe, 74
Engberg, Norma J., 141
Enlightener (Carson City). See *Carson City Enlightener*, 48
Enterprise (Elko). See *Elko Enterprise*, 69
Enterprise (Fernley), 85
Enterprise (Gabbs). See *Gabbs Valley Enterprise*, 86
Enterprise (Goldfield). See *Goldfield Enterprise & Esmeralda County News*, 109
Enterprise (Lida). See *Lida Enterprise*, 42
Enterprise (Searchlight). See *Searchlight Enterprise*, 225
Enterprise (Virginia City). See *Territorial Enterprise*, 253, 270
Erlich, Elizabeth, 232
Esmeralda Daily Union. See *Esmeralda Union*, 4
Esmeralda Herald (Aurora), 6
Esmeralda Herald (Hawthorne), 115
Esmeralda News (Hawthorne), 115
Esmeralda Star (Aurora), 1
Esmeralda Star (Dyer), 63
Esmeralda Union (Aurora), 4
Estes, Ethel, 15
Estill, Hollis H., 165
Eureka Daily Leader, 77
Eureka Daily Republican, 76
Eureka Daily Sentinel Supplement. See *Eureka Sentinel*, 74
Eureka Leader. See *Eureka Daily Leader*, 77
Eureka Miner, 79
Eureka Sentinel, 74
Eureka Tri-Weekly Standard, 79
Evans, Colonel, 3

INDEX / 319

Evasovich, John, 84
Evening Bulletin (Virginia City). See *Virginia Evening Bulletin*, 256
Evening Lode (Delamar). See *De Lamar Lode*, 61
Evening Report (Virginia City), 268
Evening Telegram (Reno), 184
Everitt, Elizabeth, 204
Expositor (Ely). See *Ely Mining Expositor*, 72
Express (Caliente). See *Caliente Express*, 25
Express (Gerlach). See *Gerlach Express*, 93
Express (Safford). See *Safford Express*, 223
Eye Opener (Tobar), 239
Ezell, James, 281
Ezell, W. C., 88

Fabulous Las Vegas Magazine, 131
Fagan, Thomas M., 193
Fagan, William, 285
Fairbanks, Fred W., 59, 81, 288
Fairchild, J. D., 7, 8
Fairchild, Mahlon D., 17, 18, 19, 246
Fairchild, Oscar L. C., 7, 8, 17, 247, 248
Fairplay Prospector (Atwood), 1
Fairplay. See Atwood
Fairview Miner, 80
Fairview News, 80
Fall, John C., 251
Fallon Citizen, 84
Fallon Eagle, 82
Fallon Eagle-Standard, 84
Fallon Herald, 81
Fallon Shopper. See *Shopper*, 85
Fallon Standard, 81
Farington, F. C., 258
Farrington, C. W., 195
Faulkner, William, 89
Fay, Nate W., 152
Federation (Reno). See *Reno Federation*, 185
Federationist (Reno). See *Nevada Federationist*, 196
Felesina, Peter V., 44, 45
Fellows, W. H. H., 175
Felton, Paul H., 88
Fenimore, Ebenezer (Old Virginny), 122
Ferguson Lode (Delamar), 61
Ferguson, George S., 278
Fernley Enterprise. See *Enterprise*, 85
Fernley Newspaper, 86
Ferral, Robert, 4
Field of Gold (Goldfield), 109
Field, Cathy Post, 139
Field, John T., 150
Fighting Mechanic (Reno), 197
Fine, William, 213
Fink, A. L., 129
Firewheel (Nixon), 158
Fisher, Arline, 214
Fisk, Fred E., 77, 78
Fisler, P. C., 241
Fitch, Thomas, 19, 257, 258
Flanigan, J. B., 225

Flannigan, George A., 72
Fleming, Jack, 284
Flight Times (Reno), 209
Flodin, C. W., 195, 196, 197
Flower, Sidney, 47, 48, 106
Flowers, L. V., 83
Floyd, J. N., 171
Flyer (Reno), 204
Fontecilla, Harry, 248
Foote, H. L., 40
Footlight (Virginia City), 262
Forbes, William J., 11, 12, 33, 112, 223, 226, 227, 246, 249, 256, 260
Fording, W. H., 101, 241
Fording, W. J., 70
Forman, Sands W., 262
Forrest, W. R., 54
Fortnightly Market Review (Reno), 187
Forum (Sparks), 231
Foster, M. G., 71
Fowler, Irene, 142
Fox, J. T., 197
Frady, Steven R., 36
Francis, Frank, 13, 124, 144
Francis, Herbert, 61
Frantzen, Earl A., 67
Fraternal Visitor (Gold Hill), 100
Frazer, Guernsey, 118
Freaner, U. B., 1
Free Lance (Carson City). See *Carson Free Lance*, 42
Free Lance (Reno), 181
Free Press (Elko), 67
Free Press (Las Vegas, 1950), 131
Free Press (Las Vegas, 1970–71). See *Las Vegas Free Press*, 136
Freeman, Robert, 23
Freeman, S. H., 196
Freeman, Will, 130
French, George D., 135
Freudenthal, H. E., 164
Friday (Reno), 208
Friel, William, 284
Frontline (Las Vegas), 141
Fulton, Robert L., 177, 179
Fulton, S. H., 12, 35
Fun and Gaming (Reno), 214
Fundial (Reno). See *Reno Fundial*, 206

Gabbs Valley Enterprise, 86
Gailbraith, Fred, 204
Gallagher, J. B., 288
Gallagher, James F., 235
Gardner, C. H., 93, 181
Gardner, Charles E., 289
Gardner, Paul K., 146, 147
Gardnerville Press, 87
Gardnerville Record, 87
Garinger, J. C., 108
Garrett, Charles, 249
Garrett, Elton M., 21, 22
Garrison, C. W., 165
Garside, Frank F., 21, 62, 94, 116, 126,

127, 128, 148, 149, 218, 240, 242, 243, 244
Garside, S. F., 158
Garside, Sherwin, 28
Garwood, Mrs. M. M., 185
Gay Times (Las Vegas). See *Vegas Gay Times*, 140
Gazette (Carson City). See *Carson Evening Gazette*, 48
Gazette (Goodsprings). See *Goodsprings Gazette*, 110
Gazette (Reno). See *Reno Evening Gazette*, 177
Gazette (Treasure City). See *White Pine Gazette*, 246
Geft, W. A., 43
Gelwicks, Dan, 89
Genoa Journal, 92
Genoa Scorpion. See *Scorpion*, 89
Genoa Weekly Courier, 92
George, E. T., 12, 142
Gerber, A. E., 284
Gerlach Express, 93
Germain, Ray, 158, 244
Germain, Virginia, 244
Getchell, Noble H., 15, 20
Ghost Town Gazette (Kingston), 124
Gibbons, Thomas A., 214, 215
Gibson, A. B., 14, 120, 218, 241
Gibson, Charles H., 14
Gifford, Harry, 45
Gilbert Record, 94
Gillespie, William M., 258
Gillis, Bill, 205
Gillis, William, 22
Ging, Aaron, 213
Ginn, John I., 246, 251, 259, 260, 261, 263
Glaser, J., 213
Glen, Robert, 4, 180, 264
Glenn, Hugh, 6
Glenn, Malcom M., 6, 115
Glenn, W. N., 33
Glessner, S. A., 32, 256
Glessner, Sam S., 255
Glickfeld, Larry, 120
Glimpse, Herb, 205
Globe (Empire City). See *Empire City Globe*, 74
Godcharles, H. S., 152
Goebel, Russell R., 214
Golconda Illustrated Gazette, 94
Golconda News. See *News*, 95
Golconda Rustler. See *Rustler*, 96
Gold Center News, 96
Gold Circle Miner (Midas), 153
Gold Circle News (Midas), 153
Gold Circle Porcupine (Midas), 153
Gold Creek News, 96
Gold Hill Daily News (1863–82), 97
Gold Hill Message. See *Daily Morning Message*
Gold Hill News (1974–78), 100. See also *Gold Hill Daily News*, 97

Gold-Cañon Switch (Johntown), 122
Golden Echo (Gold Hill), 100
Goldfield Chronicle, 106
Goldfield Enterprise & Esmeralda County News, 109
Goldfield Gossip, 105
Goldfield Hotel Life, 108
Goldfield News, 101
Goldfield News Letter, 108
Goldfield News and Weekly Tribune. See *Goldfield News*, 101
Goldfield Post, 109
Goldfield Review (Goldfield), 107
Goldfield Review (Columbia), 55
Goldfield Sun, 103
Goldfield Tribune, 105
Goldfield Vigilant, 103
Goldman, J. R., 52
Goldyke Sun, 109
Gomez, Jo, 117
Goodman, Joseph T., 253, 254
Goodrich, Eugene, 61, 164, 165
Goodsprings Gazette, 110
Goodwin, Charles C., 254, 276
Goodwin, Nat C., 187
GOPaper (Las Vegas), 137
Gordon, Laura De Force, 33
Gorman, George, 164
Gorman, Thomas K., 202
Gotwaldt, William McClure, 44, 149, 150, 185, 219, 230, 241, 281
Graff, Fred, 204
Graham, James, 58
Graham, Michael S., 217
Graham, Robert, 26
Granata, John, 195
Granite Times, 110
Grantsville Bonanza, 111
Grantsville Sun, 110
Graves, Chet R., 152
Graves, George S., 149
Gray, A. B., 29, 47, 60, 288
Greater Nevada (Carson City), 48
Green Felt (Las Vegas), 140
Green Felt News (Reno). See *Green Sheet*, 216
Green Sheet (Reno), 216
Green, James T., 35, 60, 114
Greenfield. See Yerington
Greenspun, Herman M. (Hank), 131, 132, 158
Gregory, William, 276
Grey, O. H., 78
Griffen, Frank, Jr., 88
Griffen, James B., 266
Grover, C. W., 65
Grutt, Eugene, 173
Guinan, Guy, 48
Gunn, Johnny, 272

Hadley, Caroline J., 214
Hagerman, Fred W., 180
Hahnlen, Jacob F., 257, 260

Haight, Henry H., 5
Haines, A. E., 49, 85, 155, 274
Haines, V. E., 49, 155
Hale, Harold P., 65, 67, 146
Haley, James F., 54, 72, 187, 191, 282
Haley, Phil S., 108
Hall, Kathy Ledford, 161
Halleck Gossip, 86
Hallenbeck, Darrell, 143, 161
Halloway, Rex, 206
Halpin,——, 266
Ham, Timothy L., 255, 256
Hamann, Joy, 135
Hamlyn, John, 73
Hampel, Andy, 186
Hancock, W. C., 15
Hann, Bill, 50
Hanson, Herb, 134
Hanson, Ken, 284
Harriman Herald (Sparks), 230
Harriman. See Sparks
Harrington, W. P., 123, 172, 262
Harris,——, 178
Harris, Charles N., 41, 43
Harris, Ed, 84
Harris, Ray D., 151, 252
Harris, T. S., 6
Harrison, Pat, 205
Harroun, Edward R., 281
Harroun, Genevieve, 281
Hart, Edwin L., 137
Hart, Fred H., 8, 227, 254
Hastings, O. E. F., 256
Haswell, F. B., 256
Hatch, John, 2, 4
Hauser, Warren, 288
Hawkins, Hiram R., 97
Hawley, A. T., 34, 91
Haworth, Alice, 8, 15
Haworth, Lester W., 8, 14, 148, 155, 241
Hawthorne Herald, 115
Hawthorne News, 116
Hawthorne Oasis. See *Oasis,* 113
Hawthorne–Lucky Boy News, 148
Hawthorne–Lucky Boy Post, 116
Hayden, Edward W., 177
Hazen Harvest, 118
Hazlett, A. Lester, 189
Headlight (Sparks, 1904–05), See *Sparks Headlight,* 230
Headlight (Sparks, 1908), 232
Hearth and Home (Sparks), 234
Hecht, James, 58
Hedrick, Harry, 173, 174
Helene. See Delamar
Henderson Herald. See *Las Vegas Tribune,* 130
Henderson Home News, 119
Henderson Star, 119
Hendersonian (Henderson), 118
Hendrix, O. H. P., 26
Henley, William, Jr., 284
Henley, William J., 232
Henry, Jules, 50

Herald (Aurora). See *Esmeralda Herald,* 6
Herald (Battle Mountain). See *Battle Mountain Herald,* 14
Herald (Caliente). See *Caliente Herald,* 27
Herald (Carson City). See *Daily Evening Herald,* 39
Herald (Fallon). See *Fallon Herald,* 81
Herald (Hawthorne, 1883–84). See *Esmeralda Herald,* 115
Herald (Hawthorne, 1909). See *Hawthorne Herald,* 115
Herald (Henderson). See *Las Vegas Tribune,* 130
Herald (Hornsilver). See *Hornsilver Herald,* 119
Herald (Lewis). See *Lewis Herald,* 142
Herald (Mazuma). See *Mazuma Herald,* 151
Herald (Overton). See *Moapa Valley Herald,* 161
Herald (Palmetto). See *Palmetto Herald,* 162
Herald (Rhyolite). See *Rhyolite Herald,* 218
Herald (Sparks). See *Harriman Herald,* 230
Herald (Virginia City). See *Daily Evening Washoe Herald,* 258
Herald (Wells). See *Nevada State Herald,* 278
Hercules Miner, 119
Here and Now (Reno), 203
Herr, U. C., 72
Herzig, Jacob S. (George Graham Rice), 104, 187
Hews, Bert F., 251
Hiatt, Larry, 285
Hibbard, A. A., 191
Hickey, R. A., 201
Higginbotham, Janis, 51, 233
High Sierra Times (Incline Village), 120
Hilbish, William B., 199
Hill, George B., 41
Hill, J. H., 91
Hill, John J., 162, 163, 251, 281
Hill, Nancy, 156
Hillen, A. G., 129
Hinchcliffe, C. W., 8
Hobart, William W., 78
Hogan, Henry Hardy, 179, 182
Hogan, Robert, 10
Holland, Pat, 19, 164, 165, 226, 227, 261, 264
Holoran, J. F. O., 164
Home and the Range (Reno), 212
Home Builder (Carlin). See *Western Home Builder,* 30
Home Builder (Reno). See *Nevada Home Builder,* 196
Hoole, S. F., 179
Hopkins, A. D., 139
Hopkins, Al R., 101
Hornsilver Herald, 119
Horsley, Charles Lee, 168
Hose, A. C., 25, 26
Hot Stuph (Reno), 188

Hougate, Deke, Jr., 158
Hoyt, A. V., 53
Hudgins, Houlden, 70
Huling, James T., 255, 256, 266, 269
Humboldt Bulletin (Winnemucca), 284
Humboldt Mail (Winnemucca), 282
Humboldt National (Winnemucca), 280
Humboldt Register (Unionville), 249
Humboldt Register (Winnemucca), 280
Humboldt Register and Workingman's Advocate (Unionville), 250
Humboldt Standard (Winnemucca), 283
Humboldt Star (Winnemucca), 283
Humboldt Star and Battle Mountain Scout (Winnemucca), 285
Humboldt Sun (Winnemucca), 286
Hummel, Ed G., 47
Hummel, Nicholas A., 230, 231, 273, 274
Humphrey, F. G., 20
Hunt,———, 56
Hunter, J. R., 118, 144, 252
Hunting, George C., 189

Igoa, Cathy, 278
Impact (Reno), 213
Inch, Merrill, 158, 207
Inch, Patricia, 207
Independent (Carson City). See *Carson Daily Independent,* 33
Independent (Cherry Creek), 53
Independent (Elko). See *Elko Independent,* 64
Independent (Las Vegas), 132
Independent (Pioche). See *Lincoln County Independent,* 168
Independent (Reno, 1955–58), 208
Independent (Reno, 1938). See *Nevada Independent,* 203
Independent (Sutro). See *Sutro Independent,* 237
Independent (Virginia City). See *Daily Independent,* 263
Index (Carson City). See *Daily Index,* 41
Index (Wells). See *Wells Index,* 277
Indian Advance (Stewart), 236
Indian Call (Schurz), 224
Ingram, Ken, 81
Inland Empire (Hamilton), 111
Intermountain Liberal (Reno), 199
Italian-French Colony (Reno), 189

Jackson, Austin, 152
Jackson, Joseph J., 231
Jackson, Joseph J., Jr., 232
Jacobs, L. A., 46
Jacobson,———, 56
Jacobson, Ira N., 9, 75, 79, 210, 232, 244, 245
Jacobson, Mrs. Ira N., 244
James, Alfred, 31, 89, 90, 253
James, Dick, 254
James, Richard A., 256
Jarbidge Miner, 122

Jay, Alex, 235
Jeans, F. D., 58
Jenkins, Frank, 186
Jenkins, Frank G., 281
Jenkins, Peter R., 284, 285
Jensen, Rex, 143
Jernegan, W. L., 31, 32
Jernegan, William L., 89, 90, 253
Jesch, Gary, 217
Jessup News, 122
Joachim, Louis, 264
Joachimsen, Joseph P., 10
Johnson, E. Norman, 49, 209
Johnson, G. S., 102, 192
Johnson, H. H., 157
Johnson, H. W., 34, 98
Jones, A. D., 164, 166
Jones, A. P., 42
Jones, Don, 207
Jones, John P., 35, 97
Jones, K. C., 50
Jones, Kevin, 204
Jones, Marsha, 136
Jones, Orlando Ezra, 6, 113, 114, 255, 256
Jones, Ruth Giles, 209
Jones, Uther, 165, 168
Jones, W. D., 8, 10
Jonsson, Kenneth A., 217
Jordan, Joseph S., 152, 173
Journal (Boulder City). See *Boulder City Journal,* 21
Journal (Carson City). See *Nevada State Journal,* 36
Journal (Genoa). See *Genoa Journal,* 92
Journal (Las Vegas). See *Las Vegas Journal,* 128
Journal (Orovada). See *Orovada Weekly Journal,* 160
Journal (Pioche). See *Pioche Journal,* 166
Journal (Reno, 1870+). See *Nevada State Journal,* 175
Journal (Reno, 1910). See *Reno Industrial Journal,* 191
Journal (Rochester). See *Rochester Journal,* 220
Journal (Searchlight). See *Searchlight Journal,* 225
Julian, Charlie, 51
Julien, Thomas V., 180, 280
Jumbo Miner, 123
Jurdan, A. W., 127
Justice, James, 165

Kane, H. F., 21, 219
Karrasch, Karl K., 204
Karson Sity Gazoot (Carson City), 48
Kaufman, Thomas C., 22
Kearns, W. H., 262
Keegan, William R., 278
Keene, Guy T., 218
Keeney, Russ, 233
Keith, Charles H., 65, 68, 95, 146, 156
Kelley, E. D., 64, 175, 250, 280, 281

Kellogg, Wesley, 77
Kelly, J. Wells, 258
Kelly, Ralph, 210
Kemp, Mrs. G. R., 86
Kenny, John D., 152
Keno, Joe, 116
Kent, Marge, 131
Kent, Parmenter, 47, 105, 106
Kenyon, Frank A., 6, 66, 164, 165, 228
Kettle, Fred W., 286
Key (Sparks), 235
Key Magazine (Reno), 217
Keys to Hidden Treasure (Las Vegas), 127
Keyser-Cooper, Mark, 286
Keyser-Cooper, Terri, 15
Kies, George O., 4
Kilborn, George, 176
Kilborn, Mrs. George, 176
Kimball. See Kimberly
Kimberly News, 124
Kimzey, Louis L., 134
King, Clarence S., 186
King, Richard, 118, 130, 158
King, W. T., 47
Kingsland, ——, 109
Kingsley, W. Harold, 118
Kinnear, C. J., 81
Kinsey, Stephen A., 89
Kirk, E. Kirman, 191
Knocker (Manhattan), 150
Knuz, John, 109
KOLO Times (Reno), 210
Koontz, Louis K., 109
Kosmo, James E., 133
Krane, Elliot S., 139
Kruglak, Michael, 36
Kungle, C. H., 259

La Verdad (Las Vegas), 136
Lage, Walter, 165
Lahontan Valley News (Fallon), 84
Lahontan Valley Shopper (Fallon), 83
Laird, James L., 32, 255
Lake Mead Monitor (Logandale), 143
Lake Mead Monitor (Overton), 161
Lake Peak News, 125
Lamb, W. C., 241
Lambert, Darwin, 73
Lamy, George I., 87
Landeck, Don, 216
Landel, Gilbert, 58
Lander Free Press (Battle Mountain), 12
Lander. See Tenabo
Lang, Joane, 216
Lankford, Harold V., 101, 203
Lantern (Reno), 188
Lariat (Virginia City), 265
Larraz, Rolando, 136
Lary,——, 183
Las Vegan, 140
Las Vegas Age, 126
Las Vegas Changing Times, 135
Las Vegas Family Shopper (North Las Vegas), 159
Las Vegas Free Press, 136
Las Vegas Fun Times, 140
Las Vegas Hangover, 130
Las Vegas Israelite, 134
Las Vegas Journal, 128
Las Vegas Life Magazine, 135
Las Vegas Magazine, 133
Las Vegas Mirror, 140
Las Vegas News, 129
Las Vegas News. See *North Las Vegas News*, 158
Las Vegas Panorama, 135
Las Vegas Playgirl (Carson City), 51
Las Vegas Playground, 134
Las Vegas Review (1909–29), 126
Las Vegas Review (1969). See *Quarterly Las Vegas Review*, 136
Las Vegas Review-Journal, 128
Las Vegas Star. See *Star*, 136
Las Vegas Sun, 131
Las Vegas Times (1905–06), 125
Las Vegas Times (1932), 129
Las Vegas Today, 139
Las Vegas Tribune, 130
Las Vegas Voice, 134
Las Vegas West, 141
Lashmutt, Van B., 277
Latimer, Jan, 217
Latta, Mrs. M. E., 93
Laub, William M., Jr., 138
Laurie, Don, 124
Law, J. G., 175
Laworth, Lester S., 230
Lawrence, R. S., 266
Laws, Joshua G., 277
Leader (Elko). See *Elko Leader*, 66
Leary, Marilyn Herlihy, 233
Leavy, James, 36, 50, 128
Ledger (Reno). See *Reno Ledger*, 183
Lee, A. W., 46
Lee, Charles, 39
Lee, J. Otto, 81
Lee, L. Eugene, 178, 180
Lee, William L., 45, 46, 87
Lee, William T., 180
Legend (Virginia City). See *Virginia City Legend*, 272
Legionnaire (Reno). See *Sagebrush Legionnaire*, 199
Lemaire, A. D., 13
Lemaire, H. R., 13
Lemmon, Hal A., 38, 44, 46
Leonard, Lloyd, 72, 232
Leonard, Paul A., 72, 73, 176, 178
Leonard, Volney B., 103
Leonard W. A., 71
Leonesio, L. J., 82
Lerude, Warren L ., 176, 178
Levy, Leo S., 189
Lewis Herald, 142
Lewis, Irwin G., 35, 148, 172
Lewis, John C., 32, 34, 175, 228, 264, 277
Lewis, Robert L., 160

Lewis, W. C., 101, 105, 175
Lida Enterprise, 142
Life (Reno). See *Reno Life,* 202
Lightfoot, John H., 127
Lill, George R. 94, 232
Lincoln County Independent (Pioche), 168
Lincoln County Record (Pioche), 164
Linn, Otis L., 200
Linthicum, J. F., 256, 257
Little Joker (Battle Mountain), 14
Little Mining Bradstreet (Goldfield), 107
Little, O. C., 197
Little, Walter, 51
Littlefield, E. A., 66, 175, 247
Littlefield, L. B., 66
Local Advertiser (Virginia City), 259
Local Messenger (Delamar), 62
Local Messenger (Pioche), 167
Local News (Pioche), 166
Local Picture (Reno), 217
Locke, R. P., 228
Locker, William, 121
Lode (Delamar, 1892–93). See *Ferguson Lode,* 61
Lode (Delamar, 1894–1906). See *De Lamar Lode,* 61
Lode (Ellendale). See *Ellendale Lode,* 70
Lode (Helene). See *Ferguson Lode,* 61
Lode (Pioche), 167
Lode-Express (Caliente). See *Caliente Lode-Express,* 26
Long, George W., 106
Long, Huey, 132
Longenbaugh, May, 236
Loomis, H. B., 77
Lorena Miner, 144
Loucks, Guy D., 132
Loughrin, Margaret E., 173, 174
Loustalot, Louis, 10
Love (Reno), 213
Lovejoy, E. P., 273
Lovejoy, John K., 36, 257, 258, 276
Lovejoy, Owen, 276
Lovelock Review, 145
Lovelock Review-Miner, 146
Lovelock Standard, 145
Lovelock Tribune, 144
Lowe, Theodore, 55, 108, 169, 170
Lower Taxes (Logandale), 143
Lowery, Robert E., 256, 260
Lucas, C. G. 163
Lucky Boy News. See *Hawthorne–Lucky Boy News,* 148
Lucky Boy Post. See *Hawthorne–Lucky Boy Post,* 116
Luckyboy Mining Record, 147
Lydon, B. J., 132
Lyman, James, 204
Lynch, Denny, 162
Lynch, J. M., 54, 70, 71
Lynch, Philip, 97
Lynch, Mrs. Philip, 97
Lyon County Monitor (Yerington), 288
Lyon County Sentinel (Dayton), 58
Lyon County Times (Dayton), 59
Lyon County Times (Silver City), 228
Lyon County Times (Yerington). See *Yerington Times,* 288
Lyon County Wasp (Yerington), 289

MacBride, Frank, 196
MacDonald, John H., 210, 234
MacKenzie, D., 104
Mack, Effie Mona, 271
Mackay, Eric Reay, 191
Macura, William, 202
Maddrill, John W., 8
Magazine Las Vegas, 132
Magnet (Sparks), 232
Magowan, Tom, 132
Mahanny, John A., 262, 263
Mahoney,——, 12, 13
Mahoney, John, 268
Mail (Mountain City). See *Mountain City Mail,* 157
Maley, Glenn E., 285
Mangler (Wabuska). See *Wabuska Mangler,* 273
Manhattan Magnet, 150
Manhattan Mail, 148
Manhattan News, 149
Manhattan Post, 149
Manhattan Times, 149
Mann, Alvin D. 49, 117
Mann, Kurt C. S., 207
Manning, A. H., 177
Mannix, Frank P., 16, 25, 218
Many Smokes (Reno), 212
Market Letter (Goldfield), 102
Market Letter (Pioneer). See *Pioneer Market Letter,* 169
Marriage, E. Charles D., 27
Marsden, Walter L., 78, 222
Marshall, Carol, 146
Marshall, J. V., 57
Marshall, Joseph, 146
Martens, F. E., 88
Martin, Al H., 196
Martin, Annie H., 44
Martin, J. J., 198
Martin, John, 224
Martin, John C., 101, 105
Martinez, Mrs. Theodore, 188
Mason Valley News, 150
Mason Valley News (Yerington), 289
Mason Valley Tidings (Yerington), 287
Maute, Andrew, 8, 20, 33, 111
Mayer, Erskine, 69
Mayer; S. C., 69
Mayhugh, John S., Jr., 62
Mazuma Herald, 151
Mazuma World, 151
McAfee, James, 237, 238, 265
McBeth, Robert, 280
M'Cann, J. S., 98
McCarran, Patrick, 132
McCarthy, Alfred J., 29, 114

INDEX / 325

McCarthy, Denis E., 114, 253, 254, 262
McCarthy, Mrs. Denis E., 262
McCarthy, J. A., 288
McCarthy, J. J., 109
McCarthy, Joseph R. (U.S. Senator), 132
McCarthy, John A., 114
McCarthy, Pat S., 202, 203
McCauley, Anthony, 53
McCausland, Harry, 265
McClain, Liz, 158
McClatchy, James, 233
McClellan, George, 35
McClinton, J. G., 5
McCloskey, Jack R., 116, 117
McClure, Joseph, 37
McCone, Dollie A., 268
McCoy, G. R., 26
McCraney, H. A., 149
McCrosky,——, 77
McCulloch, Frank, 206, 207
McCully, George T., 181
McDermott, John A., 88
McDivitt, C. J., 240
McDonald, C. M., 71
McDonald, Calvin B., 265
McDonald, D. J., 209
McDonald, D. M., 152, 185
McDonald, Joseph F., 176, 178
McElwain, Edward F., 19, 34, 35, 36, 226, 276
McEwen, Arthur, 46
McIntosh, C. H., 145
McKechic, F. W., Jr., 176
McKenna, Dan G., 16, 248
McKenney, L. C., 74
McKinnon, John E., 254
McLain, A. J., 226
McLain, Joseph A., 158
McMahon, June, 286
McMahon, Mark, 286
McManon, Mort D., 55
McMurry, John G., 173, 174
McNair, William D., 195
McNeary,——, 289
McNeely,——, 151
McNeil, Lee D., 196
McNeil, Lois, 199
McNeil, W. T., 30, 192, 196, 199
McParlin, T. J., 239
McQueary, Niki, 222
McWade, John M., 215, 217
Measure For Measure (Battle Mountain), 11
Meder, Horace, 47
Memorandum (Pioche), 167
Mendive, Madlen, 233
Mennell, Mark S., 137
Menzel, Frederick H., 88
Menzel, Waldemar E., 88
Mercer, Frank B., 237, 238
Merida, Maria, 141
Merigold,——, 43
Merry, Harriet, 130
Message (Gold Hill). See *Daily Morning Message*, 98
Messenger (Battle Mountain). See *Battle Mountain Messenger*, 12
Metcalf, Vernon, 198
Metropolis Chronicle, 152
Micawber, J. Wilkins, Jr., 166
Mighels, Henry R., Jr., 35, 36, 45, 81
Mighels, Henry R., 35, 37, 38
Mighels, Ida B., 36
Mighels, Nellie V., 35
Mighels, Roy R., 148, 172
Mildren, Howard E., 225
Mildren, Sinah, 225
Miles, H. W., 61
Miles, Zane 36, 51
Millard, Mike, 140
Millard, Nancy, 140
Miller,——, 40
Miller, A. Grant, 191, 231
Miller, Charles J., 33
Miller, Dean W., 133
Miller, Elmer D., 211
Miller, George E., 10
Miller, John S., 36, 52, 73
Miller, Monnie D., 84
Miller, Vern A., 84
Millers Booster, 154
Millman, William, 140
Mills, A. J., 42
Minden Times, 155
Miner, Fred L., 149, 194, 200
Miner (Bullfrog). See *Bullfrog Miner* (Rhyolite), 218
Miner (Carrara). See *Carrara Miner*, 31
Miner (Cherry Creek). See *Cherry Creek Miner*, 54
Miner (Columbus). See *Borax Miner*, 55
Miner (Contact). See *Contact Miner*, 57
Miner (Eureka). See *Eureka Miner*, 79
Miner (Fairview). See *Fairview Miner*, 80
Miner (Hercules). See *Hercules Miner*, 119
Miner (Jarbidge). See *Jarbidge Miner*, 122
Miner (Jumbo). See *Jumbo Miner*, 123
Miner (Lorena). See *Lorena Miner*, 144
Miner (Mazuma). See *Seven Troughs Miner*, 151
Miner (Mina). See *Western Nevada Miner*, 154
Miner (National). See *National Miner*, 157
Miner (Nelson). See *Eldorado Canyon Miner*
Miner (Olinghouse). See *Olinghouse Miner*, 160
Miner (Quartz Mountain). See *Quartz Mountain Miner*, 171
Miner (Rawhide). See *Rawhide Miner*, 174
Miner (Reno). See *Western Miner*, 194
Miner (Rochester, 1913–14). See *Rochester Miner*, 219
Miner (Rochester, 1917–19). See *Rochester-Packard Miner*, 220
Miner (Tenabo). See *Bullion District Miner*, 239
Miner (Tonopah). See *Tonopah Miner*, 240

Miner (Transvaal). See *Transvaal Miner*, 245
Miner (Vernon, 1907–09). See *Seven Troughs Miner*, 252
Miner (Vernon, 1907). See *Vernon Miner*, 252
Miner (Ward). See *Ward Miner*, 274
Miner (Wonder). See *Wonder Miner*, 287
Mineral County Democrat (Hawthorne). See *Mineral County Forum*, 117
Mineral County Forum (Hawthorne), 117
Mineral County Independent (Hawthorne), 116
Mineral County Independent and Hawthorne News. See *Mineral County Independent*, 116
Mineral County News (Mina), 155
Mines and Market (Goldfield), 106
Mining and Industrial Review (Reno), 184
Mining Digest (Reno), 189
Mining Expositor (Ely). See *Ely Mining Expositor*, 72
Mining Financial News (Reno), 190
Mining News (Rosebud). See *Rosebud Mining News*, 221
Mining News (State Line), 235
Mining News (Tuscarora, 1883), 248
Mining News (Tuscarora, 1907–08). See *Tuscarora Mining News*, 248
Mining News (Wonder). See *Wonder Mining News*, 286
Mining Press (Reno), 203
Mining Record (Ely). See *Ely Record*, 71
Mining Record (Lucky Boy). See *Luckyboy Mining Record*, 147
Mining Record (Tonopah). See *Nevada Mining Record*, 243
Mining Record (Winnemucca). See *Nevada Mining Record*, 285
Mining Report (Ruby Hill). See *Ruby Hill Mining Report*, 221
Mining Reporter (Silver City), 229
Mining Reporter (Tonopah). See *Tonopah Mining Reporter*, 243
Mining Review (Tuscarora), 247
Mining Review (Virginia City). See *Nevada Mining Review*, 263
Mining Topics (Unionville), 251
Mirror (Las Vegas). See *Las Vegas Mirror*, 140
Mitchell, F. H., 14
Mitchell, Henry 177
Mix, Newman H., 21, 142, 148, 162, 229
Moapa Valley Herald (Overton), 161
Molinelli, Lambert, 78, 223
Monahan, Ogden, 48
Monarch Tribune, 155
Monday Budget (Virginia City, 1917–18), 269
Monday Budget (Virginia City, 1927–29), 269
Monitor (Logandale). See *Lake Mead Monitor*, 143
Monitor (Yerington). See *Lyon County Monitor*, 288
Monroe, Warren L., 65
Montrose, George A., 44
Mooney, Homer, 176, 194
Moore, Boyd, 193
Moore, Henry S., 266
Moore, Pleasant, 98
Moore, Warren L., 284
Moracci, Francisco M., 188, 189, 231
Morden, C. A., 78
Morgan, Oscar R., 178
Morgan, William, 124
Morris, C. N., 42
Morris, James, 241
Morris, Jesse A., 141
Morris, Richard, 211, 212
Morrisett, Oscar, 109
Morrison, Donald E., 146
Morrison, John P., 259
Mottsville Star, 156
Mountain Champion (Belmont), 19
Mountain City Mail, 157
Mountain City Times, 156
Mountain Magic (Reno), 205
Moyer, Norville W., 205, 207
Moyle, E. J., 75
Mulcahy, Edwin C., 232
Mulcahy, Howard, 232
Mulcahy, P. H., 100, 232
Muller, H., 78
Mundall, John H., 97
Mundt, Jerry, 16
Mundt, Jo, 16
Murray, Jack, 133
Murray, James D., 166
Murrish, Ed, 151
Musgrove, Mark W., 12, 17, 153, 160, 166, 189, 221, 222, 274, 275
Myers, Peter, 251, 281
Myers, W. F., 19
Mygatt, Peter, 73

Nance, Eva, 234
Nation, Oliver R., 165
National Miner, 157
Native Nevadan (Reno), 211
Neddenriep, F. J., 36
Needham, Oliver, 115
Neh-Muh News (Schurz), 224
Nellis Century (Las Vegas), 133
Nelson, H., 62
Nelson, Thomas, 281
Net (Tonopah), 243
Netherton, Stanley, 288
Nevada American (Stewart), 237
Nevada Appeal (Carson City), 35
Nevada Beverage Index (Reno), 207
Nevada Bugle (Reno), 192
Nevada Business News (Las Vegas). See *Western Business News*, 137
Nevada-California Miner (Reno), 190
Nevada Capitol News (Carson City), 50
Nevada Churchman (Reno), 189
Nevada Citizen (Las Vegas), 132

Nevada Citizen (Reno), 183
Nevada Colony News (Fallon), 83
Nevada-Contact Miner Review, 57
Nevada Copper News (Acme), 1
Nevada Democrat (Carlin), 30
Nevada Democrat (Las Vegas), 133
Nevada Democrat (Reno, 1914–15), 194
Nevada Democrat (Reno, 1875). See *Daily Nevada Democrat,* 177
Nevada Democratic Record (Tonopah), 245
Nevada Farmer and Stockman (Elko), 69
Nevada Federal Journal (Sparks), 234
Nevada Federationist (Reno, 1915–17), 195
Nevada Federationist (Reno, 1917), 196
Nevada Forum (Sparks). See *Forum,* 231
Nevada Home Builder (Reno), 196
Nevada Horse Life (Reno), 216
Nevada Hunting and Fishing (Reno), 206
Nevada Independent (Reno), 203
Nevada Independent and Reno Reporter, 207
Nevada Index-Union (Carson City), 43
Nevada Jewish Chronicle (Henderson), 119
Nevada Labor Record (Reno), 201
Nevada Legionnaire (Sparks), 233
Nevada Legionnaire (Lovelock), 147
Nevada Liberal (Reno). See *Intermountain Liberal,* 199
Nevada Life (Las Vegas), 130
Nevada Lutheran (Gardnerville), 88
Nevada Magazine (Minden), 155
Nevada Magazine (Winnemucca), 282
Nevada Methodist (Sparks), 231
Nevada Miner (Golconda), 95
Nevada Miner (Reno). See *Mining and Industrial Review,* 184
Nevada Mines and Farms (Reno), 190
Nevada Mining and Market Review (Goldfield), 103
Nevada Mining Bulletin (Goldfield), 107
Nevada Mining Bulletin (Las Vegas), 129
Nevada Mining Investor (Reno), 186
Nevada Mining Market Outlook (Reno), 186
Nevada Mining News (Goldfield), 104
Nevada Mining News (Reno), 187, 192
Nevada Mining Press (Reno), 198
Nevada Mining Record (Tonopah), 243
Nevada Mining Record (Winnemucca), 285
Nevada Mining Record & Reporter (Tonopah), 244
Nevada Mining Review (Virginia City), 263
Nevada Mining Securities Review (Goldfield), 104
Nevada Mobile Home News (Reno), 213
Nevada Mobile Home Times (North Las Vegas). See *Nevada Times,* 159
Nevada Monthly (Virginia City), 267
Nevada New Era (Kennedy), 123
Nevada New Era (Lovelock), 144
Nevada News (Winnemucca), 283
Nevada News Letter and Advertiser (Reno), 193
Nevada Observer (Reno), 184, 197
Nevada Outdoor Adventure (Reno), 214

Nevada Patriot (Carson City), 39
Nevada Pionier (Virginia City), 257
Nevada Post (Virginia City), 264
Nevada Profiles (Reno), 215
Nevada Progressive (Austin), 11
Nevada Progressive (Battle Mountain), 15
Nevada Prohibitionist (Genoa), 93
Nevada Pulpit (Carson City), 38
Nevada Rancher (Sparks), 235
Nevada Record (Tonopah). See *Nevada Democratic Record,* 245
Nevada Register (Reno), 202
Nevada Report (Las Vegas), 135
Nevada Republican (Genoa). See *Carson Valley Farmer,* 91
Nevada Review Monthly (Reno), 200
Nevada Rockroller (Reno), 193
Nevada Sage (Reno), 214
Nevada Searchlight (Reno), 199
Nevada Silver Tidings (Elko), 68
Nevada Slogan (Kearns), 123
Nevada Socialist (Reno, 1914), 193
Nevada Socialist (Reno, 1916), 195
Nevada Sportsman (Sparks), 233
Nevada Staats Zeitung (Virginia City, 1864), 259
Nevada Staats-Zeitung (Virginia City, 1875), 264
Nevada State Builder (Reno), 201
Nevada State Fair Herald (Reno), 178
Nevada State Herald (Wells), 278
Nevada State Journal (Carson City), 36
Nevada State Journal (Reno), 175
Nevada State Labor News (Reno), 204
Nevada State News (Reno), 207
Nevada State Public Observer (Sparks), 234
Nevada State Veteran, 50
Nevada Statesman (Carson City), 51
Nevada Statesman (Virginia City), 265
Nevada Stockgrower (Reno), 198
Nevada Times (North Las Vegas), 159
Nevada Topics and Advertiser (Reno), 198
Nevada Tribune (Carson City). See *Daily Nevada Tribune,* 37
Nevada Union (Carson City), 43
Nevada Veteran (Las Vegas), 130
Nevada Veteran and Labor News (Reno), 202
Nevada Veterans' Journal (Reno), 210
Nevada Veteran's Journal (Tonopah), 245
Nevada Voice (Reno), 200
Nevada Workman (Goldfield), 108
Nevada's Senior Journal (Las Vegas), 139
Nevadan (Reno), 196, 197
Nevadan (Tonopah). See *Tonopah Nevadan,* 242
Nevadian (Reno), 217
Nevadian Times (Carson City), 49
Nevadian Times (Fernley), 85
Nevadian Times (Wadsworth), 274
Nevin, Vincent C., 270
New Daily Appeal (Carson City). See *Nevada Appeal,* 35
New Era (Kennedy). See *Nevada New Era,*

123
New Era (Lovelock). See *Nevada New Era*, 144
New Indian (Stewart), 236
New Nevada (Goldfield), 103
New West (Reno), 192
Newlands, Francis G., 183
Newman, Cy, 141
News (Duck Valley). See *Duck Valley News*, 62
News (Boulder City). See *Boulder City News*, 22
News (Caliente). See *Caliente News*, 27
News (Carson City, 1891–1930). See *Carson City News*, 44
News (Carson City, 1961). See *Carson City News*, 51
News (Chafey). See *Chafey News*, 52
News (Dutch Creek). See *Dutch Creek News*, 63
News (East Ely). See *White Pine News*, 64
News (Ely). See *White Pine News*, 70
News (Fairview). See *Fairview News*, 80
News (Genoa). See *Carson Valley News*, 91
News (Golconda), 95
News (Gold Center). See *Gold Center News*, 96
News (Gold Creek). See *Gold Creek News*, 96
News (Gold Hill, 1863–82). See *Gold Hill Daily News*, 97
News (Gold Hill, 1974–78). See *Gold Hill News*, 100
News (Goldfield). See *Goldfield News*, 101
News (Hamilton). See *White Pine News*, 112
News (Hawthorne, 1887–89). See *Esmeralda News*, 115
News (Hawthorne, 1928–35). See *Hawthorne News*, 116
News (Ione). See *Nye County News*, 120
News (Jessup). See *Jessup News*, 122
News (Kimball). See *Kimberly News*, 124
News (Kimberly). See *Kimberly News*, 124
News (Lake Peak), 125
News (Las Vegas, 1979), 141
News (Las Vegas, 1941). See *Las Vegas News*, 129
News (Mahhattan). See *Manhattan News*, 149
News (Mason Valley). See *Mason Valley News*, 150
News (Mina). See *Mineral County News*, 155
News (North Las Vegas). See *North Las Vegas News*, 158
News (Pine Grove). See *Pine Grove News*, 163
News (Rawhide). See *Rawhide News*, 173
News (Reno). See *Reno News*, 201, 209
News (Rochester). See *Rochester Mining News*, 220
News (Rosebud). See *Rosebud Mining News*, 221
News (Ruby Hill). See *Ruby Hill Mining News*, 222
News (Ruby Valley). See *Ruby Valley News*, 222
News (Searchlight). See *Searchlight News*, 225
News (Taylor). See *White Pine News*, 238
News (Treasure City). See *White Pine News*, 246
News (Virginia City). See *Virginia City News*, 270
News (White Plains). See *Churchill News*, 279
News (Whitney). See *Whitney News*, 279
News (Winnemucca). See *Nevada News*, 283
News (Yerington). See *Mason Valley News*, 150
News Advertiser (Reno), 202
News and Tribune (Goldfield). See *Goldfield News*, 101
News-Bulletin (Searchlight). See *Searchlight News-Bulletin*, 226
News Notes (Schurz), 224
News Reporter (Dayton), 59
Newsbits (Beatty). See *Beatty Newsbits*, 16
Newsletter (Reno). See *Native Nevadan*, 211
Nicholson, J. T., 199
Nicklin, C. W., 16, 25, 126, 218
Nicklin, T. G., 16, 245
Niemeyer, John, 191
Niles, Edward, 40, 41
Nixon, George S., 281
Noble, Lieutenant, 3
Norcross, Charles A., 38, 177, 182, 186
Nores, E. L., 165
Nores, Richard, 168
Norris, Fred J., 254
North Lake Tahoe Bonanza (Incline Village), 120
North Las Vegas News, 158
North Las Vegas Sun, 158
North Las Vegas Valley Times, 159
North Tahoe World (Crystal Bay), 58
Northern Nevada Home (Reno), 215
Northern Nevada Labor News (Reno), 211
Northern Nevada Shopping News (Reno), 214
Northern Nevada Weekly Mine Review (Lovelock), 146
Norton, Harry J., 228, 229
Noyes,——, 254
Nugent, James E., 281
Nugget (Osceola). See *Osceola Nugget*, 160
Nugget (Round Mountain), 221
Numa News (Schurz). See *Neh-Muh News*, 224
Numa Ya'-Dua' (Yerington). See *Numu Ya Dua'*, 289
Numu Ya Dua' (Yerington), 289
Nye County News (Ione), 120

O'Brien, James, 241
O'Brien, James F., 101, 288
O'Connell, Kenneth, 131

O'Connor, Mike, 140
O'Donnol, Dion, 205
O'Hara, Allen J., 22
O'Malley, Pat, 205, 206
Oak (Logandale), 143
Oasis (Hawthorne), 113
Oasis Advertiser (Boulder City), 23
Obelisk (Carrara). See *Carrara Obelisk*, 31
Observer (Reno). See *Nevada Observer*, 184, 197
Occasional (Virginia City), 267
Occidental (Virginia City), 257
Oddie, Tasker, 192, 240
Off the Strip (Las Vegas), 141
Official Las Vegas Entertainment and Events Guide, 138
Ogilvie, Norman, 199
Olcovich, I., 44, 45, 46, 47
Olcovich, Selig, 44, 45, 46, 47
Old Pah Utah (Washoe City), 276
Olinghouse Miner, 160
Olsson, Phil, 214
Oman, G. W., 93
Oracle (State Line). See *State Line Oracle*, 236
Ormsby County Ledger (Carson City), 47
Ormsby, William M., 31, 90
Oro City Times, 160
Orovada Weekly Journal, 160
Orphans' Appeal (Virginia City), 268
Orr, William E., 165
Osborne, H. Z., 28
Osborne, Lester, 281
Osborne, T. J., 164
Osceola Nugget, 160
Our Town (Reno), 214
Outlook (Sun Valley). See *Valley Outlook*, 237
Overlay (Las Vegas), 139
Overpeck, Jan, 233

Pace, O. Burt, 165
Pace (Reno). See *Reno Pace*, 208
Pacific Coast Advertiser (Virginia City), 263
Packard. See Rochester
Paggi, M. 188, 231
Pahrump Tribune, 162
Pahrump Valley Star, 161
Pahrump Valley Times, 161
Paine, C. S., 59
Paiute (Schurz), 224
Palm, Bob, 141
Palmetto Herald, 162
Pandora (Reno), 183
Paradise Reporter, 162
Paradise Sunshine, 163
Parish Guide (Carson City), 40
Parish Rubric (Carson City), 46
Park, J. D., 13
Parke, W. W., 146
Parker, Charles A., 256
Parker, James E., 3, 5, 164

Parker, Rich, 73
Parker, Tom C., 14
Parkinson, Edward J., 37, 38, 182
Parkinson, R. R., 37, 38
Patrick, Fanny B., 200
Patrick, Holmes C., 33, 112
Patrick, L. L., 102
Patrick, S. C., 64
Patterson, Charles W., 26, 145, 287, 288
Patterson, Mrs. Charles W., 288
Patterson, Ed, 288
Patton, H. W., 230
Paycrack (Rochester). See *Rochester Paycrack*, 220
Payette, Mike, 15, 271
Payne, George H., 36, 49
Payne, George M., 222
Paynter, George R., 254
Payton, Michael, 146
Payton, Tony, 88, 146
Pearson,——, 144
Peltier, George W., 144
Penrose, William J., 78, 79, 222
People's Advocate (Austin), 10
People's Advocate (Winnemucca), 282
People's Paper (Gold Hill), 100
People's Press (Pioche). See *Pioche People's Press*, 168
People's Tribune (Gold Hill), 99
Perino, Aldo A., 270
Perkins, A. B., 31
Perkins, Charles L., 35, 37, 64, 66, 249, 250
Perkins, H. A., 224, 225
Perkins, L., 204
Perry, Les, 132
Perry, S. D., 165
Peters, C. E., 151
Peters, Francis L., 27
Petillo, Ralph, 135, 140, 141
Pettee, Charles James, 61
Pettee, James, 164
Petterson, C. H., 219
Phillips, Alfred H., 8
Phillips, W. C., 7
Phoenix, John (Lieutenant Derby, Squibob), 2, 3, 5
Picotte, T. E., 228, 237, 264
Pike, W. H. A., 273
Pine Grove News, 163
Pioche Boomlet, 166
Pioche Journal, 166
Pioche Messenger. See *Local Messenger*, 167
Pioche People's Press, 168
Pioche Record. See *Lincoln County Record*, 164
Pioche Review, 165
Pioche Times, 167
Pioche World, 166
Pioneer Market Letter, 169
Pioneer Press, 169
Pioneer Times, 170
Pioneer Topics, 169
Pitchford, W. H., 112, 164, 223, 246

Pittman, Key, 170
Pittman, Vail M., 72, 73, 168
Plaindealer (Reno, 1881–84), 179
Plaindealer (Reno, 1895–99), 182
Plant, John W., 262, 266
Platt, Bill, 216
Platt, Samuel, 45, 178
Playgirl (Carson City). See *Las Vegas Playgirl*, 51
Plummer, George F., 70
Plunkett, T. C., 248
Plunkett, W. D., 248
Pollock, C. E., 272
Porter, A. O., 177
Porter, Samuel T., 68
Portfolio (Carson City), 40
Post (Carson City, 1885). See *Carson Post*, 43
Post (Carson City, 1864–65). See *Daily Morning Post*, 34
Post (Elko). See *Elko Post*, 66
Post (Ely). See *Ely Post*, 73
Post (Goldfield). See *Goldfield Post*, 109
Post (Manhattan). See *Manhattan Post*, 149
Post (Silver Peak). See *Silver Peak Post*, 229
Post (Virginia City). See *Nevada Post*, 264
Potosi Nix Cum Rouscht (Potosi), 171
Powell, Charles H., 189
Powning, C. C., 66, 175, 178
Pratt, A. C., 42, 91, 92
Pratt, William P., 97, 98, 261, 267
Preble, C. S., 177
Prell, Allan, 211
Prentice, F. A., 277
Presley, C. A., 204
Press (Blair). See *Blair Press*, 21
Press (Carson City). See *Carson Press*, 45
Press (Gardnerville). See *Gardnerville Press*, 87
Press (Gerlach). See *Valley Press*, 94
Press (Pioneer). See *Pioneer Press*, 169
Press (Rawhide). See *Rawhide Daily Press*, 173
Preston, Harry W., 26
Price, Charlie, 97
Prill, Arthur, 53
Pringle, Carol Marshall, 146
Profiles (Reno). See *Nevada Profiles*, 215
Progress (Caliente). See *Caliente Progress*, 25
Progress (Wells). See *Wells Progress*, 278
Progressive (Austin). See *Nevada Progressive*, 11
Progressive (Battle Mountain). See *Nevada Progressive*, 15
Progressive West (Reno), 185
Prohibitionist (Genoa). See *Nevada Prohibitionist*, 93
Prospector (Atwood). See *Fairplay Prospector*, 1
Prospector (Caliente), 26
Prospector (Carson City), 52
Protes, Abraham, 88

Pry (Reno), 204
Pueschel,——, 178
Pulpit (Carson City). See *Nevada Pulpit*, 38
Purcell, Louis, 231
Putnam, Charles A. V., 33, 39, 111, 260
Pyramid Lake News (Nixon). See *Firewheel*, 158

Quarterly Las Vegas Review, 136
Quartz Mountain Miner, 171

Ragsdale, John C., 76, 77, 249, 280
Rainbow (Carson City), 50
Ramos, Librado, 141
Ramos, Rose, 141
Ramsey Recorder, 172
Ramsey, Hugh A. R., 185
Raney, V. H., 210
Rangno, Louis, 130
Ransom, W. M., 213
Ranson, Marilyn, 278
Rapida, Bob, 58
Rawhide Daily Press, 173
Rawhide Miner, 174
Rawhide News, 173
Rawhide Press-Times, 174
Rawhide Rustler, 172
Rawhide Times, 173
Raycraft, Kenneth, 48
Reber, Frank L., 58, 125, 153, 157
Record (Bellehelen). See *Bellehelen Record*, 17
Record (Caliente). See *Caliente Record*, 27
Record (Ely). See *Ely Record*, 71
Record (Gardnerville). See *Gardnerville Record*, 87
Record (Gilbert). See *Gilbert Record*, 94
Record (Pioche). See *Lincoln County Record*, 164
Record (Reno, 1878). See *Daily Evening Record*, 179
Record (Reno, 1908). See *Reno Record*, 189
Record-Courier (Gardnerville), 88
Recorder (Ramsey). See *Ramsey Recorder*, 172
Rector, W. F., 127
Reed, E. F., 179
Reek, George, 78
Reese River Reveille (Austin), 7
Reflex (Taylor). See *White Pine Reflex*, 238
Reflex (Ward). See *Ward Reflex*, 275
Regan, T. E., 264
Register (Carson City). See *Daily State Register*, 37
Register (Reno). See *Nevada Register*, 202
Register (Winnemucca). See *Humboldt Register*, 280
Reilly, H. C., 72
Reminder (Boulder City). See *Boulder City Reminder*, 22
Reminder (Reno). See *Reno Reminder*, 205
Remington, H. P., 269
Reno Amusements, 194

Reno Annual Advertiser, 179
Reno Bazaar, 180
Reno Call, 186
Reno Crescent, 175
Reno Daily Record. See *Daily Evening Record,* 179
Reno Democrat (1883–84), 180
Reno Democrat (1914–15). See *Nevada Democrat,* 194
Reno Evening Gazette, 177
Reno Federation, 185
Reno Fundial, 206
Reno Industrial Journal, 191
Reno Ledger, 183
Reno Life, 202
Reno Magazine (1976), 215
Reno Magazine (1979+), 217
Reno Nevada Weekly, 191
Reno News, 201, 209
Reno Pace, 208
Reno Record, 189
Reno Reminder, 205
Reno Reporter, 205
Reno Reveille. See *Reveille,* 187
Reno State Economist, 201
Reno This Week, 207
Reno Times, 180
Reno Whooperup, 190
Reporter (Belmont). See *Silver Bend Reporter,* 17
Reporter (Paradise). See *Paradise Reporter,* 162
Reporter (Reno). See *Reno Reporter,* 205
Reporter (Shermantown). See *Shermantown Reporter,* 226
Reporter (Silver City, Mar-Aug 1876), 229
Reporter (Silver City, Sep-Dec 1876). See *Mining Reporter,* 229
Republican (Austin). See *Austin Republican,* 9
Republican (Eureka). See *Eureka Daily Republican,* 76
Republican (Winnemucca). See *Silver State,* 281
Republican Press (Eureka), 78
Republican Principles (Virginia City), 268
Reveille (Austin). See *Reese River Reveille,* 7
Reveille (Reno), 187
Review (Clarois). See *Clarois Review,* 54
Review (Goldfield). See *Goldfield Review,* 107
Review (Las Vegas). See *Las Vegas Review,* 126; *Quarterly Las Vegas Review,* 136
Review (Lovelock). See *Lovelock Review,* 145
Review (Pioche). See *Pioche Review,* 165
Review (Reno). See *Nevada Review Monthly,* 200
Review (Vernon). See *Vernon Review,* 252
Review-Miner (Lovelock). See *Lovelock Review-Miner,* 146
Reynolds,——, 118
Reynolds, Donald W., 36, 50, 52, 72, 73, 128, 284

Rhodes, Travis, 258
Rhyolite Bulletin. See *Rhyolite Daily Bulletin,* 219
Rhyolite Daily Bulletin, 219
Rhyolite Herald, 218
Rice, George Graham (Jacob S. Herzig), 104, 172, 176, 187, 190
Rice, Gordon A., 59
Richards,——, 40
Richards, Bob, 271
Richards, Emily, 202
Richardson, E. N., 244
Richardson, Eli N., 83
Richie, R. L., 203
Rickard, Edward, 77
Ricketts, V. L., 101, 105
Riddle, Frank W., 145
Riddle, George E., 144
Riddle, Homer T., 145
Riddle, Howard N., 65, 68, 145, 151, 152, 252, 281
Riddle, Merchant S., 60, 68, 282, 283
Ridgway, J. E., 59
Rieck, Elizabeth Michael, 15
Riggle, A. B., 196
Roach, Frank W., 281
Robbins, E. E., 231
Robbins, John, 280
Roberts, Edwin E., 35
Roberts, Gerald A., 9, 244, 245
Roberts, Jeanette, 205
Roberts, William G., 75, 244
Robertson, Stuart, 285
Robinette, Roger, 76
Robins, W. W., 12
Robinson, Bryant, 143
Robinson, F. H., 101
Robinson, Marshall, 35, 41, 42
Rochester Journal, 220
Rochester Miner, 219
Rochester Mining News, 220
Rochester Paycrack, 220
Rochester-Packard Miner, 220
Rocket (Hawthorne), 117
Rockroller (Reno). See *Nevada Rockroller,* 193
Roff, Nate W., 184
Rogan, Marian, 285
Rogers, Lloyd A., 205
Rolfe, Tallman H., 246
Roney, F. G., 79
Root, William B., 71
Rose, George H., 281
Rose, George M., 221, 283
Rosebud Mining News, 221
Rosenthal, S. H., 115
Ross, W. W., 33
Round Mountain Nugget. See *Nugget,* 221
Ruby Hill Mining News, 222
Ruby Hill Mining Report, 221
Ruby Valley News, 222
Rulon, Phillip M., 217
Runnels, W. H., 180
Rushlight (Virginia City), 266

Russell, Charles H., 72
Russell, George B., 49, 65, 67, 68, 95, 283
Russell, George T., 147
Russell, Grover T., 147
Rustler (Golconda), 96
Rustler (Rawhide). See *Rawhide Rustler,* 172
Rustler (Yerington). See *Yerington Rustler,* 287
Rutherford, George W., 8, 13, 281
Rutledge, Clyde R., 272

Safeguard (Virginia City). See *Daily Safeguard,* 260
Safford Express, 223
Sage (Reno). See *Nevada Sage,* 214
Sagebrush Legionnaire (Reno), 199
Sagebrush Stockman (Reno), 181
Sain, Charles MacKnight, 96, 127, 143, 144, 156
Sain's Weekly Letter (Logandale), 143
Saling, Milo P., 205, 206, 270
Samuels, Herb, 207
Sanchez, Louis, 138
Sander, Fred C., 82
Sandidge, D. M., 98
Sanford, George L., 44, 123, 178
Sanford, Graham, 178
Sanford, John, 178
Sanford, Leigh, 178
Sanford, Robert, 86, 289
Sanford, Robert H., 82
Saturday Reporter (Sparks), 233
Saxton, J. B., 5
Sayre, D. L., 29, 111, 181, 287
Schell Creek Prospect (Shellbourne), 223
Schenk, Roy W., 70
Schmidt, Larrie H., 141
Schon, Mike, 233
Schuster, Richard J., 176, 178
Schwalenberg, L. G., 72
Scorpion (Genoa), 89
Scott, E. A., 12, 13
Scott, J. Winfield, 262
Scout (Battle Mountain). See *Battle Mountain Scout,* 14
Scrimgeour, Alex, 229
Scrugham, James G., 128, 176
Searchlight (Reno). See *Nevada Searchlight,* 199
Searchlight Bulletin, 224
Searchlight Enterprise, 225
Searchlight Journal, 225
Searchlight News, 225
Searchlight News-Bulletin, 226
Searchlight. See *Searchlight Bulletin,* 224
Sears, S. S., 65
Sears, Willis, 107
Segretti, Marguerite C., 138
Selkirk, Bert N., 88
Selkirk, Sue, 88
Sellinger, Marvin, 138
Semi-Monthly Bulletin (Goldfield), 103
Sentinel (Como). See *Como Sentinel,* 56

Sentinel (Dayton). See *Lyon County Sentinel,* 58
Sentinel (Eureka). See *Eureka Sentinel,* 74
Sentinel (Reno), 209
Sentinel (Virginia City). See *Sun Mountain Sentinel,* 271
Sessions, David, 38
Seven Troughs District News (Mazuma), 151
Seven Troughs Miner (Mazuma), 151
Seven Troughs Miner (Vernon), 252
Sewall, G. T., 32
Shannon,——, 266
Sharon, William E., 97, 177, 254
Sharp, Darlene, 222
Shaw, Bob, 211
Shaw, Henry G., 254
Shaw, James T., 44
Sheehan, Jack E., 140
Sheerin, Chris H., 67
Shelly, Bruce, 233
Shelly, Carl, 147, 232, 233
Shelor, Douglass, 187, 191
Sheplow, Sam, 204
Sherman, A. A., 64, 165
Sherman, Edwin A., 1, 2
Shermantown Reporter, 226
Sherwin, John R., 138
Shettel, Florence King, 205
Shipaugh,——, 189
Shire, David, 15
Shirton, Ed M., 201, 278
Shopper (Fallon), 85
Shopper (Las Vegas), 131
Shopping News (Reno), 203
Shopping News Reminder (Reno), 206
Showtime (Reno), 213
Sibert Scorpion. See *Desert Scorpion,* 28
Siebert, Eleanor, 48
Siebert, Frederick, 48
Sierra Magazine (Reno), 209
Sierra Scene (Reno), 215
Sierra Shopper (Sparks), 235
Sills, M. W., 269
Silveira, Berta, 226
Silver Age (Carson City), 32
Silver Bend Reporter (Belmont), 17
Silver Bow Standard, 227
Silver Circle Mobile Home News (Reno), 214
Silver Peak Post, 229
Silver Plume (Eureka), 77
Silver State (Unionville), 251
Silver State (Winnemucca), 281
Silver State Forum (Carson City), 52
Silver State News (Winnemucca). See *Silver State,* 281
Simpson, A. J., 79
Simpson, Robert W., 112, 164, 238, 246, 275
Sisson, Frank, 181
Skillman, Archibald, 53, 74, 75, 112, 227
Skillman, Ed A., 75
Skillman, Willis L., 75

Skookum Times, 230
Slipstream (Pioche), 168
Smaill, R. Leslie, 81, 149, 227, 288
Smith, A. L., 188
Smith, Arthor, 64
Smith, Claude H., 81
Smith, Dean K., 35, 47
Smith, Fred W., 128
Smith, George H., 88
Smith, George M., 60, 87, 92, 93
Smith, Horace, 284
Smith, P. W., 279
Smith, Thomas, 175
Smith, William R., 50
Snell, Earle, 199
Snowbound (Reno), 181
Snyder, E. C., 68
Snyder, Ken, 84
Sommer, H. C., 144
Southern Nevada Labor Beacon (Las Vegas), 133
Southern Nevada Labor News (Las Vegas), 133
Southworth, Charles E., 87, 88
Southworth, Stoddard, 87, 88
Spark of Genius (Austin), 9
Sparks Advertiser, 233
Sparks Dispatch, 230
Sparks Headlight (1904–05), 230
Sparks Headlight (1908). See *Headlight,* 232
Sparks Tribune, 232
Spear, Frank W., 239
Speidel, Merritt C., 176, 178
Spellier, Louis A., 80
Spencer, Ernest T., 284
Spencer, Wayne, 73
Spillman, Charles F., 142, 198
Sporting Bulletin (Goldfield), 104
Sprague, Charles S., 101, 108
Sprague's Newsletter (Goldfield), 108
Spring Mountain Gazette (Las Vegas), 138
Springmeyer, George, 88
Sproule, Charles H., 12, 13, 67, 265
Sproule, Herbert C., 49
Squibob (Lieutenant Derby, John Phoenix), 2, 3, 5
Squires, Charles P., 22, 126
Stack, Garrett M., 146
Stage (Virginia City), 266
Stallings, Larry, 215
Standard (Eureka). See *Eureka Tri-Weekly Standard,* 79
Standard (Fallon). See *Fallon Standard,* 81
Standard (Lovelock). See *Lovelock Standard,* 145
Standard (Silver Bow). See *Silver Bow Standard,* 227
Standerwick, H. M., 230
Stanley, D. S., 229
Stanley, Warren, 158
Star (Aurora, 1886). See *Aurora Star,* 6
Star (Aurora, 1862–64). See *Esmeralda Star,* 1

Star (Dyer). See *Esmeralda Star,* 63
Star (Ellendale). See *Ellendale Star,* 69
Star (Henderson). See *Henderson Star,* 119
Star (Las Vegas), 136
Star (Mottsville). See *Mottsville Star,* 156
Star (Pahrump). See *Pahrump Valley Star,* 161
Star (Reno, 1904), 185
Star (Reno, 1884–85). See *Daily Morning Star,* 180
Star (Washoe City). See *Washoe Weekly Star,* 276
Star (Winnemucca). See *Humboldt Star,* 283
State Democrat (Carson City), 35
State Line Oracle, 236
Stauffer, J. W., 198
Steed, Jay E., 73
Steinick, William E., 160
Stenhouse, S. M., 78
Steninger, E. M., 67
Steninger, Eber B., 67
Steninger, Mel, 67
Sterling, John, 12
Sterling, Mike, 120
Stevens, J. E., 170, 171
Stevens, Maury, 135
Stevens, Muriel, 135
Stevenson,——, 236
Stevenson, C. C., 267
Stevenson, Charles C., 97, 261
Stevenson, Louis, 182
Stevenson, Pat, 84
Stewart, W. Frank, 264, 265
Stewart, W. J., 70
Stimson, Joel, 160
Stinson, William E., 129
Stitser, Avery D., 15, 284
Stitser, F. C., 281
Stitser, Rollin Charles, 15, 65, 284
Stock Ledger (Virginia City), 266
Stock Report (Virginia City), 265
Stockman (Reno). See *Sagebrush Stockman,* 181
Stoddard, Charles H., 175, 280
Stollery, Bobbie, 58
Stollery, Stub, 58
Stone, Bernard M., 31
Stone, Elizabeth, 209
Stoneham, W. J., 241
Storey, Everett L., 132
Storm, Brian, 205
Story, J., 77
Street, Henry C., 35, 37, 64, 250, 261
Strong, Ed A., 57
Studebaker, I. J., 160
Suffragist (Ely). See *White Pine Suffragist,* 73
Sullivan, James H., 262, 268
Sullivan, L. M., 104
Sun (Austin). See *Austin Sun,* 11
Sun (Carson City), 44
Sun (Goldfield). See *Goldfield Sun,* 103
Sun (Goldyke). See *Goldyke Sun,* 109

Sun (Grantsville). See *Grantsville Sun,* 110
Sun (Las Vegas). See *Las Vegas Sun,* 131
Sun (North Las Vegas, 1949–59). See *North Las Vegas News,* 158
Sun (North Las Vegas, 1950–51). See *North Las Vegas Sun,* 158
Sun (Tonopah). See *Tonopah Sun,* 241
Sun (Tybo). See *Tybo Sun,* 249
Sun (Winnemucca). See *Humboldt Sun,* 286
Sun Bear, 212
Sun Mountain Sentinel (Virginia City), 271
Sunderland, Calvin, 82, 286
Sunderland, Mike, 286
Sunshine (Paradise). See *Paradise Sunshine,* 163
Sutherland, William, 268, 269
Sutro Independent, 237
Sutro, Adolph, 237, 263, 264
Suverkrup, Arthur N., 36, 88
Suverkrup, John W., 88
Swayze, H. F., 275
Sweeney, Edward C., 235
Sweeney, James, 48
Swetlik, Robert, 213
Swick, R. W., 197

Taggert, Jesse, 254
Tahoe-Carson Chronicle. See *Carson Chronicle,* 49
Tahoe Chronicle (State Line). See *Carson Chronicle,* 49
Talbott, J. A., 170, 171
Tandy, Doug H., 8, 11, 15, 201, 203, 270
Taylor, Marshall, 138
Taylor, A., 77
Taylor, E. W., 115
Taylor, Howard Pitney, 254, 255, 256
Taylor, J. T., 196
Taylor, Jock, 9, 207, 232, 270
Taylor, John M., 49
Taylor, Richard B., 139, 140
Taylor, William B., 64, 65, 66, 76, 164, 165, 249
Teague, Merrill A., 175, 187, 190
Telegram (Elko), 69
Telegram (Reno). See *Evening Telegram*
Telegram (Shermantown). See *White Pine Evening Telegram,* 226
Telegraph Gossip (Rawhide), 174
Tell, Alice, 136
Tell, Jack, 135
Tell, Jay, 136
Terrell, Clyde R., 16, 101, 244
Terrell, S. W., 244
Territorial Enterprise (Carson City), 31
Territorial Enterprise (Genoa), 89
Territorial Enterprise (Winnemucca), 285
Territorial Enterprise (Virginia City, 1860–1916), 253
Territorial Enterprise (Virginia City, 1946), 270
Territorial Enterprise and Virginia City News, 271
Thatcher, William M., 8, 9, 11
Theatre Herald (Reno), 198
This Is Las Vegas, 134
Thomas, Arthur, 200
Thomas, Chuck, 232
Thomas, John, 165
Thomas, Lloyd B., 190
Thompson, Charley, 166
Thompson, Ed, 62
Thompson, H. B., 26
Thompson, John A., 89
Thompson, Munroe, 255
Thorne, V., 204
Thorpe, Bill, 89, 212
Thurston, George A., 254
Tichenor, McHenry, 176
Tidings (Deeth). See *Deeth Tidings,* 60
Tidings (Elko). See *Nevada Silver Tidings,* 68
Tieben, John Kite, 289
Tilden, R. L., 251
Times (Aurora). See *Aurora Weekly Times,* 4
Times (Belleville). See *Belleville Times,* 17
Times (Bristol). See *Bristol Times,* 24
Times (Carson City, 1880–81). See *Carson Times,* 40
Times (Carson City, 1977). See *Carson Times,* 52
Times (Crescent). See *Crescent Times,* 52
Times (Dayton). See *Lyon County Times,* 59
Times (Divide City). See *Divide City Times,* 62
Times (Ely). See *Ely Daily Times,* 73
Times (Granite). See *Granite Times,* 110
Times (Hawthorne). See *Times of Mineral County,* 117
Times (Las Vegas). See *Las Vegas Times,* 125, 129
Times (Manhattan). See *Manhattan Times,* 149
Times (Minden). See *Minden Times,* 155
Times (Mountain City). See *Mountain City Times,* 156
Times (North Las Vegas). See *North Las Vegas Valley Times,* 159
Times (Oro City). See *Oro City Times,* 160
Times (Pahrump). See *Pahrunp Valley Times,* 161
Times (Pioche). See *Pioche Times,* 167
Times (Pioneer). See *Pioneer Times,* 170
Times (Rawhide). See *Rawhide Times,* 173
Times (Reno). See *Reno Times,* 180
Times (Silver City). See *Lyon County Times,* 228; *Washoe Times,* 227
Times (Skookum). See *Skookum Times,* 230
Times (Tobar). See *Tobar Times,* 239
Times (Tonopah). See *Tonopah Daily Times,* 242
Times (Tuscarora). See *Tuscarora Times,* 247

Times (Virginia City). See *Virginia City Times,* 271
Times (Washoe City). See *Washoe Times,* 275; *Washoe Weekly Times,* 277
Times (Yerington). See *Yerington Times,* 288
Times-Bonanza (Tonopah). See *Tonopah Times-Bonanza,* 243
Times Bonanza (Virginia City). See *Virginia City Times Bonanza,* 272
Times of Mineral County (Hawthorne), 117
Times-Review (Tuscarora). See *Tuscarora Times-Review,* 247
Tobar Times, 239
Tobin, W. H., 53
Todman, John C., 28
Toll, David W., 100
Tonopah Bonanza, 240
Tonopah Daily Times, 242
Tonopah Miner, 240
Tonopah Mining Reporter, 243
Tonopah Nevadan, 242
Tonopah Sun, 241
Tonopah Times-Bonanza, 243
Topics (Columbia). See *Columbia Topics,* 55
Topics (Pioneer). See *Pioneer Topics,* 169
Town Talk (Reno), 203
Towner, Norman, 203
Townsend, Edward W., 266
Townsend, James W. E., 42, 177, 253
Traders' Daily Gossip (Goldfield), 104
Transvaal Miner, 245
Transvaal Tribune, 245
Travers, James, 221
Trebell, T. S., 126
Trego, Robert H., 284, 285
Trembly, Henry, 110
Trespass (Virginia City). See *Daily Trespass,* 260
Tri-State Miner (Reno), 200
Tri-Town Times (Fernley), 86
Tribune (Duluth). See *Duluth Tribune,* 63
Tribune (Goldfield). See *Goldfield Tribune,* 105
Tribune (Las Vegas). See *Las Vegas Tribune,* 130
Tribune (Lovelock). See *Lovelock Tribune,* 144
Tribune (Monarch). See *Monarch Tribune,* 155
Tribune (Pahrump). See *Pahrump Tribune,* 162
Tribune (Reno). See *Daily Nevada Tribune,* 182
Tribune (Sparks). See *Sparks Tribune,* 232
Tribune (Transvaal). See *Transvaal Tribune,* 245
Triplett, Charles J., Jr., 278
Triplett, Charles J., 278
Triplett, F. H., 10, 15
Triplett, Frances, 278
Triplett, Ola F., 278
Triplett, Phil S., 68, 277, 278

Triplett, Rose Marie, 278
Trippel, Eugene J., 24
True Fissure (Candelaria), 28
Truman, David S., 282
Trussell, David, 120
Truth (Reno), 192
Tubman, Thomas M., 188
Tuck, Curtis, 85
Turner, DeWitt C., 191
Turner, H. W., 164
Tuscarora Mining News, 248
Tuscarora Times, 247
Tuscarora Times-Review, 247
Twain, Mark (Samuel Clemens), 74, 99, 253, 254, 257
Two O'clock News (Virginia City), 259
Tybo Sun, 249

Uhlhorn, John F., 265
Union (Carson City). See *Nevada Union,* 43
Union (Virginia City). See *Comstock Union,* 267
Union (Virginia City). See *Virginia Daily Union,* 255

Valentine, Thomas B., 256
Valjean, A., 64, 70
Valley Green Sheet (Sparks), 235
Valley Outlook (Sun Valley), 237
Valley Press (Gerlach), 94
Van Devort, T. D., 35, 55, 107, 240, 241
Van Duzer, Clarence D., 95, 184, 282
Van Sooy, Neal, 36, 50
Vance,——, 181
Vanderlieth, Edward D., 77, 78
Vardy, George R., 278
Vaux, Glenn C., 134, 211
Vegas Gay Times, 140
Vegas Visitor, 134
Vegas Wild, 137
Vernon Miner, 252
Vernon Review, 252
Vestergaard, Julius, 84
Veteran's Journal (Las Vegas), 135
Vida Nueva (Las Vegas), 141
Vieira,——, 47
View Magazine (Reno), 212
Vigilant (Goldfield). See *Goldfield Vigilant,* 103
Vigilant Reporter (Reno), 208
Villager (Crystal Bay), 58
Villasenor, E. Ricardo, 136
Virginia City Chronicle, 271. See also *Virginia Evening Chronicle,* 261
Virginia City Crier, 272
Virginia City Legend, 272
Virginia City News, 270
Virginia City Times, 271
Virginia City Times Bonanza, 272
Virginia Daily Union, 255
Virginia Evening Bulletin, 256

Virginia Evening Chronicle, 261
Virginia Weekly Messenger. See *Nevada Statesman,* 265
Vogliotti, Gabriel R., 135
Voice of the People (Reno), 191
Voorhees, W. T., 53

Wabuska Mangler, 273
Wadsworth Dispatch (1892–1904), 273
Wadsworth Dispatch (1920). See *Dispatch,* 274
Waggoner, R. L., 288
Walch, Jack, 143
Waldo, H. A., 177, 179, 180, 251, 280
Walker Lake Bulletin (Hawthorne), 114
Walker Lake Mining Record. See *Luckyboy Mining Record,* 147
Walker, Charles A., 70
Walker, Dale, 216
Walker, F. H., 197
Walker, Peggy, 216
Wallace, Bill, 129
Wallace, W. W., 125
Walters, Caroline, 206
Walters, Stewart, 206
Ward Miner, 274
Ward Reflex, 275
Warren, George, 268
Warren, H., 163
Warren, Wallie, 207
Washoe County Citizen (Reno), 210
Washoe Herald (Virginia City). See *Daily Evening Washoe Herald,* 258
Washoe Star (Washoe City). See *Washoe Weekly Star,* 276
Washoe Stock Circular (Virginia City), 258
Washoe Times (Silver City), 227
Washoe Times (Washoe City, 1862–63), 275
Washoe Times (Washoe City, 1865). See *Washoe Weekly Times,* 277
Washoe Weekly Star (Washoe City), 276
Washoe Weekly Times (Washoe City), 277
Wasp (Yerington). See *Lyon County Wasp,* 289
Wasson, John, 279
Wasson, Joseph, 5, 279
Watts, H. H., 264
Watts, W. W., 77
Waysom, Dolly, 208
We Are Free (Las Vegas), 138
We, The People (Virginia City), 272
Weaver, Paul E., Jr., 204
Weaver, Paul E., Sr., 204
Webb, Joseph, 89, 122
Webster, William Stuart, 23, 63, 172, 175, 184
Weekly (Carson City, 1900–18). See *Carson Weekly,* 47
Weekly (Carson City, 1891–99), 45
Weekly 6 Shooter (Mountain City), 156
Weekly Gazette and Stockman. See *Reno Evening Gazette,* 177

Weekly Market Letter (Goldfield), 102
Weekly Market Review (Goldfield), 102
Wehking, Henry G., 185
Weide, B. G., 237
Weissman, Len, 130
Welch, J. Herbert, 190, 286
Wells Index, 277
Wells Progress, 278
Welter, Arthur J., 284
Wendell, Jack J., 234
Wentworth, Chapman, 120
Wescott, O. K., 166
West, Charles I., 134
West, Debbie, 224
West, Walter L., Jr., 235
West, The Voice of Western America (Las Vegas), 132
West Coast Poetry Review (Reno), 213
Western Business News (Las Vegas), 137
Western Financier (Reno), 195
Western Home Builder (Carlin), 30
Western Miner (Reno), 194
Western Mines and Markets (Reno), 200
Western Nevada Miner (Mina), 154
Western Wildlife (Reno), 216
Weston, H. L., 56, 57, 58, 59
Westover, J., 27
Westover, Mrs. J., 27
Wharton,——, 289
What's Happening (Las Vegas), 138
Wheeler, D. N., 69
Wheeler, Richard, 91
White Pine Evening Telegram (Shermantown), 226
White Pine Gazette (Treasure City), 246
White Pine Miner (Ely), 71
White Pine News (Cherry Creek), 53
White Pine News (East Ely), 64
White Pine News (Ely), 70
White Pine News (Hamilton), 112
White Pine News (Taylor), 238
White Pine News (Treasure City), 246
White Pine Reflex (Taylor), 238
White Pine Suffragist (Ely), 73
White Ribbon (Carson City), 46
White, Charles H., 23
Whitehead, J. B., 180
Whitney News, 279
Whooperup (Reno). See *Reno Whooperup,* 190
Wick, Merna N., 207
Wiegand, Conrad, 99, 100
Wight, Katha, 158
Wignall, Barbara, 65
Wignall, Max, 65
Wilcox, Walter, 72, 73
Wilkinson, George W., 133
Wilkinson, Marc, 130, 226
Williams,——, 102
Williams, David S., 27
Williams, Delbert E., 82, 87, 93
Williams, Mrs. Delbert E., 82
Williams, Edna D., 27
Williams, F. O., 68

Williams, Jonathan, 31, 32, 90, 253, 254
Williams, M. R., 208
Williams, R. J., 210
Williams, Ray A., 50
Williamson, David E. W., 176, 178
Williamson, Frances A., 183
Williamson, Mary L., 183
Wilson, Adair, 7
Wilson, E. B., 276
Windle, R. E. L., 15, 101, 221, 281, 283, 284
Winnemucca Argent, 279
Winnemucca Republican. See *Silver State,* 281
Winni Minimart (Winnemucca), 286
Wintersteen, John, 51
Witherell, J. B., 56
Wixon, Tom, 52
Wogan, Maurya, 72, 205, 284
Wollard, I. B., 253
Wonder Miner, 287
Wonder Mining News, 286
Woodburn, William, 259
Woodward, D. L., Jr., 232, 233
Woodward, Donald, 51, 52, 88, 232
Woodward, Lynn, 51
Woodward, R. M., 156
Woolcock, Fred E., 13
Woolf, D. B., 257

Woolley, Jim, 129
Worden, John E., 82
Workman (Goldfield). See *Nevada Workman,* 108
World (Mazuma). See *Mazuma World,* 151
World (Pioche). See *Pioche World,* 166
Wright,——, 281
Wright, C. C. S., 65, 145, 247
Wright, Carole, 158, 211
Wright, J. A., 10
Wright, John, 120
Wright, Michael A., 215
Wright, William (Dan De Quille), 253, 267
Wyatt, Frank, 166

Yacenda, Adam, 159
Yerington Rustler, 287
Yerington Times, 288
Yogi (Carson City), 47
Young, Brigham, 2
Young, C. S., 42, 177
Young, Carl, 193
Young, J. B., 81
Young, Janie E., 216, 217

Zenoff, Morry M., 22, 119